Fodor's

HONG KONG

FODOR'S HONG KONG
Editors: Caroline Trefler

Editorial Contributors: Stephen Brewer, Doretta Lau, Denise Leto, Samantha Leese, Maloy Luakian, Dorothy So, Jason Spotts, Kate Springer

Production Editor: Carrie Parker
Maps & Illustrations: David Lindroth, *cartographer;* Rebecca Baer, *map editor;* William Wu, *information graphics*
Design: Fabrizio La Rocca, *creative director;* Tina Malaney, Chie Ushio, Jessica Ramirez, Ann McBrde-Alayon, Liliana Guia, *designers;* Melanie Marin, *associate director of photography;* Jennifer Romains, *photo research*
Cover Photos: Front cover: (Chinese Junk and skyline of Central District and Victoria Harbor): SCPhotos/Alamy. Back cover (from left to right): Roger Price/Flickr [Attribution License]; Charlotte Marillet/Flickr [Attribution-ShareAlike License]; Hong Kong Tourism Board. Spine: sutsaiy/Shutterstock.
Production Manager: Angela L. McLean

23rd Edition

ISBN 978-0-7704-3208-9

ISSN 1070-6887

SPECIAL SALES
This book is available at special discounts for bulk purchases for sales promotions or premiums. Special editions, including personalized covers, excerpts of existing books, and corporate imprints, can be created in large quantities for special needs. For more information, write to Special Markets/Premium Sales, 1745 Broadway, MD 3-1, New York, NY 10019, or e-mail specialmarkets@randomhouse.com.

AN IMPORTANT TIP & AN INVITATION
Although all prices, opening times, and other details in this book are based on information supplied to us at press time, changes occur all the time in the travel world, and Fodor's cannot accept responsibility for facts that become outdated or for inadvertent errors or omissions. So **always confirm information when it matters,** especially if you're making a detour to visit a specific place. Your experiences—positive and negative—matter to us. If we have missed or misstated something, **please write to us.** Share your opinion instantly through our online feedback center at fodors.com/contact-us.

PRINTED IN COLOMBIA

10 9 8 7 6 5 4 3 2 1

CONTENTS

MAPS

ABOUT THIS GUIDE

Fodor's Ratings

Everything in this guide is worth doing—we don't cover what isn't—but exceptional sights, hotels, and restaurants are recognized with additional accolades. **Fodor's Choice★** indicates our top recommendations; ★ highlights places we deem highly recommended; and **Best Bets** call attention to notable hotels and restaurants in various categories. Care to nominate a new place? Visit Fodors.com/contact-us.

Trip Costs

We list prices wherever possible to help you budget well. Hotel and restaurant price categories from $ to $$$$ are noted alongside each recommendation. For hotels, we include the lowest cost of a standard double room in high season. For restaurants, we cite the average price of a main course at dinner or, if dinner isn't served, at lunch. For attractions, we always list adult admission fees; discounts are usually available for children, students, and senior citizens.

Hotels

Our local writers vet every hotel to recommend the best overnights in each price category, from budget to expensive. Unless otherwise specified, you can expect private bath, phone, and TV in your room. For expanded hotel reviews, facilities, and deals visit Fodors.com.

Restaurants

Unless we state otherwise, restaurants are open for lunch and dinner daily. We mention dress code only when there's a specific requirement and reservations only when they're essential or not accepted. To make restaurant reservations, visit Fodors.com.

Top Picks		Hotels &
★ Fodor's Choice		**Restaurants**
		☎ Hotel
Listings		⤵ Number of
✉ Address		rooms
✉ Branch address		‖◎‖ Meal plans
☎ Telephone		✕ Restaurant
🖷 Fax		⟋ Reservations
⊕ Website		🏛 Dress code
✉ E-mail		▭ No credit cards
🎫 Admission fee		$ Price
☉ Open/closed		
times		**Other**
Ⓜ Subway		⇨ See also
⊹ Directions or		☞ Take note
Map coordinates		🏌 Golf facilities

Credit Cards

The hotels and restaurants in this guide typically accept credit cards. If not, we'll say so.

Experience
Hong Kong

HONG KONG TODAY

You may have caught glimpses of Hong Kong in old Jackie Chan or Chow Yun-fat movies, the city set against a clattering backdrop of surreal high-rises and bamboo scaffolding, but the silver screen only scratches the surface of this fast-paced metropolis. Beneath the iconic attractions and pop-culture phenomena, this multifaceted city is full of surprises, and yet extremely accessible to travelers who haven't spent much time in Asia.

Today's Hong Kong . . .

. . . is truly cosmopolitan. Living up to the title of Asia's World City, Hong Kong is a buzzing stage that attracts millions of visitors from all over the globe. Business travelers pass through frequently because it's so close to China, and Hong Kong's soaring market development makes it one of the world's leading financial hubs. Of course, just as many people come here for leisure travel. Navigation is easy within the city center since road signs, maps, and directions on public transportation are spelled out in Chinese and English. Most major tourist attractions—including museums, parks, and performance venues—also have bilingual directories and information centers. While the city has a distinct tradition of its own, you'll also find foreign influences everywhere, whether it's in the form of European fashion houses, clubs that play the latest American hits, or top-grade sushi restaurants that rival those in Tokyo.

. . . is a shopper's paradise. You can score great bargains here in Hong Kong on everything from electronics to clothing—and there's no sales tax, which is all the more reason to shop your heart out. You'll find all the world-renowned brands here at large-scale shopping malls and Rodeo Drive—like stretches along Canton Road and Fashion Walk, but it's worth visiting the loud and crowded local markets, where you can haggle for cheap trinkets. If you go to larger markets like the one on Temple Street in Yau Ma Tei and Tung Choi Street in Mong Kok, most of the vendors are used to tourists and can speak basic phrases of English. Cutting-edge fashionistas might want to look into the independent boutiques hidden away in small complexes such as Island Beverly mall in Causeway Bay. These stores sell clothes and jewelry by local designers and one-of-a-kind pieces sourced from Korea and Japan. Be warned though that a lot of these shops don't open until late afternoon.

WHAT WE'RE TALKING ABOUT NOW

Forget France: wine connoisseurs are looking to Hong Kong for opportunities to buy, sell, and trade rare vintages. The great grape boom started when the government got rid of the wine tax back in 2008, and in the years since then the increase of industry knowledge and interest has firmly established this city as Asia's epicenter of fine wines. Aside from reds, whites, and bubbles, Hong Kong's beer and spirit market is also taking off with a growing number of restaurants and bars dedicating themselves to high-quality craft bottles.

It may not sound immediately obvious but this city boasts a rich contemporary art scene that includes large-scale exhibitions and auctions that attract collectors from all over the world. The industry

. . . is at a political crossroads. Although Hong Kong was officially returned to China in 1997, following 156 years under British rule, there is still some palpable tension between locals and the mainland. A large part comes from the clash of cultures and the feeling that the overwhelming influx of mainland visitors has put a strain on the city's resources (most notably on baby milk formula and hospital space for pregnant women). And despite being classified as a Special Administrative Region (SAR) that is given some political autonomy from China, the Communist Party has made several attempts to impose its policies on Hong Kong—all of which have been strongly resisted by the local community. A recent example of this was the protest against implementing Chinese national education in schools. Thankfully, both sides have remained civil and even when rallies occur, they're usually peaceful and well-organized demonstrations that are effective without being violent.

. . . is getting greener. Despite its expansive rural landscape, Hong Kong has always been identified more as a concrete jungle plagued by urban development and inner-city pollution than as an eco-destination. But the times they are a-changin' and residents have really stepped up their efforts to turn their home into an eco-friendly city. The most notable change is the increase of interest in farming and a back-to-basics lifestyle, especially from the younger community. Weekend trips to farms out in the New Territories are gaining popularity as a way to relieve stress from the hustle and bustle of city life. And while Hong Kong's size makes it difficult to find arable land, some enterprising farmers are looking up and building rooftop gardens right in the heart of the city. Restaurants are also doing their part with more chefs designing menus based on sustainable seafood and locally grown produce.

received another push this year as world-renowned art show Art Basel made its official Hong Kong debut, taking over from the previous success of the Art HK fair. And with construction for the West Kowloon Cultural District (which will include a museum and arts education facility) underway, there's plenty for the creative crowd to look forward to.

The gay community comes out loud and proud against the city's more conservative parties. The Pride Parade of 2012 saw a record turnout with legislative councilors and notable celebs—including Tat Ming Pair's vocalist Anthony Wong and Cantopop songstress Denise Ho—banding together to speak up for gay rights and same-sex marriage.

WHAT'S WHERE

1 Western. Just west of the skyscrapers, this older and quieter neighborhood of Hong Kong Island is known for its steep and narrow roads, Chinese medicine markets, antiques shops, temples, and the tram.

2 Central. Hong Kong's world-famous finance hub extends through Admiralty and boasts skyline high-rises, luxury-brand flagship stores, and grand hotels with gourmet restaurants, all connected by footbridges. Head up the Mid-Levels Escalators and take the funicular to Victoria Peak for postcard views of the city and harbor.

3 Wan Chai, Causeway Bay, and Eastern. Wan Chai still has its strip of harmless red-light venues, though not so far away are design shops and wine bars. Trendy young locals flock to Causeway Bay's shopping hubs, Sogo, and Times Square. Residential Eastern has a growing restaurant and arts scene.

4 Tsim Sha Tsui. Moving across the harbor to Kowloon, Tsim Sha Tsui begins at the 50-year-old Star Ferry Terminal followed by the eastward promenade along the Avenue of Stars, which offers front-row views of the famous Hong Kong Island skyline.

5 **Yau Ma Tei, Mong Kok, and Northern Kowloon.** Yau Ma Tei and Mong Kok are the epicenters of night and day markets, where you can score souvenirs and knick-knacks on the cheap. North of here are residential areas and attractions including the famed Kowloon Walled City Park and Wong Tai Sin Temple.

6 **New Territories.** Hong Kong's least developed areas are the sites of still-inhabited historic villages and relatively unspoiled natural beauty, in addition to the Ten Thousand Buddhas Monastery and Hong Kong Heritage Museum in the new town of Sha Tin.

7 **Southside.** Stanley, with its colonial remnants, outdoor market, waterfront restaurants, and annual Dragon Boat races, may be Southside's obvious destination. But don't let it stop you from visiting beaches, from Repulse Bay to Shek O, at the start (or finish) of the Dragon's Back scenic hiking trail. Or play with the pandas at Ocean Park.

8 **Lantau Island.** Of the Hong Kong archipelago of 260 islands, Lantau is by far the largest. It's home to the Big Buddha and spectacular mountain views from hiking trails beyond the Ngong Ping 360 cable car ride. It's also where you'll find Disneyland.

HONG KONG PLANNER

Looks Deceive

On the surface Hong Kong is a big chaotic Chinatown punctuated by imposing skyscrapers and shopping malls. A closer look reveals the marks of a century of colonialism and several thousand years of Chinese ancestry. Then, notice that rural mountains, forests, and outlying islands comprise more than 70% of Hong Kong's land mass.

Wording It Right

Learn to recognize a few basic Cantonese expressions such as "*lei-ho?*" ("hello, how are you?") and "*mm-goi*" ("excuse me" or "thank you"). Hong Kong's official languages are Chinese and English, but the native dialect is Cantonese. Mandarin Chinese has gained popularity here and in Macau.

In hotels, large stores, international restaurants, and clubs, most people speak English. Many taxi and bus drivers and staffers in small shops, cafés, and market stalls do not.

Ask MTR (Mass Transit Railway) employees or English-speaking policemen, identifiable by their red striped epaulets, for directions. Get your concierge to write down your destination in Chinese if you're headed off the main trail.

Visitor Information

Swing by the Hong Kong Tourist Board (HKTB) visitor center before even leaving the airport. It publishes stacks of helpful, free exploring booklets and maps, offers free classes and workshops on local culture, runs a plethora of tours, and operates a multilingual helpline. Its detailed, comprehensive website is a fabulous resource. If you're planning on visiting several museums in a week, pick up a Museum Weekly Pass, which gets you into seven museums for HK$30. Buy it at participating museums or at the HKTB visitor center at the Tsim Sha Tsui Star Ferry Concourse.

Hong Kong Tourist Board (*HKTB*). ✉ *Hong Kong International Airport, Arrivals Level, Terminal 1, Lantau* ☎ *2508– 1234 hotline daily 9–6* ⊕ *www.discoverhongkong.com* ⊗ *Daily 8 am–9 pm* ✉ *The Peak Piazza, Victoria Peak, Central* ⊗ *Daily 9–9* ✉ *Star Ferry Concourse, Tsim Sha Tsui* ⊗ *Daily 8–8.*

Open Hours

Business hours for most shopping malls and boutiques are from 11 am until 8 or 9 pm, though hours may be extended during weekends and festive seasons. Small, family-owned businesses might close for big public holidays—especially Chinese New Year—but major operations and chain stores usually stay open year-round.

Hong Kong will keep you well-fed through the day and deep into the night. Breakfast can start as early as 8 am with options such as Cantonese dim sum or scrambled eggs on toast with a glass of milk tea. In between lunch and dinner, most cha chaan tengs (Hong Kong–style cafés) offer an afternoon tea menu, which is basically the regular menu at a discounted price. Typical closing time for restaurants is 10:30 or 11 pm, but you'll find plenty of late-night dining establishments, including street snack stalls that sell fish balls on a stick until well past midnight.

After dinner, take advantage of Hong Kong's buzzing nightlife scene. Bars and clubs stay open until the wee hours of the morning. Or you can rent out a private room and sing the whole night away at one of the many karaoke lounges in town.

Getting Around

Hong Kong's streets may seem utterly chaotic, but the public transport system is not. Be sure to purchase a rechargeable Octopus card, which can be used on all buses, trains, and trams, the ferry, and even to make purchase at vending machines, convenience stores, fast-food restaurants, and the racetrack.

The quickest and perhaps safest way to travel is with the ever-reliable MTR (underground railway), which links to most of the areas you'll want to visit. There's no timetable because trains run so frequently. Signs and announcements are in both Chinese and English, and posted maps help visitors navigate outside the stations, too.

Although you can cross the harbor on the MTR, the Star Ferry is a cheaper ride, with the added bonus of being able to enjoy the fantastic harbor views during the 10-minute journey between Hong Kong Island and Tsim Sha Tsui. To get to the outlying islands, take a sampan or hire an air-conditioned junk for the day.

If you prefer street-level travel, the city's air-conditioned double-decker buses can take you anywhere, provided you know which number and route to take. On the northern side of Hong Kong Island, you can also take the tram (listen for the distinctive "ding-ding"), a fun and inexpensive way to get from one side of the island to the other—and it's the same route that the MTR follows, so you should be able to walk to an MTR station from any tram stop between Sheung Wan and Shau Kei Wan.

If you do get lost, you can always hail a cab. Prices are reasonable if you're not traveling too far, and tipping is not required. Not all drivers are willing to cross the harbor, though, so be sure to ask before getting in, and, unless it's a designated cross-harbor vehicle, expect to be charged for the return-trip toll as well.

Perhaps best of all, Hong Kong is a city that's easy to explore by foot. In Central, use the covered walkways that run from buildings in the business district all the way to Mid-Levels, thus avoiding stoplights, exhaust fumes, and weather conditions (but not crowds). The same can apply to the pedestrian overpasses all around the city.

When to Go

High season, from September through late December, sees sunny, dry days and cool, comfortable nights. January and February are mostly cool and damp, with periods of overcast skies. March and April are pleasant, and by May the temperature is consistently warm and comfortable.

June through August are the cheapest months for one reason: they coincide with the hot, sticky, and very rainy typhoon (hurricane) season. Hong Kong is prepared for blustery assaults; if a big storm approaches, the airwaves crackle with information, and your hotel will post the appropriate signals (a No. 10 signal indicates the worst winds; a black warning means a rainstorm is brewing). This is serious business—bamboo scaffolding and metal signs can hurtle through the streets, trees can break or fall, and large areas of the territory can flood. Museums, shops, restaurants, and transport shut down at signal No. 8, but 7-Elevens and cinemas typically stay open.

Hong Kong Temperatures

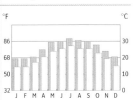

HONG KONG
TOP ATTRACTIONS

Mid-Levels Escalators

(**A**) The longest outdoor covered escalator system in the world covers half a mile of moving stairs, walkways, and passageways from the business hub of Central to the residential heights of Mid-Levels. Step off a few flights up from Central in SoHo or on Hollywood Road for gallery hopping, eating out, or club crawling.

Victoria Peak

(**B**) At 552 meters (1,810 feet) above sea level, the peak is Hong Kong Island's highest hill above the harbor. Buy a ticket for the 125-year-old Peak Tram, take in the postcard views, then take a scenic nature walk or bus ride back down to Central.

Mong Kok Markets

(**C**) Flowers, birds, goldfish, turtles, and jade by day; clothes, sneakers, toys, and knickknacks by night. And there's always food around Temple Street. Visit the stronghold of the Triads (secret-society gangs) on Nathan Road, or wander down Sai Yeung Street, which is full of snacks, buskers, and touts.

Kowloon Walled City Park

(**D**) Exempted from British rule and abandoned by the Chinese following their treaty in 1842, the Walled City grew into a lawless, labyrinthine slum occupied by Triads, gambling houses, brothels, and disease. In 1995 it was resurrected as a peaceful and expansive Qing Dynasty–style garden. The documentary photos and restored South Gate remnants exhibit how far the park has come.

Tian Tan Buddha

(**E**) The Ngong Ping 360 cable car ride can take you only so far. The true path to divine ascension is by way of 268 steps leading up to the 275-ton Tian Tan Buddha statue (the Big Buddha), which sits on a hill next to the Po Lin Buddhist Monastery. Nearby is the Wisdom Path, a beautiful walk that offers splendid views.

Stanley

Come to this waterside town to see classic colonial buildings, wander through the eclectic market, dine on the waterfront, and swim at the beach where hundreds of Dragon Boats race every spring.

Dragon's Back Trail

(F) This hiking trail across the southeast end of Hong Kong Island will give you a whole new perspective of Hong Kong, though you don't need to be an athlete to walk the undulating ridge.

Duk Ling

(G) Sail Victoria Harbour on Hong Kong's last authentic red-sailed junk. The Duk Ling was built in Macau over half a century ago and was restored to her original glory in the late 1980s. It's now the symbol of the Hong Kong Tourist Board, which offers HK$100 one-hour rides exclusively for tourists.

Ocean Park

(H) This popular theme park has exciting rides as well as up-close access to some of the world's most fascinating animals. The park is best known for its marine life exhibits, the grand aquarium, and the spectacular dolphin shows. Make sure to pay a visit to the giant panda habitat, too.

Wong Tai Sin Temple

(I) One of the busiest religious shrines in the city, Wong Tai Sin Temple is perpetually packed with dedicated worshippers looking to have their prayers answered. The complex itself is a stunning structure that houses the teachings of Taoism, Buddhism, and Confucianism. The temple can get crazily crowded during major Chinese festivities so check the lunar calendar before you go if you want to avoid the madness.

TOP EXPERIENCES

Yum Cha

No trip to Hong Kong is complete without a *yum cha* (translates into "drink tea") experience. Along with their tea, guests nibble on small plates of delicacies and bamboo steamers of designed-to-share dim sum. Traditionally, *yum cha* is available for breakfast and lunch, but there are many dedicated restaurants that serve made-to-order dim sum all through the day.

Ride the Star Ferry

The iconic Star Ferry has been shuttling passengers across Victoria Harbour for more than a century. Today's green and white boats are relics of the 1950s and '60s. Take one from either Wan Chai or Central to Tsim Sha Tsui, then turn around and admire that famous Hong Kong skyline. At night, catch the 8 pm Symphony of Lights show.

Take the Tram

These rattling cars have become giant rolling advertisements, carrying everyone from schoolboys to grannies through all the main street action straight across Hong Kong Island. Climb aboard at off-peak hours on an early weekday afternoon for a leisurely ride from the busy Western Market terminus to the green fields of Happy Valley or Victoria Park.

Nightlife in Lan Kwai Fong

Hong Kong has no shortage of after-hour hangouts but for the most concentrated stretch of clubs and bars, head to Lan Kwai Fong. Options here range from casual beer joints to happening dance clubs, and everything is concentrated in a small area so it's easy to hop from one venue to the next.

Mid-Levels Escalators

The longest outdoor covered escalator system in the world covers half a mile of moving stairs, walkways, and passageways from the business hub of Central to the residential heights of Mid-Levels. Step off a few flights up from Central in SoHo or on Hollywood Road to check out the galleries, restaurants, and bars. Note that the escalators go in only one direction during rush hour, so you have to take the stairs in the opposite direction.

Go to the Races

Even if you're not a gambler, it's worth heading to Hong Kong's tracks in Happy Valley and Sha Tin. It's a multimillion-dollar-a-year business, and the season runs from September through June and draws serious crowds. In the public stands the vibe is electric and loud, thanks to the gamblers shouting and waving their newspapers madly.

FREE AND ALMOST FREE

It's easy to spend money in the big city: shopping, entrance fees, food, shows, late-night cocktails. But if you'd like to put your wallet away for a while, here are some of our favorite options.

Art

Visitors are free to browse antiques and art works by Asian prodigies at private galleries in Central, SoHo, and Sheung Wan. Kowloon Park's winding Sculpture Walk features 20 works—including an Eduardo Paolozzi—against a leafy backdrop. And be sure to keep your eyes open at the malls, most notably Harbour City and Times Square, where you'll see Hong Kong's version of public art.

Bird-Watching

See our feathered friends up close and personal without leaving town—either at the Yuen Po Street Bird Garden in Kowloon or at the Edward Youde Aviary in the heart of Hong Kong Park.

Bright Lights

Victoria Harbour's Symphony of Lights is performed every evening at 8 to a crowd of mesmerized visitors and proud residents. Music and narration blast through low-fi outdoor speakers as 44 skyscrapers are synchronized to light up on cue. Watch from the waterfront promenade in Tsim Sha Tsui, Golden Bauhinia Square in Wan Chai, or the InterContinental Hotel's lobby lounge.

Culture Classes

The tourist board runs free classes on feng shui, kung fu, Cantonese opera, and Chinese tea appreciation. If you prefer a more immersive experience, a tai chi master will guide you through the moves at the Sculpture Court, just outside the Hong Kong Museum of Art, every Monday, Wednesday, and Friday morning at 8. Contact the HKTB (☎ 2508–1234) for details.

Enlightenment

Inner peace is priceless, and though it's customary to make a small donation, all of Hong Kong's temples are free. So is the peaceful Chi Lin Nunnery in Kowloon, as well as the Big Buddha and Wisdom Path on Lantau Island, although you have to pay to get there first.

Heritage

Visit the Hong Kong Heritage Museum in Sha Tin on a Wednesday, when admission is free of charge for the whole family. This expertly curated museum chronicles Hong Kong's changing face, from scattered fishing and farming communities to booming towns. The Hong Kong Museum of Art, Museum of History, Museum of Coastal Defence, Science Museum, Space Museum, and Dr. Sun Yat-sen Museum also offer free admission on Wednesday.

Views

It doesn't cost a cent to ride up to the Bank of China's 43rd-floor observation deck, or to visit the Hong Kong Monetary Authority on the 55th floor of the International Finance Centre, for fabulous harbor views over to Kowloon. Get the reverse vista from the Tsim Sha Tsui waterfront promenade. For a glorious panoramic bay view of Victoria Park, visit the 5th and 6th floors of the main library in Causeway Bay.

Walkabouts

In town, you can take in colonial architecture during an hour-long stroll through Western between the University of Hong Kong and Western Market. Or try walking across Central through buildings linked by covered pedestrian passages. You can also head for the hills and hike along the Dragon's Back or up to Lion Rock.

BEST FESTS AND FÊTES

Traditional Festivals

Cheung Chau Bun Festival. Thousands make the yearly trip to Cheung Chau Island for the exuberant Cheung Chau Bun Festival, a four-day-long Taoist thanksgiving feast. A procession of children dressed as gods winds its way toward Pak Tai Temple, where 60-foot towers covered in sweet buns quiver outside—the idea is that people climb the towers to get to the buns; the higher the bun the better the fortune bestowed on the person. (8th day of 4th moon, usually May).

Chinese New Year. The loudest and proudest traditional festival, Chinese New Year, brings Hong Kong to a standstill each year. Shops shut down, and everywhere you look there are red and gold signs, kumquat trees, and pots of yellow chrysanthemums, all considered auspicious. On the lunar new year's eve the crowds climax at the flower markets and fairs; on the first night there's a colorfully noisy parade; on the second night the crowds ooh and ahh at the no-costs-spared fireworks display over the harbor. (1st day of 1st moon, usually late Jan.–early Feb.).

Ching Ming. Ancestor worship is important in Hong Kong culture, and on Ching Ming families meet to sweep the graves of departed relatives and burn paper offerings in respect for them. (3rd moon, Apr. 4 or 5).

Dragon Boat Festival. The Dragon Boat Festival pits long, multi-oared, dragon-head boats against one another in races to the shore; the biggest event is held at Stanley Beach. The festival commemorates the hero Qu Yuan, a poet and scholar who drowned himself in the 3rd century BC to protest government corruption. These days it's one big beach party. (5th day of 5th moon, usually June).

Lantern Festival. The Chinese New Year festivities end with the overwhelmingly red Lantern Festival. Hong Kong's parks—especially Victoria Park—become a sea of light as people, mostly children, gather with beautifully shaped paper or cellophane lanterns. It's also a traditional day for playful matchmaking, so it's particularly auspicious for single people. (15th day of 1st moon, usually Feb.).

Mid-Autumn Festival. During the Mid-Autumn Festival, families and friends gather to admire the full moon while munching on moon cakes, which are traditionally stuffed with lotus-seed paste, though new-fangled "snowy skin" varieties are also popular. Colorful paper lanterns fill Hong Kong's parks, and a 220-foot-long "fire dragon" dances through the streets of Tai Hang near Victoria Park. (15th day of 8th moon, usually Sept.–Oct.).

Non-Traditional Events

Clockenflap. Hong Kong's answer to Glastonbury, Clockenflap has brought major musical acts to the city, including Primal Scream, Santigold, and the Cribs. Concert-goers can sit on grassy patches surrounding the stages or can check out the multimedia art exhibitions and film tent. (Usually Nov. or Dec.) ⊕ *www. clockenflap.com.*

Wine and Dine Festival. Every year, the Hong Kong Tourism Board throws a month-long culinary extravaganza packed with restaurant deals, tours, and food-themed street carnivals. The highlight event is the four-day Wine and Dine Festival, which has colorful booths offering tasty snacks and tipples. Try some, buy some, and feast to your heart's content. (Usually late Oct.–early Nov.).

TOURING HONG KONG

With so many things to see and do in bustling Hong Kong, it can be daunting to tackle it all by yourself. If you want to leave the planning to someone else, there are some excellent guided tours catering to all sorts of interests.

General Tours

Big Bus Tour. These double-decker tourist buses cover three routes—Hong Kong Island, Kowloon, and Stanley—with recorded commentary in ten languages. Tourists can hop on or off at any stop along the way to take in the neighborhood sights. There's also a night-time bus tour that takes visitors through the neon-lit streets of Tsim Sha Tsui, Mong Kok, and Yau Ma Tei. ☎ 2723–2108 ⊕ www.bigbustours.com.

Gray Line Heritage Tour. Perfect for history buffs, the Gray Line Heritage Tour takes visitors to the sites of Hong Kong's five great clans in the New Territories. The route stops at several well-preserved monuments, including Tai Fu Tai—the home of a Man clan scholar in the late 1800s. Tours are scheduled on Monday, Wednesday, Friday, and Saturday. ⊠ 5th fl., Cheong Hing Building, 72 Nathan Rd., Tsim Sha Tsui ☎ 2368–7111 ⊕ www.grayline.com.hk.

Kowloon Market Walk. With its cacophonous Cantonese soundtrack and bright neon signs, Kowloon can be a bit chaotic for the first-time visitor but a guided Market Walk will take you through the nooks and crannies of Yau Ma Tei and Mong Kok. You'll shop at famed street markets that sell everything from fine jade to cheap clothing and goldfish in plastic bags. ☎ 9187–8641 ⊕ www.walkhongkong.com.

Nature Walks

Tai Po Kau Nature Walk. Walk Hong Kong hosts guided trails through the Tai Po Kau forest in the New Territories. The forest is known for its variety of flora and fauna and is popular for bird-watching. A visit to a butterfly garden is included in the half-day tour. ☎ 9187–8641 ⊕ www.walkhongkong.com.

Offbeat Tours

★ **Fodor's Choice** **Dialogue in the Dark Exhibition.** A truly unique way to experience Hong Kong, Dialogue in the Dark is a simulated tour from the perspective of the visually impaired. The "walk" covers five iconic scenes of the city, including a ride on the star ferry and a trip to a market. The tour is conducted in pitch-black darkness, allowing visitors to experience the surroundings through their four other senses. ⊠ Shop 215, 2nd fl., The Household Centre, Nob Hill, 8 King Lai Path, Mei Foo, Mei Foo ☎ 2310–0833 ⊕ www.dialogue-in-the-dark.hk ⊗ Closed Mon.

Secret Tour. Secret Tour skips the major sights, focusing instead on Hong Kong's hidden gems. Themed tours range from 70s Hong Kong to cemetery walks, and usually include a meal at a restaurant. ⊕ www.secrettourhk.com.

Foodie Tasting Tour. Celebrating the vibrant flavors of Hong Kong, the Foodie Tasting Tour takes visitors to six restaurants in Central and Shueng Wan, with a certified foodie guide who will help you decipher menus and talk you through the traditional eating customs. All meals are included in the ticket price. Arrive hungry: you'll be feasting on everything from wonton noodles to freshly steamed dim sum. ☎ 2850–5006 ⊕ www.hongkongfoodietours.com ⊗ Closed Sun.

HONG KONG WITH KIDS

One child's buzz is another child's bore, so plan a variety of amusements to keep everyone entertained. Hong Kong has two major amusement parks, but so many more opportunities to laugh and learn at museums, parks, and wildlife reserves. See the main listings for more information.

Hong Kong Disneyland

Hong Kong's version of Magic Kingdom, on Lantau Island, is as polished as all the other Disneys but much smaller. You can easily go on every ride at least once and see all the attractions in a day. If your kids are theme park–savvy, the tame rides here won't win their respect, but there is lots to entertain littler kids. Space Mountain is the most thrilling ride, though the U-shaped RC Racer at Toy Story Land also gets a few screams. Otherwise, watch the Festival of the Lion King, or just wait for the fireworks.

Hong Kong Park

This large public park has stunning architecture against a backdrop of lush greenery. The highlight is the Edward Youde Aviary, home to about 600 birds of 90 species indigenous to the endangered Malesian rainforests around Southeast Asia. Plant lovers should pay the Forsgate Conservatory a visit.

Hong Kong Wetland Park

While Tin Shui Wai is known as one of Hong Kong's poorest communities, the Wetland Park's opening helped raise its image with a vast Wetland Reserve home to numerous species of native wildlife. The park has a visitor center, which includes an auditorium and several indoor galleries offering edu-taining exhibits, as well as a café, play area, resource center, and souvenir shop. ⊠ *Wetland Park Road, Tin Shui Wai, New Territories* ☎ *2708–8885, 3152–2666* ⊕ *www.wetlandpark.com* ☎ *HK$30* ☽ *Wed.–Mon. 10–5.* Ⓜ *Tin Shui Wai.*

Hong Kong Zoological and Botanical Gardens

Hong Kong has grown around these gardens, which opened in 1864, and although they're now watched over by skyscrapers, a visit here is still a delightful escape. Burmese pythons, Chinese alligators, Bali mynahs, Bornean orangutans, ring-tailed lemurs, and lion-tailed macaques are among its 400 birds, 70 mammals, and 50 reptiles in the zoo enclosures.

Ocean Park

This homegrown marine theme park offers a balance of toned-down thrills and high-octane rides suitable for toddlers to teenagers as well as a giant aquarium and the popular giant-panda enclosure. The park stretches out over 200 hilly acres, which you can gaze down at from the cabins of the mile-long cable car that connects the tamer Lowlands area to the action-packed Headland.

Science Museum

Kids can spend a full day bouncing from one exhibition zone to another at this science-themed museum. Take the fitness challenge or learn about light, sound, and motion through interactive presentations and activities. The museum is closed on Thursdays; Wednesday is free admission.

Yuen Po Street Bird Garden

The air starts to fill with warbling and tweeting about a block from this narrow public park, where there are about 70 stalls selling various species of birds, mostly smaller ones, in addition to cages, seed, and accessories. Look for talking mynahs, budgies, and parrots toward the far end of the garden, where these species have more space to perch on independent stands to which they're chained.

UNDERSTANDING FENG SHUI

Feng shui (pronounced *foong soy* in Cantonese, *fung shway* in Mandarin, and literally translated as "wind" and "water") is the art of placing objects in such a way as to bring about yin-yang balance. In the West, feng shui seems like just another interior-design fad; in Hong Kong it's taken very seriously and is believed to affect everything from health to financial prospects.

One school of thought looks at buildings in relation to mountains or bodies of water. It's ideal, for example, for a building to face out to sea with a mountain behind it. (Is it coincidence that this allows for the best views and breezes?) Another school focuses on shapes in the immediate environment; triangles, for instance, give off bad feng shui. Both schools are concerned with the flow of energy. Entrances are placed to allow positive energy to flow in, and objects such as mirrors are used to deflect negative energy. Cities are often short of such natural feng shui improvers as babbling brooks, but not to worry: a fish tank is a fine alternative.

Feng Shui Structures

Feng shui has a huge influence on Hong Kong's architecture. Rumor has it that during construction of the Hongkong & Shanghai Bank (HSBC) Main Building, the escalators were reset so that they would be at an angle to the entrance. Because evil spirits can only travel in a straight line, this realignment was thought to prevent waterborne spirits from flowing in off Victoria Harbour. The escalators are also believed to resemble two whiskers of a powerful dragon, sucking money into the bank. Atop the building and pointing toward the Bank of China Tower are two metal rods that look like a window-washing apparatus: the rods are a classic feng shui technique designed to

deflect the negative energy—in this case, from the Bank of China—away and back to its source.

On the other side of the harbor, the International Commerce Centre (ICC), which usurped the IFC's title as Hong Kong's tallest skyscraper, is governed by similar feng shui principals. A small terrace garden and fountain at the foot of the building provide a sense of harmony between the natural elements while the main entrances are located in auspicious positions that supposedly attract luck and fortune. But in a place like Hong Kong, where the cityscape is always evolving, it's important to remember that a building's feng shui can change constantly with its surroundings.

TO YOUR HEALTH

In recent years Traditional Chinese Medicine (TCM) has caused a lot of holistic hype in the West. Around here, though, it's been going strong for a while—more than 2,000 years, to be precise. Although modern Hong Kongers may see western doctors for serious illnesses, for minor complaints and everyday pick-me-ups they still turn to traditional remedies.

To get to the root of your body's disequilibrium, a TCM practitioner takes your pulse in different places, examines your tongue, eyes, and ears, and talks to you. Your prescription could include herbal tonics, teas, massage, dietary recommendations, and acupuncture.

Key Concepts Taoists believe that the world is made up of two opposing but interdependent forces: negative *yin*, representing darkness and the female, and positive *yang*, standing for light and masculinity. Both are essential for good health: when one becomes stronger than the other in the body, we get sick.

Another concept is *qi*, the energy or life force behind most bodily functions. It flows through channels or meridians: if these are blocked, ill health can ensue. Acupuncture along these meridians is a way of putting your qi in order.

It's not all inner peace—to be healthy you need to be in harmony with your environment, too. The Five Elements theory divides up both the universe and the body into different "elemental" categories: water, wood, fire, earth, and metal. Practitioners seek to keep all five elements in balance.

Learning and Consultations

Eu Yan Sang Integrated Medical Centre. If you don't know your qi from your chin, and you're not sure if you need a dried seahorse or a live snake, head to the Eu Yan Sang Integrated Medical Centre. Glass cases at this reputable store display reindeer antlers, dried fungi, ginseng, and other medicinal mainstays. Grave but helpful clerks behind hefty wooden counters will happily sell you purported cures for anything from the common cold to impotence (the cure for the latter is usually slices of reindeer antler boiled into tea). There are other smaller branches all over Hong Kong, which offer over-the-counter consultations in English. ⊠ *152–156 Queen's Rd. Central, Central* ☎ *3521–1233, 3521–1236 hotline* ⊕ *www.euyansang.com* ☼ *Mon.–Sat. 10–2, 3–7* Ⓜ *Sheung Wan, Exit E2.*

⚠ Chinese medicines aren't regulated by the Hong Kong government. Anything that sounds dubious or dangerous might be just that.

Brush up on traditional treatments at the **Hong Kong Museum of Medical Sciences**, in Central. The least morbid and most enlightening exhibits compare Chinese and western medical practices, and show Chinese medicines of both animal and plant origin. Elsewhere, dusty displays of old medical equipment send macabre thrills up your spine. Reaching this museum is a healthy experience in itself: you pant up several blocks' worth of stairs to the Edwardian building in which it is located. Get here on the Mid-Levels Escalators: alight at Caine Road and walk west a few blocks to Ladder Street. The museum is just down the first flight of stairs, on the left. (See the full listing for details).

Hong Kong University Chinese Medicine Clinic and Pharmacy. The Hong Kong University Chinese Medicine Clinic and Pharmacy is a training clinic run by the most respected medical school in town. It also has master practitioners of acupuncture and orthopedics on hand. Consultations start at HK$200, visits to the masters at HK$500 (not including medicine). ⊠ *Unit 50–53, 2nd fl., Admiralty Centre, Harcourt Rd., Admiralty, Central* ☎ *3761–1188* ⊗ *Mon.–Sat. 10–2, 3–8, Sun. 9:30–1:30* Ⓜ *Admiralty, Exit A.*

Acupuncture and Massage

Happy Foot. At the root of Chinese acupressure and acupuncture is reflexology, which is based on the theory that there are reflex points on the feet, hands, and head linked to every part of the body. Thus a good foot, hand, or head massage is believed to effectively relieve tension or even treat illness. Foot massage need not be torture in the gentle hands of Happy Foot, where the goal is to make your whole body feel relaxed, from the feet up. Massages start at HK$198 for 50 minutes. ⊠ *11th fl., Jade Centre, 98 Wellington St., Central* ☎ *2544–1010* ⊕ *www.happyfoot.hk* ⊗ *Daily 10–midnight* Ⓜ *Central.*

Quality Chinese Medical Centre. Acupuncture, acupressure, and herbal medicine are just some of the offerings at the Quality Chinese Medical Centre. Consultations start at HK$80; expect to pay around HK$290 for acupuncture. ⊠ *Unit A, 5th fl., Jade Centre, 98 Wellington St., Central* ☎ *2881–8267 English hotline* ⊕ *www. qualitytcm.com* Ⓜ *Central.*

Medicine and Remedies

Good Spring Company Limited. Downing a bittersweet glass of herbal health tonic is a normal part of many a Hong Konger's day. Good Spring Company Limited offers blends for flu, headaches, colds, and coughs. A small paper cup usually starts at HK$6. Don't be put off by the black *gui ling gao* (turtle jelly): these wobbly puddings are commonly consumed for their medicinal properties. ⊠ *8 Cochrane St., Central* ☎ *2544–3518.*

Hung Fook Tong. You'll find Hung Fook Tong outlets in most MTR stations. The store offers TCM remedies for the cosmopolitan consumer with convenient, bottled herbal teas and additive-free soups packaged for easy reheating. Each product comes with a different list of medicinal benefits so ask the staff to recommend the best brew for you. ⊠ *Shop 58, Hong Kong Station, Central* ☎ *2526–6036* ⊕ *www. hungfooktong.com.*

Tong Ren Tang. Established in 1669, Tong Ren Tang has long been one of mainland China's most respected traditional medicine companies. There are stores all across the city stocking packaged pills, health foods (including bird's nest) and specialty wines designed to be good for what ails you. ⊠ *163 Des Voeux Rd. Central, Central* ☎ *3105–0016* ⊕ *www.tongrentang.com.*

BEACHES

Hong Kong has many fantastic beaches with gorgeous views of the sea dotted with small green islands. On the southern coast of the main island, the most accessible and most popular are Stanley and Repulse Bay. Just to the west is the smaller, less-crowded Deep Water Bay, and farther west is the more intimate South Bay. On the southeast coast of the island, Turtle Cove is isolated and beautiful, and Shek O's beach has a community feel. You can reach most beaches by bus or taxi (HK$150 and up). See the full listings for more information.

▌▌▌TIP➡ Hong Kong's Environmental Protection Department has set some tough guidelines and goals for cleaning up area waters. For more info, including beach-by-beach pollution ratings, check out the EPD's website: www.epd.gov.hk/epd.

Southside
Just east of Ocean Park, this bay was the setting for the William Holden film *Love Is a Many Splendored Thing* (1955). Nearby are the manicured greens of the Deep Water Bay Golf Course. The area has become a multimillionaires' enclave, and is home to Hong Kong's richest man, Li Ka-shing, a real-estate tycoon.

Repulse Bay, in Southside, is named after the British warship HMS *Repulse* and not, as some say, after its slightly murky waters. If you come out here, the **Verandah**, a replica of the eating and drinking establishment that once graced the iconic Repulse Bay Hotel, is a great place for traditional English afternoon tea.

In Shek O village you can find old mansions, small shops and a few popular Chinese and Thai restaurants. Follow the curving path from the town square across a footbridge to Tai Tau Chau, really a large rock with a lookout over

the South China Sea. Also near town are the Shek O Golf and Country Club and the superb Shek O Country Park, with great trails and bird-watching. From Central, take MTR to Shau Kei Wan, then take Bus 9 to the last stop (about 30 minutes).

Stanley is known primarily for its market but past the market, on Stanley Main Street, a strip of restaurants and pubs faces the bay. Stanley's main beach is the site of Hong Kong's official Dragon Boat races, usually held in June.

The New Territories
Hap Mun Wan. Half Moon Bay, as Hap Mun Wan, is called in English, is a brilliant, golden-sand beach near Sai Kung Town on the Sai Kung peninsula. Sampans to Half Moon depart from the Sai Kung waterfront, beside the bus station. If you're sharing a sampan with other passengers, remember the color of the flag on the roof: that's the color you need for your return ferry. Shared sampans cost HK$40. *From Central, take MTR to Hang Hau, then Exit B1 and Minibus 101M to Sai Kung Town.* ✉ *New Territories.*

Sha Ha. The main reason people visit this beach on the Sai Kung peninsula is for the windsurfing. Grab something to eat at the restaurants and bars that dot the beach. *From Central, take MTR to Hang Hau, then Exit B1 and Minibus 101M to Sai Kung Town. It's a 10 min walk along the shore to Sha Ha.* ✉ *New Territories.*

Silverstrand. Though rocky in spots, this beach at the east end of Sai Kung has soft sand and is crowded on summer weekends. Walk down a steep set of steps to reach the small stretch of beach where families enjoy all manner of floating beds and tubes in the sea.

REGION/BEACH	Travel Time from Central	Peaceful	Swimmable	Lifeguards	Showers/ Restrooms
Southside					
Deep Water Bay	20 mins.	crowded	often	yes	yes
Repulse Bay	30 mins.	crowded	often	yes	yes
South Bay	30 mins.	crowded	yes	yes	yes
Shek O	60 mins.	crowded	yes	yes	yes
Stanley	40–45 mins.	crowded	yes	yes	yes
New Territories					
Clear Water Bay	70–80 mins.	crowded	yes	yes	yes
Hap Mun Wan	60–75 mins.	often	yes	yes	yes
Sha Ha	60–75 mins.	often	yes	no	no
Silverstrand	60 mins.	crowded	yes	yes	yes
Outer Islands					
Cheung Chau: Tung Wan	60–75 mins.	crowded	yes	yes	yes
Lamma: Hung Shing Ye	60–75 mins.	often	yes	yes	yes
Lamma: Lo So Shing	60–75 mins.	often	yes	yes	yes
Lantau: Cheung Sha Wan	60–75 mins.	often	yes	yes	yes

From Central, take MTR to Hang Hau, then Exit B1 and Minibus 11M toward the University of Science and Technology. ⊠ *New Territories.*

Lantau Island

Popular Cheung Sha, on Lantau Island, is only a short taxi or bus ride from the Silvermine Bay ferry pier. Its mile-long expanse is excellent for swimming.

Silvermine Beach. The stretch of beach on Lantau can be seen from the ferry as you approach the island, though because of its proximity to the pier and other fishing boats, the waters aren't as clean as those at Cheung Sha. You can rent bikes at the Silvermine Beach Hotel and explore the village of Mui Wo. *Take ferry from Central's Pier 6 to Mui Wo. Buses meet ferry every half hour on weekdays and Sat.; on Sun., buses leave when full.* ⊠ *Lantau.*

HIKING

Although most visitors to Hong Kong don't come for the lush lowlands, bamboo and pine forests, rugged mountains with panoramas of the sea, or secluded beaches, nature is never very far from all the city's towering skyscrapers. About 40% of Hong Kong's territory is protected in 23 parks, including four marine parks and one marine reserve.

Don't expect unspoiled wilderness, however. Few upland areas escape Hong Kong's plague of hill fires for more than a few years at a time. Partly because of these fires, most of Hong Kong's forests, except for a few spots in the New Territories, have no obvious wildlife other than birds—and mosquitoes. Still, you can enjoy magnificent views along many of the hiking trails, most of which are easily accessible by public transportation.

Getting Ready

Necessities include sunglasses, hat, bottled water, bug repellent, a day pack, and sturdy hiking boots. Weather tends to be warm during the day and cool toward nightfall. Check the weather before you set off; the Hong Kong Observatory (⊕ www.hko.gov.hk) has special forecasts for hiking and mountaineering.

It's important to stay in touch while out in the wilderness so bring walkie-talkies or well-charged mobile phones. Check the Office of the Communications Authority website (⊕ www.ofca.gov.hk), which has a mobile network coverage survey along popular trails.

Finally, remember to familiarize yourself with your trail to avoid getting lost. Pick up a guide like *Hong Kong Hikes* from any bookstore.

Government Publications Centre. You can buy trail maps at the Government Publications Centre. Ask for blueprints of the trails and the Countryside Series maps. Note that the HM20C series has handsome four-color maps, but they're not very reliable. The HKTB also provides maps with good walking trails and hikes. ⊠ *Unit 626, 6th fl., North Point Government Offices, 333 Java Rd., North Point* ☎ *2537–1910* ⊕ *www.bookstore.gov.hk.*

Trails

★ Fodor's Choice **Dragon's Back.** One of the most popular trails crosses the "rooftop" of Hong Kong Island. Take the Peak Tram from Central up to Victoria Peak, and tackle as much or as little of the range as you feel like—there are numerous exits "downhill" to public-transport networks. Surprisingly wild countryside feels a world away from the urban bustle below, and the panoramas—of Victoria Harbour on one side, and Southside and outlying islands on the other—are spectacular. You can follow the trail all the way to the delightful seaside village of Shek O, where you can relax over a casual dinner before returning to the city by bus or taxi. The most popular route, and shorter, is from Shek O Country Park. *Take the MTR from Central to Shau Kei Wan, then Bus 9, alight after the first roundabout, near the crematorium.*

Lion Rock. The easiest way to access the trail to Lion Rock, a spectacular summit, is from Kowloon. The hike passes through dense bamboo groves along the Eagle's Nest Nature Trail and up open slopes to Beacon Hill for 360-degree views over hills and the city. The contrasting vistas of green hills and the cityscape are extraordinary. There's a climb up the steep rough track to the top of Lion Rock, a superb vantage point for appreciating Kowloon's setting between hills and sea. The trail ends at Wong Tai Sin Taoist Temple,

where you can have your fortune told. *To start, catch the MTR to Choi Hung (25 mins from Tsim Sha Tsui) and a 10-min taxi ride up Lion Rock. From Wong Tai Sin, return by MTR.*

★ Fodor's Choice **MacLehose Trail.** Named after a former Hong Kong governor, the 97-km (60-mi) MacLehose is the grueling course for the annual charity event, the MacLehose Trailwalker. Top teams finish the hike in an astonishing 15 hours. Mere mortals should allow three to four days or simply tackle one section on a day hike.

This isolated trail starts at Tsak Yue Wu, beyond Sai Kung, and circles High Island Reservoir before breaking north. A portion takes you through the Sai Kung Country Park and up a mountain called Ma On Shan. Turn south for a high-ridge view, and walk through Ma On Shan Country Park. From here, walk west along the ridges of the mountains known as the Eight Dragons, which gave Kowloon its name.

After crossing Tai Po Road, the path follows a ridge to the summit of Tai Mo Shan (Big Hat Mountain), which, at 3,140 feet, is Hong Kong's tallest mountain. Continuing west, the trail drops to Tai Lam Reservoir and Tuen Mun, where you can catch public transport back to the city. *To reach Tsak Yue Wu, take the MTR to Hang Hau, then Exit B1 and Minibus 101M to Sai Kung Town. From Sai Kung Town, take Bus 94 to the country park.*

▐▐▐ TIP➜ An easier way to access Tai Mo Shan is via an old military road. En route you'll see the old British barracks, now occupied by the People's Liberation Army. Take the MTR to Tsuen Wan and exit the station at Shiu Wo Street, then catch Minibus 82.

Wilson Trail. The 78-km- (48-mile-) long trail runs from Stanley Gap on the south end of Hong Kong Island, through rugged peaks that have a panoramic view of Repulse Bay and the nearby islands, and to Nam Chung in the northeastern New Territories. You have to cross the harbor by MTR at Quarry Bay to complete the entire walk. The trail is smoothed by steps paved with stone, and footbridges aid with steep sections and streams. Clearly marked with signs and information boards, this popular walk is divided into 10 sections, and you can easily take just one or two (figure on three to four hours per section); traversing the whole trail takes about 31 hours.

Section 1, which starts at Stanley Gap Road, is only for the very fit. Much of it requires walking up steep mountain grades. For an easier walk, try Section 7, which begins at Sing Mun Reservoir and takes you along a greenery-filled, fairly level path that winds past the eastern shore of the reservoir in the New Territories and then descends to Tai Po, where there's a sweeping view of Tolo Harbour. Other sections will take you through the monkey forest at the Kowloon Hill Fitness Trail, over mountains, and past charming Chinese villages. *To reach Section 7, take the MTR to Tsuen Wan, then catch Minibus 82. Get off at the bus terminus and walk for 15 mins.*

CINEMA
HONG KONG

Hong Kong cinema still projects an image of classic martial arts and prolific Triad flicks, with a few auteurs capturing the nuanced poetry of life in the former British colony. Inside the territory, however, silly romantic comedies with Canto-pop stars, gory/sexy ghost films, cheesy slapstick throwaways, and a handful of thoughtful independent films also populate the screens. It goes without saying that you can learn a lot about Hong Kong by watching its local flicks in situ.

Hong Kong International Film Festival. The annual Hong Kong International Film Festival brings together some of the finest film industry talent from all over the globe. The festival usually occurs in mid-May, offering two weeks worth of movie screenings, exhibitions, and seminars, some hosted by world-renowned actors and filmmakers. ☎ 2970–3300 ⊕ *www. hkiff.org.hk.*

A Night at the Movies

Except for children's and other niche-market films dubbed in Cantonese, all non-English-language films have both Chinese and English subtitles. For showtimes and theaters, check the websites of the movie chains or theaters directly, where you can usually see the seating chart updated in real time, before either booking online by credit card or buying your tickets at the counter later (all cinemas have assigned seating). Most cinemas offer a discount on morning shows or matinees.

Broadway Cinematheque. The train-station design of this art house has won awards; inside the foyer a departure board displays the showings of primarily foreign and independent films, with a few Hollywood productions to round out the roster. You can read the latest reel-world magazines from around the globe at Kubrick,

the café-bookshop next door, which also sells film books, comics, and other alternative literature. ⊠ *Prosperous Garden, 3 Public Square St., Yau Ma Tei* ☎ *2388–3188 ticketing hotline* ⊕ *www.cinema. com.hk* Ⓜ *Yau Ma Tei.*

★ **Fodor's Choice** | **Hong Kong Film Archive.** Don't underestimate the popularity of old black-and-white films in a modern auditorium; it's best to buy your movie ticket in advance to avoid sold-out disappointment. The theater screens rare classics from the history of Hong Kong cinema and beyond, from the impressive archive of film reels and documents dating back several decades. Conscientiously curated film programs are accompanied by an exhibition in a separate gallery downstairs. ⊠ *50 Lei King Rd., Sai Wan Ho, Eastern* ☎ *2739–2139* ⊕ *www.filmarchive.gov.hk* ⊘ *Closed Tue.* Ⓜ *Sai Wan Ho.*

Palace IFC. Large, cushy brown leather seats and ushers in black suits make this boutique cinema seem more like a private screening room than a multiplex. Five screens show new releases, foreign and independent films, and occasionally even restored celluloid classics. It's pricier than most picture houses, but also much classier. ⊠ *1st fl., IFC Mall, 8 Finance St., Central* ☎ *2388–6268* ⊕ *www.cinema. com.hk* Ⓜ *Hong Kong or Central.*

GET OUT OF TOWN

Whether it's the sights of Central or the whirring sounds of Tsim Sha Tsui, spending a few days in Hong Kong's city center can be a sensory overload. If you want to escape the bustle for a little while, peace and quiet is usually just a train or a ferry ride away.

Outlying Islands

Hong Kong comprises 260 outlying islands, some of which make great escapes from the city. You'll find waterfront views, some seafood, and a little peace and quiet. Hong Kong ferries travel out from the Central pier outside Two IFC. For more information see the main listings.

Lantau is the largest of Hong Kong's islands and has a wealth of attractions, including Hong Kong Disneyland, the Giant Buddha, and the magnificent Po Lin Monastery. The island's mountains and parks also make it a hit with hikers.

For beaches and water sports, head to **Cheung Chau**. On weekends Tung Wan, its main beach, is so crowded that its sweep of golden sand is barely visible. Plenty of nearby restaurants offer refreshments, seafood, and shade. There are no cars allowed on the island, so the air is noticeably cleaner.

Lamma Island is also popular. It's about as close to a 1960s bohemian scene as Hong Kong gets—full of laid-back expats who've spawned a subculture of vegetarian restaurants, health-food shops, and craft stores. "Beach" overstates the sandy strip known as Hung Shing Yeh, also called Power Station Beach because of the massive power plant visible from it. Stay on shore if you see plastic bags or other refuse on the water. Or just head to Yung Shue Wan, the former farming and fishing village that's been an expat enclave since the early 1980s.

New Territories

North of the Kowloon Peninsula, the New Territories is made up mostly of rural landscapes and well-preserved heritage sites, though new town centers and residential complexes have grown over the past few decades.

Sha Tin is one of the most developed and densely populated districts in the New Territories. It's home to the Chinese University of Hong Kong, as well as the perpetually packed New Town Plaza shopping mall and the Sha Tin racecourse. There are interesting cultural and historical sites out here, too, including the Hakka walled villages and the Ten Thousand Buddhas Monastery. At night, there are open-air food markets serving Sha Tin's famous chicken congee and roast pigeon.

The former fishing village of **Sai Kung** is known for its seafood restaurants. The tourist-friendly town center is easily accessible by public transportation, but the district also boasts unsoiled beaches, lush country parks, and rural villages that are only accessible by foot, taxi, or boat.

Macau

Billed as the Las Vegas of Asia, this tiny city glitters with the lights from its larger-than-life hotels and casinos. Gambling is a favorite pastime here, but the island is also a fascinating cultural destination, having retained so much of its colonial Portuguese past. The cuisine here is unique—a blend of Chinese and Portuguese cooking with an emphasis on spices. Ferries depart every day from Hong Kong–Macau and Hong Kong–China ferry terminals. Single trips take approximately 45 minutes to 1 hour.

Central Hong Kong and Kowloon

WORD OF MOUTH

"You can spend hours in Hong Kong Park—watching or joining the morning crowd doing their Tai Chi, having a great run, and being struck by the contrasting harmonies of the non-stop frenzy of HK side-by-side with the serenity of the park."

—rizzuto

Updated by
Doretta Lau

The Hong Kong Island skyline, with its ever-growing number of skyscrapers, speaks to ambition and money. Paris, London, even New York were centuries in the making, while Hong Kong's towers, bright lights, and glitzy shopping emporia weren't yet part of the urban scene when many of the young investment bankers who fuel one of the world's leading financial centers were born.

Commerce is concentrated in the glittering high-rises of Central, tucked between Victoria Harbor and forested peaks on Hong Kong Island's north shore. While it's easy to think all the bright lights are the sum of today's Hong Kong, you need only walk or board a tram for the short jaunt west into Western to discover a side of Hong Kong that is more traditionally Chinese but no less high-energy. You'll discover the real Hong Kong to the east of Central, too, in Wan Chai, Causeway Bay, and beyond. Amid the residential towers are restaurants, shopping malls, bars, convention centers, a nice smattering of museums, and—depending on fate and the horse you wager on—one of Hong Kong's luckiest or unluckiest spots, the Happy Valley Racecourse.

Kowloon sprawls across a generous swath of the Chinese mainland across Victoria Harbour from Central. Tsim Sha Tsui, at the tip of Kowloon peninsula, is packed with glitzy shops, first-rate museums, and eye-popping views of the skyline across the water. Just to the north are the teeming market streets of Mong Kok and in the dense residential neighborhoods beyond, two of Hong Kong's most enchanting spiritual sights, Wong Tai Sin Temple and Chi Lin Nunnery.

As you navigate this huge metropolis (easy to do on the excellent transportation network), keep in mind that streets are usually numbered odd on one side, even on the other. There's no baseline for street numbers and no block-based numbering system, but street signs indicate building numbers for any given block.

WESTERN

Sightseeing
☆★★★

Dining
☆☆★★

Lodging
☆☆★★

Shopping
☆☆☆★

Western has been called Hong Kong's Chinatown, and despite the name this is the part of Hong Kong least affected by Western influence. Many of the narrow, jammed streets that climb the slopes of Victoria Peak seem to be light-years from the dazzle of Central, just down the road. Though developers are making short work of the traditional architecture, Western's colonial buildings, rattling trams, old-world medicine shops, and lively markets still recall bygone times. Western is a foodie's idea of heaven, as you'll soon discover when you step into Sheung Wan Wet Market on Queen's Road or browse the dried delicacies—abalone, bird's nests, sea cucumbers, mushrooms—in shops around Wing Lok Street and Des Voeux Road.

TOP ATTRACTIONS

Hong Kong Museum of Medical Sciences. You can find out all about medical practices, disease outbreaks, and breakthroughs at this private museum, which is housed in a redbrick building at the top of Ladder Street that references Edwardian style architecture. The 11 exhibition galleries cover 10,000 square feet, and present information on both Western and Chinese medical practices. ⊠ *2 Caine Lane, Mid-Levels, Western* ☎ *2549–5123* ⊕ *www.hkmms.org.hk* ⌨ *HK$10* ☉ *Tues.–Sat. 10–5, Sun. and holidays 1–5* Ⓜ *Sheung Wan, Exit A2.*

Man Mo Temple. No one knows exactly when Hong Kong Island's oldest temple was built—the consensus is sometime around the arrival of the British in 1841. The temple is dedicated to the Taoist gods of literature and war: Man, who wears green, and Mo, dressed in red. The temple bell, cast in Canton in 1847, and the drum next to it are sounded to attract the gods' attention when a prayer is being offered. ⊠ *Hollywood Rd. at Ladder St., Sheung Wan, Western* ☉ *Daily 8–6* Ⓜ *Sheung Wan, Exit A2.*

Fodor'sChoice
★

University Museum and Art Gallery, The University of Hong Kong. Chinese harp music and a faint smell of incense float through peaceful rooms filled with a small but excellent collection of Chinese antiquities. On view are ceramics and bronzes, some dating from 3,000 BC; fine paintings; lacquerware; and carvings in jade, stone, and wood. Some superb ancient pieces include ritual vessels, decorative mirrors, and painted pottery. The museum has the world's largest collection of Nestorian crosses, dating from the Mongol Period (1280–1368). These belonged

GETTING ORIENTED

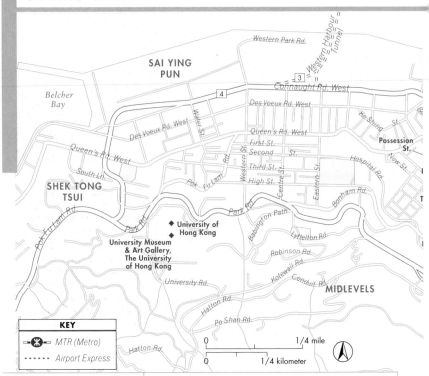

Western Park Rd.

SAI YING PUN

Belcher Bay

Connaught Rd. West

3

4

Des Voeux Rd. West

Des Voeux Rd. West

Water St.

Ko Shing St.

Queen's Rd. West

Queen's Rd. West

First St.

Possession St.

Second St.

South Ln.

Western Rd.

Third St.

Centre St.

Eastern St.

High St.

Hospital Rd.

New St.

SHEK TONG TSUI

Pok Fu Lam Rd.

Pok Fu Lam Rd.

Park Rd.

Park Rd.

Bonham Rd.

Babington Path

◆ **University of Hong Kong**

Lyttelton Rd.

University Museum & Art Gallery, The University of Hong Kong

Robinson Rd.

University Rd.

Kotewall Rd.

Conduit Rd.

MIDLEVELS

Hatton Rd.

Po Shan Rd.

Hatton Rd.

KEY

━⊗━ *MTR (Metro)*

‐‐‐‐‐ *Airport Express*

0   1/4 mile

0   1/4 kilometer

THE TERRITORY

The Mid-Levels Escalator is the unofficial boundary between Western and Central. Several main thoroughfares run through Western parallel to the shore: Des Voeux Road (where the trams run), Queen's Road, Hollywood Road, and Caine Road.

Western technically reaches all the way to Kennedy Town, where the tram lines end, but there's not much of interest for a sightseer beyond Sheung Wan.

TAKING IT IN

Colonial Architecture. You can see Western's colonial buildings on an hour-long stroll from the University of Hong Kong (take a cab or bus out). East along Bonham Road, which becomes Caine Road, are Victorian apartments. The Museum of Medical Sciences is at Caine Lane. Head down the staircase, then left onto Hollywood Road to Possession Street. Follow this downhill, doglegging right and left through Bonham Strand, onto Morrison, and to the Western Market.

Traditional Goods. An hour is enough time to wander Sheung Wan's traditional shops. In the morning, when trade's brisk, take the tram to Wilmer Street. Walk a block south and turn left onto Queen's Road West (herbal remedies, temple goods). Walk left for a block at Possession, then loop left through Bonham Strand West (ginseng), right for a block at Des Voeux, then back along Wing Lok (dried seafood). Continue on Bonham Strand (bird's nests), dipping left onto Hillier (snakes) and beyond to Man Wa Lane (chops).

2

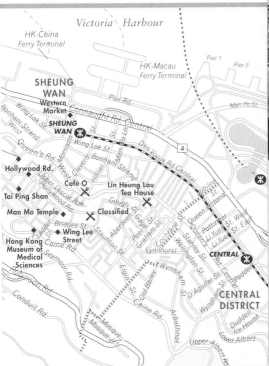

GETTING AROUND

The most scenic way to cross Western is on a tram along Des Voeux Road; the route runs all the way from Central to Sheung Wan. From Central this is probably the quickest route into Western: no traffic, no subway lines, no endless underground walks. There are stops every two or three blocks. The Sheung Wan MTR station brings you within spitting distance of Western Market. Alternately, Bus 3B runs between Jardine House in Central to the university, as does green Minibus 8. Buses 40 and 40M also run through Central to the university. Expect a taxi from Central to the area around the Mid-Levels Escalators to cost about HK$24.

QUICK BITES

Gage Street is great for Hong Kong fast food like a bowl of steaming wonton noodles, at any *dai pai dong* (street-stall restaurant).

Classified. Sit on weathered wooden benches at Classified and sample cheeses from a vast selection. Or have a coffee, a glass of wine, or a hearty pasta. ⊠ *108 Hollywood Rd., Sheung Wan, Western* ☎ *2525–3454.*

Lin Heung Lau Tea House. Cracked Formica tabletops, cranky waiters, old men reading the newspapers: There's nothing fancy about Lin Heung Lau Tea House, but it's been doing great dim sum for years. Stop by any time after 6 am and fill up on such dishes as *ha gau* (steamed shrimp dumplings) and *cha siu bau* (barbecue pork buns), washed down with lots of tea. ⊠ *160 Wellington St., Sheung Wan, Western* ☎ *2544–4556.*

to a heretical Christian sect who came to China from the Middle East during the Tang Dynasty (618–907).

There are usually two or three well-curated temporary exhibitions on view; contemporary artists who work in traditional mediums are often featured. ■ TIP➜ Don't miss part of the museum: the collection is spread between the T.T. Tsui Building and the Fung Ping Shan Building, which you access via a first-floor footbridge. The museum is a bit out of the way—20 minutes from Central via Buses 3B, 23, 40, 40 M, or 103, or a 15-minute uphill walk from Sheung Wan MTR—but it's a must for the true Chinese art lover. ⊠ *94 Bonham Rd., Pokfulam, Western* ☎ *2241–5500* ⊕ *www.hku.hk/hkumag* ☒ *Free* ☉ *Mon.–Sat. 9:30–6, Sun. 1–6* Ⓜ *Sheung Wan.*

WORTH NOTING

Hollywood Road. Hong Kong's best antiques shops and classical-art galleries are on this street, named for the holly trees that once grew here. The farther west you go, the less genuine things get. Porcelain, curios, and not-very-old trinkets masquerading as artifacts make up most of the offerings on Upper Lascar Row, a flea market commonly known as Cat Street. ⊠ *Hollywood Rd. between Arbuthnot Rd. and Queen's Rd. Wes, Sheung Wan, Western* Ⓜ *Sheung Wan, Exit A2.*

Possession Street. A sign here marks where Captain Charles Elliott stepped ashore in 1841 to claim Hong Kong for the British empire. This was once the waterfront, but aggressive reclamation has left the spot several blocks inland. At the top of the street stands Hollywood Centre, home to a number of shops and galleries and the non-profit contemporary art space Asia Art Archive. ⊠ *Possession St., between Queen's Rd. Central and Hollywood Rd., Sheung Wan, Western* Ⓜ *Sheung Wan, Exit A2.*

Tai Ping Shan. The maze of streets west of Man Mo Temple is known as Tai Ping Shan (the Chinese name for Victoria Peak, which towers above it). It's a sleepy area that's filled with small shops. One of the city's oldest residential districts has undergone major gentrification in recent years. ⊠ *Tai Ping Shan St. between Upper Station St. and Square St., Sheung Wan, Western* Ⓜ *Sheung Wan, Exit A2.*

The University of Hong Kong. It's worth a trip out to the western end of the Mid-Levels to see the imposing Edwardian buildings, most along Bonham Road, of the University of Hong Kong, where competition for a place is fierce. The institution opened in 1912 with the Faculty of Medicine. Today the exteriors of University Hall, Hung Hing Ying Building, and Tang Chi Ngong Building are on the government's "Declared Momument List." ⊠ *Bonham Rd. at Pok Fu Lan Rd., Pok Fu Lam, Western* ☎ *2859–2111* ⊕ *www.hku.hk.*

Western Market. The Sheung Wan district's iconic market, a hulking brown-and-white colonial structure, is a good place to get your bearings. Built in 1906, it functioned as a produce market for 83 years. Today it's a shopping center selling trinkets and fabrics—the architecture is what's worth the visit. Nearby are the Chinese herbal medicine on Ko Shing Street and Queen's Road West; dried seafood on Wing Lok Street and Des Voeux Road West; and ginseng and bird's nest on Bonham Strand West. ✉ *323 Des Voeux Rd. Central, Sheung Wan, Western* ☉ *Daily 10 am–midnight* Ⓜ *Sheung Wan, Exit B or C.*

Wing Lee Street. Just minutes away from Man Mo Temple is one of the last streets in Hong Kong where every building features 1950s architecture. In 2010 the buildings on this tucked-away street were saved from being demolished, following a series of protests and a plea from the filmmakers of the award-winning local film *Echoes of the Rainbow*. ✉ *Wing Lee St., above Hollywood Rd. between Ladder and Shing Wong Sts., Sheung Wan, Western* Ⓜ *Sheung Wan, Exit A2.*

CENTRAL

Sightseeing
★★★★
Dining
☆★★★
Lodging
☆★★★
Shopping
★★★★

Hong Kong's historical heart has been a world center of trade and commerce since the mid-19th-century British-colonial era. Streets and squares are lined with architectural landmarks that these days are overshadowed by soaring masterpieces of contemporary architecture. Somehow the mishmash works. Central is still, yes, the city center, packed with businesspeople, shoppers, and tourists. Bankers and diplomats rub elbows with *tai-tai*—local-speak for ladies who lunch, but the term can certainly apply to men as well—who can work off a meal shopping at designer-packed malls or luxury emporiums selling made-to-measure Chinese-style suits and cheongsams. With the harbor on one side and Victoria Peak on the other, Central also provides unrivaled views—once you get high enough to see them, whether from a skyscraper or the hillsides that provide a backdrop to the district.

TOP ATTRACTIONS

Central Star Ferry Pier. Take in the view of the Kowloon skyline from this pier, from which sturdy green-and-white Star Ferries cross the harbor. Naturally, the views are even better from the open water. ⊠ *Man Kwong St. between Rumsey and Man Yiu Sts., Central* ☎ *2367–7065 for ferries, 2118–6201 for tours* ⊕ *www.starferry.com.hk* Ⓜ *Hong Kong Station, Exit A2.*

2

Fodor'sChoice
★
Flagstaff House Museum of Tea Ware. All that's good about British colonial architecture is exemplified in the simple white facade, wooden monsoon shutters, and colonnaded verandas. More than 600 pieces of delicate antique teaware from the Tang (618–907) through the Qing (1644–1911) dynasties fill rooms that once housed the commander of the British forces. ■**TIP➔** Skip the lengthy, confusing tea-ceremony descriptions; concentrate on the porcelain itself. Look out for the unadorned brownish-purple clay of the Yixing pots: unglazed, their beauty hinges on perfect form. There's a playroom on the ground floor with interactive computer stations on the history of tea. ✉ *Hong Kong Park, 10 Cotton Tree Dr., Central* ☎ *2869–0690* ⊕ *www.lcsd. gov.hk/ce/Museum/Arts/en/tea/tea01.html* ⬚ *Free* ⊙ *Wed.–Mon. 10–6* Ⓜ *Admiralty, Exit C1.*

⟳
Fodor'sChoice
★
Hong Kong Park. A welcome respite from the Central skyscrapers occupies the site of Victoria Barracks, a garrison; the buildings from 1842 and 1910 still stand. The park is home to the Flagstaff House Museum of Tea Ware and the Edward Youde Aviary. ✉ *19 Cotton Tree Dr., Central* ☎ *2521–5041* ⬚ *Free* ⊙ *Daily 6 am–11 pm* Ⓜ *Admiralty, Exit C1.*

Mid-Levels Escalators. The unimaginatively named Mid-Levels district is midway up the hill between Victoria Peak and the Western and Central districts. Running through it is the escalator, which connects the now-defunct Central Market (at the border of Central and Western) with several main residential roads. Free of charge and protected from the elements, this series of moving walkways makes the uphill journey a cinch. Before 10 am they move only downward, carrying workers bearing coffee to work. ✉ *Next to 100 Queen's Rd. Central, Central* ⊙ *6–midnight* Ⓜ *Central, Exit D1.*

SoHo. The area south of (i.e., above) Hollywood Road is the epicenter of Hong Kong's latest gastro revolution. The bars here are a chiller alternative to the crowded drinking spots in Lan Kwai Fong (Central's nightlife epicenter) and generally close by 2 am. Trendy boutiques are tucked between the eateries, some featuring local designers and one-of-a kind goods. ✉ *South of Hollywood Rd. and north of Caine Rd., just off Mid-Levels Escalators, SoHo, Central* ⊕ *www.ilovesoho.hk* Ⓜ *Central, Exit D1.*

Fodor'sChoice
★
Star Ferry. Since 1898 the Star Ferry pier has been the public gateway to Hong Kong Island from Kowloon. If it's your first time in the city, taking the Star Ferry across Victoria Harbour and back is a must. It's a beautiful and relaxing 10-minute trip on vintage vessels, whose average age is 50 years old. An evening ride is the most spectacular, when the city's neon and skyscrapers light up the skyline across the water, especially if you can time your ride to coincide with the 8 pm Symphony of Lights show.

For a poetic portrayal of the back-and-forth Star Ferry routine from an outsider's point of view, see the 2005 French film *La Moustache*, which was shot on location.

The new Central Star Ferry Terminal is at Piers 7 and 8 of the Outlying Islands Ferry Piers. On ferries between Central and Tsim Sha Tsui there are two classes: first-class seats (HK\$2.50–HK\$3) on the roomier upper

GETTING ORIENTED

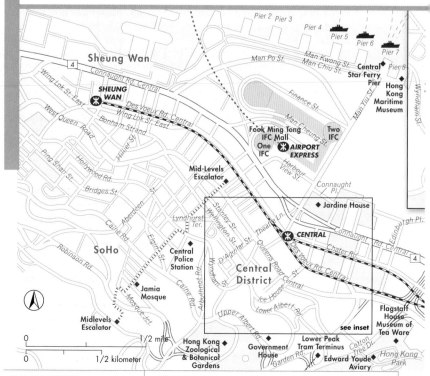

THE TERRITORY

The Mid-Levels Escalators forms the boundary of Central with Western. Streets between Queen's Road Central and the harbor are laid out more or less geometrically. To the south of Queen's Road, lanes climbing the slopes of Victoria Peak are steep and don't appear to follow any sort of pattern. Overhead walkways connect Central's major buildings, an all-weather alternative to the chaotic streets below.

QUICK BITES

At lunchtime people flood the cul-de-sac that is known as Rat Alley (Wing Wah Lane off D'Aguilar Street). Choose from Thai, Malay, Indian, Chinese, or American places.

Tsui Wah. No visit to Central is complete without a bowl of noodles at Tsui Wah, open 24 hours. ⊠ Ground fl., 15–19 Wellington St., Central ☎ 2525–6338 ⊕ www. tsuiwahrestaurant.com.

Genki Sushi. Need an instant sushi fix? Pull up a stool at the conveyor belt at Genki Sushi. ⊠ Ground fl., Far East Finance Centre, 16 Harcourt Rd., Admiralty ☎ 2865–2933 ⊕ www.genkisushi.com.hk.

2

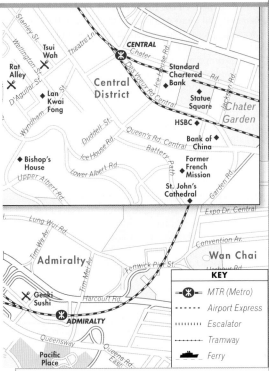

TAKING IT IN

Colonial Central. *South China Morning Post* columnist Jason Wordie (⊕ *www.jasonswalks. com*) leads three-hour tours loaded with anecdotes.

The Urban Runway. Cross Central without touching street level. Start in the IFC Mall; leave by Pret A Manger on the southeast side, turn right into the walkway, pass the General Post Office and Jardine House, and enter on the Armani floor of the Chater Building. The door between Emporio and Fiori leads to Alexandra House; take the stairs to the right of Dolce & Gabbana up into the Landmark, go straight ahead toward Harvey Nichols, then turn right at Anya Hindmarch, and walk into the Central Building. Turn left, go up the stairs past Clarins, and into Central Tower. Turn right in the elevator lobby and take the bridge into the Entertainment Building, which drops you in Lan Kwai Fong. Time your 15-minute walk to finish at 6 pm—happy hour.

KEY

⊛	MTR (Metro)
- - - - -	Airport Express
⋯⋯⋯⋯	Escalator
- - - - -	Tramway
🚢	Ferry

GETTING AROUND

Central MTR station is a mammoth underground warren with a host of far-flung exits. A series of travelators join it with Hong Kong Station, under the IFC Mall, where Tung Chung Line and Airport Express trains arrive and depart. Rattling old trams along Des Voeux Road reliably get you into Western or as far east as Wan Chai in minutes.

Star Ferry vessels to Kowloon leave Pier 7 every 6 to 12 minutes.

deck have more of a breeze, and an air-conditioned compartment in front; second-class seats (HK$2–HK$2.40) on the lower deck tend to be stuffier and noisy because they're near the engine room. ■ TIP➜ For trips from Central to Tsim Sha Tsui, seats on the eastern side have the better views. Across the way, the pier is a convenient starting point for any tour of Kowloon. As you face the bus station, Ocean Terminal, where luxury cruise ships berth, is on your left; inside this terminal, and in the adjacent Harbour City complex, are miles of air-conditioned shopping arcades. Across the street, the Peninsula hotel is the classic destination for afternoon tea. Or simply stroll eastward along the Avenue of Stars for an extended waterfront view of the famous Hong Kong skyline. ☎ 2367–7065 ⊕ www.starferry.com.hk ⊗ Central to/from Tsim Sha Tsui, daily 6:30 am–11:30 pm.

Fodor's Choice **Victoria Peak and the Victoria Peak Tram.** As you step off the Peak Tram,
★ a sharp intake of breath and bout of sighing over the view will cure the feeling that you left your stomach somewhere down in Central. Whatever the time, whatever the weather, be it your first visit or your 50th, this is Hong Kong's one unmissable sight. Spread below you is a glittering forest of skyscrapers; beyond them the harbor and—on a clear day—Kowloon's eight mountains. At the top you enter the Peak Tower, a mall full of restaurants and shops; there's a viewing platform on the roof. Outside the Tower, another mall faces you. Well-signed nature walks around the Peak are wonderful respites from the commercialism. On a rainy day wisps of cloud catch on the buildings' pointy tops; at night both sides of the harbor burst into color. Consider having dinner at one of the restaurants near the Upper Terminus.

■ TIP➜ Bypass the overpriced tourist traps inside Sky Terrace and Gallery and head straight up the escalators to the rooftop, which looks down over the Pok Fu Lam country park and reservoir, and, on a clear day, Aberdeen.

Soaring 550 meters (1,805 feet) above sea level, the peak looks over Central and beyond. The steep funicular tracks up to the peak start at the **Peak Tram Terminus,** near St. John's Cathedral on Garden Road. Hong Kong is proud that its funicular railway is the world's steepest. Before it opened in 1888, the only way to get up to Victoria Peak was to walk or take a bumpy ride in a sedan chair on steep steps. At the Lower Terminus, the Peak Tram Historical Gallery displays a replica of the first-generation Peak Tram carriage. On the way up, grab a seat on the right-hand side for the best views of the harbor and mountains. The trams, which look like old-fashioned trolley cars, are hauled the whole way in seven minutes by cables attached to electric motors. En route to the Upper Terminus, 396 meters (1,300 feet) above sea level, the cars pass four intermediate stations, with track gradients varying from 4 to 27 degrees.

Before buying a return ticket down on the tram, consider taking one of the beautiful low-impact trails back to Central. Buses also go down. You'll be treated to spectacular views in all directions on the **Hong Kong Trail,** an easygoing 40- to 60-minute paved path that begins and ends at the Peak Tram Upper Terminus. Start by heading north along fern-encroached Lugard Road. There's another stunning view of Central

From Victoria Peak, Hong Kong Island's multiple levels of skyscrapers stretch out below.

from the lookout, 20 minutes along, after which the road snakes west to an intersection with Hatton and Harlech roads. From here Lantau, Lamma, and—on incredibly clear days—Macau come into view. The longer option from here is to wind your way down Hatton to the University of Hong Kong campus in Western District.

Bus 15C, usually, but not always, a red double-decker with an open top, shuttles you between the Peak Tram Lower Terminal and Central Bus Terminal near the Star Ferry Pier, every 15 to 20 minutes, for HK$4.20. ⊠ *Tram between Garden Rd. and Cotton Tree Dr., Central* ☎ *2522–0922* ⊕ *www.thepeak.com.hk* ⊠ *HK$28 one-way, HK$40 round-trip* ⊘ *tram daily every 10–15 mins, 7 am–midnight.*

WORTH NOTING

Asia Society Hong Kong Center. A revitalized former explosives magazine compound is the pleasant setting for exhibitions pertaining to Asian countries and cultures. Views from the lush Joseph Lau Roof Garden are spectacular; a walk on the grounds is a must. The Center's Ammo Cafe is a lovely spot for lunch or a drink. ⊠ *9 Justice Dr., Admiralty* ☎ *2103–9511* ⊕ *asiasociety.org/hong-kong* ⊠ *HK$30* ⊘ *Tues.–Fri. 11–6, Sat.–Sun. 10–6* Ⓜ *Admiralty, Exit F.*

Bank of China Building. Along Statue Square's southern end are the three buildings of Hong Kong's note-issuing banks. The art deco building is the former headquarters of the Bank of China, which was built in the 1950s and renovated in 1998. The building now houses offices, as well as the exclusive China Club, a member's-only restaurant. ⊠ *1 Bank St., Central* Ⓜ *Central, Exit K.*

Bishop's House. This yellow Victorian building with brown trim has been the official residence of the Anglican bishop since 1851. A stone staircase with magnificent balustrades is adorned with four old-fashioned gas lamps that have been lighting the way since the late 1870s. ⊠ *1 Lower Albert Rd., Central* Ⓜ *Central, Exit D1.*

Central Ferry Pier. The pier juts out into the harbor in front of the International Finance Centre. Ferries regularly leave from here to Lantau, Lamma, and Cheung Chau islands. The Star Ferry Pier is just steps away (⇨ *See above*). ⊠ *Man Kwong St. between Rumsey and Man Yiu Sts., Central* Ⓜ *Hong Kong Station, Exit A2.*

Central Police Station. The colonial building just after Wyndham Street that becomes Hollywood Road is a must-have location in any self-respecting Hong Kong cop movie. It was the neighborhood headquarters from 1864—when part of it was built—through 2004. Currently it is closed except during special events, and is slated to reopen in 2015 as an arts and culture hub. ⊠ *10 Hollywood Rd., Central* ⊕ *www.centralpolicestation.org.hk* ⊗ *Not open to public except during events* Ⓜ *Central, Exit D1.*

Cheung Chau. This small, carless island southwest of Hong Kong is best known as the home of windsurfing Olympic gold medalist Lee Lai-shan. The island community lives mostly on the sandbar that connects the two hilly tips of this 1.2-mile-long, dumbbell-shape landmass. It's a one-hour ferry ride from Central's Pier 5 outside Two IFC, and the town harbor is lined with seafood restaurants and shops.

On weekends Tung Wan, Cheung Chau's main beach, is so crowded that its sweep of golden sand is barely visible. At one end of the beach is the Warwick Hotel. Plenty of nearby restaurants offer refreshments, seafood, and shade. There are no private cars allowed on this island, so the air is noticeably cleaner.

Edward Youde Aviary. This pleasant attraction in Hong Kong Park boasts numerous varieties of birds in an environment filled with plants, trees, and even a forest streambed. ⊠ *10 Cotton Tree Dr., Central* ☏ *2521–5041* ⊕ *www.lcsd.gov.hk/parks/hkp* 🎫 *Free* ⊗ *Daily 9–5* Ⓜ *Admiralty, Exit C1.*

Former French Mission Building. A tree-lined lane called Battery Path runs uphill parallel to Queen's Road Central behind the HSBC building. The British built it when they arrived in 1841 to move their cannons uphill—hence the name. At the top of Battery Path sits the Former French Mission Building, an elegant redbrick building with white columns and green shutters on the windows. Finished in 1917, the government-declared monument is now home to the Court of Final Appeal. ⊠ *1 Battery Path, Central* Ⓜ *Central, Exit D1.*

Government House. The handsome white Victorian occupying the land between Upper and Lower Albert roads was constructed in 1855 as the official residence of British governors, and is now home to the Hong Kong chief executive. During the Japanese occupation the house was significantly rebuilt, so it exhibits a Japanese influence, particularly in the roof eaves. The gardens are opened to the public once a year in March, when the azaleas bloom. ⊠ *Upper Albert Rd., Mid-Levels,*

Spend a few minutes, an hour, or a day people-watching in Hong Kong Park.

Central ⊕ *www.ceo.gov.hk/gh/eng* ⊗ *Not open to public except during special occasions* Ⓜ *Central, Exit D1.*

Hong Kong Maritime Museum. Previously located in Stanley, the museum, which explores Hong Kong's rich 2,000 year maritime history, re-opened at the end of February 2013 at the old Hung Hom Star Ferry Pier. One of its gems is an ink painting scroll called *Pacifying the South China Sea*, which chronicles the nine-day Battle of Lantau. The scroll has been digitized and transformed into a 360-degree animation experience. ⊠ *Central Pier No. 8, Central* ☎ *3713–2500* ⊕ *www.hkmaritimemuseum.org/eng* 🕮 *HK$30.*

Hong Kong Zoological and Botanical Gardens. This welcoming green space includes a children's playground and numerous gardens, but the real attractions are the dozens of mammals, birds, and reptiles housed in zoological exhibits. Buses 3B, 12, and 13 run from various other stops in Central; the walk from the Central MTR stop is quite a distance and uphill. ⊠ *Albany Rd. between Robinson and Upper Albert Rds., Central* ☎ *2530–0154* 🕮 *Free* ⊗ *Daily 6 am–10 pm* Ⓜ *Central.*

HSBC. The spectacular strut-and-ladder facade of this Norman Foster building is one of the most important structures in 20th-century architecture. Walk under it and look up into the atrium through the curved glass floor, or go inside for a view of the building's mechanics. ⊠ *1 Queen's Rd. Central, across from Statue Square, Central* 🕮 *Free* ⊗ *Weekdays 9–5:30, Sat. 9–12:30* Ⓜ *Central, Exit K.*

International Finance Centre. One building towers above the rest of Central's skyline: Two IFC, or the second tower of the International Finance Centre. The tall, tapering structure has been compared to at least one—unprintable—thing and is topped with a clawlike structure straight out of Thundercats. Designed by Argentine architect Cesar Pelli (of London's Canary Wharf fame), its 88 floors top a whopping 1,362 feet. Opposite stands its dinky little brother, the 38-floor One IFC. The massive IFC Mall stretches between the two, and Hong Kong Station is underneath. If you wish to see the breathtaking views from Two IFC, you can visit the Hong Kong Monetary Authority (✉ *55/F, Two IFC* ☎ *2878–1111* ⊕ *www.info.gov.hk/hkma*). While there, take a quick look at exhibits tracing the history of banking in Hong Kong. Upon arrival, you may need to register your passport with the concierge. ✉ *8 Finance St., Central* ⊕ *www.ifc.com.hk* ☐ *Free* ☉ *Hong Kong Monetary Authority weekdays 10–6, Sat. 10–1* Ⓜ *Hong Kong Station, Exit A2.*

Jamia Mosque. The Mid-Levels Escalator goes right by the religious institution on Shelley Street. The original 1840s structure was rebuilt in 1915 and shows its Indian heritage in the perforated arches and decorative facade work. The mosque isn't open to non-Muslims, but it occupies a small verdant enclosure that's a welcome retreat. ✉ *30 Shelley St., above Caine Rd. next to escalator, Central* Ⓜ *Central, Exit D1.*

Jardine House. Just behind the IFC is a notable '60s skyscraper recognizable by its many round windows. The 52-level building is home to Jardine, Matheson & Co., the greatest of the old British *hongs* (trading companies) that dominated trade with imperial China. Once linked to opium trafficking, the firm is now a respected investment bank. ✉ *1 Connaught Place, Central* ☎ *2500–0555* Ⓜ *Hong Kong Station, Exit A2.*

Lan Kwai Fong. In Hong Kong the word "nightlife" is synonymous with LKF, a few narrow lanes filled with bars and clubs just up the hill from the intersection of Queen's Road Central and Pedder Street. Veering right at the top gets you to Wyndham Street and the start of a series of high-caliber antiques and Oriental-rug shops, as well as more drinking spots. ✉ *Lan Kwai Fong and D'Aguilar St. between Wyndham and Wellington Sts., Central* ⊕ *www.lankwaifong.com* Ⓜ *Central, Exit D1.*

Queen's Road. Hong Kong's answer to New York's 5th Avenue and London's King's Road are the first few blocks of Chater Road, Des Voeux Road Central, and Queen's Road Central (the thoroughfares that stretch west from Statue Square). Most high-end designers have boutiques in the priceless über-posh minimalls like the Landmark or Alexandra House. A stone's throw away, but at the other end of the income scale, are Li Yuen Street East and Li Yuen Street. Known as the Lanes, they're packed with stalls selling cheap cheongsams (sexy, slit-skirt, silk dresses with Mandarin collars) and Hello Kitty merchandise. On the south side of Queen's Road is steep Pottinger Street, a haberdasher's dream. ✉ *Queen's Rd. Central, Chater Rd., and Des Voeux Rd. Central, between Peel and Bank Sts., Central* Ⓜ *Central, Exit D1.*

St. John's Cathedral. A peaceful gap in the skyscrapers—on Garden Road and up from Queen's Road Central—accommodates the graceful Gothic form of this Anglican church. Completed in 1849, the cathedral is made of Canton bricks in the shape of a cross. The doors are made from

DID YOU KNOW?

Serenity is hard to come by in bustling Hong Kong, but locals and visitors alike can get a bit of peace in Hong Kong Park. The park's waterfall and lake are just the beginning. Anyone can join in the tai chi practices, make feathered friends at Edward Youde Aviary, or sip a spot of tea at the tea shop inside the Flagstaff House Museum of Tea Ware.

timber salvaged from the World War II-era British warship HMS *Tamar.* ⊠ *4–8 Garden Rd., Central* ☎ *2523–4157* ⊕ *www.stjohnscathedral.org. hk* 🖼 *Free* ⊘ *Mon., Tues., Thurs., Fri. 7–6, Wed. 7–6:30, Sat.–Sun. 7–7* Ⓜ *Central, Exit K.*

Standard Chartered Bank. The rose-color wedgelike building was completed in 1990 and designed by P&T Architects and Engineers. A pair of stained-glass windows by Remo Riva represents visions of "Hong Kong Today" and "Hong Kong Tomorrow." ⊠ *4 Des Voeux Rd., Central* Ⓜ *Central, Exit K.*

Statue Square. The land was gifted to the public by the Hongkong & Shanghai Bank (HSBC, whose headquarters dominate the southern end), with the proviso that nothing built on it could block the bank's view of the water. The Victorian–Chinese hybrid building on Statue Square's east side was built for the Supreme Court in 1912 and is now home to the 70-member Legislative Council (LegCo), often the focus of the demonstrations that have become a fixture of Hong Kong life since 1997. In front of the council building is the Cenotaph, a monument to all who lost their lives in the two World Wars. ⊠ *Between Chater Rd. and Des Voeux Rd. Central, next to Prince's Building at 10 Chater Rd., Central* Ⓜ *Central, Exit K.*

DID YOU KNOW?

Statue Square took its name from bronze figures of British royalty that stood here before the Japanese occupation, when they were removed and melted down. The only figure exempt was stern Sir Thomas Jackson (1841–1915), who looks over the square toward HSBC—he was the chief manager for more than 30 years.

WAN CHAI, CAUSEWAY BAY, AND EASTERN

Sightseeing
☆★★★

Dining
★★★★

Lodging
☆★★★

Shopping
☆★★★

Explore beyond Western and Central and you'll discover that Wan Chai, Causeway Bay, Happy Valley, and the neighborhoods of Eastern are equally as vibrant and reveal another facet of Hong Kong. Though Wan Chai is known primarily for its nightlife (think red lights and photos of semi-naked women outside clubs), it is also home to the Convention Centre and arts institutions. Causeway Bay, one of the city's liveliest areas, is a shopping and dining mecca, and the Happy Valley horse races, a big part of Hong Kong life, are just a short walk away.

WAN CHAI

All in all, Hong Kong's notorious center of lowlife is fairly tame these days, a bustling mix of hotels, shops, and convention facilities. This doesn't mean that the old neighborhood has lost all its character. A few blocks back from Wan Chai's new office blocks are crowded alleys where you can still experience old Hong Kong and stumble across a wet market, a tiny furniture-maker's shop, an age-old temple, and yes, the strip joints, bars, and gambling dens that have long made the quarter popular with denizens of the night. Like all of Hong Kong, Wan Chai is quite safe after dark, but single women strolling the streets in the wee hours might get unwanted attention from groups of drunken tourists.

TOP ATTRACTIONS

Hong Kong Arts Centre. The Arts Centre is a vibrant building housing several galleries, including the Goethe Institute, a cinema, and two performing arts venues. ⊠ *2 Harbour Rd., Wan Chai* ☎ *2582–0200* ⊕ *www.hkac.org.hk/en/index.php* 🎫 *Free* ☉ *Daily 8 am–11 pm* Ⓜ *Wan Chai, Exit C.*

GETTING ORIENTED

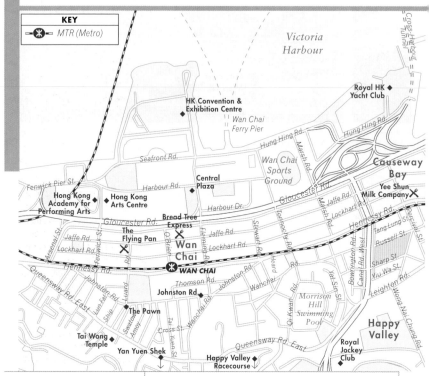

KEY

----★---- MTR (Metro)

Victoria Harbour

HK Convention & Exhibition Centre

Wan Chai Ferry Pier

Royal HK ◆ Yacht Club

Cross Harbour Tunnel

Hung Hing Rd.

Seafront Rd.

Wan Chai Sports Ground

Marsh Rd.

Causeway Bay

Fenwick Pier St.

Hong Kong Academy for Performing Arts

Hong Kong Arts Centre

Harbour Rd.

Central Plaza

Harbour Dr.

Gloucester Rd.

Jaffe Rd.

Lockhart Rd.

Yee Shun Milk Company ✕

Gloucester Rd.

Bread Tree Express

The Flying Pan ✕

Jaffe Rd.

Jaffe Rd.

Lockhart Rd.

Hennessy Rd.

Tang Lung St.

Russell St.

Lockhart Rd.

Wan Chai

O'Brien Rd.

Fleming Rd.

Stewart Rd.

Luard Rd.

Heard Rd.

Sharp St.

Canal Rd. West

Yiu Wa St.

★ **WAN CHAI**

Henessy Rd.

Queensway Rd. East

Johnston Rd.

Lun Fat

Ship St.

Swatow

Amoy

Thomson Rd.

Johnston Rd. ◆

Johnston Rd.

Wanchai Rd.

Tai Yuen St.

Wanchai Rd.

Yat-Sin St.

Morrison Hill Swimming Pool

Leighton Rd.

Wong Nai Chung Rd.

Happy Valley

The Pawn ◆

Cross St.

Queensway Rd. East

Royal Jockey Club

Tai Wong Temple ◆

Yan Yuen Shek

Happy Valley ◆ Racecourse ↓

THE TERRITORY	TAKING IT IN
Wan Chai's trams run mostly along Hennessy Road, with a detour along Johnston Road at the neighborhood's western end. Queen's Road East runs parallel to these two streets to the south, and a maze of lanes connects it with Hennessy. The thoroughfares north of Hennessy—Lockhart, Jaffe, and Gloucester, which is a freeway— are laid out in a grid. Causeway Bay's diagonal roads make the neighborhood hard to navigate, but it's small; wander around and before long you'll hit something familiar.	**Once Upon a Time in the East.** There were settlements here long before the British arrived, and the area was strategically important after colonization. Find out about it all from local historian Jason Wordie (⊕ www.jasonswalks.com), who runs tours through Wan Chai, Causeway Bay, and Shau Kei Wan. **A Wan Chai Wander.** Rattle to Wan Chai by tram along roads dense with jutting signs. Get off at Southorn Playground, and wander the lanes south of Johnston Road before heading up Luard Road and over walkways to the Hong Kong Academy for Performing Arts and Hong Kong Arts Centre, in adjacent buildings. The Hong Kong Convention and Exhibition Centre is a few minutes away—wander its harborside promenade. If you're here at dusk, Wan Chai's drinking holes will be lighting up as you walk back to the MTR along Fleming Road. Look up at Central Plaza on your right.

2

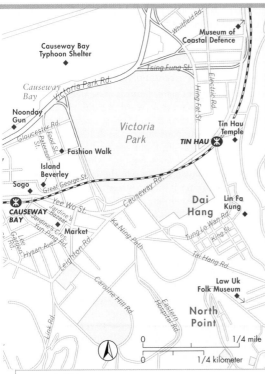

Map labels:
- Museum of Coastal Defence
- Whitfield Rd.
- Causeway Bay Typhoon Shelter
- Tsing Fung St.
- Electric Rd.
- Causeway Bay
- Victoria Park Rd.
- Hing Fat St.
- Tin Hau Temple
- Noonday Gun
- Gloucester Rd.
- Food St.
- Paterson St.
- Victoria Park
- TIN HAU
- Fashion Walk
- Island Beverley
- Sogo
- Great George St.
- Causeway Rd.
- CAUSEWAY BAY
- Yee Wo St.
- Dai Hang
- Lin Fa Kung
- Jardine's Bazaar
- Jardine's Cres.
- Ka Ning Path
- Tung Lo Wan Rd.
- Market
- Hysan Ave.
- Yun Ping Rd.
- Lee Garden Rd.
- Leighton Rd.
- Tai Hang Rd.
- King St.
- Law Uk Folk Museum
- North Point
- Caroline Hill Rd.
- Eastern Hospital Rd.
- Link Rd.

0 ————— 1/4 mile
0 ————— 1/4 kilometer

GETTING AROUND

Both Wan Chai and Causeway Bay have their own MTR stops, but a pleasant way to arrive from Central is on the tram along Hennessy Road. If you're going beyond Wan Chai, check the sign at the front: some continue to North Point and Shau Kei Wan, via Causeway Bay, while others go south to Happy Valley.

The underground MTR stations are small labyrinths, so read the signs carefully to find the best exit. Traffic begins to take its toll on journey times to places beyond Causeway Bay, and the MTR is often the quickest way to travel.

QUICK BITES

Flying Pan Wan Chai. In a nightspot-packed district, a café serving breakfast round-the-clock is bound to be a hit. The Flying Pan Wan Chai has waffles, blintzes, 24 different omelets, bagels, muffins, grilled sandwiches—the list goes on. Throw in squishy sofas and a jukebox, and this becomes the perfect spot to hit after bar hopping. ⊠ *3rd fl., 81–85 Lockhart Rd., Wan Chai* ☎ *2528–9997.*

Bread Tree Express. Hong Kong–style baked pastas, sandwiches, and inexpensive tea sets are oh-so satisfying at Bread Tree Express. Seating is limited at lunch, but this is the perfect spot for a late-afternoon nibble. ⊠ *G/F 134 Jaffe Rd., Wan Chai* ☎ *2529–8848.*

Yee Shun Milk Company. Yee Shun Milk Company sounds kooky, but you can't leave Causeway Bay without dessert at this crowded little diner. The signature dish is steamed milk with ginger juice. Alternatively, there's steamed egg, a local custard. ⊠ *506 Lockhart Rd., Causeway Bay* ☎ *2591–1837.*

WORTH NOTING

Central Plaza. Clad in reflective gold, silver, and copper-color glass, the triangular building at Harbour and Fleming roads is glitzy to the point of tastelessness. On completion in 1992 it was briefly the city's tallest building, but then Two IFC beat it by 130 feet. Note the colorful fluorescent tube lights atop the building; they actually make up a clock so complicated that no one knows how to tell time using it. ⊠ *18 Harbour Rd., Wan Chai* ☎ *2586–8111* ⊕ *www.centralplaza.com.hk.*

Hong Kong Convention and Exhibition Centre. Land is so scarce in Hong Kong that developers usually only build skyward, but the HKCEC is an exception, sitting on a spit of reclaimed land jutting into the harbor. Curved-glass walls and a swooping roof make it look like a tortoise lumbering into the sea or a gull taking flight, depending on whom you ask. Of all the international trade fairs, regional conferences, and other events held here, by far the most famous was the 1997 Handover ceremony. An obelisk commemorates it on the waterfront promenade, which also affords great views of Kowloon.

Outside the center stands the *Golden Bauhinia*. This gleaming sculpture of the Bauhinia flower, Hong Kong's symbol, was a gift from China celebrating the establishment of the Hong Kong SAR in 1997. The police hoist the SAR flag daily at 7:50 am. On the first of every month there is an enhanced flag raising ceremony at 7:45 am. ⊠ *1 Expo Dr., Wan Chai* ☎ *2582–8888* ⊕ *www.hkcec.com.hk* Ⓜ *Wan Chai, Exit A.*

Johnston Road. Trams clatter along this busy road, which is choked with traffic day and night. It's also packed with shops selling food, cell phones, herbal tonics, and bargain-basement clothes. Rattan furniture, curtains, picture frames, paper lanterns, and Chinese calligraphic materials make up the more traditional assortment at Queen's Road East, which runs parallel to Johnston Road. The lanes that stretch between the two roads are also lined with stalls, forming a mini-market of clothing and accessories. ⊠ *Johnston Rd. between Heard and Gresson Sts., Wan Chai* Ⓜ *Wan Chai, Exit A3.*

The Pawn. In a previous incarnation, this heritage building was home to a pawnshop. It is now a refurnished dining establishment serving modern British cuisine. The rooftop is official public space; you may visit it even if you are not a patron of the restaurant. ⊠ *62 Johnston Rd., Wan Chai* ☎ *2866–3444* ⊕ *www.thepawn.com.hk* ☉ *Mon.–Sat. 11 am–2 am, Sun. 11am–midnight* Ⓜ *Wan Chai, Exit A3.*

Yan Yuen Shek. High above Wan Chai halfway to Victoria Peak is the suggestively shaped monolith known as Yan Yuen Shek, or Lovers' Rock. It's a favorite with local single women, who visit to burn joss sticks and make offerings in hope of finding a husband. The easiest way up is on Minibus 24A from the Admiralty MTR station. ⊠ *South of Bowen Rd. between Wan Chai Gap and Stubbs Rds., Wan Chai.*

DID YOU KNOW?

Wan Chai was once one of the five *wan*—areas the British set aside for Chinese residences—but it developed a reputation for vice and attracted sailors on shore leave during the Vietnam War. How times have changed: Wan Chai is still as risqué an area as Hong Kong has to offer, but that says more about the city's overall respectability than it does about the available indulgences. For all its bars and massage parlors, Wan Chai is now so safe that it seems a pale version of the "Wanch" of Richard Mason's novel *The World of Suzie Wong.* Today many venture to the area for arts and culture at Hong Kong Academy for Performing Arts and the Hong Kong Arts Centre.

CAUSEWAY BAY

Shoppers crowd the streets of Causeway Bay, the area east of Wan Chai, seven days a week. There are also lots of restaurants and the odd sight. The action happens in a five-block radius of the intersection of Hennessy Road and Percival Street. Another of the area's specialties are upstairs cafés (inside combo commercial/residential buildings), often populated by teens and twentysomethings, and mazelike micromalls of independent fashion, jewelry, and gadgets.

TOP ATTRACTIONS

Fodor'sChoice **Happy Valley Racecourse.** The biggest attraction east of Causeway Bay
★ for locals and visitors alike is this local legend, where millions of Hong Kong dollars make their way each year. The exhilarating blur of galloping hooves under jockeys dressed in bright silk jerseys is a must-see. The races make great Wednesday nights out on the town. Aside from the excitement of the races, there are restaurants, bars, and even a racing museum to keep you amused. The public entrance to the track is a 20-minute walk from Causeway Bay MTR Exit A (Times Square), or simply hop on the Happy Valley tram, which terminates right in front. ⊠ *Sports Rd. at Wong Nai Chung Rd., Happy Valley, Causeway Bay* ⌂ *HK$10* ☺ *Wed. 5:15 or 5:30 during racing season* Ⓜ *Causeway Bay, Exit A.*

Victoria Park. Hong Kong Island's largest park is a welcome breathing space on the edge of Causeway Bay and bounded by Hing Fat, Gloucester, and Causeway roads. It's beautifully landscaped and has recreational facilities for soccer, basketball, swimming, lawn bowling, and tennis. At dawn every morning hundreds practice tai chi chuan here. It's also the site of midautumn's Lantern Carnival, with the trees a mass of colorful lights. Just before Chinese New Year (late January to early February), the park hosts a huge flower market. On the eve of Chinese New Year, after a traditional family dinner at home, much of Hong Kong happily gathers here to shop and wander into the early hours of the first day of the new year. ⊠ *1 Hing Fat St., Causeway Bay* ☎ *2890–5824* ⊕ *www.lcsd.gov.hk/parks/vp/en/index.php* ⌂ *Free* ☺ *24 hours* Ⓜ *Tin Hau, Exit A2.*

WORTH NOTING

Causeway Bay Typhoon Shelter. Hong Kong's maritime past and present are much in evidence on Causeway Bay's waterfront. Sampan dwellers and old-fashioned junks once gathered during bad weather in the Causeway Bay Typhoon Shelter. Most boat-dwellers have moved to dry land, so these days yachts and speedboats moor here. A few traditional sampans, crewed primarily by elderly women, still ferry owners to their sailboats. ⊠ *Near entrance of Cross Harbour Tunnel, Causeway Bay* Ⓜ *Causeway Bay, Exit D1.*

Hope that luck will be a lady and stick with you at Happy Valley Racecourse.

Noonday Gun. A block east of the Royal Hong Kong Yacht Club stands the Noonday Gun, which Noël Coward made famous in his song *Mad Dogs and Englishmen*; it's still fired at noon every day. It is said that the tradition began when a Jardine employee fired a gun in salute of the company's head arriving at the port, angering a member of the Royal Navy. ⊠ *Kellet Island, Causeway Bay* Ⓜ *Causeway Bay, Exit D1.*

DID YOU KNOW?

Opium-smuggler-turned-investment-bank Jardine Matheson once had its warehouses in Causeway Bay. The company moved to Central decades ago, but left a legacy of street names: there's Jardine's Bazaar and Jardine's Crescent, two of Causeway Bay's best shopping streets, and Yee Wo Street with the firm's Chinese name.

EASTERN

The densely populated neighborhoods east of Causeway Bay are largely residential and commercial, with a good number of shopping malls and restaurants that cater to residents. You'll also find art galleries and bookshops installed in converted industrial buildings, and some fascinating museums that are well worth seeking out.

TOP ATTRACTIONS

Law Uk Folk Museum. This restored Hakka house was once the home of the Law family, who arrived here from Guangdong in the mid-18th century. It's the perfect example of a triple-*jian*, double-*lang* residence. Jian are enclosed rooms—here, the bedroom, living room, and workroom at the back. The front storeroom and kitchen are the lang, where the walls don't reach up to the roof, and thus allow air in. Although the museum is small, informative texts outside and displays of rural furniture and farm implements inside give a powerful idea of what rural Hong Kong was like. It's definitely worth a trip to bustling industrial Chai Wan, at the eastern end of the MTR, to see it. Photos show what the area looked like in the 1930s—

HEADING EAST

The island's far eastern districts—North Point, Quarry Bay, Shau Kei Wan, and Chai Wan—are all undeniably parts of the "real" Hong Kong, which means they're full of offices, apartment blocks, and factories.

these days a leafy square is the only reminder of the woodlands and fields that once surrounded this buttermilk-color dwelling. ⊠ *14 Kut Shing St., Chai Wan, Eastern* ☎ *2896–7006* ⊕ *www.lcsd.gov.hk/CE/ Museum/History/en/luf.php* ⊡ *Free* ⊗ *Mon.–Wed., Fri.–Sat. 10–6, Sun. 1–6* Ⓜ *Chai Wan, Exit B.*

WORTH NOTING

☾ **Museum of Coastal Defence.** Shau Kei Wan is home to the Museum of Coastal Defence in the converted Lei Yue Mun Fort. The museum is in the redoubt, a high area of land overlooking the narrowest point of the harbor; you take an elevator and cross an aerial walkway to reach it. As well as the fascinating historical displays indoors, there's a historical trail complete with tunnels, cannons, and observation posts. ⊠ *175 Tung Hei Rd., Shau Kei Wan, Eastern* ☎ *2569–1500* ⊕ *hk.coastaldefence.museum* ⊡ *HK$10; free Wed.* ⊗ *Fri.–Wed. 10–5* Ⓜ *Shau Kei Wan.*

KOWLOON

Sightseeing
☆★★★
Dining
★★★★
Lodging
★★★★
Shopping
☆★★★

Just across the harbor from Central, this piece of Chinese mainland takes its name from the string of mountains that bound it in the north: *gau lung,* "nine dragons" (there are actually eight mountains, the ninth represents the emperor who named them). Kowloon is less sophisticated than its island-side counterpart, but its dense, gritty, urban fabric can feel more authentically Chinese. It's also the backdrop for Hong Kong's best museums and most interesting spiritual sights, as well as street upon street of hard-core consumerism in every imaginable guise. There are several neighborhoods here that are easy to get to and well worth exploring.

TSIM SHA TSUI

You'll probably come to this district hugging the waterfront at the southern tip of Kowloon (in Chinese the name means "pointed sandy mouth") to see one or more of Hong Kong's top museums. These collections are within easy reach of one another amid high-rises, hotels, shops, and Kowloon Park, a coveted parcel of green space. One of the best things to see in Tsim Sha Tsui (often referred to simply as TST) is Central: there are fabulous cross-harbor views from the **Star Ferry Pier** as well as from the ferries themselves. The sweeping pink-tile **Hong Kong Cultural Centre** and the Former KCR (Kowloon–Canton Railway) Clock Tower are the first landmarks along the breezy pedestrian **TST East Promenade,** which starts at the Avenue of Stars and stretches a couple of miles east. ■ TIP➔ Try to visit the promenade once in the daytime and once at 8 pm for the Symphony of Lights, a nightly show in which

GETTING ORIENTED

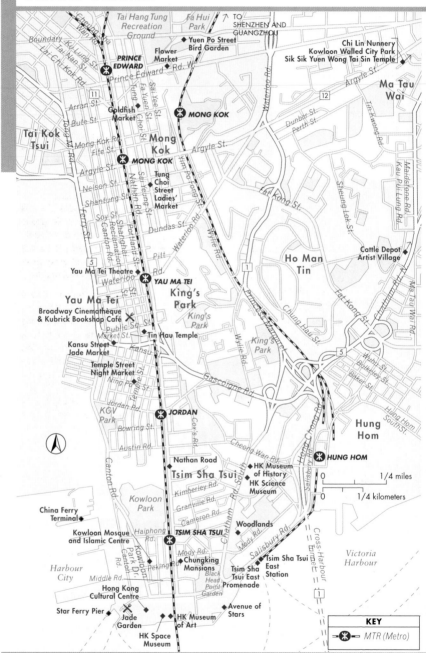

KEY

🔆➡ _MTR (Metro)_

GETTING AROUND

The most romantic way from Hong Kong Island to southern Tsim Sha Tsui (TST) is by Star Ferry. There are crossings from Central every 6–12 minutes and a little less often from Wan Chai.

TST is also accessible by MTR. Underground walkways connect the station with the Tsim Sha Tsui East station on the East Rail Line, where trains depart every 10–15 minutes for the eastern New Territories. The Kowloon Airport Express station is amid a construction wasteland west of TST, connecting with Austin station on the West Rail; for now hotel shuttles link it to the rest of Kowloon.

The MTR is your best bet for Jordan, Yau Ma Tei, Mong Kok, and other sights in far-flung Kowloon, including Wong Tai Sin Temple, and Chi Lin Nunnery.

QUICK BITES

Kubrick Bookshop Café. Arty tomes surround the tables at the Kubrick Bookshop Café. It's attached to the city's best art-house cinema. Tuck into sandwiches, pasta dishes, and cakes. The coffee's great, too. ⊠ *Broadway Cinemathèque, 3 Public Square St., Yau Ma Tei* ☎ *2384–8929* ⊕ *www.kubrick.com.hk.*

Jade Garden. Jade Garden is a popular dim sum chain. Come early on weekends. ⊠ *5th fl., Star House, opposite Star Ferry Concourse, Tsim Sha Tsui* ☎ *2730–6888.*

THE TERRITORY

From the Star Ferry Pier, the Tsim Sha Tsui (TST) waterfront extends a few miles to TST East. Shops and hotels line Nathan Road, which runs north from the waterfront through the market districts of Jordan, Yau Ma Tei, and Mong Kok. Wong Tai Sin Temple and Chi Lin Nunnery are just to the east of Mong Kok.

TAKING IT IN

Walk the Talk. Walk the Talk tours use your mobile phone or its iPhone App as an audio guide. The tours are packed with serious history and kooky anecdotes. ⊕ *www.walkthetalk.hk.*

Hong Kong Tourism Board (*HKTB*). Kowloon looks great from the harbor, and the Hong Kong Tourism Board runs a junk ride ($100) on the *Duk Ling* on Thursdays and Saturdays. A passport is required for registration. ⊠ *TST Star Ferry Concourse* ☎ *2508–1234* ⊕ *www.discoverhongkong.com.*

44 skyscrapers light up on cue as a commentator introduces them in time to a musical accompaniment.

TOP ATTRACTIONS

Duk Ling. The *Duk Ling* is a fully restored authentic fishing junk, originally built in Macau in the 1950s, whose large red sails are a sight to behold. For HK$50, the HKTB offers visitors aged 3 to 75 one-hour sails from Kowloon Pier (Thursday at 2 pm and 4 pm, Saturday at 10 am and noon) and from Central's Pier 9 (Thursday at 3 pm and 5 pm, Saturday at 11 am and 1 pm). Register first at the Hong Kong Tourist Board (HKTB) Visitor Centre in Tsim Sha Tsui, and bring your passport to prove you're from out of town. ⊠ *Tsim Sha Tsui* ☎ *2573–5282* ⊕ *www.dukling.com.hk.*

Fodor's Choice **Hong Kong Museum of Art.**

★ ⇨ *See highlighted feature in this section.*

Hong Kong Museum of History. The permanent Hong Kong Story features spectacular life-size dioramas that include village houses and a Central shopping street in colonial times, while the ground-floor Folk Culture section is a Technicolor introduction to the history and customs of Hong Kong's main ethnic groups. Upstairs, gracious stone-walled galleries whirl you through the Opium Wars and the beginnings of colonial Hong Kong. ▮▮TIP➡ Unless you're with kids who dig models of cavemen and bears, skip the prehistory and dynastic galleries. Reserve energy for the last two galleries: a chilling account of life under Japanese occupation and a colorful look at Hong Kong life in the '60s.

Budget at least two hours to stroll through—more if you linger in each and every gallery. Pick your way through the gift shop's clutter to find local designer Alan Chan's T-shirts, shot glasses, and notebooks. His retro-kitsch aesthetic is based on 1940s cigarette-girl images. To get here from the Tsim Sha Tsui MTR walk along Cameron Road, then left for a block along Chatham Road South. A signposted overpass takes you to the museum. ⊠ *100 Chatham Rd. S, Tsim Sha Tsui* ☎ *2724–9042* ⊕ *hk. history.museum* ☙ *HK$10; free Wed.* ☽ *Mon. and Wed.–Sat. 10–6, Sun. and holidays 10–7* Ⓜ *Tsim Sha Tsui, Exit B2.*

☙ **Kowloon Park.** These 33 acres are just behind Nathan Road, at TST's north end. They're crisscrossed by paths and meticulously landscaped but this is still a refreshing retreat after a bout of shopping. In addition to a fitness trail, soccer pitch, playgrounds, an aviary, and a maze garden, on Sundays and public holidays there are stalls with arts and crafts. ⊠ *22 Austin Rd., Tsim Sha Tsui* ☎ *2724–3344* ⊕ *www.lcsd.gov. hk/parks/kp/en* ☙ *Free* ☽ *5 am–midnight* Ⓜ *Tsim Sha Tsui MTR, Exit A1, Jordan, Exit C1.*

WORTH NOTING

Avenue of Stars. You have to look down to appreciate the city's walk of fame. Countless local film stars have pawed the wet concrete—you may not recognize many names unless you're a fan of Hong Kong films, but the homage shows how big the local film industry is. ⊠ *TST East Promenade outside New World Renaissance Hotel, Tsim Sha Tsui* ⊕ *www.avenueofstars.com.hk/eng/home.asp* Ⓜ *Tsim Sha Tsui, Exit E.*

HONG KONG MUSEUM OF ART

✉ *10 Salisbury Rd., Tsim Sha Tsui* ☎ *2721–0116* ⊕ *hk.art. museum* 🎫 *HK$10* ⊙ *Fri. and Mon.–Wed. 10–6, Sat. and Sun 10–7* Ⓜ *Tsim Sha Tsui MTR, Exit F.*

2

TIPS

■ Traditional Chinese landscape paintings are visual records of real or imagined journeys—a kind of travelogue. Pick a starting point and try to travel through the picture, imagining the journey the artist is trying to convey.

■ There is a collection search system on the first floor, as well as a research center.

■ Guided tours can help you understand art forms with which you're not familiar (in English Tuesday through Sunday at 11 am). Check the website for the schedule of more detailed visits to specific galleries—they change every month. If you prefer to tour alone, consider an English-language audio guide: it's informative, if a little dry, and it costs only HK$10.

An extensive collection of Chinese art is packed inside this boxy tiled building on the Tsim Sha Tsui waterfront in Kowloon. The collections contain a heady mix of Qing ceramics, 2,000-year-old calligraphic scrolls, and contemporary canvases. It's all well organized into thematic galleries with clear, if uninspired, explanations. Hong Kong's biggest visiting exhibitions are usually held here too. The museum is a few minutes' walk from the Star Ferry and Tsim Sha Tsui MTR stop.

Highlights

The Chinese Antiquities Gallery is the place to head if ceramics are your thing. A series of low-lit rooms on the third floor houses ceramics from Neolithic times through the Qing dynasty. Unusually, they're displayed by motif rather than by period: dragons, phoenixes, lotus flowers, and bats are some of the auspicious designs. Bronzes, jade, lacquerware, textiles, enamel, and glassware complete this collection of decorative art.

In the **Chinese Fine Art Gallery** you get a great introduction to Chinese brush painting, often difficult for the Western eye to appreciate. Landscape paintings from the 20th-century Guangdong and Lingnan schools form the bulk of the collection, and modern calligraphy also gets a nod.

The **Contemporary Hong Kong Art Gallery** showcases a mix of traditional Chinese and western techniques. Paintings account for most of the pieces from the first half of the 20th century, when local artists used the traditional mediums of brush and ink in innovative ways. Western techniques dominate later work, the result of Hong Kong artists' having spent more time abroad.

Hong Kong Science Museum. The exhibits are kid-friendly and hands-on and include an energy machine, a miniature submarine, and cognitive and memory tests. That said, this is more of a rainy-day time-killer than a must-see. ⊠ *2 Science Museum Rd., corner of Cheong Wan Rd. and Chatham Rd., Tsim Sha Tsui* ☎ *2732–3232* ⊕ *hk.science.museum* 🖃 *HK$25; free Wed.* ⊘ *Mon.–Wed. and Fri. 10–7, Sat.–Sun. 10–9* Ⓜ *Tsim Sha Tsui, Exit B2.*

Hong Kong Space Museum. A structure behind the art museum that looks like an oversize golf ball sliced in half houses a planetarium, a solar telescope, and an Omnimax theater. It's all fairly unremarkable, though, and children under 3 aren't allowed to view the Omnimax shows. ⊠ *10 Salisbury Rd., Tsim Sha Tsui* ☎ *2721–0226* ⊕ *hk.space. museum* 🖃 *HK$10* ⊘ *Mon. and Wed.–Fri 1–9, Sat.–Sun. 10–9* Ⓜ *Tsim Sha Tsui MTR, Exit F.*

Kowloon Mosque and Islamic Centre. Hong Kong's largest Islamic worship center stands in front of Kowloon Park. Visitors can call ahead to arrange for a tour of the premises or simply drop by to see the building, which is also known as the Kowloon Masjid and Islamic Centre, and was designed by noted Indian architect I. M. Kadri. In addition to prayer halls, the complex includes a medical clinic and a library. ⊠ *105 Nathan Rd., Tsim Sha Tsui* ☎ *2724–0095* ⊕ *kowloonmosque. com* 🖃 *Free* ⊘ *5 am–10 pm* Ⓜ *Tsim Sha Tsui, Exit A1.*

Nathan Road. The famous Kowloon road runs several miles north from Salisbury Road in TST, all the way to Mong Kok. It's filled with hotels, restaurants, shopping malls, and boutiques—retail space is so costly that the southern end is dubbed the Golden Mile. The mile's most famous tower block is ramshackle Chungking Mansions, packed with cheap hotels and Indian restaurants. The building was a setting for local director Wong Kar-Wai's film *Chungking Express.* To the left and right are mazes of narrow streets with even more shops selling jewelry, electronics, clothes, souvenirs, and cosmetics. ⊠ *Nathan Rd. between Salisbury Rd. and Boundary St., Tsim Sha Tsui* Ⓜ *Tsim Sha Tsui, Jordan, Yau Ma Tei, Mong Kok, Prince Edward.*

YAU MA TEI

North of Tsim Sha Tsui, the vibrant area of Yau Ma Tei teems with people and is home to several street markets. The area of Yau Ma Tei around Jordan Road is often referred to as Jordan. The Jordan MTR stop is a good place to start your exploring.

TOP ATTRACTIONS

Temple Street. Temple Street, in the heart of Yau Ma Tei, is home to Hong Kong's biggest night market. Stalls selling kitsch of all kinds set up in the late afternoon in the blocks north of Public Square Street. Fortune-tellers, prostitutes, and street doctors also offer their services here. ⊠ *Temple St. between Jordan Rd. and Kansu St., Yau Ma Tei* Ⓜ *Yau Ma Tei, Exit C; Jordan, Exit A.*

Tin Hau Temple. This incense-filled site is dedicated to Taoist sea goddess Tin Hau, queen of heaven and protector of seafarers. The crowds here

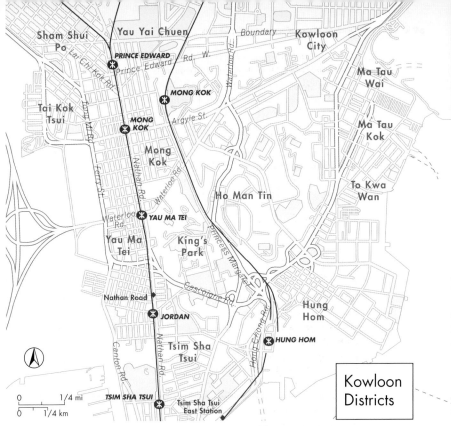

Kowloon
Districts

Sham Shui Po
Yau Yai Chuen
Boundary
Kowloon City
PRINCE EDWARD
Prince Edward Rd.
Rd. W.
Ma Tau Wai
Tai Kok Tsui
MONG KOK
Ma Tau Kok
MONG KOK
Argyle St.
Mong Kok
Lai Chi Kok Rd.
Tong Mi Rd.
Ferry St.
Nathan Rd.
Waterloo Rd.
Ho Man Tin
To Kwa Wan
YAU MA TEI
Yau Ma Tei
King's Park
Princess Margaret
Waterloo Rd.
Nathan Road
Gascoigne Rd.
Hung Hom
JORDAN
Hong Kong Rd.
Tsim Sha Tsui
Nathan Rd.
HUNG HOM
Canton Rd.
TSIM SHA TSUI
Tsim Sha Tsui East Station

0   1/4 mi
0   1/4 km

testify to her being one of Hong Kong's favorite deities—indeed, this is one of around 40 temples dedicated to her. Like all Tin Hau temples, this one once stood on the shore. Kowloon reclamation started in the late 19th century, and now the site is more than 3 km (2 mi) from the harbor. The main altar is hung with gold-embroidered red cloth and usually piled high with offerings. There are also two smaller shrines inside the temple honoring earth god Tou Tei and city god Shing Wong. Both the temple and stalls in the eponymous market outside are fortune-telling hot spots: you may well be encouraged to have a try with the chim. Each stick is numbered, and you shake them in a cardboard tube until one falls out. A fortune-teller asks you your date of birth and makes predictions from the stick based on numerology. Alternatively, you could have a mystically minded bird pick out some fortune cards for you. ■ TIP➜ It's a good idea to agree on prices first; bargaining with fortune-tellers is common. ⊠ *Market St. between Temple St. and Nathan Rd., Yau Ma Tei* ☉ *Daily 7–5:30* Ⓜ *Yau Ma Tei, Exit C.*

WORTH NOTING

Kansu Street Jade Market. From priceless ornaments to fake pendants, if it's green and shiny, it's here. Quality and prices at the stalls vary hugely, so if you're not with a jade connoisseur, stick with the cheap and cheerful. ⊠ *Kansu St. between Battery St. and Reclaimation St., Yau Ma Tei* ☒ *Free* ☉ *Daily 10–5* Ⓜ *Yau Ma Tei, Exit C.*

Shanghai Street. Traditional trades are plied along this street. There are blocks dominated by tailors or shops selling Chinese cookware or everything you need to set up a household shrine. Nearby Ning Po Street is known for its paper kites and for the colorful paper and bamboo models of worldly possessions (boats, cars, houses) that are burned at Chinese funerals. ⊠ *Shanghai St. between Jordan Rd. and Argyle St., Yau Ma Tei* Ⓜ *Yau Ma Tei.*

Yau Ma Tei Theatre. The government has converted this former movie theater (which had shown adult films for some years before falling into disuse) into a 300-seat venue for Chinese opera performances. A historic redbrick building next door serves as the theater's administration building. ⊠ *6 Waterloo Rd., Yau Ma Tei* ☎ *2264–8108* ⊕ *www.lcsd.gov.hk/ ymtt* ☉ *Daily 1–8* Ⓜ *Yau Ma Tei, Exit B2.*

MONG KOK

Mong Kok lives up to its Chinese name, which translates roughly as "busy corner." Long city blocks here are known for bustling markets that sell clothing, flowers, pets, and temple goods. The neighborhood is the epicenter of Hong Kong street fashion—the trends that originate from these bustling streets are known as "MK style." Mong Kok is technically the last district of Kowloon: Boundary Street marks the beginning of the New Territories, though these days the urbanized areas are known as New Kowloon.

WORTH NOTING

Fa Yuen Street. This street that runs parallel to Tung Choi Street Ladies' Market, between Argyle Street and Shan Tung Street, is sneaker central; sports shops sell some brands you know and lots you don't. If you're not sporty, the stretch between Mongkok Road and Nullah Road offers cheap versions of the latest clothing fashion trends. ⊠ *Fa Yuen St. between Mongkok Rd. and Shan Tung St., Mong Kok* ☒ *Free* Ⓜ *Mong Kok, Exit D3.*

Flower Market. Stalls containing local and imported fresh flowers, potted plants, and even artificial blossoms cover Flower Market Road, as well as parts of Yuen Po Street, Yuen Ngai Street, Prince Edward Road West, and Playing Field Road. ⊠ *Flower Market Rd. between Yuen Ngai St. and Yuen Po St., Mong Kok* ☒ *Free* ☉ *Daily 7–7* Ⓜ *Mong Kok East, Exit C; Prince Edward, Exit B1.*

☺ **Goldfish Market.** A few dozen shops on Tung Choi Street and Nullah Road sell the ubiquitous fish, which locals believe to be lucky. In addition to feed and aquariums, the market is home to other varieties of animals. ⊠ *Tung Choi St. and Nullah Rd., Mong Kok* ☒ *Free* ☉ *10:30–10* Ⓜ *Mong Kok East, Exit C; Prince Edward, Exit B2.*

Tung Choi Street Ladies' Market. Despite the name, stalls are filled with no-brand clothes and accessories for both sexes. The shopping is best between Dundas and Argyle. ⊠ *Tung Choi St. between Dundas St. and Argyle St., Mong Kok* ☒ *Free* Ⓜ *Mong Kok.*

CHI LIN NUNNERY

✉ *5 Chi Lin Dr., Diamond Hill, Northern Kowloon* ☎ *2354-1888* 🎫 *Free* 🕐 *Nunnery daily 9–4:30, lotus-pond garden daily 7–7* Ⓜ *Diamond Hill, Exit C2.*

TIPS

■ Left of the Main Hall is a don't-miss hall dedicated to Avalokitesvra, better known in Hong Kong as Kwun Yum, goddess of mercy and childbearing, among other things. She's one of the few exceptions to the rule that bodhisattvas are represented as asexual beings.

■ Be sure to keep looking up—the latticework ceilings and complicated beam systems are among the most beautiful parts of the building. Combine Chi Lin Nunnery with a visit to Sik Sik Yuen Wong Tai Sin Temple, only one MTR stop or a short taxi ride away.

Not a single nail was used to build this nunnery, which dates from 1934. Instead, traditional Tang Dynasty architectural techniques involving wooden dowels and bracket work hold its 228,000 pieces of timber together. Most of the 15 cedar halls house altars to *bodhisattvas* (those who have reached enlightenment)—bronze plaques explain each one.

Highlights

Feng shui principles governed construction. The buildings face south toward the sea, to bring abundance; their backs are to the mountain, provider of strength and good energy. The temple's clean lines are a vast departure from most of Hong Kong's colorful religious buildings—here polished wood and gleaming Buddha statues are the only adornments.

The **Main Hall** is the most imposing—and inspiring— part of the monastery. Overlooking the smaller second courtyard, it honors the first Buddha, known as Sakyamuni. The soaring ceilings are held up by 28 cedar columns, measuring 18 feet each. They also support the roof—no mean feat, given that its traditionally made clay tiles make it weigh 176 tons.

Courtyards and gardens, where frangipani flowers scent the air, run beside the nunnery. The gardens are filled with bonsai trees and artful rockeries. Nature is also present inside: the various halls and galleries all look onto two courtyards filled with geometric lotus ponds and manicured bushes.

Sik Sik Yuen Wong Tai Sin Temple is one of Hong Kong's most famous Taoist temples.

🕙 **Yuen Po Street Bird Garden.** Next to the Flower Market, more than 70 stalls sell different types of twittering, fluttering birds of numerous colors, shapes, and sizes. Birdcages and food, from seeds to live grasshoppers, are also for sale. ✉ *Yuen Po St. between Boundary St. and Prince Edward Rd. West, Mong Kok* 🕙 *Daily 7 am–8 pm* Ⓜ *Mong Kok East, Exit C; Prince Edward, Exit B1.*

NORTHERN KOWLOON

There's much to do in Kowloon beyond Tsim Sha Tsui and Mong Kok. Wong Tai Sin Temple and Chi Lin Nunnery, just a few subway stops to the east of Mong Kok, are two of Hong Kong's must-do spiritual sights. The Kowloon Walled City Park and Cattle Depot Artist Village are surrounded by fairly uninspiring residential and commercial districts but well worth a trip.

TOP ATTRACTIONS

Fodor'sChoice **Chi Lin Nunnery.**

★ ⇨ *See highlighted lising in this section.*

Kowloon Walled City Park. Arguably Hong Kong's most beautiful park, designed in Qing-dynasty style, is near the old Kai Tak Airport, between Tung Tau Tsuen and Tung Tsing roads. The park opened in 1995, and in previous centuries was a walled military site, then a notorious slum. Today the major attraction is the Yamen, an example of southern Chinese architecture of the 19th century, and is the only remaining structure from the original Walled City. There are also a number of traditional gardens on the grounds, and eight walks showcasing different flora, as well as free 45-minute guided tours. Hong Kong's Thai community is based in the streets south of the park, and there are countless hole-in-the-wall Thai restaurants. Bus 113 stops nearby, or take the MTR to Kowloon Tong and take a cab. ⊠ *Tung Tau Tsuen Rd. between Junction Rd. and Tung Tsing Rd., Kowloon City, Northern Kowloon* ☎ *2716–9962* ⊕ *www.lcsd.gov.hk/parks/kwcp/en/* 💲 *Free* ⊙ *6:30 am–11 pm.*

DID YOU KNOW?

Only the occasional patch of daylight was visible from the labyrinthine alleys of the Kowloon Walled City, Hong Kong's most notorious slum. Originally a 19th-century Chinese fortress, the city wasn't included in the British lease of the New Territories, thus it remained part of China and out of bounds to the Hong Kong police. The Triads ruled its unlicensed doctors and dentists, opium dens, brothels, gambling houses, and worse.

Fodor's Choice
★

Sik Sik Yuen Wong Tai Sin Temple. There's a practical approach to prayer at one of Hong Kong's most exuberant places of worship. Here the territory's three major religions—Taoism, Confucianism, and Buddhism—are all celebrated under the same roof. You'd think that ornamental religious buildings would look strange with highly visible vending machines and LCD displays in front of them, but Wong Tai Sin pulls it off in cacophonous style. The temple was established in the early 20th century, on a different site, when two Taoist masters arrived from Guangzhou with the portrait of Wong Tai Sin—a famous monk who was born around AD 328—that still graces the main altar. In the '30s the temple was moved here; continuous renovations make it impossible to distinguish old from new.

Start at the incense-wreathed main courtyard, where the noise of many people shaking out *chim* (sticks with fortunes written on them) forms a constant rhythmic background. After wandering the halls, take time out in the Good Wish Garden—a peaceful riot of rockery—at the back of the complex. At the base of the complex is a small arcade where soothsayers and palm readers are happy to interpret Wong Tai Sin's predictions for a small fee. At the base of the ramp to the Confucian Hall, look up behind the temple for a view of Lion Rock, a mountain in the shape of a sleeping lion. ■ TIP→ If you feel like acquiring a household altar of your own, head for Shanghai Street in Yau Ma Tei, the Kowloon district north of Tsim Sha Tsui, where religious shops abound. ⊠ *Wong Tai Sin Rd., Wong Tai Sin, Northern Kowloon* ☎ *2327–8141* 💲 *Donations expected. Good Wish Garden HK$2* ⊙ *Daily 7–5:30* Ⓜ *Wong Tai Sin, Exit B2 or B3.*

WORTH NOTING

Cattle Depot Artist Village. A former location for the slaughter of cattle has been transformed into a home for a number of artists' studios, a theater, and some of Hong Kong's best galleries, including 1a Space and Videotage. Individual artists and galleries keep erratic hours, and what you see will depend on who's open to the public at any given time. Take the MTR to Jordan and catch a cab, or take a bus that goes through To Kwa Wan, such as the 101. ⊠ *63 Ma Tau Kok Rd., To Kwa Wan, Northern Kowloon* 💲 *Free* ⊙ *Daily 10–7.*

Day Trips

WORD OF MOUTH

"We took the MTR to Lantau Island to go to the Big Buddha. We took the cable car up—stunning views of the islands. It is amazing how much 'wilderness' there is on the islands!"

—Florida1

Updated by
Doretta Lau

Beyond all the towering skyscrapers and bustling markets, 70 percent of Hong Kong's land is rural, rugged, and relatively unspoiled. Easy day trips from one of the most startlingly busy and modern metropolises in the world take you to pristine beaches, hillside forests, and still-quiet fishing villages. No matter what sort of experience you crave, Hong Kong's vast and efficient transport network puts just about any place you want to visit within easy reach.

Beach lovers usually head to the south side of Hong Kong Island, where the seaside towns of Shek O and Stanley command two peninsulas and are surrounded by popular stretches of sand. Of course, you never get too far from civilization in Hong Kong—the ever popular Ocean Park, an aquarium and water park, and a lush golf course are set amid the beautiful Southside scenery.

Lantau is the largest of Hong Kong's 200 islands and has long been a favorite getaway for city dwellers who want to escape to the forested landscapes and mountain vistas. The island is famous as the home of the world's favorite mouse, at Disney World, and for the world's largest Buddha, the Tian Tian Buddha at Ngong Ping. Near these sights are towering peaks offering mountain hikes and nice beaches backed by quiet fishing villages. You can take in the scenery from the Ngong Ping 360 cable car, a 5.7 km ride filled with fantastic views of Lantau's steep northern coast.

Many of Hong Kong's lushest, trail-laced parks are tucked away in the New Territories, at the eastern end of Kowloon. Here you can also catch glimpses of traditional life in rustic villages, visit incense-filled temples, or lie on pristine beaches.

SOUTHSIDE

Sightseeing
☆★★★

Dining
☆☆★★

Lodging
☆☆☆★

Shopping
☆☆☆★

For all the unrelenting urbanity of Hong Kong Island's north coast, the south coast is a rolling landscape of green hills dropping down to picturesque bays and sandy beaches. With beautiful sea views, Southside is a breath of fresh air—literally and figuratively—and coveted turf for some of Hong Kong's wealthiest residents. The pace is slower than it is in more congested parts of the city, and there are lots of sea breezes and opportunities to take sampan rides, play a round of golf, swim, or simply enjoy the scenery.

TOP ATTRACTIONS

Ocean Park. Most Hong Kongers have fond childhood memories of this aquatic theme park. It was built by the omnipresent Hong Kong Jockey Club on 170 hilly acres overlooking the sea just east of Aberdeen. Highlights include the four resident giant pandas; Marine World's enormous aquarium; Ocean Theatre, where dolphins and seals perform; and such thrill rides as the gravity-defying Abyss Turbo. The park is accessible by a number of buses including the 72, 72A, 260, and 629; get off at the stop after the Aberdeen tunnel. ▐ **TIP** If you have kids, plan to spend the whole day here. ✉ *Ocean Park Rd., Aberdeen, Southside* ☎ *3923–2323* ⊕ *www.oceanpark.com.hk* ⊠ *HK$280 adults; HK$140 kids* ⊙ *Daily 10–7.*

Stanley. This peninsula town lies south of Deep Water and Repulse bays. There's great shopping in the renowned Stanley Market, whether you want casual clothes, sneakers, cheap souvenirs, cheerful bric-a-brac— even snow gear. Stanley's popular beach is the site of the Dragon Boat Races every June. To get here from Exchange Square Bus Terminus in Central, take Bus 6, 6A, 6X, 66, 64, or 260. ✉ *Southside.*

WORTH NOTING

Aberdeen. On side streets you'll find outdoor barbers at work and any number of dim sum restaurants. You'll also see traditional sights like the Aberdeen Cemetery, with its enormous gravestones, and yet another shrine to the goddess of the sea: the Tin Hau Temple. During the Tin Hau Festival in April and May, hundreds of boats converge along the shore here.

Aberdeen's harbor contains about 3,000 junks and sampans. Several generations of one family can live on each junk (you may recall when Angelina Jolie's character, Lara Croft, stepped aboard such a boat in *Tomb Raider 2*). ✉ *Southside.*

Ap Lei Chau Island. A bridge connects Aberdeen with this island (Duck's Tongue Island in English), where boat-builders work in the old way.

GETTING ORIENTED

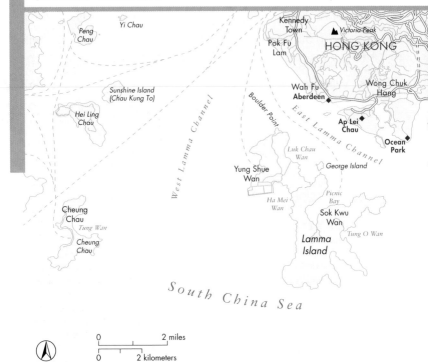

TAKING IT IN	TRANSPORTATION FROM CENTRAL TO ...
It's best to pick one hub out here, and explore in and around it: Aberdeen with its junks and sampans on the southwest coast; Stanley and its market on the south central coast; or Shek O with its beaches and parkland far to the southeast.	**Aberdeen:** 30 minutes via Bus 70 or 91. (Ap Lei Chau is 15 minutes from Aberdeen on Bus 90B or 91; 10 minutes by sampan).
	Deep Water Bay: 20 minutes via Bus 6, 64, 260, or 6A.
	Ocean Park: 30 minutes via Bus 6A, 6X, 70, 75, 90, 97, or 260.
Gray Line Tours. Gray Line Tours has day trips of Hong Kong Island including Man Mo Temple, the Peak, Aberdeen, Repulse Bay, Stanley Market, and dim sum lunch at Jumbo Kingdom floating restaurant in Aberdeen for HK$590 per adult. ☎ 2368–7111 ⊕ www.grayline. com.hk.	**Repulse Bay:** 30 minutes via Bus 6, 6A, 6X, 66, 64, or 260.
	Shek O: 50 minutes via MTR to Shau Kei Wan and then Bus 9 to the last stop.
	Stanley: 40 minutes via Bus 6, 6A, 6X, 66, 64, or 260.
	Note that express buses skip Aberdeen and Deep Water Bay, heading directly to Repulse Bay and Stanley. Buses run less frequently in the evening, so it's more convenient to grab a taxi (they're everywhere, unless it is 4 pm, when taxi drivers change shifts).

QUICK BITES

In **Stanley Market** there are dozens of cheap local and international eateries. For more upscale yet still casual joints, head to Stanley Main Road.

The Verandah at the Repulse Bay. Treat yourself to British high tea at the Verandah. Tea is served Wednesday to Saturday from 3 to 5:30 and Sunday from 3:30 to 5:30. ⊠ *109 Repulse Bay Rd., Southside* ☎ *2292–2822* ⊕ *www.therepulsebay.com.*

Black Sheep Restaurant. A favorite place for lunch, drinks, or just alfresco lounging is this pleasantly small place that offers an eclectic menu and a relaxed vibe. ⊠ *Ground fl., 330, Southside, Shek O* ☎ *2809–2021.*

GOLFERS TAKE NOTE

Deep Water Bay Golf Club. Deep Water Bay is flanked to the north by the Deep Water Bay Golf Club, which is owned by the Hong Kong Golf Club. The most convenient course to play if you're staying on Hong Kong Island has nine challenging holes. It's a members' club (some of Hong Kong's richest businessmen play here), but it's casual, and visitors with handicap certificates are admitted on weekdays from 9 to 2 (walk-in only).

Greens fees are HK$550 for 18 holes. Club rental will cost you another HK$200; a caddy, still another HK$180. The club also has two restaurants (one serving Chinese fare, the other western dishes), plus a members-only fitness center and swimming pool. ⊠ *19 Island Rd., Deep Water Bay* ☎ *2812–7070* ⊕ *www.hkgolfclub.org.*

Repulse Bay is one of Hong Kong's lovely but frequently overlooked beaches.

Unspoiled just a decade and a half ago, Ap Lei Chau is now covered with public housing, private estates, and shopping malls. ⊠ *Southside*.

Deep Water Bay. Just east of Ocean Park is this lovely beach. It's a good place to have a barbecue or swim under the watchful eye of a lifeguard. To get here, take Bus 6, 64, 260, or 6A from Exchange Square Bus Terminus in Central. ⊠ *Southside* ☎ *2812–0228*.

Repulse Bay. The tranquil area is home to a landmark apartment building with a hole in it. Following the principles of feng shui, the opening was incorporated into the design so the dragon that lives in the mountains behind can readily drink from the bay. The popular restaurant The Verandah (⇨ *Quick Bites)* is a great place for a meal with majestic bay views. The beach is large and wide, but be warned: it's the first stop for most Southside visitors. Huge statues of Tin Hau—Goddess of the Sea and Goddess of Mercy—at the east end of the beach border on gaudy. In the 1970s, when worshippers were planning to erect just one statue, they worried she'd be lonely, so an additional statue was created to keep her company. To get here, take Bus 6, 6A, 6X, 66, 64, or 260 from Exchange Square Bus Terminus in Central. ⊠ *Beach Rd. at Seaview Promenade, Repulse Bay, Southside* ☎ *2812–2483*.

DID YOU KNOW?

The Chinese name for Stanley translates as "Red Pole." Depending on to whom you're talking, it refers to the red flowers on two silk-cotton trees here or to a nearby hill that turns red at sunset, acting as a beacon for sailors. The English name comes from Lord Stanley, a 19th-century British official.

Shek O. The seaside locale is Southside's easternmost village. Weekend beachgoers and hikers crowd the Thai restaurant on the left as you enter town. Every shop here sells the same inflatable beach toys—the bigger the better, it seems. Cut through town to a windy road that takes you to the "island" of Tai Tau Chau, really a large rock with a lookout over the South China Sea. Just over a century ago, this open water was ruled by pirates. You can hike through nearby Shek O Country Park, where the bird-watching is great, in less than two hours. To get here from Central, take the MTR to Shau Kei Wan, then take Bus 9 to the last stop (about 30 min). ⊠ *Southside.*

3

LANTAU ISLAND

Sightseeing
★★★★
Dining
☆☆☆★
Lodging
☆☆☆★
Shopping
☆☆☆★

Manic development is changing Lantau, but the island is still known as the "lungs of Hong Kong" because of the abundant forests, relative dearth of skyscrapers, and laid-back attractions—beaches, fishing villages, and hiking trails. At Ngong Ping, a mini-theme park keeps the island's most famous sight, the Giant Buddha, company. Not to be outdone, Disney has opened a park and resort on the northeast coast, near the airport. At 142 square km (55 square miles), Lantau is almost twice the size of Hong Kong Island, so there's room for all this development, and the island remains a welcome green getaway.

TOP ATTRACTIONS

☺ **Hong Kong Disneyland.** Though Hong Kong's home to Mickey Mouse is tame compared with other Magic Kingdoms, it's fast bringing Mai Kei Lo Su—as the world's most famous mouse is known locally—to a mainland audience. Younger kids will find plenty of amusement, but their older siblings and parents will have to settle for just one thrill ride, Space Mountain. If you need to visit a theme park in Hong Kong, Ocean Park in Aberdeen (⇨ *Southside, above*) is a better bet. ⊠ *Fantasy Rd., Lantau Island* ⊕ *park.hongkongdisneyland.com* ✆ *HK$399 adults, HK$285 kids* ☉ *Daily 10–8 or 9* Ⓜ *Disneyland Resort.*

Fodor's Choice **Tian Tan Buddha.**
★ ⇨ *See highlighted listing in this chapter.*

WORTH NOTING

Cheung Sha Beach. Two miles of golden sand 8 km (5 miles) southwest of Mui Wo make this one of Hong Kong's longest beaches. It gets breezy here, so windsurfers often don't have to contend with crowds.

TIAN TAN BUDDHA

✉ Ngong Ping, Lantau Island
☎ 2109–9898 Ngong Ping
hotline ⊕ www.plm.org.hk/
eng/home.php ⊠ Monastery
and path free. Walking with
Buddha: HK$35 ⊗ Buddha
daily 10–5:30, monastery and
path daily 8–6 Ⓜ Tung Chung.

TIPS

■ You can get here on the
Ngong Ping 360 sky rail from
a terminal adjacent to the
MTR station in Tung Chung
or via Buses 2 and 23 from
Mui Wo and Tung Chung,
respectively.

■ The only way to the upper
level, right under the Buddha,
is through an underwhelming
museum inside the podium.
You only get a couple of feet
higher up.

■ The booth at the base of
the stairs is only for tickets for
lunch—wandering around the
Buddha is free.

■ The monastery's vegetarian restaurant is a clattering
canteen with uninspiring fare.
Pick up sandwiches at the
Citygate Mall, Tung Chung, or
eat at a restaurant in Ngong
Ping Village.

Hong Kongers love superlatives, even if making them
true requires strings of qualifiers. So the Tian Tan Buddha is the world's largest Buddha—that's seated, located
outdoors, and made of bronze. Just know the vast silhouette is impressive. Steep stairs lead to the lower
podium, essentially forcing you to stare up at all 202
tons of Buddha as you ascend. At the top, cool breezes
and fantastic views over Lantau Island await.

Highlights

Po Lin Monastery. It's hard to believe today, but from
its foundation in 1927 through the early '90s, this monastery was virtually inaccessible by road. These days,
it's at the heart of Lantau's biggest attraction. The monastery proper has a gaudy, commercial, orange temple
complex. Still, it's the Buddha people come for.

Wisdom Path. This peaceful path runs beside 38 halved
tree trunks arranged in an infinity shape on a hillside.
Each is carved with Chinese characters that make up
the Heart Sutra, a 5th-century Buddhist prayer that
expresses the doctrine of emptiness. The idea is to walk
around the path—which takes five minutes—and reflect.
Follow the signposted trail to the left of the Buddha.

Ngong Ping Village. People were fussing about this
attraction before its first stone was laid. Ngong Ping
Village is a moneymaking add-on to the Tian Tan
Buddha. Walking With Buddha is intended to be an
educational stroll through the life of Siddhartha Gau-
tama, the first Buddha, but it's more of a multimedia
extravaganza that shuns good taste with such kitsch as
a self-illuminating Bodhi tree and piped-in incense. No
cost has been spared in the dioramas that fill the seven
galleries—ironic, given that each represents a stage of
the Buddha's path to enlightenment and the eschewing
of material wealth.

GETTING ORIENTED

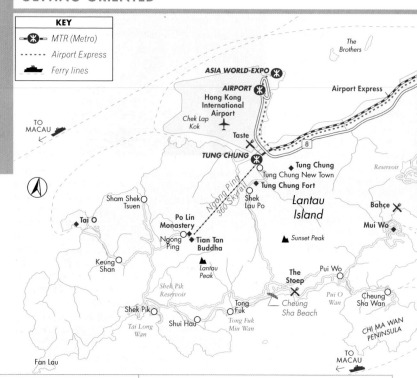

KEY	
☒ *MTR (Metro)*	
---- *Airport Express*	
⛴ *Ferry lines*	

THE TERRITORY	TOURS TO TAKE IT IN
Lantau is connected to Kowloon by the lengthy Tsing Ma Bridge. Most Lantau roads lead to and from Tung Chung, the new high-rise town on the north shore, just west of the bridge and close to Hong Kong International Airport. The Tung Chung Road winds through mountains and connects north Lantau with the southern coast. Here, the South Lantau Road stretches from the town of Mui Wo (where ferries from Central arrive) in the east to Tai O in the west, passing Cheung Sha Beach and Ngong Ping.	**Hong Kong Dolphinwatch.** Candy-pink dolphins might sound like something Disney cooked up, but Lantau's cutest residents are the endangered species *Sousa chinensis,* native to the Pearl River estuary. Only a few hundred are left, but experienced ecotourism company Hong Kong Dolphinwatch has a 97-percent sighting rate on their three-hour cruises (HK$380). ☎ 2984–1414 ⊕ www.hkdolphinwatch.com. **Splendid Tours.** To see Lantau's big sights whistle-stop style, try Splendid Tours. A daylong trip (HK$750, including lunch) takes in the Tsing Ma Bridge, Cheung Sha Beach, Tai O village, and Ngong Ping. ☎ 2316–2151 ⊕ www.splendid.hk.

✉ *Ground fl., 38 Peel St., Central* ☎ *2851–6882* Ⓜ *Central.*

Chine Gallery. Dealing in antique furniture and rugs from China, this dark, stylish gallery accommodates international clients by coordinating its major exhibitions with the spring and fall auction schedules of Christie's and Sotheby's. ✉ *42A Hollywood Rd., Central* ☎ *2543–0023* ✍ *info@chinegallery.com* ⊕ *www.chinegallery.com* ☉ *Closed Sun.* Ⓜ *Central.*

Connoisseur Art Gallery. This well-known gallery represents a small batch of modern, mostly figurative Chinese artists, though it also showcases the dreamlike work of Swedish painter Dorina Mocan and dabbles in photography. Recent exhibitions have featured farflung talents, from eastern Asia to South America. The gallery started to push out of its—and Hong Kong's—comfort zone with the opening of Connoisseur Contemporary a few doors down in 2008; it features the often controversial creative output of the sociopolitical group referred to as the "eighties generation"—mainland Chinese emerging artists born in the 1980s under the one-child policy and known for subversive works. ✉ *G3 Chinachem Hollywood Ctr., 1 Hollywood Rd., Central* ☎ *2868–5358* ✍ *info@connoisseur-art.com* ⊕ *www.connoisseur-art.com.*

Galerie La Vong. The works of today's leading Vietnamese artists, many of whose creations reveal an intriguing combination of French Impressionist and traditional Chinese influences, are the focus here. ✉ *13th fl., 1 Lan Kwai Fong, Central* ☎ *2869–6863* Ⓜ *Central.*

The Green Lantern. Irish expat Olive Forrest has cleverly retained original elements of the former print shop in which her store is housed. With her unique sense of style, Forrest brings together Chinese and Tibetan antiques, contemporary lighting designed in-house, silk soft furnishings, high-quality OM Living bed linens, and home accessories, such as contemporary lamp stands in brass. ✉ *72 Peel St., SoHo, Central* ☎ *2526–0277* Ⓜ *Central, Exit D1.*

Grotto Fine Art. Director and chief curator Henry Au-yeung writes about, curates, and gives lectures on 20th-century Chinese art. His tucked-away gallery focuses exclusively on local Chinese artists, with an interest in the newest and most avant-garde works. Look for paintings, sculptures, prints, photography, mixed-media pieces, and conceptual installations. ✉ *2nd fl., 31C–D Wyndham St., Central* ☎ *2121–2270* ⊕ *www.grottofineart.com* Ⓜ *Central.*

Hanart TZ Gallery. This is a rare opportunity to compare and contrast cutting-edge and experimental art from mainland China and Hong Kong selected by one of the field's most respected authorities. Unassuming curatorial director Johnson Chang Tsong-zung also cofounded the Asia Art Archive, and has curated exhibitions at the São Paolo and Venice biennials. ✉ *4th fl., Pedder Building, 12 Pedder St., Central* ☎ *2526–9019* ⊕ *www.hanart.com* Ⓜ *Central.*

Cat Street antiques shops in Sheung Wan offer cheaper wares than those on Hollywood Road.

Hanlin Gallery. For Japanese works of art, antiques, modern ceramics, and woodblocks, visit this refined, calm gallery run by specialist Carlos Prata since 1986. His collection and expertise extend to decorative Chinese art, including furniture, fans, textiles, and silver. ⊠ *Ground fl., 56–58 Hollywood Rd., Central* ☎ *2522–4479* ⊕ *www.hanlingallery. com* ☉ *Closed Sun.* Ⓜ *Central, Exit D1.*

Honeychurch Antiques. Highly respected dealers Lucille and Glenn Vessa (one of the few accredited appraisers here) were the first to set up shop on Hollywood Road nearly half a century ago. The gallery has managed to keep its original location, with a front-row seat to the neighborhood's transformation into the art hub it is today. This shop still provides fine Chinese, Japanese, and Southeast Asian antique silver, porcelain, and unaltered furniture with four additional floors of show space next door. ⊠ *Ground fl., 29 Hollywood Rd., Central* ☎ *2543–2433* ⊕ *www. honeychurch.com* Ⓜ *Central.*

New Gallery on Old Bailey. Gallery director Elizabeth Sham attracts prominent and innovative contemporary artists to display their work at this well-established gallery, which draws an appreciative crowd of local and international patrons. ⊠ *Basement fl. and ground fl., 17 Old Bailey St., Central* ☎ *2234–9889* ⊕ *www.newgalleryonoldbailey.com* ☉ *Closed Sun.* Ⓜ *Central.*

Oi Ling Fine Chinese Antique. This beautiful showroom displays Chinese antique furniture, scholar's items, terracotta, bronze, and archaeological stone works. Owner Oi Ling Chiang gives frequent talks. ⊠ *Ground fl., 52 Hollywood Rd., Central* ☎ *2815–9422* ⊕ *www.oilingantiques. com* Ⓜ *Central.*

Picture This Gallery. It's a one-of-a-kind source for vintage posters—mainly with travel and movie themes—early photography of Hong Kong and elsewhere in China, antique maps, prints and engravings, antiquarian books, and limited-edition reproductions or works by artists such as Dong Kingman. You might imagine a dusty library, but Christopher Bailey's welcoming shop and gallery is spacious, bright, and organized. In recent years, Bailey's offerings have shifted toward contemporary photography featuring exhibitions from the likes of Keith Macgregor, Yau Leung, and *National Geographic*'s Michael Yamashita. ⊠ *13th fl., 9 Queen's Rd., Central* ☎ *2525–2820* ⊕ *www.picturethiscollection. com* ⊙ *Closed Sun.* Ⓜ *Central* ⊠ *2nd fl., Prince's Bldg., 10 Chater Rd., Central* ☎ *2525–2803* Ⓜ *Central.*

Plum Blossoms Gallery. You can't miss this gallery's unique, asymmetrical window. The airy, New York–style space displays groundbreaking contemporary Chinese art alongside ancient Asian textiles and rugs. Ask the refreshingly knowledgeable staff to escort you upstairs to see more. ⊠ *Shop G6, 1 Hollywood Rd., Central* ☎ *2521–2189* ⊕ *www. plumblossoms.com* ⊙ *Closed Sun.* Ⓜ *Central.*

Sandra Walters Consultancy Ltd. Sandra Walters, a longtime figure on the art scene, represents a stable of Asian and international artists encompassing a variety of periods and styles. Make an appointment with her or one of her team to advise you on small to significant investments. ⊠ *501 Hoseinee House, 69 Wyndham St., Central* ☎ *2522–1137* ⊙ *Closed Sun.* Ⓜ *Central, Exit D2.*

Schoeni on Old Bailey Street. Known for vigorously promoting Chinese art on a global scale, this gallery, founded by Manfred Schoeni in 1992, has represented and supported various artists from mainland China with styles ranging from neorealism to conceptualism. Manfred's daughter Nicole now pinpoints exciting new artists for her prominent clientele. You're likely to pass the Hollywood Road branch first, but the Old Bailey Street gallery, up the hill, is the bigger and better of the two. ⊠ *21–31 Old Bailey St., Central* ☎ *2869–8802* ⊕ *www.schoeniartgallery.com* ⊙ *Closed Sun.* Ⓜ *Central.*

Sin Sin Fine Art. Works by diverse emerging and established artists from Indonesia, Thailand, mainland China, Hong Kong, and France reveal the aesthetic tastes of the lively Hong Kong designer and entrepreneur, Sin Sin. There are also regular exhibitions and artist talks. In the nearby Annex, you'll see more-progressive installations, objects, and performance art. ⊠ *Ground fl., 53–54 Sai St., Mid-Levels, Central* ☎ *2858–5072* ⊕ *www.sinsin.com.hk* Ⓜ *Sheung Wan, Exit A2.*

Sotheby's. The respected auction house opened here in 1973. Its teams work with Chinese ceramics, jade carvings, snuff bottles, and classical and contemporary paintings. The auction house, now accompanied by a 15,000-sq-ft art gallery, deals in watches and jewelry, including jadeite and western pieces. Head here for lectures, exhibitions, cultural events, and for the rare chance to gaze upon Sotheby's diamonds. ⊠ *5th fl., Pacific Place, 88 Queensway, Admiralty, Central* ☎ *2524–8121* ⊕ *www. sothebys.com* Ⓜ *Admiralty.*

DID YOU KNOW?

Hong Kong's mix of western and eastern treatments puts the "ah" in spa. You can get a quick manicure or have an extravagant spa day. Or rejuvenate weary feet with traditional Chinese reflexology. Hotel spas stay open a few hours later than the stand-alone establishments, so you don't have to curtail shopping. With treatments for men and treatment rooms for couples, the boys don't need to feel left out, either. Warning: you'll be spoiled for life.

Teresa Coleman Fine Arts Ltd. Specialist Teresa Coleman sells embroidered costumes from the Imperial Court, antique textiles, painted and carved fans, lacquered boxes, and engravings and prints in her centrally located gallery. She has a streetside shop at the same address for walk-ins, but this space is appointment only. ⊠ *4th fl., 55 Wyndham St., Central* ☎ *2526–2450* ✑ *tc@teresacoleman.com* ⊕ *www. teresacoleman.com* Ⓜ *Central.*

The Tibetan Gallery. At this ground-floor extension of Teresa Coleman Fine Arts you'll find antique Tibetan *thangkas* (Buddhist paintings) hanging in the windows, as well as bronzes, textiles, and exquisite rugs on display. Manager Josephine Chan is also a restoration expert. ⊠ *55 Wyndham St., Central* ☎ *2530–4863* ⊕ *www.thetibetangallery. com* Ⓜ *Central.*

Wattis Fine Art. Run by affable expert Jonathan Wattis and his wife Vicky for 25 years, Wattis Fine Art specializes in antique maps and prints and photographs of Hong Kong, China, and Southeast Asia. ⊠ *2nd fl., 20 Hollywood Rd., Central* ☎ *2524–5302* ⊕ *www.wattis.com.hk.*

Yan Gallery. This is the place for Hong Kong–based artist Hu Yongkai's charming, slightly cartoonish depictions of Chinese women in traditional settings (you've almost certainly seen fakes in a Stanley Market stall). Among emerging and established local artists the gallery, which isn't as stuffy as some and more commercial than others, also represents Bob Yan, whose extremely popular and colorful dog portraits are commissioned by private clients. ⊠ *1st fl., Chinachem Hollywood Centre, 1 Hollywood Rd., Central* ☎ *2139–2345* ⊕ *www.yangallery. com* Ⓜ *Central.*

Yue Po Chai Antique Co. One of Hollywood Road's oldest shops is at the Cat Street end, next to Man Mo Temple. Its vast and varied stock includes porcelain, stone carvings, and ceramics. ⊠ *Ground fl., 132–136 Hollywood Rd., Central* ☎ *2540–4374* Ⓜ *Central.*

Zee Stone Gallery. Massive street-level windows still hold court on what's fast becoming a sleek bar and restaurant strip. The gallery displays contemporary, often abstract, paintings from China, with a smattering of work from Burma and Vietnam. ⊠ *Ground fl., Chinachem Hollywood Centre, 1 Hollywood Rd., Central* ☎ *2810–5895* ⊕ *www.zeestone.com* Ⓜ *Central, Exit D2.*

BEAUTY AND COSMETICS

Beautiful Skin Centre. If you need a day of pampering after pounding the pavement, the hidden Beautiful Skin Centre has just the thing. Stretch out for a facial, pedicure, body massage, or let the gentle Helena use an ultrasoothing coconut wax to get you bare. ⊠ *Pacific Place, 88 Queensway, Admiralty, Central* ☎ *2877–8911* ⊕ *www.beautifulskincentre. com.hk* Ⓜ *Admiralty.*

Joyce Beauty. Love finding unique beauty products from around the world? Then this is the place for you, with cult perfumes, luxurious skin solutions, and new discoveries to be made. Bring your credit card—"bargain" isn't in the vocabulary here. ⊠ *Ground fl., New World Tower, 16–18 Queen's Rd. Central, Central* ☎ *2367–0860* ⊕ *www. joyce.com* Ⓜ *Central* ⊠ *Gateway Arcade, Harbour City, 3–27 Canton*

Rd., Tsim Sha Tsui, Kowloon ☎ *2367–8128* Ⓜ *Tsim Sha Tsui* ✉ *Festival Walk, 80 Tat Chee Ave., Kowloon Tong, Kowloon* ☎ *2265–7176* Ⓜ *Kowloon Tong.*

Mandarin Beauty Salon and Barber Shop. Enjoy views of Victoria Harbour from the 24th floor while you tame your tresses at the Mandarin Beauty Salon. No-nonsense Betty employs hair-removal techniques that are whispered about in the best of circles, and Samuel So has perfected his famous Shanghainese pedicure over the past 20 years. On the second floor in the Mandarin's 1930s Shanghai–inspired barber shop, your man is enjoying his own grooming, complete with in-mirror TVs and VIP rooms. ✉ *Mandarin Oriental, 5 Connaught Rd., Central* ☎ *2825–4800* ⊕ *www.mandarinoriental.com* Ⓜ *Central.*

Mannings. Like Watsons, this chain can be found throughout the city. It sells everything from shampoo and lotions to emery boards and cough medicine (western and Chinese brands). Some stores have pharmacies. ✉ *Shop 204, IFC Mall, 8 Finance St., Central* ☎ *2523–9672, 2299–3381 customer service and branch information* ⊕ *www.mannings.com. hk/eng* Ⓜ *Hong Kong.*

BOOKS AND STATIONERY
Indosiam Rare Books. Yves Azemar indulges his passion for rare books and prints about former French colonies in Asia in this tiny apartment, which he has converted into a library–shop. The former French schoolteacher is happy to sit and chat about this fascinating genre—the lectures are never boring. ✉ *1st fl., 89 Hollywood Rd., Central* ☎ *2854–2853* Ⓜ *Central.*

CHILDREN'S CLOTHING
Bumps to Babes. It has everything you could possibly need for babies and children, all in one place. In addition to familiar brands of clothing, diapers, toiletries, food, and toys, look for strollers, books, maternity wear, furniture, and more. ✉ *5th fl., Pedder Bldg., 12 Pedder St., Central* ☎ *2522–7112* ⊕ *www.bumpstobabes.com* Ⓜ *Central* ✉ *21st fl., Horizon Plaza, 2 Lee Wing St., Ap Lei Chau, Southside* ☎ *2552–5000* ⊕ *www.bumpstobabes.com.*

Lace Department Store. You might head straight for the embroidered linens, but back up and review the children's clothing by the door. You've seen these beautiful, traditional, hand-smocked cotton dresses and baby overalls in elegant European stores, sold at prices to make you faint. Here expect to pay as little as HK$200. As you tour the city, keep an eye out for embroidered-linens specialists who carry similar dresses. ✉ *5th fl., Crawford House, 70 Queen's Rd. Central, Central* ☎ *2523–8162* Ⓜ *Central.*

Marleen Molenaar Sleepwear. When Hong Kong–based Dutch designer and mother Marleen Molenaar discovered how limited her choices were for children's pajamas and sleepwear, she founded her own label. The gorgeous 100% cotton, high-quality classic European collections are sold around the world, in Lane Crawford's home department, and through her showroom, by appointment. ✉ *Shop 502, Tak Woo House, 17–19 D'Aguilar St., Central* ☎ *2525–9872, 9162–0350* ⊕ *www. marleenmolenaar.com* Ⓜ *Central.*

CLOTHING

Barney Cheng. One of Hong Kong's best-known, local designers, Barney Cheng creates haute-couture designs and prêt-à-porter collections with wit and elegance. When the Kennedy Center in Washington, D.C., hosted an exhibition titled "The New China Chic," Cheng was invited to display his works alongside those by the likes of Vera Wang and Anna Sui. His more recent pieces have drifted toward simplicity, with sophisticated cuts and exotic prints, such as alligator jackets and skirts. Cheng has made many a bride's dream gown, and his masterfully tailored suits of award-winning Milano wool cost from HK$100,000 to HK$400,000. Consultations are available on weekdays by appointment, but Cheng will open his doors on weekends for special occasions and VIPs. ⊠ *12th fl., World Wide Commercial Bldg., 34 Wyndham St., Central* ☎ *2530–2829* ⊕ *www.barneycheng. com* ⊘ *Closed weekends* Ⓜ *Central.*

Episode. Locally owned and designed Episode collections focus on accessories and suiting and other elegant clothing for working women and ladies who lunch. Look also for the younger and trendier Jessica collection. Though distinct, both collections pay close attention to current trends in the fashion world. ⊠ *22nd fl., Entertainment Bldg., 30 Queen's Rd. Central, Central* ☎ *2921–2010* ⊕ *www.toppy.com.hk* Ⓜ *Central* ⊠ *Gateway Arcade, Harbour City, 5 Canton Rd., Tsim Sha Tsui, Kowloon* ☎ *2926–3000* ⊕ *www.toppy.com.hk* Ⓜ *Tsim Sha Tsui.*

Fang Fong Projects. Fang Fong fell in love with the vintage feel of the SoHo district as a design graduate and vowed to move in. She chose a light-filled studio space to display her floaty, 1970s-inspired clothing line, with its bold prints and sexy wisps of lace and silk. She also brought her friends with her, or at least those who suited her vibe. Head here for Japanese kimono-inspired belts and for bags by U.K. brand Dialog, which works with scrap fabric from fair trade sources. ⊠ *Shop 1, 69 Peel St., SoHo, Central* ☎ *3105–5557.*

Hulu 10. Newcomer to historic Glenealy—center of British Hong Kong—Hulu 10 takes traditional Chinese textiles for a contemporary spin. Encased by a beautiful white brick building, the store is warm and welcoming, with dark wood floors and open space. Designed and produced locally, the garments have a throwback vibe, inspired by '60s fashion and iconic artifacts like Xian's Terracotta Warriors. Find classic Chinese tunics and silk scarves alongside more modern-looking dresses for the ladies, as well as a leaner selection of children's and menswear. ▐TIP→ This quaint little street snakes above Lower Albert Road and can be tricky to find at first. Start from the Fringe Club at Wyndham's five-way intersection and head uphill. ⊠ *Ground fl., 10 Glenealy, Central* ☎ *2179–5500* ⊕ *hulu10.com* ⊘ *Closed Sun.* Ⓜ *Central, Exit D1.*

Joyce. Local socialites and couture addicts still thank Joyce Ma, the fairy godmother of luxury retail in Hong Kong, for bringing must-have labels to the city. Others may be catching up, but her Joyce boutiques are still ultrachic havens outfitted with a Vogue-worthy wish list of designers and beauty brands. Not so much a shop as a fashion institution, hushed Joyce houses the worship-worthy creations of fashion's greatest gods and goddesses. McCartney, Miyake, Donna

Karan, McQueen, Oscar de la Renta: the stock list is practically a mantra. Joyce sells unique household items, too, so your home can live up to your wardrobe. ⊠ *New World Tower, 16 Queen's Rd., Central* ☎ *2810–1120* ⊕ *www.joyce.com* Ⓜ *Central* ⊠ *Pacific Place, 88 Queensway, Admiralty, Central* ☎ *2523–5944* Ⓜ *Admiralty* ⊠ *Gateway Arcade, Harbour City, 3–27 Canton Rd., Tsim Sha Tsui, Kowloon* ☎ *2367–8128* Ⓜ *Tsim Sha Tsui.*

Lu Lu Cheung. A fixture on the Hong Kong fashion scene for more than a decade, Lu Lu Cheung creates designs that ooze comfort and warmth. In both daytime and evening wear, natural fabrics and forms are represented in practical yet imaginative ways. ⊠ *Ground fl., 50 Wellington St., Central* ☎ *2537–7515* ⊕ *www.lulucheung.com.hk* Ⓜ *Central.*

Ranee K. Designer Ranee Kok Chui-Wah's showrooms feature one-off dresses and eclectic women's wear that bring new meanings to "East meets West." Known for her quirky cheongsams and dresses, she also collaborates with brands such as Furla. Special clients and local celebrities enjoy her custom tailoring, too. ⊠ *Ground fl., 25 Aberdeen St., Central* ☎ *2108–4068* ⊕ *www.raneek.com* Ⓜ *Central.*

Fodor's Choice
★
Shanghai Tang. Make your way past the perfumes, scarves, and silk-embroidered Chinese souvenirs to the second floor, where you'll find live Canaries tweeting from golden cages and a rainbow of fabrics at your fingertips. In addition to the brilliantly hued—and expensive—silk and cashmere clothing, you'll find custom-made suits starting at around HK$30,000, including fabric. You can also have a cheongsam (a sexy slit-skirt silk dress with a Mandarin collar) made for around HK$10,000, including fabric. Ready-to-wear Mandarin suits are in the HK$15,000–HK$20,000 range. You can find outlets scattered across Hong Kong, including the airport's Terminal One. ⊠ *1 Duddell St., Central* ☎ *2525–7333* ⊕ *www.shanghaitang.com* Ⓜ *Central* ⊠ *1881 Heritage House 1, 2A Canton Rd., Tsim Sha Tsui, Kowloon* Ⓜ *Tsim Sha Tsui.*

Siberian Fur Store Ltd. In general, furs sold by reputable Hong Kong dealers are the ideal combination of superior quality and low prices. This shop, owned and operated by a prominent local family, is famous for its high-quality furs and special attention to design. ⊠ *Ground fl., 29 Des Voeux Rd. Central, Central* ☎ *2522–1380* Ⓜ *Central* ⊠ *Ground fl., 21 Chatham Rd. S, Tsim Sha Tsui, Kowloon* Ⓜ *Tsim Sha Tsui.*

Vintage HK. As you walk along Hollywood Road past the art galleries and wine bars, take time to wander down the steep side streets. On Peel Street you'll stumble upon this one-of-a-kind treasure, which is marked by a black-and-white sign visible from Hollywood. Inside, crinkly posters, love-worn leather, and a stash of antique knickknacks will transport you to the 1970s and beyond. From retro cameras to clocks, belts to blouses, Dior to Marc Jacobs, this is a trove of near-mint-condition consignment pieces. ⊠ *57–59 Hollywood Rd., SoHo, Central* ☎ *2545–9932* Ⓜ *Central.*

Vivienne Tam. You know it when you walk into a Vivienne Tam boutique—the strong Chinese-motif prints and modern updates of traditional women's clothing are truly distinct. Don't let the bold, ready-to-wear collections distract you from the very pretty accessories, which include leather bags with Asian embellishments. Tam is one of the best-known Hong Kong designers and, even though she's now based outside the SAR, the city still claims her as its own. ✉ *Pacific Place, 88 Queensway, Admiralty, Central* ☎ *2918–0238* ⊕ *www.viviennetam. com* Ⓜ *Admiralty* ✉ *Ocean Centre, Harbour City, 2–27 Canton Rd., Tsim Sha Tsui, Kowloon* Ⓜ *Tsim Sha Tsui* ✉ *Festival Walk, 80 Tat Chee Ave., Kowloon Tong, Kowloon* Ⓜ *Kowloon Tong.*

CRAFTS AND CURIOS

Mountain Folkcraft. A little old-fashioned bell chimes as you open the door to this fantastic old shop filled with handicrafts and antiques from around China. Amid the old treasures, carved woodwork, rugs, and curios, are stunning folk-print fabrics. To reach the store from Queen's Road Central, walk up D'Aguilar Street toward Lan Kwai Fong, then turn right onto Wo On Lane. ✉ *Ground fl., 12 Wo On La., Central* ☎ *2525–3199* Ⓜ *Central.*

DEPARTMENT STORES

Fodor'sChoice ★ **Chinese Arts & Crafts.** Head to this long-established mainland company to blitz through that tiresome list of presents in one fell swoop. It stocks a huge variety of well-priced brocades, silk clothing, and cheap porcelain. In direct contrast to the thrill of digging through dusty piles at the open-air Jade Market, it provides a clean, air-conditioned environment in which to shop for classic jade jewelry—the prices aren't too outrageous. Incongruously scattered throughout the shops are specialty items like large globes with lapis oceans and landmasses inlaid with semiprecious stones for a mere HK$70,000. Other more accessible—and more packable—gifts include appliqué tablecloths and cushion covers or silk dressing gowns. ✉ *Pacific Place, 88 Queensway, Admiralty, Central* ☎ *2827–6667* ⊕ *www.cacgift.com* Ⓜ *Admiralty, Exit F* ✉ *Ground fl., Hip Shing Hong Centre, 55 Des Voeux Rd. Central, Central* ⊕ *www. cacgift.com* Ⓜ *Central* ✉ *28 Harbour Rd., Wan Chai* ⊕ *www.cacgift. com* Ⓜ *Wan Chai, Exit A5* ✉ *Star House, 3 Salisbury Rd., Tsim Sha Tsui, Kowloon* ⊕ *www.cacgift.com* Ⓜ *Tsim Sha Tsui, Exit F.*

Harvey Nichols. When this legendary British retailer announced its Hong Kong opening, locals were skeptical, saying nothing would ever live up to the original London store. But Harvey Nicks quickly had them eating their (Philip Treacy) hats with the sheer volume of hyper-cool labels the store stocks. The menswear section has been a particularly big hit with local celebs, while local *tai-tais* (ladies who lunch) have declared the fourth-floor restaurant *the* place for mid-shopping-spree coffee breaks. In 2011, the department store opened a second sprawling spot, located in Admiralty's Pacific Place mall. Head to this flagship store for quiet surrounds and 83,000 sq. ft. of top-shelf brands. ✉ *The Landmark, 15 Queen's Rd., Central* ☎ *3695–3388* ⊕ *www.harveynichols.com* Ⓜ *Central* ✉ *Pacific Place, 88 Queensway, Admiralty* ☎ *3968–2668.*

Fodor'sChoice ★ **Lane Crawford.** This prestigious western-style department store has been the favorite of local label-lovers for years—not bad for a brand that started out as a makeshift provisions shop back in 1850. The massive flagship store in the IFC Mall feels like a monument to fashion's biggest names, with exquisitely designed acres divided up into small gallery-like spaces for each designer. The phenomenal brand list includes everything from haute couture through designer denim to Agent Provocateur lingerie. Sales here are more like fashionista wrestling matches, with everyone pushing and shoving to find bargains. ⊠ *Podium 3, IFC Mall, 8 Finance St., Central* ☎ *2118–3388, 2118–7777 Lane Crawford concierge* ⊕ *www.lanecrawford.com* Ⓜ *Hong Kong, Exit A1* ⊠ *Pacific Place, 88 Queensway, Admiralty, Central* Ⓜ *Admiralty.* ⊠ *Gateway Arcade, Harbour City, 3 Canton Rd., Tsim Sha Tsui, Kowloon* Ⓜ *Tsim Sha Tsui, Exit E* ⊠ *Times Square, 1 Matheson St., Causeway Bay* Ⓜ *Causeway Bay, Exit A*

Marks & Spencer. Classic, good-quality clothing is what this British retailer has built an empire on—its underwear, in particular, is viewed as a national treasure. Although basics are on the staid side, the newer Per Una, Autograph, and Limited collections are decidedly trendier. This is one of the few stores in town to stock a full range of sizes, which includes shoes up to a US size 10. There are branches in many of Hong Kong's malls; most of the shops have a British specialty food section, too, with a good range of wines. ⊠ *22–28 Queen's Rd., Central* ☎ *2921–8323* ⊕ *www.marks-and-spencer.hk* Ⓜ *Central, Exit D1* ⊠ *Times Square, Shops 617–621 and 415–416, 1 Matheson St., Causeway Bay* ☎ *2923–7972* Ⓜ *Causeway Bay* ⊠ *Harbour City Ocean Centre, 5 Canton Rd., Tsim Sha Tsui, Kowloon* ☎ *2926–3344* Ⓜ *Tsim Sha Tsui, Exit E.*

Sincere. Hong Kong's most eclectic department store stocks everything from frying pans to jelly beans. Run by the same family for more than a century, Sincere has several local claims to fame: it was the first store in Hong Kong to give paid days off to employees, the first to hire women in sales positions—beginning with the founder's wife and sister-in-law— and the first to establish a fixed-price policy backed up by the regionally novel idea of issuing receipts. Although you probably won't have heard of its clothes or cosmetic brands, you might come across a bargain in one of its four locations strewn throughout Hong Kong. ⊠ *173 Des Voeux Rd. Central, Central* ☎ *2544–2688, 2830–1016 customer service hotline* ⊕ *www.sincere.com.hk/department/lang_en* Ⓜ *Sheung Wan.*

ELECTRONICS, CAMERAS, AND MUSIC

Flow. Track down this tiny gem for secondhand CDs, DVDs, magazines, and wall-to-wall used books in English. The range is extraordinary, and the organizational system baffling, but the owner is knowledgeable, friendly, and willing to poke among the shelves for you. Books here average around HK$40, compared to a few hundred new. ⊠ *1st fl., 38 Hollywood Rd., SoHo, Central* ☎ *2964–9483.*

HOME FURNISHINGS

Homeless. Pleasantly quirky but with a finger firmly on the pulse of the city, this small design brand emporium has its flagship in NoHo (North of Hollywood Road), one of Central's up and coming nooks. The store showcases some of its own in-house creations, but it mostly stocks pieces from modern-day design icons. Come here to pick up a Tom Dixon bowler-hat lampshade or a Pac Man–shape oven glove by Fred.

Traditional herbalists mix healing concoctions in Wan Chai shops.

Try its basement café for brunch on Saturday. ⊠ *Ground fl., 29 Gough St., NoHo, Central* ☎ *2581–1880* ⊕ *www.homeless.hk.*

Lee Fung China Ware Co., Ltd. Friendly service and a decent selection of Chinese and western-style dinnerware make this a good one-stop shop. It also carries vases and antique reproductions. ⊠ *Ground fl., 279 Des Voeux Rd. Central, Sheung Wan, Western* ☎ *2524–0630* ⊕ *Sheung Wan.*

Tai Ping Carpets. Headquartered in Hong Kong, Tai Ping is highly regarded for its custom-made rugs and wall-to-wall carpets. It takes 2½ to 3 months to make specially ordered carpets; you can specify color, thickness, and even the direction of the weave. Tai Ping's occasional sales are well worth attending; check the classified section of the *South China Morning Post* for dates. ⊠ *Prince's Bldg, 10 Chater Rd., Central* ☎ *2522–7138* ⊕ *www.taipingcarpets.com* Ⓜ *Central.*

Wah Tung Ceramic Arts. This slightly slick but reliable manufacturer and retailer of predominantly handcrafted ceramics has been in operation since the early days of trade with the West (1863). The overwhelmingly large product line includes antique replicas, vases, dinnerware, figurines, and more—all in classic Chinese motifs. ⊠ *7th fl., Lee Roy Commercial Bldg., 57–59 Hollywood Rd., Central* ☎ *2543–2823* ⊕ *www. wahtungchina.com* ☺ *Closed Sun.* Ⓜ *Central* ⊠ *16th fl., Cheung Fat Bldg., 7–9 Hill Rd., Sai Wan, Western.*

JEWELRY

Carat. Forget the cheesy cubic zirconium of the past. One look at its stark showrooms, and you'll see that Carat has mastered the creation and presentation of synthetic gemstones. Hand-assembled in precious-metal settings, the large collection spans various eras of jewelry styles. ⊠ *IFC*

Mall, Shop 1062, 8 Finance St., Central ☎2234–7372 ⊕ *www.carat.cc* Ⓜ *Central* ✉ *Gateway Arcade, Harbour City, 3 Canton Rd., Tsim Sha Tsui, Kowloon* ☎3101–1510 ⊕ *www.carat.co* Ⓜ *Tsim Sha Tsui.*

Chocolate Rain. The collections—dreamed up by a Hong Kong fine arts graduate—consist of pieces handcrafted of recycled materials, such as fabrics, bottle lids, paint buckets, and other funky finds. Head here for unique iPhone cases, one-of-a-kind bags, illustrations, and jewelry, as well as an ever-changing array of works by the designer's friends. ✉ *Ground fl., 67a Peel St., SoHo, Central* ☎2975–8318 ⊕ *www. chocolaterain.com* Ⓜ *Central.*

Chow Sang Sang. Chow Sang Sang has more than 100 shops in China. In addition to its contemporary gold, diamond, jade, and wedding collections for the local market, the manufacturer and retailer also sources international brands. ✉ *37 Queen's Rd. Central, Central* ☎3583–4150, 2192–3123 customer service and branch information ⊕ *www. chowsangsang.com* Ⓜ *Central* ✉ *Festival Walk, 2nd fl., 80 Tat Chee Ave., Kowloon Tong, Kowloon* ☎2265–8322 ⊕ *www.chowsangsang. com* Ⓜ *Kowloon Tong* ✉ *Ground fl., 525 Hennessy Rd., Causeway Bay* ☎2891–2422 ⊕ *www.chowsangsang.com* Ⓜ *Causeway Bay.*

Chow Tai Fook. Jade is not the only thing you'll see from this local chain founded in 1929. It also has fine jewelry in diamond, jadeite, ruby, sapphire, emerald, 18K gold, and more-traditional pure gold. And don't worry about tracking one down; there are more than a dozen branches on Kowloon's Nathan Road alone. ✉ *Ground fl., AON China Bldg., 29 Queen's Rd. Central, Central* ☎2523–7128 ⊕ *www.chowtaifook. com* Ⓜ *Central* ✉ *Park Lane Shopper's Boulevard, 123 Nathan Rd., Tsim Sha Tsui, Kowloon* ☎2735–7966 ⊕ *www.chowtaifook.com* Ⓜ *Tsim Sha Tsui* ✉ *Ground fl., Chow Tai Fook Centre, 580A Nathan Rd., Mong Kok, Kowloon* ☎2131–0628 ⊕ *www.chowtaifook.com* Ⓜ *Mong Kok.*

Edward Chiu. Everything about Edward Chiu is *fabulous,* from the flamboyant way he dresses to his high-end jade jewelry. The minimalist, geometric pieces use the entire jade spectrum, from deep greens to surprising lavenders. Inspired in part by Art Deco, Chiu is also famous for contrasting black-and-white jade, setting it in precious metals, and adding diamond or pearl touches. ✉ *Shop 2023, IFC Mall, 8 Finance St., Central* ☎2525–2618 ⊕ *www.edwardchiu.com* Ⓜ *Central.*

Eldorado Watch Co Ltd. At this deep emporium of watch brands, seek the advice of one of the older staffers who look like they've been there since the British landed. Brands include Rolex, Patek Philippe, Girard-Perregaux, etc. ✉ *Ground fl., Peter Bldg., 60 Queen's Rd. Central, Central* ☎2522–7155 Ⓜ *Central, Exit D2.*

Gallery One. This is the next-best option for midrange pearls if you can't make it to the Jade Market. Gallery One blends into Hollywood Road's backdrop of trinket-filled storefronts, but its selection of Japanese and freshwater pearls stands out. Prices are reasonable, and they will string together whichever combination of pearls and semiprecious stones you choose. Gallery One also carries Tibetan and Buddhist beads in wood and amber, as well as bronze sculptures. ⊠ *Ground fl., 31–33 Hollywood Rd., Central* ☎ *2545–6436* Ⓜ *Central, Exit D2.*

Jan Logan. This Australian designer has celebrities wearing her youthful yet elegant designs. Pieces contrast cultured, South Seas, and Tahitian pearls with onyx, diamonds, quartz, and other stones. ⊠ *IFC Mall, 8 Finance St., Central* ☎ *2918–4212* ⊕ *www.janlogan.com* Ⓜ *Central.*

Kai-Yin Lo. Kai-Yin Lo is famous for her Asian-inspired jewelry, combining contemporary style with ancient Chinese designs and materials such as semiprecious stones and jade. The *International Herald Tribune* has credited her with bridging the gap between fine and fashion jewelry. Lo acts as a consultant, lecturer, and writer on heritage and art and culture; sales of her jewelry continue by appointment only. ⊠ *55 Garden Rd., Central* ☎ *2773–6009* ⊕ *www.kaiyinlo-design.com.*

Karen Jewel Co. Designer Karen Lee studied jewelry making in Florence before creating her own brand in 2003. She uses a variety of precious stones, including rubies, sapphires, and emeralds, in her one-of-a-kind custom-made jewelry, which tends to have an antique look. Her showroom, where you can check out some sample pieces, is worth a visit; appointments are required, so call ahead. ⊠ *17A, 128 Wellington St., Central* ☎ *2151–9622* ⊕ *www.karenjewel.com* Ⓜ *Central.*

K.S. Sze & Sons. More salon than store, powdered elderly ladies who lunch and casually dressed tourists all come here for the same thing: quality pearls, fine jewelry, and excellent service. In addition to classic styles, K.S. Sze works closely with clients on custom orders. ⊠ *Prince's Building, 10 Chater Rd., Central* ☎ *2524–2803* Ⓜ *Central.*

Larry Jewelry. This is a long-established source for handcrafted jewelry made from high-grade precious stones. Catering to local tastes since 1967, the traditional company has a new push to attract younger customers. That said, there really is a wide enough range to please most tastes. ⊠ *Ground fl., 72 Queens Rd. Central, Central* ☎ *2521–1268* ⊕ *www.larryjewelry.com* Ⓜ *Central.* ⊠ *Ground fl., 33 Nathan Rd., Tsim Sha Tsui, Kowloon* Ⓜ *Tsim Sha Tsui*

Po Kwong Jewelry Ltd. Specializing in strung pearls from Australia and the South Seas, Po Kwong will add clasps to your specifications. They also carry pearl earrings, rings, and pendants. ⊠ *18th fl., HK Diamond Exchange Bldg., 8–10 Duddell St., Central* ☎ *2521–4686* ⊕ *www. po-kwong-pearl.com.*

Qeelin. With ancient Chinese culture for inspiration and *In the Mood for Love* actress Maggie Cheung as the muse, something extraordinary was bound to come from Qeelin. Its name was cleverly derived from the Chinese characters for male ("qi") and female ("lin"), and symbolizes harmony, balance, and peace. The restrained beauty and meaningful creations of designer Dennis Chan are exemplified in two main collections: Wulu, a minimalist form representing the mythical gourd as well as the lucky number eight; and Tien Di, literally "Heaven and Earth," symbolizing everlasting love. Classic gold, platinum, and diamonds mix with colored jades, black diamonds, and unusual materials for a truly unique effect. A sweeter addendum to the collection was added recently in the form of Bo Bo, the panda bear. ⊠ *IFC Mall, 8 Finance*

Many visitors to Hong Kong come for the tax- and duty-free jewelry.

St., Central ☎ *2389–8863* ⊕ *hk.qeelin.com* Ⓜ *Central* ✉ *Peninsula Shopping Arcade, Salisbury Rd., Tsim Sha Tsui, Kowloon* Ⓜ *Tsim Sha Tsui* ✉ *Ocean Terminal, Harbour City, 3 Canton Rd., Tsim Sha Tsui, Kowloon* Ⓜ *Tsim Sha Tsui.*

Ronald Abram. Looking at the rocks in these windows can feel like a visit to a natural history museum. Large white- and rare-color diamonds sourced from all over the world are a specialty here, but the shop also deals in emeralds, sapphires, and rubies. With years of expertise, Abrams dispenses advice on both the aesthetic merits and the investment potential of each stone or piece of jewelry. ✉ *Mezzanine, Mandarin Oriental, 5 Connaught Rd., Central* ☎ *2810–7677* ⊕ *www. ronaldabram.com* Ⓜ *Central.*

Saturn Essentials. If you're looking for a local artisan, a reasonably priced piece of silver, semiprecious stones, and sometimes even gold jewelry—or you just want a chat with a nice lady—visit Maureen "Mo" Gerrard. Her shop is opposite the salon of her son, Paul Gerrard. The shop repairs, cleans, plates, and polishes, too. ✉ *4th fl., Ming Fat Bldg., 74 Wellington St., Central* ☎ *2537–9335* ⊕ *www.saturnessentials.com* Ⓜ *Central.*

Super Star Jewelry. Discreetly tucked in a corner of Central, Super Star looks like any other small Hong Kong jewelry shop—with walls lined by display cases filled with the usual classic designs (old-fashioned to some) in predominantly gold and precious stones. What makes them stand out are the good prices and personalized service. The cultured pearls and mixed strands of colored freshwater pearls are not all shown, so ask Lily or one of her colleagues to bring them out. ✉ *The Galleria, 9 Queen's Rd. Central, Central* ☎ *2521–0507* Ⓜ *Central.*

Tayma Fine Jewellery. Unusual colored "connoisseur" gemstones are set by hand in custom designs by Hong Kong–based jeweler Tayma Page Allies. The collection is designed to bring out the personality of the individual wearer, and includes oversize cocktail rings, distinctive bracelets, pretty earrings, and more. ⊠ *Prince's Bldg., 10 Chater Rd., Central* ☎ *2525–5280* ⊕ *www.taymajewellery.com* Ⓜ *Central.*

MALLS

Fodor's Choice
★ **IFC Mall.** A quick glance at the directory—Tiffany & Co., Kate Spade, Prada, Gieves & Hawkes—lets you know that the International Finance Centre isn't for the faint of pocket. Designer department store Lane Crawford has its flagship store here, and agnès b.'s whimsical multiboutique fashion and lifestyle flagship sits under a large skylight styled after the shop owner's summer house in the south of France. Even the mall's cinema multiplex is special: the deluxe theaters have super-comfy seats with extra legroom and blankets for those chilled by the air conditioning. If you finish your spending spree at sunset, go for a cocktail at RED or Isola, two posh rooftop bars with fabulous harbor views. The Hong Kong Airport Express station (with in-town check-in service) is under the mall, and the Four Seasons Hotel connects to it. Avoid the mall between 12:30 and 2, when it's flooded with lunching office workers from the two IFC towers. ⊠ *8 Finance St., Central* ☎ *2295–3308* ⊕ *www.ifc.com.hk* Ⓜ *Hong Kong, Exit F.*

LAB Concept. Pacific Place may have put Admiralty on the map, but LAB Concept has breathed new life into the otherwise uneventful neighborhood. This 64,000-square-foot "fashion playground"—from the same masterminds behind Joyce and Lane Crawford—comprises a network of shops in the formerly forgettable Queensway Plaza and is fast becoming a major shopping destination. The white, contemporary space introduces some playful touches you won't find elsewhere, such as concierge facial stations and vending machines selling American Apparel tanks. Expect young and edgy brands, including Theory, JBrand, Scotch & Soda, Michael by Michael Kors, and Alexander Wang. Beloved beauty brands populate the FACES department, but the highlight is the mix of must-have boots, heels (even for bigfoot Americans), and accessories at Shoespace. ⊠ *Queensway Plaza, 93 Queensway, Admiralty* ☎ *2118– 6008* ⊕ *www.labconcepthk.com* Ⓜ *Admiralty, Exit C2.*

Landmark. If you haven't got a boutique in Landmark, you clearly haven't made it in the fashion world, darling. Central's most prestigious shopping site houses Celine, Loewe, Gucci, Joyce Grooming, and Harvey Nichols, among others. Even if your credit-card limit isn't up to a spree here, the hushed Café Landmark is the best place in town to watch well-coiffed tai-tais on the prowl. The large gourmet grocery store and food court, ThreeSixty, serves up Hong Kong's widest selection of organic produce and eco-friendly household products like detergent and utensils. A pedestrian bridge links the mall with shopping arcades in Landmark Prince's, Landmark Alexandra, Landmark Chater, and the Mandarin Oriental Hotel. ⊠ *8/F, One Exchange Square, Pedder St. and Des Voeux Rd., Central* ☎ *2530–4725* ⊕ *www.landmark.hk/ english/index.aspx* Ⓜ *Central, Exit G.*

Pacific Place. Once Hong Kong Island's classiest mall, Pacific Place has since been upstaged by the IFC. Yet it remains popular with well-to-do Hong Kongers, perhaps because it's quieter and more exclusive than most malls. High-end international prêt-à-porter fills most of its four floors, and department store Harvey Nichols has its Asia flagship here. Live music from its resident grand piano can still sometimes be heard wafting through the floors. When your bags are weighing you down, sandwiches, sushi, and Starbucks are on hand, as is a multiplex cinema. The JW Marriott, the Island Shangri-La, the Conrad, and the Upper House hotels are connected to this plaza, all with enticing afternoon tea options. Elevated walkways join Pacific Place with three lesser arcades: the **Admiralty Centre, United Centre,** and **Queensway Plaza.** ⊠ 88 Queensway, Admiralty, Central ☎ 2844–8900 ⊕ www.pacificplace. com.hk Ⓜ Admiralty, Exit F.

Pedder Building. Although dwarfed by flashy skyscrapers, the Pedder Building is one of Hong Kong's few remaining true neoclassical-style buildings. Once known for its discounted designer outlets and eclectic tenants, the elegant stone construction reinvented itself with a host of new faces after renovations in 2012. Though several shops kept their coveted spots—Bumps to Babes, Annette Jewellery, and the Armoury, to name a few—the Pedder Building seems to have a voracious appetite for art galleries and exhibition spaces. Ben Brown Fine Arts and Gagosian Gallery survived the transition, joined quickly by Simon Lee, Pearl Lam, and Hanart TZ, with more to come. If you need a break from all the abstract images, new-media installations, and inevitable head scratching, sneak away to Burgundy Etc and the Pacific Cigar Company smoking lounge on the fourth floor. ⊠ 12 Pedder St., Central Ⓜ Central.

SHOES AND BAGS

Hop's Handbag Co. Ltd. Uh-oh. You've over-shopped, and now packing is a problem. Hop over to Hop's for cheap luggage, from generic to name brands such as Samsonite. It also sells lots of handbags: some nameless but acceptable; others, amazing throwbacks to the '80s (and now back in fashion). ⊠ Ground fl., 12 Li Yuen St. E, Central ☎ 2523–3888 Ⓜ Central.

Kow Hoo Shoe Company. If you like shoes made the old-fashioned way, then Kow Hoo, one of Hong Kong's oldest (circa 1946), is for you. It also does great cowboy boots—there's nothing like knee-high calfskin. ⊠ 2nd fl., Prince's Bldg., 10 Chater Rd., Central ☎ 2523–0489 ⊕ kowhoo.com.hk ⊗ Closed Sun. Ⓜ Central.

Kwanpen. Famous for its crocodile bags and shoes, Kwanpen has acted as a manufacturer for famous brands since 1938, as well as being a stand-alone retailer. It also uses ostrich and leather. ⊠ Pacific Place, 88 Queensway, Admirality, Central ☎ 2918–9199 ⊕ www.kwanpen.com Ⓜ Admiralty ⊠ IFC Mall, 8 Finance St., Central Ⓜ Central ⊠ 1881 Heritage, 2A Canton Rd., Tsim Sha Tsui, Kowloon ⊕ www.kwanpen. com Ⓜ Tsim Sha Tsui.

Lianca. This is one of those unique places that make you want to buy something even if there's nothing you need. Lianca, first and foremost a manufacturer, sells well-made leather bags, wallets, frames, key chains, and home accessories in timeless, simple designs. It's an unbranded way to be stylish. ⊠ *Basement fl., 27 Staunton St., entrance on Graham St., SoHo, Central* ☎ *2139–2989* ⊕ *www.liancacentral.com* Ⓜ *Central*.

Mayer Shoes. Since the 1960s, Mayer has been making excellent custom-order shoes and accessories in leather, lizard, crocodile, and ostrich. Go to them for the classic pieces for which they became famous rather than this season's "it" bag. Prices for ladies shoes start at several hundred U.S. dollars and peak at roughly US$2,000. ⊠ *Mandarin Oriental, 5 Connaught Rd., Central* ☎ *2524–3317* Ⓜ *Central*.

Mischa Designs. Designer Michelle Lai's bags are handmade from Japanese brocade obis (sashes) and kimonos from the 1920s to the 1950s. Clutch bags such as the Dumpling or any of the reversible styles could make even the most unremarkable outfit look noteworthy. Keep an eye out for bigger totes made of obis paired with leather. You can also find her designs at Fang Fong Projects. ⊠ *Shop 1, 69A Peel St., Central* ☎ *3105–5557* ⊕ *www.mischadesigns.com*.

On Pedder. This store's brand directory reads like a fashion editor's wish list of world-famous shoe, bag, accessory, and jewelry designers. The main branch can be found in Central's Joyce boutique, but you might see the same brands at Lane Crawford—that's because they're sister companies. For the same aesthetics at lower prices, check out trendy younger sibling Pedder Red at the Gateway Arcade at Harbour City. ⊠ *On Pedder at Joyce, 1st fl., New World Tower, 18 Queen's Rd., Central* ☎ *2118–2323 for branch information* ⊕ *www.onpedder.com* Ⓜ *Central*.

Sam Wo. A veteran of this area, Sam Wo sells fashion-inspired leather bags at low prices and without the branding. You'll need a keen eye to spot the must-haves amid all the must-nots. See neighboring stalls for closer interpretations of branded bags. ⊠ *Basement, 41–47 Queen's Rd. Central, Central* ☎ *2524–0970* ⊗ *Closed Sun.* Ⓜ *Central*.

SPAS

Acupressure and Massage Centre of the Blind. Looking for a good massage without all the glitz? Visit these skilled and affordable blind masseurs trained in acupressure and Chinese massage, conveniently located in the middle of the Central Business District. Expect to pay around HK$240 per hour. ⊠ *2nd fl., Tung Ming Bldg., 40–42 Des Voeux Rd. Central, Central* ☎ *2810–6666* Ⓜ *Central*.

Four Seasons Spa. Enter via a light-wood and stark white hallway into treatment rooms that ooze modern cool. The two-hour, signature Traditional Moroccan Hamam treatment, using energizing salt scrubs and warm clay, is head-to-toe cleansing for your body and your soul. Even better? It's also supposed to ease that stubborn jet lag. The serene steam and sauna complex and harbor views will also help to alter your mood. ⊠ *Four Seasons Hotel, 8 Finance St., Central* ☎ *3196–8888* ⊕ *www. fourseasons.com* Ⓜ *Central*.

Fodor'sChoice
★
Happy Foot Reflexology Center. Who knew that pressure on your big toe could help clear your sinuses? Reflexology is Hong Kong's cheap way to relax, and Happy Foot is the legendary place to have it done. The armchairs are comfortable, and the therapists are experts, but don't expect a luxe experience. Interiors are basic, and you'll share a room

with other customers. But this is reflected in the prices too: pay about HK$250 for a 50-minute full-body massage or HK$198 for just your feet. ✉ *6th fl., 11th fl., and 13th fl., Jade Centre, 98 Wellington St., Central* ☎ *2544–1010* ⊕ *www.happyfoot.hk* Ⓜ *Central* ✉ *19th fl., Century Square, 1–13 D'Aguilar St., Central* ☎ *2522–1151* ⊕ *www. happyfoot.hk* Ⓜ *Central* ✉ *7th fl., QRE Plaza, 202 Queen's Rd. East, Wan Chai* ☎ *2573–3438.*

Fodor's Choice
★
The Mandarin Spa & the Oriental Spa. If you indulge in just one Hong Kong spa treatment, have it at one of these sister spas, at the Mandarin Oriental and the Landmark Mandarin Oriental hotels. Designed as a journey from the outer into the inner world, the experience begins on the check-in and fitness floor. You're taken up to the next level and offered a welcome tea, then guided deeper into this haven, where treatments are administered by excellent therapists in serene rooms. Try the signature Time Ritual, a holistic combination of therapies adapted to your specific needs on the day. Treatments here get you access to the vitality pool, the amethyst-crystal steam room, the authentic Turkish hammam, and more. Next door to the Mandarin, the legendary Mandarin Beauty Salon and Barber Shop offers traditional favorites. Ask for a famous Shanghainese pedicure with Samuel and his knives (yes, knives!), or see Betty for the traditional eyebrow threading. ✉ *Landmark Mandarin Oriental, 15 Queen's Rd. Central, Central* ☎ *2132–0011* ⊕ *www. mandarinoriental.com* Ⓜ *Central.*

Quality Chinese Medical Centre. Acupuncture looks alarming but is painless. Where better to try it than in China? This reputable center is also a good place to learn more about traditional Chinese medicine and herbal remedies. ✉ *5th fl., Jade Centre, 98 Wellington St., Central* ☎ *2881–8267* ⊕ *www.qualitytcm.com* Ⓜ *Central.*

TAILOR-MADE CLOTHING

Blanc de Chine. Blanc de Chine has catered to high society and celebrities, such as actor Jackie Chan, for years. That's easy when you're housed in the Prince's Building and you rely on word of mouth. The small, refined tailoring shop neatly displays exquisite fabrics from Switzerland and Italy, lovely ready-made women's wear, menswear, and home accessories. With newer stores in New York and Beijing, it appears the word is getting out. Items here are extravagances, but they're worth every penny. ✉ *Shop 123, Prince's Bldg., 10 Chater Rd., Central* ☎ *2104–7934* ⊕ *www.blancdechine.com* Ⓜ *Central, Exit K.*

Linva Tailors. It's one of the best of the old-fashioned cheongsam tailors, in operation since the 1960s. Master tailor Mr. Leung takes clients through the entire process and reveals a surprising number of variations in style. Prices are affordable, but vary according to fabric, which ranges from basics to special brocades and beautifully embroidered silks. ✉ *38 Cochrane St., Central* ☎ *2544–2456* Ⓜ *Central.*

MEN'S TAILORS
A-Man Hing Cheong Co., Ltd. People often gasp at the very mention of A-Man Hing Cheong, in the Mandarin Oriental Hotel. For some it symbolizes the ultimate in fine tailoring, with a reputation that extends back to its founding in 1898. For others it's the lofty prices that elicit a reaction. Regardless, this is a trustworthy source of European-cut suits,

custom shirts, and excellent service. ✉ *Mezzanine, Mandarin Oriental, 5 Connaught Rd., Central* ☎ *2522–3336* Ⓜ *Central.*

Ascot Chang. This self-titled "gentleman's shirtmaker" makes it easy to find the perfect shirt, even if you could get a better deal in a less prominent shop. Ascot Chang has upheld exacting Shanghainese tailoring traditions in Hong Kong since 1955, and now has stores in New York, Beverly Hills, Manila, and Shanghai. The focus here is on the fit and details, from 22 stitches per inch to collar linings crafted to maintain their shape. Among the countless fabrics, Swiss 200s two-ply Egyptian cotton by Alumo is one of the most coveted and expensive. Like many shirtmakers, Ascot Chang does pajamas, robes, boxer shorts, and women's blouses, too. It also has developed ready-made lines of shirts, T-shirts, neckties, and other accessories available for online ordering. ✉ *Shop 131, Prince's Bldg., 10 Chater Rd., Central* ☎ *2523–3663* ⊕ *www.ascotchang.com* Ⓜ *Central* ✉ *IFC Mall, 2nd fl., 1 Harbour View St., Central* ☎ *2295–3833* ⊕ *www.ascotchang.com* Ⓜ *Central* ✉ *The Peninsula Hong Kong, Salisbury Rd., Tsim Sha Tsui, Kowloon* ☎ *2366–2398* ⊕ *www.ascotchang.com* Ⓜ *Tsim Sha Tsui* ✉ *Kowloon Station, 2nd fl., 1 Austin Rd. West, Tsim Sha Tsui, Kowloon* ☎ *2196–8438* ⊕ *www.ascotchang.com* Ⓜ *Tsim Sha Tsui.*

Jantzen Tailor. Catering to expatriate bankers since 1972, this reputable yet reasonable tailor specializes in classic shirts; it also makes suits and women's garments. The comprehensive website displays its commitment to quality, such as hand-sewn button shanks, customizable interlinings, and Coats brand thread. ✉ *5th fl., 25 Des Voeux Rd., Central* ☎ *2570–5901* ⊕ *www.jantzentailor.com* Ⓜ *Central.*

Practical Tailor. As its name suggests, Practical Tailor is a refreshing change of pace from some of the stuffy and overpriced heavyweights just down the street. Popular among westerners and young professionals, the Shanghainese outfit is run by friendly and attentive co-owners Andy Shum and Jason Chan, who ensure every suit comes fully canvassed and hand stitched, inside and out. Depending on the quality of fabric—Inner Mongolia cashmere and silk from Ermenegildo Zegna will obviously run up the price—men's suits range from roughly HK$5,000 to HK$12,000. ✉ *8th fl., AIE Bldg., 33 Connaught Rd. Central, Central* ☎ *2522–3866* ⊕ *www.penhk.com* Ⓜ *Central, Exit A.*

Yuen's Tailor. Need a kilt? This is where the Hong Kong Highlanders Reel Club comes for custom-made kilts. The Yuen repertoire, however, extends to well-made suits and shirts. The tiny shop is on an unimpressive gray walkway and is filled from floor to ceiling with sumptuous European fabrics. It's a good place to have clothes copied; prices are competitive. ✉ *2nd fl., Escalator Link Alley, 80 Des Voeux Rd., Central* ☎ *2815–5388* Ⓜ *Central.*

WOMEN'S TAILORS

Irene Fashions. In addition to having the same name as the W.W. Chan women's division (⇨ *See Kowloon Peninsula*), this Irene Fashions promises much of the same guidance and workmanship. But don't confuse this popular Central tailoress with her Kowloon-side counterpart; the two are *not* related. Slightly more well known, this tailor attracts many expatriate women in search of everything from suits to evening

Tailor-Made

No trip to Hong Kong would be complete without a visit to one of its world-famous tailors, as many celebrities and dignitaries can attest. In often humble, fabric-cluttered settings, customer records contain the measurements of notables such as Jude Law, Kate Moss, David Bowie, Luciano Pavarotti, and Queen Elizabeth II.

TAILORING TIPS

If you've ever owned a custom-made garment, you understand the joy of clothes crafted to fit your every measurement. Hong Kong is best known for men's tailoring, but whether you're looking for a classic men's business suit or an evening gown, these steps will help you size things up.

■ Set Your Style. Be clear about what you want. Bring samples—a favorite piece of clothing or magazine photos. Also, Hong Kong tailors are trained in classic, structured garments. Straying from these could lead to disappointment. There are three basic suit styles. The American cut has a jacket with notched lapels, a center vent, and two or three buttons. The trousers are lean, with flat fronts. The British cut also has notched lapels and two- or three-button jackets, but it features side vents and pleated trousers. The double-breasted Italian cut has wide lapels and pleated trousers.

■ Choose Your Fabric. You're getting a deal on workmanship, so consider splurging on, say, a luxurious blend of cashmere, mink, and wool. When having something copied, though, choose a fabric similar to the original. Take your time selecting: fabric is the main cost factor. Examine fabric on a large scale; small swatches are deceiving.

■ Measure Up. Meticulous measuring is the mark of a superior craftsman, so be patient. And for accuracy, stand as you normally would (you can't suck in that gut forever).

■ Place Your Order. Most tailors require a deposit of 30%–50% of the total cost. Request a receipt detailing price, fabric, style, measurements, fittings, and production schedule. Ask for a swatch to compare with the final product.

■ Get Fit. There should be at least two fittings. The first is for major alterations. Subsequent fittings are supposed to be for minor adjustments, but don't settle for less than perfect: Keep sending it back until they get it right. Bring the right clothes, such as a dress shirt and appropriate shoes, to try on a suit. Try jackets buttoned and unbuttoned. Examine every detail. Are shoulder seams puckered or smooth? Do patterns meet? Is the collar too loose or tight? (About two fingers' space is right.)

FINDING A TAILOR

■ As soon as you arrive, visit established tailors to compare workmanship and cost.

■ Ask if the work is bespoke (made from scratch) or made-to-measure (based on existing patterns but handmade according to your measurements).

■ You get what you pay for. Assume the workmanship and fabric will match the price.

■ A fine suit requires six or more days to create. That said, be wary but not dismissive of "24-hour tailors." Hong Kong's most famous craftsmen have turned out suits in a day.

wear. Service in the cluttered atmosphere may be brusque, but it's only because they know what they're talking about. ⊠ *3rd fl., Tung Chai Bldg., 86–90 Wellington St., Central* ☎ *2850–5635* Ⓜ *Central.*

Margaret Court Tailoress. A name frequently passed on by expert Hong Kong shoppers, Margaret Wong's tailoring services span women's daywear to bridal gowns to Chinese cheongsam. Prices tend to be midrange. ⊠ *8th fl., Winner Bldg., 37 D'Aguilar St., Central* ☎ *2525–5596* Ⓜ *Central.*

Perfect Dress Alteration (aka Ann & Bon). Hong Kong's tai-tais bring their couture here for adjustments, as evidenced by the Chanel, Escada, and Versace bags hanging overhead in this cluttered little workshop buzzing with the sound of sewing machines. Although primarily known for alterations, it also offers tailoring services for women. ⊠ *2nd fl., Melbourne Plaza, 33 Queen's Rd. Central, Central* ☎ *2522–8838* Ⓜ *Central.*

Siriporn. Around the corner from the Midlevels Escalator and one of the most highly recommended Thai tailors in town, Siriporn is known for an acute sense of aesthetics, reasonable prices, and brightly colored Thai silks. It's also capable of crafting subtle garments to please minimalists. Visit by appointment only. ⊠ *Shop 1801, 18–20 Lyndhurst Terr., Central* ☎ *2866–6668* ⊕ *www.sarahsiriporn.com* Ⓜ *Central.*

WAN CHAI, CAUSEWAY BAY, AND BEYOND

WAN CHAI

No malls, no air-conditioning, no Prada—Wan Chai has all these things in its favor when shopping in Central starts to feel a bit like more of the same. Tourists don't shop here much, so you can try out your Cantonese at the rock-bottom no-name clothing outlets on the lanes between Johnston Road and Queen's Road East. Everything from underwear to evening wear is on offer. On Johnston Road, shops selling bamboo birdcages and kung fu gear pay homage to Wan Chai's traditional side, in contrast to the chic modern furniture stores that have mushroomed here. Find them spreading into the small meandering Star Street neighborhood behind Three Pacific Place (⊕ *www.starstreet.com.hk*). Rosewood furniture and camphor-wood chests are two of the specialties of the midrange furniture shops on Queen's Road East and Wan Chai Road, near Admiralty. The Suzy Wong stereotype lives on in the marine-filled tattoo parlors lining Lockhart Road. Techno-happy modern Hong Kong is alive and well at the Wan Chai Computer Centre, a collection of dozens of computing outlets on Hennessy Road.

CLOTHING

45R. Around since 1978, Japanese brand 45R has garnered a reputation for ultracomfortable, exquisitely crafted jeans. Following the successes of outposts in Paris and New York, a flagship store opened on Star Street in 2009. Amid the minimalist surrounds, find heaps of its famous hand-dyed denim as well as breezy button-downs, wooly sweaters, and understated frocks. ⊠ *7 Star St., Wan Chai* ☎ *2861–1145* ⊕ *www.45rpm.jp* Ⓜ *Wan Chai, Exit B2.*

Locals buy colorful Chinese lanterns and festive decorations for the Lunar New Year, but they also make great souvenirs.

Kapok. Hip messenger bags, soft fabrics, funky watches, comfy kicks, music, stationery—Kapok has it all. This bright local favorite is a one-stop shop for classic cotton and knits. Meanwhile, its café and gallery space on Sun Street serves up steamy French coffee, chocolate croissants, and freshly baked cupcakes. ⌧ *5 St. Francis Yard, Wan Chai* ☎ *2549–9254* ⊕ *www.ka-pok.com* Ⓜ *Wan Chai, Exit B2.*

Russell Street. Gatekeeper of the up-and-coming, Russell Street aims to introduce fresh labels to Hong Kong's style savants. Taking cues from New York and London's top fashion students, as well as established international labels—think Victoria Beckham and House of Holland—the boutique showcases eclectic designs ranging from fancy furs to colorful graphic-print dresses. Among the mix of envy-inducing pieces, look for Sophie Hulme's gorgeous leather bags and lively animal print cardigans from Sibling and Sister. ⌧ *6 St. Francis Yard, Wan Chai* ☎ *2886–0800* ⊕ *www.russell-street.com* Ⓜ *Wan Chai, Exit B2.*

Sonjia by Sonjia Norman. Walk past a local garage and snoozing dogs in this old-style Hong Kong area to find the low-key atelier of Korean-English ex-lawyer Sonjia Norman. The designer crafts quietly luxurious, one-of-a-kind pieces and modified vintage clothing under the Sonjia label. Her clothes are the epitome of understated stealth wealth. A new adjacent store houses Norman's home and living collection, including tableware, linens, and all sorts of pillows and cushions. ⌧ *Ground fl., 2 Sun St., Wan Chai* ☎ *2529–6223* ⊕ *www.sonjiaonline. com* Ⓜ *Wan Chai.*

Vie. Modern and minimalist, Vie's decor is in perfect harmony with its Nordic apparel. The combination boutique and gallery on St. Francis

Yard is a spinoff of Vein, and offers up a mix of Scandinavian luxury labels and home accessories. The lineup changes every four to six weeks, but you can usually find at least a dozen stalwart, simple-yet-elegant brands, including Filippa K, Aarikka, and Won Hundred. Expect straight lines, a gray-scale palette, and unexpected pops of color. ⊠ *Shop 2, St. Francis Yard, Wan Chai* ☎ *2804–1038* ⊕ *www.bvein.com* Ⓜ *Wan Chai, Exit B2.*

ELECTRONICS, CAMERAS, AND MUSIC

Kung Fu Supplies Co. You've seen *Enter the Dragon* a hundred times, and you practice your karate chops daily. Time to get the drum, cymbal, leather boots, sword, whip, double dagger, studded bracelet, and *kempo* gloves. Kung Fu Supplies Co. can kit you out. ⊠ *192 Johnston Rd., Wan Chai* ☎ *2891–1912* ⊕ *www.kungfu.com.hk.*

Monocle. A London-based media brand that does it all: magazine publishing, online news, radio, CDs, cafés, plus retail outlets in Tokyo, Toronto, and New York. Hong Kong devotees rejoiced when the brand opened a retail-cum-office on Star Street's St. Francis Yard in 2010. This contemporary spot offers up stylish accessories like beloved linen-bound notebooks, greeting cards, embossed card cases, and walnut-trimmed heritage radios. Whether shopping for trendy tote bags or excellent reading material, you'll be in good company. ⊠ *Shop 1, Bo Fung Mansion, 1–4 St. Francis Yard, Wan Chai* ☎ *2804–2323* ⊕ *www.monocle. com* Ⓜ *Wan Chai.*

Fodor'sChoice ★ **Wanchai Computer Centre.** You'll find honest-to-goodness bargains on computer goods and accessories in the labyrinth of shops spanning several floors. And you can negotiate prices. Your computer can be put together by a computer technician in less than a day if you're rushed; otherwise, two days is normal. The starting price is HK$3,000 depending on the hardware, processor, and peripherals you choose. This is a great resource, whether you're a techno-buff who's interested in assembling your own computer (a popular pastime with locals), or a technophobe looking for discounted earphones. ⊠ *130 Hennessy Rd., Wan Chai* Ⓜ *Wan Chai, Exit A5.*

HOME FURNISHINGS

Nlostnfound Living & Co. Some of the items at Nlostnfound could use a bath, but the clutter has a lot of character. Take the time to browse through the jumble of old-world trinkets—1940s clocks, Shanghai lamps, 20s-era luggage trunks, antique furniture, colorful wind-up walking toys, typewriters, and postcards—and you'll likely find something worth salvaging. ⊠ *3 St. Francis Yard, Wan Chai* ☎ *2574–1328* ⊕ *www.nlostnfound.com* Ⓜ *Wan Chai.*

OVO. Push past a giant weathered steel door to enter this atmospheric, high-ceiling showroom, which feels like a cross between a museum and a temple. The fusion and contrasts of Southeast and West permeate every surface of the minimalist furniture, home furnishings, and accessories designed by the in-house team. Items are smart and rarely fussy. Beautiful, unvarnished blocks of wood, for example, are proposed as side tables. A few minutes' walk away you'll also find the newer **OVO Studio** (⊠ *The Arcade, 100 Cyberport* ☎ *2529–6060 Western*), or OS, with its more European mix of in-house and international contemporary designs from brands like Tom Dixon, Fritz Hansen, and Andreu World. ✉ *Ground fl., 16 Queen's Rd. E, Wan Chai* ☎ *2526–7226* ⊕ *www.ovo.com.hk* Ⓜ *Wan Chai, Exit B1.*

JEWELRY

Wing On Jewelry Ltd. There's a nostalgic charm to the butterflies, birds, and natural forms fashioned from jade, pearls, precious stones, and gold here. Everything looks like an heirloom inherited from your grandmother. With on-site gemologists and artisans, and a commitment to post-sale service, this store has a long list of repeat customers. If, however, you lean toward Scandinavian aesthetics and clean lines, this probably isn't the place for you. ✉ *146 Johnston Rd., Wan Chai* ☎ *2572–2332* ⊕ *www.wingonjewelry.com.hk* Ⓜ *Wan Chai* ✉ *459 Hennessy Rd., Causeway Bay* Ⓜ *Causeway Bay.*

SHOES AND BAGS

Lili Lili Shoes. The Chan Brothers have an illustrious history in Hong Kong and have certainly left a trail of satisfied customers in their wake; however reviews these days speak of hit and miss experiences there. Prices have also shot up over the last few years (from around HK$1,300 for sandals and HK$2,000 for high heels). Still, when they are good, they are very, very good. ✉ *Admiralty Centre, 18 Harcourt Rd., Wan Chai* ☎ *2865–3989* Ⓜ *Admiralty.*

CAUSEWAY BAY

Hong Kong fashionistas hungry for new labels choose Causeway Bay over Central any day. Quirky-but-cool Asian brands that won't arrive stateside for years are the pull at Japanese department store Sogo and micromalls like the Island Beverley. The low-profile storefronts on Yiu Wa Street belie its *hot* reputation for homegrown clothing and housewares. Similar up-and-coming boutiques are scattered along Vogue Alley, at the intersection of Paterson and Kingston streets. Local shops that have already made their names around here include innovating lifestyle specialist G.O.D. (Goods Of Desire), which has a big branch on Leighton Street.

Megamall Times Square soars behind all this—its mix of designer and midrange gear makes it a good one-stop shop destination. Other good bets for clothing are the big branches of local chains like Giordano on Jardine's Crescent. Prices in the stalls and poky shops along here and Jardine's Bazaar are unbeatable. Cheap souvenir stalls are another boon. You can see how real Hong Kongers do their food shopping at the "wet market" (so called because the vendors are perpetually hosing down their produce) at the end of these streets. Locals also head to Hennessy Road for jewelry, watches, luggage, stereos, cameras, and electronic goods.

BEAUTY AND COSMETICS

Aroma Natural Skin Care. This store has been the secret weapon of skin regime enthusiasts for years, with stock from some of the industry's most venerated brands, many of them hard to track down. Find your Dr. Hauschka, Bioderma, Aveda, and Skin Ceuticals here, as well as the mandatory spectrum of whitening products. ✉ *Shop 863 Island Beverly Ctr., 1 Great George St., Causeway Bay* ☎ *2506–0699* ⊕ *www.aroma-natural.com.hk* Ⓜ *Causeway Bay.*

Kwong Sang Hong. This shop carries Hong Kong's first local cosmetics line, also known as Two Girls Brand. The colorful, old-fashioned packaging, which is reminiscent of traditional Chinese medicines, is more remarkable than the products. That said, the line's classics—including hair oil, talcum powder, and face cream—do make lovely gifts. ✉ *Causeway Place, Hong Kong Mansion, 2–10 Great George St., Causeway Bay* ☎ *2504–1811* ⊕ *www.twogirls.hk* Ⓜ *Causeway Bay.*

Sa Sa Cosmetics. The fuchsia-pink signs that announce Hong Kong's best and largest cosmetic discounter will become familiar sights on any shopping expedition. Look for deals on everything from cheap glittery makeup to sleek designer lines. Fragrances are a particularly good buy; prices are usually even lower than those at airport duty-free shops. ✉ *Shop G01, Hang Lung Centre, 2–20 Paterson St., Causeway Bay* ☎ *2577–2286, 2505–5023 customer service and branch info* ⊕ *www.sasa.com* Ⓜ *Causeway Bay* ✉ *1st fl., Chung King Express, 36–44 Nathan Rd., Tsim Sha Tsui, Kowloon* Ⓜ *Tsim Sha Tsui.*

CLOTHING

G2000. This inexpensive chain carries men's and women's business wear in Asian sizes. It's a great place to look for suits with matching shirts (and ties) for a good price. Expect a mix of city-chic and casual, and especially good fits for anyone petite. ✉ *24–26 East Point Rd., Causeway Bay* ☎ *2972–2576* ⊕ *www.g2000.com.hk* Ⓜ *Causeway Bay* ✉ *2nd fl., Gateway Arcade, Harbour City, 5 Canton Rd., Tsim Sha Tsui, Kowloon* ☎ *2730–4759* ⊕ *www.g2000.com.hk* Ⓜ *Tsim Sha Tsui.*

Giordano. Hong Kong's version of the Gap is the most established and ubiquitous local source of basic T-shirts, jeans, and casual wear. Like its U.S. counterpart, the brand now has a bit more fashion sense and slick ad campaigns, but still offers reasonable prices. A few of its hundreds of stores are listed here, but you'll have no problem finding one on almost every major street. A new line, **Giordano Concepts,** offers more stylish (and pricier) urban wear in neutral colors like black, gray, and white. Customer service is generally good, even if the young, energetic staff screeches "hello" then "bye-bye" at every customer in a particularly jarring way. ✉ *Ground fl., Island Beverly, 1 Great George St., Causeway Bay* ☎ *2923–7445* ⊕ *www.giordano.com.hk* Ⓜ *Causeway Bay* ✉ *Ground fl., 43–45 Queen's Rd. Central, Central* ⊕ *www.giordano.com.hk* Ⓜ *Central, Exit D2* ✉ *Ground fl., Manson House, 74–78 Nathan Rd., Tsim Sha Tsui, Kowloon* ☎ *2926–1028* ⊕ *www.giordano.com.hk* Ⓜ *Tsim Sha Tsui.*

Giordano Ladies. If Giordano is the Gap, Giordano Ladies is the Banana Republic, albeit with a more Zen approach. Find clean-line modern classics in neutral black, gray, white, and beige; each collection is brightened by a single highlight color, red one season, blue the next, and so on. Everything is elegant enough for the office and comfortable enough for the plane. ✉ *Shop 32A, JP Plaza, 22 and 32 Paterson St., Causeway Bay* ☎ *2922–1018* ⊕ *www.giordanoladies.com* Ⓜ *Causeway Bay* ✉ *1st fl., Manson House, 74–78 Nathan Rd., Tsim Sha Tsui, Kowloon* ☎ *2926–1331* ⊕ *www.giordano.com.hk* Ⓜ *Tsim Sha Tsui.*

Olivia Couture. The surroundings are functional, but the gowns, wedding dresses, and cheongsams by local designer Olivia Yip are lavish. With a growing clientele, including socialites looking to stand out, Yip is quietly making a name for herself and her Parisian-influenced pieces. ✉ *Ground fl., Bartlock Centre, 3 Yiu Wah St., Causeway Bay* ☎ *2838–6636* ⊕ *www.oliviacouture.com* Ⓜ *Causeway Bay.*

Pink Martini. Step into this blush-colored boudoir for fresh young fashions with spunk, courtesy of brands like Laguna Moon, Daily Dolly, and Kikka. It also has a small range of costume jewelry, clutches, and jackets, all nicely aimed at bringing out your inner girl. ✉ *Shop 2, ground fl., Bartlock Centre, 3 Yiu Wa St., Causeway Bay* ☎ *2574–1498* ⊕ *www.pinkmartini.com.hk.*

Spy Henry Lau. Local bad boy Henry Lau brings an edgy attitude to his fashion for men and women. Bold and often dark, with a touch of bling, his clothing and accessories lines are not for the fainthearted. ✉ *1st fl., Cleveland Mansion, 5 Cleveland St., Causeway Bay* ☎ *2317–6928* ⊕ *www.spyhenrylau.com* Ⓜ *Causeway Bay, Exit E.* ✉ *21 Staunton St., Soho, Central* Ⓜ *Central*

Uniqlo. If you are a Giordano or Bossini fan, don't miss this Japanese chain. Uniqlo carries a wide variety of inexpensive, fashionable casual wear for women, men, and children. New locations have been opening rapidly throughout the city since 2007. Popular items include T-shirts, jeans, and pajamas. ✉ *2nd fl., Lee Theatre Plaza, 99 Percival St., Causeway Bay* ☎ *2577–5811* ⊕ *www.uniqlo.com.hk* Ⓜ *Causeway Bay* ✉ *2nd fl., Miramar Shopping Centre, 132 Nathan Rd., Tsim Sha Tsui, Kowloon* Ⓜ *Tsim Sha Tsui.*

DEPARTMENT STORES

Fodor'sChoice
★

City'super. Wherever you're from and whatever you're missing, whether it's fresh oysters from France or Japanese cosmetics, this gourmet supermarket and international variety store is the place to begin your search. Locals and tourists looking for gadgets, inexpensive jewelry and accessories, and quirky products like bottled water for pets often find them here, and this store will never bore you. The Times Square location often has international-theme food festivals. Be sure to check out the Japanese imported sweets like Royce Chocolate's unusual chocolate chips. ✉ *IFC Mall, Shop 1041–1049, 8 Finance St., Central* ☎ *2234–7128* ⊕ *www.citysuper.com.hk* Ⓜ *Hong Kong, Exit A1* ✉ *Basement One, Times Square, Causeway Bay* ☎ *2506–2888* ⊕ *www.citysuper.com.hk* Ⓜ *Causeway Bay, Exit A* ✉ *Harbour City, 3rd fl., 3 Canton Rd., Tsim Sha Tsui, Kowloon* ☎ *852–2375* ⊕ *www.citysuper.com.hk* Ⓜ *Tsim Sha Tsui, Exit A1.*

LCX. This spacious store combines local and international fashion, beauty products, and dining under one roof. Clothing brands like Bauhaus, American Eagle, French Connection, Initial, and Cocktail all have their own areas here, along with TonyMoly, Demologica, Too Cool For School, Max Factor, Lush, and other cosmetics lines. It also has a handful of restaurants, including Itacho Sushi and Suzuki Cafe. ✉ *3rd fl., Ocean Terminal, Harbour City, 2–27 Canton Rd., Tsim Sha Tsui, Tsim Sha Tsui* ☎ *2890–5200* ⊕ *www.lcx.com.hk* Ⓜ *Tsim Sha Tsui.*

Sogo. A lynchpin of the Causeway Bay shopping scene, Japanese brand Sogo's main branch has 16 floors of clothing, cosmetics, and housewares. The vast basement-level grocery store keeps the Japanese expat community happily fed. There's a dazzling variety of Chinese, Japanese, and international brands—the store is particularly strong on street wear, makeup, and accessories. The downside is that it's all squeezed into a tiny retail space, which can make shopping here cramped work. The considerably smaller Tsim Sha Tsui branch is in the basement shopping arcade under the Space Museum. ⊠ *555 Hennessy Rd., Causeway Bay* ☎ *2833–8338* ⊕ *www.sogo.com.hk* Ⓜ *Causeway Bay, Exit D* ⊠ *12 Salisbury Rd., Tsim Sha Tsui, Kowloon* Ⓜ *East Tsim Sha Tsui, Exit J.*

ELECTRONICS, CAMERAS, AND MUSIC

Broadway. Like its more famous competitor, Fortress, Broadway is a large electronic-goods chain. It caters primarily to the local market, so some staff members speak better English than others. Look for familiar name-brand cameras, computers, sound systems, home appliances, and mobile phones. Just a few of the many shops are listed here. ⊠ *7th fl., Times Square, 1 Matheson St., Causeway Bay* ☎ *2506–0228* ⊕ *www.ibroadway.com.hk* Ⓜ *Causeway Bay, Exit A* ⊠ *3rd fl., Ocean Centre, Harbour City, Canton Rd., Tsim Sha Tsui, Kowloon* ☎ *2736–7733* ⊕ *www.broadway.com.hk* Ⓜ *Tsim Sha Tsui* ⊠ *Ground fl., 78 Sai Yeung Choi St. S, Mong Kok, Kowloon* ☎ *2381–6760* ⊕ *www.broadway.com.hk* Ⓜ *Mong Kok.*

Fodor's Choice ★ **Fortress.** Part of billionaire Li Ka-shing's empire, this extensive chain of shops sells electronics with warranties—a safety precaution that draws the crowds. It also has good deals on printers and accessories, although selection varies by shop. You can spot a Fortress by looking for the big orange sign. For the full list of shops, visit the website. ⊠ *Times Square, 7th and 8th fl., 1 Matheson St., Causeway Bay* ☎ *2506–0031* ⊕ *www.fortress.com.hk* Ⓜ *Causeway Bay* ⊠ *3rd fl., Ocean Centre, Harbour City, 5 Canton Rd., Tsim Sha Tsui, Kowloon* ☎ *3101–1413* Ⓜ *Tsim Sha Tsui* ⊠ *Chung Kiu Commercial Bldg., 47–51 Shan Tung St., Mong Kok, Kowloon* ☎ *2781–1730* Ⓜ *Mong Kok* ⊠ *Lower ground fl., Melbourne Plaza, 33 Queen's Rd. Central, Central* ☎ *2121–1077* Ⓜ *Central.*

COMPUTERS **DG Lifestyle Store.** An appointed Apple Center, DG carries Mac and iPod products. High-design gadgets, accessories, and software by other brands are add-ons that meld with the sleek Apple design philosophy. ⊠ *9th fl., Times Square, 1 Matheson St., Causeway Bay* ☎ *2506–1338* ⊕ *www.dg-lifestyle.com* Ⓜ *Causeway Bay* ⊠ *Shop 120, Pacific Place, Admiralty, Central* ☎ *2918–4811* ⊕ *www.dg-lifestyle.com* Ⓜ *Admiralty* ⊠ *Ground fl., Mikiki Mall, 638 Prince Edward Rd. East, San Po Kong, Kowloon* ☎ *2331–8628* ⊕ *www.dg-lifestyle.com* Ⓜ *Kowloon Bay.*

HOME FURNISHINGS

Franc Franc. This Japanese home and living store is sort of like a higher-end IKEA, with everything you'd need to equip your downtown apartment, from bookshelves to bubble bath. The funky, colorfully modern designs and intriguing gadgets will keep all types of shoppers entertained, and it's quite a feat to leave the store with empty hands. ☒ *2nd fl., Hang Lung Centre, 2–20 Paterson St., Causeway Bay* ☎ *3427–3366* ⊕ *www.francfranc.com* Ⓜ *Causeway Bay.*

G.O.D. This pioneering lifestyle brand plays with ideas, designs, and words drawn from Hong Kong's unique heritage, with imaginative and retro, yet functional, results. Its huge product range consists mostly of home furnishings and tableware, though there are some fashion items; the men's and women's boxer shorts are particularly cute. Affordable creations, such as red rubber trays for making "double happiness" character ice cubes, Buddha statues irreverently painted in Day-Glo tones, and old-fashioned Chinese textiles reimagined in modern settings, manage to be both nostalgic and contemporary. Buy a trendy gift or unique vintage-style postcards for the folks back home. ☒ *Ground fl. and 1st fl., Leighton Centre, 77 Leighton Rd., entrance on Sharp St. E, Causeway Bay* ☎ *2890–5555* ⊕ *www.god.com.hk* Ⓜ *Causeway Bay* ☒ *Ground fl. and 1st fl., 48 Hollywood Rd., Central* ☎ *2805–1876* ⊕ *www.god.com.hk* Ⓜ *Central* ☒ *Basement fl., Silvercord, 30 Canton Rd., Tsim Sha Tsui, Kowloon* ☎ *2784–5555* ⊕ *www.god.com.hk* Ⓜ *Tsim Sha Tsui.*

JEWELRY

City Chain Co. Ltd. With more than 200 shops in Asia and locations all over Hong Kong, City Chain Co. Ltd. has a wide selection of watches for various budgets, including Ellesse, Cyma, and Solvil & Titus. ☒ *Times Square, 1 Matheson St., Causeway Bay* ☎ *2506–3553* ⊕ *www.citychain.com* Ⓜ *Causeway Bay, Exit A* ☒ *Ground fl., Yat Fat Bldg., 44–46 Des Voeux Rd. Central, Central* ☎ *2537–6518* ⊕ *www.citychain.com* Ⓜ *Central, Exit C* ☒ *1st fl., Festival Walk, 80 Tat Chee Ave., Kowloon Tong, Kowloon* ☎ *2907–8912* ⊕ *www.citychain.com* Ⓜ *Kowloon Tong, Exit C1.*

King Fook Jewellery. When considering jewelry stores, longevity is a good thing. King Fook has been around since 1949, promising stringent quality control, quality craftsmanship, and professional service. **Masterpiece by King Fook,** the higher-end King Fook line, sells first-grade diamonds and precious jewelry. ☒ *Ground fl. and 1st fl., Windsor House, 311 Gloucester Rd., Causeway Bay* ☎ *2576–1032* ⊕ *www.kingfook.com* Ⓜ *Causeway Bay* ☒ *Ground fl., 30–32 Des Voeux Rd., Central* Ⓜ *Central.*

MALLS

Hysan Place. Across the street from Causeway Bay's popular Sogo looms neighborhood newcomer Hysan Place. This gleaming 17-story mall devotes the fourth and fifth floors to Japanese and Korean designers. Try on urban-chic garb from Daily Dolly, Snidel, and Deicy, then head up to the sixth floor for pampering. Dubbed the Garden of Eden, this level is overflowing with name-brand beauty products, lingerie, dessert counters, bathing suits, and nail salons. For a fix of fresh air, step out onto the Sky Garden on the fourth level, or slip into the three-level Eslite bookstore—open 24 hours a day—to relax with a book and a cuppa. ☒ *500 Hennessy Rd., Causeway Bay* ☎ *2886–7222* ⊕ *hp.leegardens.com.hk* Ⓜ *Causeway Bay, Exit D2 or F.*

Lee Gardens One and Two. These two adjacent malls are a firm favorite with local celebrities. They come as much for the mall's low-key atmosphere—a world away from the bustle of Central—as for the clothes. And with so many big names under one small roof—Gucci, Jean-Paul Gaultier, Vivienne Tam, Armani, and Hermès, to name but a few—who can blame them? The second floor of Lee Gardens Two is taken up with designer kiddie wear. The two buildings, one on either side of Hysan Avenue, are linked by a second-floor footbridge. ⊠ *33 Hysan Ave., Causeway Bay* ☎ *2907–5227* ⊕ *www.leegardens.com.hk* Ⓜ *Causeway Bay, Exit F.*

Fodor's Choice
★

Times Square. This gleaming mall packs in most of Hong Kong's best-known stores into 12 frenzied floors, organized thematically. Lane Crawford and Marks & Spencer both have big branches here, as does favored local deli City'super. Many restaurants are located in the basement, giving way to names like Gieves & Hawkes and Burberry on the second floor, and midrange options like Zara higher up. The electronics, sports, and outdoors selection is particularly good. An indoor atrium hosts everything from heavy-metal bands to fashion shows to local movie stars; there's also a dozen or so eateries: try the innovative SML (or Small Medium Large) for its large terrace and good selection of wines. The huge Page One bookshop is on the ninth floor. ⊠ *1 Matheson St., Causeway Bay* ☎ *2118–8900 Customer Service Hotline* ⊕ *www.timessquare.com.hk* Ⓜ *Causeway Bay, Exit A.*

MARKETS

Jardine's Bazaar and Jardine's Crescent. These two small parallel streets are so crammed with clothing stalls it's difficult to make your way through. Most offer bargains on the usual clothes, children's gear, bags, and cheap souvenirs like chopstick sets. The surrounding boutiques are also worth a look for local and Japanese fashions, though the sizes are small. ⊠ *Jardine's Bazaar, Causeway Bay* Ⓜ *Causeway Bay, Exit F.*

SHOES AND BAGS

Milan Station. Even if you're willing to shell out for an Hermès Kelly bag, how can anyone expect you to survive the waitlist? Milan Station resells the "it" bags of yesterday that have been retrieved from Hong Kong's fickle fashionistas. Inexplicably, the shop entrances were designed to look like MTR stations. The concept has been so successful, unimaginatively named copycats have sprung up, such as Paris Station. Discounts vary according to brand and trends, but the merchandise is in good condition. ⊠ *Ground fl., Percival House, 77–83 Percival St., Causeway Bay* ☎ *2504–0128, 2730–8037 customer service* ⊕ *www.milanstation.net* Ⓜ *Causeway Bay* ⊠ *Ground fl., 26 Wellington St., Central* ☎ *2736–3388* ⊠ *Ground fl., Pakpolee Commercial Centre, 1A Sai Yeung Choi St. South, Mong Kok, Kowloon* ☎ *2782–0033* Ⓜ *Mong Kok* ⊠ *Ground fl., 81 Chatham Rd., Tsim Sha Tsui, Kowloon* ☎ *2730–2528* Ⓜ *Tsim Sha Tsui.*

Prestige Shoe Co. Ltd. Like the Happy Valley shoemakers, Prestige does fashion-forward, acceptable-quality, reasonably priced shoes. Unlike its valley brethren it's more convenient, with several locations around town. ⊠ *1st fl., Island Beverley Centre, 1 Great George St., Causeway Bay* ☎ *2523–3003* Ⓜ *Central* ⊠ *Shop 149, World Wide House, 19 Des Voeux Rd. Central, Central* ☎ *2523–3003.*

4

CLOSE UP

Shopping Hong Kong's Markets

Chinese markets are hectic and crowded, but great fun for the savvy shopper. The intensity of the bargaining and the variety of goods available are well worth the detour.

Nowadays Hong Kongers may prefer to flash their cash in department stores and designer boutiques but, generally, markets are still the best places to shop. Parents and grandparents, often toting children, go to their local neighborhood wet market almost daily to pick up fresh items such as tofu, fish, meat, fruit, and vegetables. Food markets are also great places to mix with the locals and engage with the touts.

Some markets have a mish-mash of items; others are more specialized, dealing in one particular ware. Prices paid are always a great topic of conversation. A compliment on a choice article will often elicit the price paid in reply, and a discussion may ensue on where to get the same thing at an even lower cost.

GREAT FINDS

The prices we list *below* are meant to give you an idea of what you can expect to pay for certain items. Actual post-bargaining prices will of course depend on how well you haggle, while pre-bargaining prices are often based on how much the vendor thinks he or she can get out of you.

Jade. A symbol of purity and beauty for the Chinese, jade comes in a range of colors. Subtle and simple bangles vie for attention with large sculptures in markets. A lavender jade Guanyin (Goddess of Mercy) pendant runs about HK$260 and a green jade bangle about HK$280 before bargaining.

Silk. You'll find silk items at certain markets, from purses to slippers to traditional dresses. Silk brocade costs around HK$35 per meter, a price that's generally negotiable only if you buy large quantities.

Mah-Jongg Sets. The clack-clack of mah-jongg tiles can be heard late into the night in many public housing estates during the summer. Cheap plastic sets go for about HK$50. Far more aesthetically pleasing are ceramic sets in slender drawers of painted cases. These run about HK$250 after bargaining, from a starting price of HK$450.

"Maomorabilia." The Chairman's image is available on badges, bags, lighters, watches, ad infinitum. Pop art–like figurines of Mao and his Red Guards clutching red books are kitschy but iconic. For sound bites and quotes from the Great Helmsman, buy the Little Red Book itself. Pre-bargaining, a badge costs HK$25, a bag HK$50, and a ceramic figurine HK$380. Just keep in mind that many posters are fakes.

Pearls. Many freshwater pearls are grown in Taihu; seawater pearls come from Japan or the South Seas. Some have been dyed and others mixed with semi-precious stones. Designs can be pretty wild and the clasps are not of high quality, but necklaces and bracelets are cheap. Post-bargaining, a plain, short strand of pearls should cost around HK$40.

Propaganda and Comic Books. Follow the adventures of Master Q, or look for scenes from Chinese history and lots of *gongfu* (Chinese martial arts) stories, like *Longfumun* (Dragon Tiger Gate). Most titles are in Chinese and often in black and white, but can be bargained down to around HK$15.

Retro Finds. Odd items from the prewar '30s to the booming '70s include treasures like antique furniture, wooden toys, and tin advertising signs. Small items such as teapots can be bought for around HK$250. Retro items are harder to bargain down for than mass-produced items.

SHOPPING KNOW-HOW

At the Markets: Make sure to put money and valuables in a safe place. Pickpockets and bag-slashers are becoming more common. When purchasing, check for fake items, for example, silk and pearls.

Bringin' Home the Goods: Although that faux-Gucci handbag is tempting, remember that some countries have heavy penalties for the import of counterfeit goods. Likewise, that animal fur may be cheap, but you may get fined a lot more at your home airport than what you paid for it. Counterfeit goods are generally prohibited in the United States, but there's some gray area regarding goods with a "confusingly similar" trademark. Each person is allowed to bring in one such item, as long as it's for personal use and not for resale.

When to Go: Avoid weekends if you can and try to go early in the morning, from 8 am to 10 am, or early evening for the night markets. Rainy days are also good bets for avoiding the crowds and getting better prices.

HOW TO BARGAIN

Successful bargaining requires knowing your prices and never losing your cool. Here's a step-by-step guide to getting the price you want and having fun at the same time.

Do's

■ Start by deciding how much you're willing to pay for an item.

■ Let the vendor know you're interested.

■ The vendor will quote you a price, sometimes using a calculator.

■ At this point it's up to you to express either incredulity or loss of interest. But be forewarned, the vendor plays this game, too.

■ Name a price that's around 70% of the original price—lower if you feel daring.

■ Pass the calculator back and forth until you reach an agreement.

Don'ts

■ Don't enter into negotiations if you aren't seriously considering the purchase.

■ Don't haggle over small sums of money.

■ If the vendor isn't budging, walk away; he'll likely call you back.

■ It's better to bargain if the vendor is alone. He's unlikely to come down on the price if there's an audience.

■ Saving face is everything in China. Remain pleasant and smile often.

■ Buying more than one of something can get you a better deal.

■ Dress down and leave your jewelry and watches in the hotel safe on the day you go marketing. You'll get a lower starting price if you don't flash your wealth.

Rabeanco. Hong Kong–based Rabeanco has a reasonably priced line of beautiful, quality bags in Italian leather. Expect designs that are contemporary and colorful, but never flashy or absurd. Buy yours now before the world discovers them. ⊠ *Ground fl., 33 Sharp St. E, Causeway Bay* ☎ *3586–0281, 2245–5085 customer service and branch information* ⊕ *www.rabeanco.com* Ⓜ *Causeway Bay* ⊠ *1st fl., Man Yee Arcade, 68 Des Voeux Rd. Central, Central* ☎ *2259–5388* Ⓜ *Central* ⊠ *Ground fl., Hong Kong Pacific Centre, 28 Hankow Rd., Tsim Sha Tsui, Kowloon* ☎ *3586–0281* Ⓜ *Tsim Sha Tsui.*

EASTERN

MALLS

Cityplaza. An ice-skating rink and a multiplex theater are two of the reasons why Cityplaza is the city's most popular family mall. So popular, in fact, that it's best to steer clear on weekends, when you have to fight through the crowds. Toys and children's clothing labels are well represented, as are midrange local and international adult brands. There are also branches of Marks & Spencer, local department store Wing On, Japanese supermarket Apita, Japanese stationery and accessory shop Muji, and popular Food Republic with 21 Asian food stalls and mini restaurants perfect for a quick bite. ⊠ *18 Tai Koo Shing Rd., Tai Koo, Eastern* ☎ *2568–8665* ⊕ *www.cityplaza.com.hk* Ⓜ *Tai Koo.*

Island Beverley Centre. This hip micromall played a big part in putting Causeway Bay on the fashion map. Shoe-box-size boutiques fill its four cramped floors—some showcase small, local designers; others stock Japanese and Korean brands hard to find overseas. Edgy club wear competes for the space with cutesy numbers for girls who just don't want to grow up. Indeed, many of the clothes look like they'll only fit local schoolgirls, but not to worry: Island Beverley has a great selection of bags, accessories, and jewelry. ⊠ *1 Great George St., Causeway Bay* Ⓜ *Causeway Bay.*

Windsor House Computer Plaza. Clean, wide corridors distinguish this less frantic computer arcade from the others. It has three floors of computer products with a wide selection of Mac and PC computer games, video games, laptops, desktops, and accessories. This is a reputable center with competitive prices. ⊠ *10th to 12th fl., Windsor House, 311 Gloucester Rd., Causeway Bay* ☎ *2895–6796* Ⓜ *Causeway Bay.*

Perfect Shoes & Handbags Co., Ltd. One of the best shoe shops in Happy Valley is known to Hong Kongers yet still a well-kept secret. Don't let the address confuse you; this is the beginning of the Wong Nai Chung Road strip of shoe shops. ⊠ *G/F, 3 Leighton Rd., Causeway Bay* ☎ *2577–1771* Ⓜ *Causeway Bay.*

SHOES AND BAGS

Brand Off Tokyo. This Japanese chain hit town in 2008; like Milan Station, it carries secondhand goods from luxury brands like Louis Vuitton, Hermès, Chanel, Prada, and Dior. The shop is also a member of the Association Against Counterfeit Product Distribution, a Japanese organization that uses scientific evidence to determine whether products are genuine or knockoffs. ⊠ *1st fl., Shop 120, Cityplaza, 18 Tai Koo Shing Rd., Tai Koo, Eastern* ☎ *2967–6137* ⊕ *www.brandoff.com.hk* Ⓜ *Tai Koo.*

Stanley Village Market draws visitors and locals with its bargain prices.

SOUTHSIDE

Stanley Village Market is the reason most visitors come south. Trawling its crowded tourist-laden lanes for clothes, sportswear, and table linen can take half a day—more if you stop to eat. Classy reproductions of traditional Chinese furniture (with price tags to match) are the main draw at the Repulse Bay's shopping arcade, nearby. Farther west is Ap Lei Chau, a small residential island on reclaimed land, known for the vast furniture and antique warehouse Horizon Plaza and its designer outlets, including Joyce, funky furniture from Tequila Kola, and Shambala's seemingly Arabian warehouse brimming with antique treasures. On the upper floors, you'll also find fashion outlets, such as Armani, Ralph Lauren, Dolce & Gabbana, and Diesel. A bridge connects it to Hong Kong Island proper.

ANTIQUES DEALERS AND ART

Art Statements Gallery. Far afield on the southern side of Hong Kong island, this gallery makes up for its discreet location with often boundary-pushing works of art by conceptual Asian artists, as well as leading artists from Europe and North America. Since opening the gallery in 2004, founder Dominique Perregaux has brought a fresh perspective to the local art scene. ⊠ *8th fl., Gee Chang Hong Centre, 65 Wong Chuk Hang Rd., Aberdeen, Southside* ☎ *2696–2300* ⊕ *www.artstatements. com* ☽ *Closed Sun.*

Manks Ltd. Open to walk-ins seven days a week, this warehouse in the Wong Chuk Hang industrial district features 20th-century decorative arts, European antiques, and Scandinavian furniture, all proffered by the delightful Susan Man. For those who'd prefer to stick closer to the center of town, there's also a showroom in Wan Chai. ⊠ *3rd fl., The Factory, 1 Yip Fat St., Wong Chuk Hang, Southside* ☎ *2522–2115* ⊕ *www.manks.com.*

CLOTHING

Hoi Yuen Emporium Co. Of all the cheaper alternatives to Shanghai Tang, this is the best. It has a fantastic selection of Mao collared jackets for boys and girls. Chinese-style onesies come in muted, non-cartoonish colors, and cost less than HK$80. ⊠ *Stanley Market, 64 Stanley Main St., Stanley, Southside* ☎ *2813–0470.*

Joyce Warehouse. Fashionistas who've fallen on hard times can breathe a sigh of relief. Joyce's outlet on Ap Lei Chau, the island offshore from Aberdeen in Southside, stocks last season's duds from the likes of Jil Sander, Armani, Max Mara, Phillip Lim, and Anna Sui. Prices for each garment are reduced by about 10% each month, so the longer the piece stays on the rack, the less it costs. Bus 90B gets you from Exchange Square to Ap Lei Chau in 25 minutes; then hop a taxi for the four-minute taxi ride to Horizon Plaza. ⊠ *21st fl., Horizon Plaza, 2 Lee Wing St., Southside* ☎ *2814–8313* ⊕ *www.joyce.com.*

CRAFTS AND CURIOS

Good Laque. These elegant lacquerwares make wonderful gifts. The reasonably priced decorative home accessories, tabletop items, and picture frames come in classic red, black, and metallic colors as well as silver and gold. ⊠ *Ground fl., Stanley Market, 40–42D Stanley Main St., Southside, Stanley* ☎ *2899–0632* ⊕ *www.goodlaque.com* ⊠ *16th fl., Horizon Plaza, 2 Lee Wing St., Ap Lei Chau, Southside* ☎ *3106–0163.*

HOME FURNISHINGS

CarpetBuyer Limited. With a modern approach to an age-old business, a son of the Oriental Carpet Trading House family sells high-quality carpets from China, India, Iran, and Pakistan at warehouse prices. ⊠ *17th fl., Unit 1718, Horizon Plaza, 2 Lee Wing St., Ap Lei Chau, Southside* ☎ *2850–5508* ⊕ *www.carpetbuyer.com.*

Gaffer Ltd. The city's first gallery specializing in studio glass—which is gaining respect in the collecting world—has moved to the Western district and broadened its focus. The two-level gallery still hosts a backdrop of modern glass sculptures by artists from Southeast Asia, Australia, and the United States, but also showcases a variety of paintings from primarily Chinese-Australian artists. Expect everything from watercolor to abstract, pop art to traditional oil. ⊠ *Ground fl., 13 Western St., Sai Ying Pun, Western* ☎ *2521–1770* ⊕ *gaffer.com.hk* Ⓜ *Sheung Wan.*

Mrs. Chan. One of the top children's clothing stalls in Stanley Market sells everything from play-date clothes to Christmas Day bests. Push your way through the piles and hanging examples of tasteful, brand-name pieces for babies, boys, and girls. Come here first, then do some comparison shopping before pulling out your wallet. ⊠ *Stall opposite Stanley Municipal Services Bldg., 6 Stanley Main St., Southside, Stanley* ☎ *6082–7503.*

MARKETS

Fodor's Choice ★ **Stanley Market.** This was once Hong Kong's most famed bargain trove for visitors, but its ever-growing popularity means that Stanley Village Market no longer has the best prices around. Still, you can pick up some good buys in sportswear, casual clothing, textiles, and paintings if you comb through the stalls. Good-value linens—especially appliqué tablecloths—also abound. Dozens and dozens of shops line a main street so narrow that awnings from each side meet in the middle, and on busy days your elbows will come in handy. Weekdays are a little more relaxed. One of the best things about Stanley Market is getting here: the winding bus ride from Central (routes 6, 6X, 6A, or 260) or Tsim Sha Tsui (route 973) takes you over the top of Hong Kong Island, with fabulous views on the way. ⊠ *Stanley Market, Southside* ⊕ *www. hk-stanley-market.com.*

4

KOWLOON PENINSULA

Kowloon is home to the famous Nathan Road, the postcard image of a busy Hong Kong street, where bright neon lights adorn every building. It's also the main artery through a throbbing cluster of markets and shopping streets, where it's all about bargains and knockoffs. Locals usually don't shop on Nathan Road. Kowloon is also the place for outdoor markets, drawing locals and in-the-know visitors who are willing to bargain for their bargains. In addition to good sales at outdoor vending areas such as the Temple Street Night Market and the Ladies' Market, cultural shopping experiences abound in places such as the Bird Garden or the Jade Market.

▓ TIP➔ Visiting all the outdoor markets in Kowloon in one day may be exhausting. You're better off picking three sites you want to spend some time in rather than rushing through them all.

TSIM SHA TSUI

Lighted up in neon and jam-packed with shops, garish Nathan Road is Tsim Sha Tsui's main drag, usually crammed with tourists and sketchy salespeople alike. "What a drag" is the phrase that often comes to mind when shopping here: sky-high prices and shop assistants bent on ripping you off leave you wishing you'd gone elsewhere. Slip down the side streets, though, and things get better. Granville and Cameron roads are home to cheap clothing outlets, while Japanese imports and young designers fill the boutiques at the funky minimall called Rise. Chinese emporiums Yue Hwa and Chinese Arts & Crafts have big branches here—both are great places to stock up on cheap souvenirs.

Although Tsim Sha Tsui is known for its low-end shopping, that doesn't mean luxury goods are out of the picture. The Peninsula Arcade, Joyce, the vast Harbour City shopping center, and the impressive, colonial-style 1881 Heritage arcade all have a big-name count fit to rival Central's. One contrast is found in the shoppers, who tend to be a bit lower key. Bespoke tailoring is another Tsim Sha Tsui specialty—quality varies enormously, so try to choose somewhere well established, like Sam's.

DID YOU KNOW?

Hong Kong is a leading producer of pure-gold items, and Nathan Road between Mong Kok and TST is one of *the* places to buy golden baubles. Local law requires all jewelers to indicate the number of carats and the manufacturer on gold products. In addition to checking for these markings, ask for an invoice listing the weight and price of each item.

BEAUTY AND COSMETICS

FACES. This sprawling one-stop shop, just a stone's throw from the Kowloon Star Ferry terminal, carries a long list of high-profile and niche beauty brands. ✉ *Ocean Terminal, Harbour City, 5 Canton Rd., Tsim Sha Tsui* ☎ *2118–5622* Ⓜ *Tsim Sha Tsui.*

CLOTHING

Dorfit. A longtime cashmere manufacturer and retailer, Dorfit caters to a variety of men's, women's, and children's tastes. Knitwear here comes in pure cashmere as well as blends, so be sure to ask which is which. ✉ *6th fl., Mary Bldg., 71–77 Peking Rd., Tsim Sha Tsui* ☎ *2312–1013* ⊕ *www.dorfit.com.hk* Ⓜ *Tsim Sha Tsui* ✉ *1st fl., 10 Wellington St., Central* ☎ *2501–0018* Ⓜ *Central.*

Initial. This team of local designers creates simple but whimsical men's and women's clothing with a trendy urban edge. The bags and accessories strike a soft vintage tone, fitting the store's fashionably worn interiors, casually strewn secondhand furniture, and sultry jazz soundtrack. ✉ *The Park Lane Hong Kong, 31 Gloucester Rd., Causeway Bay* ☎ *2882–9044* ⊕ *www.initialfashion.com* Ⓜ *Causeway Bay* ✉ *3rd fl., Ocean Terminal, Harbour City LCX, 2–27 Canton Rd., Tsim Sha Tsui* Ⓜ *Tsim Tsa Shui.*

Fodor'sChoice ★ **Pearls & Cashmere.** Warehouse prices in chic shopping arcades? It's true. This old Hong Kong favorite is elegantly housed in hotels on both sides of the harbor. In addition to quality men's and women's cashmere sweaters in classic designs and in every color under the sun, they also sell reasonably priced pashminas, gloves, and socks, which make great gifts for men and women. In recent years the brand has developed the more fashion-focused line, BYPAC. ✉ *Mezzanine, Peninsula Hotel Shopping Arcade, Salisbury Rd., Tsim Sha Tsui* ☎ *2723–8698* Ⓜ *Tsim Sha Tsui* ✉ *Mezzanine, Mandarin Oriental, 5 Connaught Rd., Central* ☎ *2525–6771* Ⓜ *Central.*

CRAFTS AND CURIOS

Tittot. This Taiwanese brand has taken modern Chinese glass art global. Glass works here are made using the laborious lost-wax casting technique, used by artists for centuries to create a bronze replica of an original wax or clay sculpture. The collection includes tableware, paperweights and decorative pieces, glass Buddhas, and jewelry, and can be purchased in Lane Crawford department stores. ✉ *Lane Crawford, 1 Matheson St., Times Square, Causeway Bay* ☎ *2118-3638* ⊕ *www.tittot.com* Ⓜ *Causeway Bay.*

ELECTRONICS, MUSIC, AND ACCESSORIES

Hong Kong Records. You'll find a good selection of current local and international CDs and DVDs at this age-old company. A lower profile also means prices are sometimes lower than in flashier retailers. ✉ *Gateway Arcade, Harbour City, 3 Canton Rd., Tsim Sha Tsui* ☎ *2175–5700* ⊕ *www.hongkongrecords.hk* Ⓜ *Tsim Sha Tsui.*

JEWELRY

Artland Watch Co Ltd. Artland Watch Co Ltd. Elegant but uncomplicated, the interior of this established watch retailer is like its service. The informed staff will guide you through the countless luxury brands on show and in the catalogs from which you can also order. Prices here aren't the best in Hong Kong, but they're still lower than at home. ✉ *Ground fl., Mirador Mansion, 54-64B Nathan Rd., Tsim Sha Tsui* ☎ *2366–1074* Ⓜ *Tsim Sha Tsui.*

Prince Jewellery and Watch Company. This shop carries timepieces made by more than 50 international brands such as Omega, Chopard, and Breguet, IWC, in addition to other jewelry, which may entertain those accompanying the avid watch-shopper. ✉ *Ground fl., Bo Yip Bldg, 10 Peking Rd., Tsim Sha Tsui* ☎ *2369–2123* ⊕ *www.princejewellerywatch. com* Ⓜ *Tsim Sha Tsui.*

TSL Jewellery. One of the big Hong Kong chains, TSL (Tse Sui Luen) specializes in diamond jewelry, and manufactures, retails, and exports its designs. Its range of 100-facet stones includes the Estrella cut, which reflects nine symmetrical hearts and comes with international certification. Although its contemporary designs use platinum settings, TSL also sells pure, bright, yellow-gold items targeted at Chinese customers. ✉ *G5–G7, Park Lane Blvd., Nathan Rd., Tsim Sha Tsui* ☎ *2332–4618* ⊕ *www.tsljewellery.com* Ⓜ *Tsim Sha Tsui* ✉ *Ground fl., 1 Yee Woo St., Causeway Bay* Ⓜ *Causeway Bay.*

MALLS

Elements. This upscale shopping mall is in the Kowloon West residential and commercial district, and just above Kowloon's Airport Express train and check-in station. The mall is beautifully designed, and is divided into five different zones based on the elements: metal, wood, water, earth, and fire. This is one-stop shopping as far as international luxury brands are concerned, with Valentino, Mulberry, Prada, and Gucci, just to name a few. ✉ *1 Austin Rd. W, Tsim Sha Tsui* ☎ *2735– 5234* ⊕ *www.elementshk.com* Ⓜ *Kowloon.*

Fodor's Choice ★ **Harbour City.** The four interconnected complexes that make up Harbour City contain almost 500 shops between them—if you can't find it here, it probably doesn't exist. Pick up a map on your way in, as it's easy to get lost. **Ocean Terminal,** the largest section, runs along the harbor and is divided thematically, with kids' wear and toys on the ground floor, and sports and cosmetics on the first. The top floor is home to white-hot street-wear store LCX *(⇨ above)*. Near the Star Ferry pier, the **Marco Polo Hong Kong Hotel Arcade** has branches of the department store Lane Crawford. Louis Vuitton, Prada, and Burberry are some of the posher boutiques that fill the **Ocean Centre** and **Gateway Arcade,** parallel to Canton Road. Most of the complex's restaurants are here, too. A cinema and three hotels round up Harbour City's offerings. Free Wi-Fi is available. ✉ *3–27 Canton Rd., Tsim Sha Tsui* ⊕ *www.harbourcity. com.hk* Ⓜ *Tsim Sha Tsui.*

Mira Mall. Not to be confused with neighboring Miramar Shopping Centre, the Mira Mall opened in 2012 as an extension of the Mira Hotel. This new addition to the Tsim Sha Tsui shopping scene aims at Hong Kong's young elite with the likes of a two-story Twist, Tommy Hilfiger, and Coach. Asian talent is a focal point at the four-story galleria, with designers such as Ika Butoni and her colorful Indonesian creations. Noteworthy international brands include NorieM, Laura

Ashley, Cocomojo, and Sebago, and don't miss the 22,000-square-foot Collect Point flagship store in the basement. ⊠ *118 Nathan Rd., Tsim Sha Tsui* ☎ *2315–5868* ⊕ *www.mira-mall.com* Ⓜ *Tsim Sha Tsui.*

Rise Commercial Building. Many a quirky Hong Kong street-wear trend is born in this fabulous micromall. Don't let its grubby exterior put you off: this arcade is a haven of Asian cool. Japanese designers are particularly well represented—look out for überhip brand A Bathing Ape, which does some of the funkiest T-shirts around. Handmade shoes and oversized retro jewelry are other fixtures—and all at bargain prices. ⊠ *5–11 Granville Circuit, off Granville Rd., Tsim Sha Tsui* Ⓜ *Tsim Sha Tsui.*

MARKETS

Arts & Crafts Fair. Small stalls from local cottage industries sell handicrafts each Sunday and on public holidays outside the Cultural Centre on the Tsim Sha Tsui waterfront. Portrait artists are at hand to capture your likeness, and there's other artwork, jewelry, and knickknacks. Each stall holder is chosen by a panel of judges who look to promote Hong Kong artists and small businesses. ⊠ *Hong Kong Cultural Centre Piazza, 10 Salisbury Rd., Tsim Sha Tsui* ☎ *2734–2843* ⊗ *Closed Mon.– Sat.* Ⓜ *Tsim Sha Tsui, Exit E.*

TAILOR-MADE CLOTHING

MEN'S TAILORS **David's Shirts Ltd.** Customers have been enjoying the personalized service of David Chu since 1961. All the work is done in-house by Shanghainese tailors with at least 20 years' experience each. There are more than 6,000 imported European fabrics to choose from, each prewashed. Examples of shirts, suits, and accessories—including 30 collar styles, 12 cuff styles, and 10 pocket styles—help you choose. Single-needle tailoring; French seams; 22 stitches per inch; handpicked, double-stitched shell buttons; German interlining—it's all here. Your details, down to on which side you wear your wristwatch, are kept on file should you wish to use its mail-order service in the future. ⊠ *Ground fl., Wing Lee Bldg., 33 Kimberley Rd., Tsim Sha Tsui* ☎ *2367–9556* ⊕ *www.davidsshirts. com* Ⓜ *Tsim Sha Tsui* ⊠ *Mezzanine, Mandarin Oriental, 5 Connaught Rd., Central* ☎ *2524–2979* Ⓜ *Central.*

Maxwell's Clothiers Ltd. After you've found a handful of reputable, high-quality tailors, one way to choose between them is price. Maxwell's is known for its competitive rates. It's also a wonderful place to have favorite shirts and suits copied and for straightforward, structured women's shirts and suits. It was founded by third-generation tailor Ken Maxwell in 1961 and follows Shanghai tailoring traditions, while also providing the fabled 24-hour suit upon request. The showroom and workshop are in Kowloon, but son Andy and his team take appointments in the United States, Canada, Australia, and Europe twice annually. The motto of this family business is, "Simply let the garment do the talking." ⊠ *7th fl., Han Hing Mansion, 38–40 Hankow Rd., Tsim Sha Tsui* ☎ *2366–6705* ⊕ *www.maxwellsclothiers.com* Ⓜ *Tsim Sha Tsui.*

Fodor'sChoice **Sam's Tailor.** Unlike many famous Hong Kong tailors, you won't find the ★ legendary Sam's in a chic hotel or sleek mall. But don't be fooled. These digs in humble Burlington House, a tailoring hub, have hosted everyone

Don't skimp on custom clothing. Rely on the expert tailors listed *in this chapter* for classic, tailor-made Chinese clothing.

from U.S. presidents (back as far as Richard Nixon) to performers such as the Black Eyed Peas, Kylie Minogue, and Blondie. This former uniform tailor to the British troops once even made a suit for Prince Charles in a record hour and 52 minutes. The men's and women's tailor does accept 24-hour suit or shirt orders, but will take about two days if you're not in a hurry. Founded by Naraindas Melwani in 1957, "Sam" is now his son, Manu Melwani, who runs the show with the help of his own son, Roshan, and about 57 tailors behind the scenes. In 2004 Sam's introduced a computerized bodysuit that takes measurements without a tape measure. (It uses both methods, however.) These tailors also make biannual trips to Europe and North America. (Schedule updates are listed on the website.) ⊠ *Burlington House, 94 Nathan Rd., Tsim Sha Tsui* ☎ *2367–9423* ⊕ *www.samstailor.com* Ⓜ *Tsim Sha Tsui.*

W. W. Chan & Sons Tailors Ltd. Chan is known for excellent-quality suits and shirts and classic cuts and has an array of fine European fabrics. It's comforting to know that you'll be measured and fitted by the same master tailor from start to finish. The Kowloon headquarters features a mirrored, hexagonal changing room so you can check every angle. Tailors from here travel to the United States several times a year to fill orders for their customers; if you have a suit made here and leave your address, they'll let you know when they plan to visit. ⊠ *2nd fl., Burlington House, 92–94 Nathan Rd., Tsim Sha Tsui* ☎ *2366–9738, 2366–2634* ⊕ *www.wwchan.com* Ⓜ *Tsim Sha Tsui.*

Amazing Grace. A charismatic collection of handicrafts from around Asia surrounds you in this store, which first opened in the '70s. With locations in terminal one and two, both airport stores house a colorful assortment of Balinese sarongs, signature Suzie Wong cheongsams, hand-painted silk muumuus, Christmas ornaments, beaded Indian accessories, and a wide variety of jade, abalone-shell and silver chopsticks. Find just about anything amid this potpourri of Asian keepsakes. ⊠ *7th fl., Shop 192, East Hall, Hong Kong International Airport Terminal One, Lantau Island* ☎ *2186–6675* ⊕ *www. amazinggracehk.com.*

WOMEN'S TAILORS

Irene Fashions. In 1987 the women's division of noted men's tailor W.W. Chan branched off and was renamed Irene Fashions. You can expect the same level of expertise and a large selection of fine fabrics. Experienced at translating ideas and pictures into clothing, in-house designers will sketch and help you develop concepts. Like its parent company, Irene promises that the same tailor will take you through the entire process, and most of the work is done on-site. ⊠ *Burlington House, 2nd fl., 92–94 Nathan Rd., Tsim Sha Tsui* ☎ *2367–5588* ⊕ *www.wwchan.com* Ⓜ *Tsim Sha Tsui.*

Mode Elegante. Don't be deterred by the somewhat dated mannequins in the windows. Mode Elegante is a favorite source for custom-made suits among women and men in the know. Tailors here specialize in European cuts. You'll have your choice of fabrics from the United Kingdom, Italy, and elsewhere. Your records are put on file so you can place orders from abroad. It'll even ship the completed garment to you almost anywhere on the planet. Alternatively, you can make an appointment with director Gary Zee, one of Hong Kong's traveling tailors, who makes regular visits to North America, Europe, and Japan. ⊠ *11th fl., Star House, 3 Salisbury Rd., Tsim Sha Tsui* ☎ *2366–8153* ⊕ *www.modeelegante.com* Ⓜ *Tsim Sha Tsui.*

YAU MA TEI, MONG KOK, AND NORTHERN KOWLOON

The bright-lights-big-city look of Tsim Sha Tsui gives way to housing blocks and tenements hung with aging signs north of Jordan Road. Streets are crowded and traffic is manic, but this down-to-earth chaos is what makes shopping in these north Kowloon neighborhoods rewarding. Well, that and all the bargains at the area's markets. Yau Ma Tei has jade and pearls at Kansu Street; and bric-a-brac and domestic appliances fill atmospheric Temple Street nightly. Farther north are blocks and blocks of brandless clothes and accessories at the Fa Yuen Street Ladies' Market. Parallel Tung Choi Street has cut-price sporting goods. Goldfish, flowers, and birds each have their own dedicated market in Prince Edward, north of Mong Kok. Yue Hwa's five-story Jordan shop is one of the best places in Hong Kong for cheap gifts. The arrival of the cavernous Langham Place changed the local landscape here; the user-friendly megamall has lashings of natural light and a sanctuary-like food hall.

YAU MA TEI
DEPARTMENT STORES

Fodor'sChoice
★

Yue Hwa Chinese Products Emporium. Five floors contain Chinese goods, ranging from clothing and housewares through tea and traditional medicine. The logic behind the store's layout is hard to fathom, so go with time to rifle around. As well as the predictable tablecloths, silk pajamas, and chopstick sets, there are cheap and colorful porcelain sets and offbeat local favorites like mini-massage chairs. The top floor is entirely given over to tea—you can pick up a HK$50 packet of leaves or an antique Yixing teapot stretching into the thousands. ⊠ *301–309 Nathan Rd., Jordan, Yau Ma Tei* ☎ *3511-2222* ⊕ *www.yuehwa.com* Ⓜ *Jordan.*

ELECTRONICS, CAMERAS, AND MUSIC

Kubrick. This is the closest thing to a bilingual community bookshop you're likely to find in Hong Kong, with its stock of alternative-spirited books, graphic novels, magazines, music, and DVDs in a variety of foreign languages. It's also attached to a cinema that regularly shows art-house flicks and a casual café serving basic pastas and sandwiches, and hosting occasional poetry readings or music gigs. Come here to get a good, if slightly unpolished, sense of the city's art culture, and pick up an interesting gift—perhaps a book exploring "a Swiss-Chinese Intercultural Encounter About the Culture of Food" or a photo documentary of Hong Kong's informal rooftop communities. When seeking directions, ask for the Broadway Cinemateque. ⊠ *Shop H2, Prosperous Garden, 3 Public Square St., Yau Ma Tei* ☎ *2384-8929* ⊕ *www.kubrick.com.hk* Ⓜ *Yau Ma Tei* ⊠ *6th fl., Millennium City 5 APM, 418 Kwun Tong Rd., Kwun Tong, Northern Kowloon* ☎ *3148-1289* Ⓜ *Kwun Tong.*

JEWELRY

Kansu Street Jade Market. Jade in every imaginable shade of green, from the milkiest apple tone to the richest emerald, fills the stalls of this Kowloon market. If you know your stuff and haggle insistently, you can get fabulous bargains. Otherwise, stick to cheap trinkets. Some of the so-called "jade" sold here is actually aventurine, bowenite, soapstone, serpentine, and Australian jade—all inferior to the real thing. ⊠ *Kansu St. off Nathan Rd., Yau Ma Tei* Ⓜ *Yau Ma Tei.*

Sandra Pearls. You might be wary of the lustrous pearls hanging at this little Jade Market stall. The charming owner, Sandra, does, in fact, sell genuine and reasonably priced cultured and freshwater pearl necklaces and earrings. Some pieces are made from shell, which Sandra is always quick to point out, and could pass muster among the snobbiest collectors. ⊠ *Stall 437 and 447, Jade Market, Kansu St., Yau Ma Tei* ☎ *9485-2895* Ⓜ *Yau Ma Tei.*

SHAM SHUI PO

Two stops from Mong Kok on the MTR is Sham Shui Po, a labyrinth of small streets teeming with flea markets and wholesale shops where you can buy anything from electronics to computers to clothing. The Golden Computer Arcade, stuffed with small computer hardware shops, is favored by local mouse potatoes. Prices are competitive, but parts usually come without a warranty.

MONG KOK

CLOTHING

Bossini. A Giordano competitor, Bossini takes a very similar, light approach to casual clothing, as indicated by its brand philosophy, "Be Happy." Expect colorful collections for women, men, and children. ✉ *6–12A Sai Yeung Choi St., Mong Kok* ☎ *2710–8466* ⊕ *www.bossini.com* Ⓜ *Mong Kok*

✉ *Ground fl., On Lok Yuen Bldg., 27A Des Voeux Rd. Central, Central* ☎ *2524–9313* Ⓜ *Central* ✉ *Ground fl., Cityplaza, 18 Tai Koo Shing Rd., Tai Koo, Eastern* ☎ *2967–9789* Ⓜ *Tai Koo.*

Me & George. Anyone who enjoys a good thrift-store rummage will delight in the messy abandon of Me & George (also known as Mee & Gee), not to mention the rock-bottom prices. Clothing items here start at HK$10. Yes, you heard right! Expect a mix of poorly made factory rejects and vintage dresses, shoes, and handbags, and enjoy trying to discern between the two. Fitting is not usually allowed (as is the case with most small fashion import outlets), but staff are often tolerant of quick try-ons in front of a mirror. ✉ *64 Tung Choi St., Mong Kok.*

DEPARTMENT STORES

Seibu. This Japanese department store is actually owned by local tycoon Dickson Poon, who counts Harvey Nichols among his other possessions. Beauty counters, shoes, handbags, and western ready-to-wear labels make up the bulk of its offerings. Expect hip street wear as well as more professional looks. ✉ *1st and 2nd fl., Langham Place, 555 Shanghai St., Mongkok, Kowloon* ☎ *2971–3888* Ⓜ *Mongkok.*

ELECTRONICS, CAMERAS, AND MUSIC

Mong Kok Computer Centre. This labyrinth of small shops and narrow corridors is somewhat claustrophobic, but it has many good deals on computers and software. Ask for a warranty, and read it carefully. ✉ *8–8A Nelson St., Mong Kok* ☎ *2781–0706* ⊕ *www.mongkokcc.com* Ⓜ *Mong Kok.*

HOME FURNISHINGS

Yuen Po Street Bird Garden. Though mostly built as a neighborhood park in which bird-owning residents can meet and "walk" their caged pets, the Urban Renewal Authority also included some 70 stalls to be used by those who lost trade when the famous Hong Lok Street songbird stalls were demolished in a revitalization project in the late nineties. Though it sells various kinds of feathered creatures, you can also pick up the picturesque, empty carved cages and put them to better (empty) use in your home decor. Access the main entrance from Boundary Street, a short walk from the Prince Edward MTR station. ✉ *Yuen Po St., Mong Kok* ☎ *2302–1762* ⊕ *www.lcsd.gov.hk/parks/ypsbg/en* Ⓜ *Prince Edward.*

SHOES AND BAGS

Right Choice Export Fashion Co. Take a moment to look past the plastic stilettos worthy of an exotic dancer, and you might just discover unfathomably cheap yet stylish shoes (even if they'll only last one season). The sandals are especially pretty and can cost as little as HK$60. Look for shops like this near most market streets. ⊠ *Ground fl., 187 Fa Yuen St., Mong Kok* ☎ *2394–6953* Ⓜ *Prince Edward.*

Sportshouse. Come here for trendy sneakers and other casual footwear by brands like Nike, Puma, Adidas, Converse, and Birkenstock. ⊠ *Ground fl., 61 Fa Yuen St., Mong Kok* ☎ *2332–3099* ⊕ *www.sportshouse.com* Ⓜ *Mong Kok* ⊠ *Shop B01, Basement fl., The Elegance, Sheraton Hong Kong Hotel and Towers, 20 Nathan Rd., Tsim Sha Tsui* ☎ *2311–2902* Ⓜ *Tsim Sha Tsui* ⊠ *5th fl., New Town Plaza Phase I, 18 Sha Tin Centre St., Sha Tin, New Territories* ☎ *2691–6856* Ⓜ *Shatin.*

MALLS

Langham Place. This mall's light beige sandstone stands in stark contrast to the pulsating neon signs and crumbling residential blocks around it. Yet Langham Place has fast become a fixture of Mong Kok's chaotic shopping scene, with nearly 300 shops packed into 15 floors. It's especially popular with hipsters, who come for the local and Japanese labels in offbeat boutiques ranged around a spiral walkway on the 11th and 12th floors. Extra-long escalators—dubbed "Xpresscalators"—whisk you quickly up four levels at a time. The elegant glass-and-steel skyscraper across the road is the Langham Place Hotel, whose stylish dining patio, The Backyard, offers the serenest of outdoor sanctuaries in one of the region's most congested neighborhoods. ⊠ *8 Argyle St., Mong Kok* ☎ *3520–2800* ⊕ *www.langhamplace.com. hk* Ⓜ *Mong Kok.*

MARKETS

Flower Market. Huge bucketfuls of roses and gerbera spill out onto the sidewalk along Flower Market Road, a collection of street stalls selling cut flowers and potted plants. Delicate orchids and vivid birds of paradise are some of the more exotic blooms. During Chinese New Year there's a roaring trade in narcissi, poinsettias, and bright yellow chrysanthemums, all auspicious flowers. ⊠ *Flower Market Rd., off Prince Edward Rd. W, Mong Kok* Ⓜ *Prince Edward.*

 Goldfish Market. Goldfish are considered good luck in Hong Kong (though aquariums have to be positioned in the right place to bring good luck to the family), and this small collection of shops is a favorite local source. Shop fronts are decorated with bag upon bag of glistening, pop-eyed creatures, waiting for someone to take them home. Some of the fishes inside shops are serious rarities and fetch unbelievable prices. ⊠ *Tung Choi St., Mong Kok* Ⓜ *Mong Kok.*

Ladies' Market. Block upon block of tightly packed stalls overflow with clothes, bags, and knickknacks along Tung Choi Street in Mong Kok. Despite the name, there are clothes for women, men, and children here. Most offerings are imitations or no-name brands; rifle around enough and you can often pick up some cheap and cheerful basics. Haggling is the rule here: a poker face and a little insistence can get you dramatic

Go fish at the Goldfish Market in Mong Kok.

discounts. At the corner of each block and behind the market are stands and shops selling the street snacks Hong Kongers can't live without. Pick a place where locals are munching and point at whatever takes your fancy. Parallel **Fa Yuen Street** is Mong Kok's unofficial sportswear market. ✉ *Tung Choi St., Mong Kok* Ⓜ *Mong Kok.*

Fodor's Choice **Temple Street Night Market.** Each night, as it gets dark, the lamps strung
★ between the stalls of this Yau Ma Tei street market slowly light up, and the air fills with the smells wafting from myriad food carts. Hawkers try to catch your eye by flinging clothes up from their stalls. Cantonese opera competes with pop music, and vendors' cries and shoppers' haggling fills the air. Adding to the color here are the fortune-tellers and the odd magician or acrobat who has set up shop in the street. Granted, neither the clothes nor cheap gadgets on sale here are much to get excited about, but it's the atmosphere people come for—any purchases are a bonus. The market stretches for almost a mile and is one of Hong Kong's liveliest nighttime shopping experiences. ✉ *Temple St., Mong Kok* Ⓜ *Jordan.*

NORTHERN KOWLOON

ELECTRONICS, CAMERAS, AND MUSIC

Golden Computer Arcade. It's the most famous—some would say infamous—computer arcade in town. Know what you want before you go to avoid being dazed by the volume of computer equipment and software. ✉ *146–152 Fuk Wa St., Sham Shui Po, Northern Kowloon* ☏ *2729–2101* ⊕ *www.goldenarcade.org* Ⓜ *Sham Shui Po.*

MALLS

Fodor's Choice
★

Festival Walk. Don't be put off by Festival Walk's location in residential Kowloon Tong—it's 20 minutes from Central on the MTR. Make the effort to get here: Festival Walk has everything from Giordano (Hong Kong's answer to the Gap) to Vivienne Tam. By day the six floors sparkle with sunlight, which filters through the glass roof. Marks & Spencer and

DKNY serve as anchors; Armani Exchange and ck Calvin Klein draw the elite crowds; while Camper and agnès b. keep the trend spotters happy. Hong Kong's best bookstore, Page One, has a big branch downstairs. The mall also has one of the city's largest ice rinks, as well as a multiplex cinema, perfect if you're shopping with kids who want a respite from the sometimes scorching-hot weather. ⊠ *80 Tat Chee Ave., Kowloon Tong, Northern Kowloon* ☎ *2844–2200* ⊕ *www. festivalwalk.com.hk* Ⓜ *Kowloon Tong.*

Mega Box. This 18-story mall is a great option for family shopping expeditions: those with minimal shopping stamina can amuse themselves at the video arcade, the IMAX theater, or the skating rink, and there are also numerous eateries. However, unlike other malls that are walking distance from MTR stations, visitors need to take its free shuttle from the Kowloon Bay MTR station. To catch the shuttle, exit the MTR station at Exit A and go through Telford Plaza; you can always ask the Plaza concierge if you're confused. Shuttles run about every 10 minutes. ⊠ *38 Wang Chiu Rd., Kowloon Bay, Northern Kowloon* ☎ *2989–3000* ⊕ *www.megabox.com.hk* Ⓜ *Kowloon Bay.*

Where to Eat

WORD OF MOUTH

"For Peking duck, try Spring Deer. Like a restaurant out of the '40s (and I don't think they've changed the curtains since) with florescent lighting, older waiters in white coats, lots of locals at big tables, ducks coming out of the kitchen by the dozens, and only a wee smattering of tourists."

—LAleslie

Updated by
Dorothy So

No other city in the world boasts quite as eclectic a dining scene as Hong Kong. Luxurious fine-dining restaurants opened by celebrity chefs such as Gray Kunz and Joël Robuchon are just a stone's throw from humble local eateries doling out thin noodles and some of the best wonton shrimp dumplings, or delicious slices of tender barbecued meat piled atop bowls of fragrant jasmine rice.

One of the key lessons here is never judge a book by its cover—the most unassuming eateries are often the ones that provide the most memorable meals. At noodle-centric restaurants, fish-ball soup with ramen noodles is an excellent choice, and the goose, suckling pig, honeyed pork, and soy-sauce chicken are good bets at the roast-meat shops. A combination plate, with a sampling of meats and some greens on a bed of white rice, is generally a foolproof way to go if you're not sure what to order. Street foods are another must-try; for just a couple of bucks, you can sample curry fish balls, skewered meats, stinky tofu, and all sorts of other delicious tidbits. If you have the chance, visit a *dai pai dong* (outdoor food stall) and try the local specialties.

For fine dining with a unique Hong Kong twist, you can always hit up places like the exclusive and extravagant Krug Room or try Alvin Leung's one-of-a-kind "X-treme Chinese" fare at Bo Innovation.

Finally, remember that Hong Kong is the world's epicenter of dim sum. While you're here you must have at least one dim sum breakfast or lunch in a teahouse. Those steaming bamboo baskets you see conceal mouth-watering dumplings, buns, and pastries—all as comforting and delicious as they are exotic.

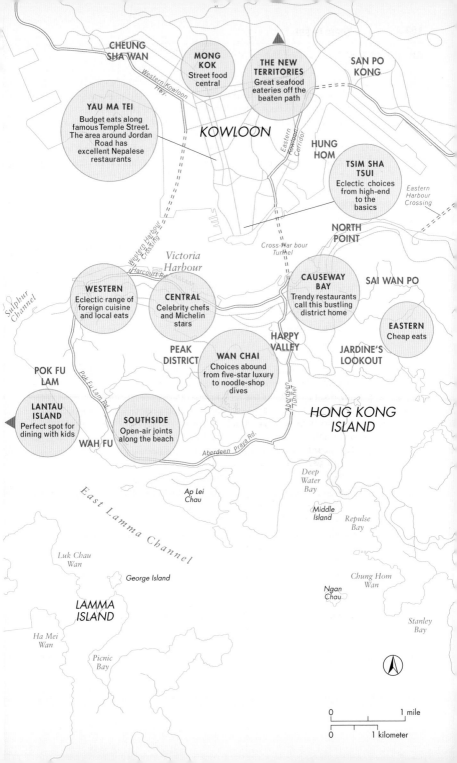

CHEUNG SHA WAN

MONG KOK
Street food central

THE NEW TERRITORIES
Great seafood eateries off the beaten path

SAN PO KONG

Western Kowloon Hwy.

YAU MA TEI
Budget eats along famous Temple Street. The area around Jordan Road has excellent Nepalese restaurants

KOWLOON

HUNG HOM

TSIM SHA TSUI
Eclectic choices from high-end to the basics

Eastern Kowloon Corridor

Eastern Harbour Crossing

Western Harbour Crossing

Harcourt Rd.

Victoria Harbour

Cross-Harbour Tunnel

NORTH POINT

WESTERN
Eclectic range of foreign cuisine and local eats

CENTRAL
Celebrity chefs and Michelin stars

CAUSEWAY BAY
Trendy restaurants call this bustling district home

SAI WAN PO

Sulphur Channel

PEAK DISTRICT

HAPPY VALLEY

WAN CHAI
Choices abound from five-star luxury to noodle-shop dives

EASTERN
Cheap eats

JARDINE'S LOOKOUT

POK FU LAM

Pok Fu Lam Rd.

LANTAU ISLAND
Perfect spot for dining with kids

WAH FU

SOUTHSIDE
Open-air joints along the beach

Aberdeen Tunnel

HONG KONG ISLAND

Aberdeen Praya Rd.

Deep Water Bay

Ap Lei Chau

Middle Island

Repulse Bay

East Lamma Channel

Luk Chau Wan

George Island

Chung Hom Wan

Ngan Chau

LAMMA ISLAND

Ha Mei Wan

Picnic Bay

Stanley Bay

0   1 mile

0   1 kilometer

PLANNING

HOURS

A typical Hong Kong breakfast is often congee (a rice porridge), noodles, or plain or filled buns. Most hotels serve western-style breakfasts, however, and coffee, pastries, and sandwiches are readily available at local coffee-shop chains and western cafés. Lunchtime is between noon and 2 pm; normal dinner hours are from 7 until 11 pm, but Hong Kong is a 24-hour city, and you'll be able to find a meal here at any hour. Dim sum can begin as early as 7:30 am and, though it's traditionally a daytime food, you'll find plenty of specialist restaurants that serve dim sum late into the evening.

PRICES, TIPPING, AND TAX

Many restaurants in Hong Kong serve main dishes that are meant to be shared, so take this into account with respect to prices. It's also worth noting that some specialty dishes are outrageously expensive—abalone, bird's-nest soup, shark's-fin soup. And when you get your check, don't be shocked that you've been charged for everything, including tea, rice, and those side dishes placed automatically on your table. At upmarket and western-style restaurants tips are appreciated (10% is generous); the service charge on your bill doesn't go to the waitstaff.

RESERVATIONS

Book ahead during Chinese holidays and the eves of public holidays, or at high-end hotel restaurants like the Krug Room or Caprice. Certain classic Hong Kong preparations (e.g., beggar's chicken, whose preparation in a clay pot takes hours) require reserving not just a table but the dish itself. Do so at least 24 hours in advance. You'll also need reservations for a meal at one of the so-called private kitchens—unlicensed culinary speakeasies, which are often the city's hottest tickets. Book several days ahead, and be prepared to pay a deposit. Reservations are virtually unheard of at small, local restaurants.

SHARE AND SHARE ALIKE

In China food is meant to be shared. Instead of ordering individual main dishes, it's usual for those around a table—whether 2 or 12 people—to share several. Four people eating together, for example, might order a whole or half chicken, another type of meat, a fish dish, a vegetable, and fried noodles—all of which would be placed on the table's lazy Susan. Restaurants may adjust portions and prices according to the number of diners.

Western-style cutlery is common in many—but not all—upmarket Chinese restaurants in Hong Kong, but what better place to practice your chopstick skills? Serving chopsticks are usually provided for each dish. You should use these to serve yourself and others. If no serving chopsticks are provided, serve yourself using your own chopsticks; just be sure to use the ends that you haven't put into your mouth.

WHAT TO WEAR

Casual dress—sports shirts, T-shirts, clean jeans, and the like—is acceptable almost everywhere in Hong Kong, although shorts and sneakers or flip-flops will feel out of place at trendy venues and five-star restaurants where people dress to impress. Generally, the dress code in Hong Kong is stylish but quite conservative.

WINE OR BEER?

Traditionally, markups on wine have been high here, and wine lists uninspired. French reds have long had a cachet in Hong Kong, but since the abolishment of wine tax in 2008, the city's wine selection has become increasingly democratic and now includes many New World selections that are often better suited to the local cuisine and the climate. More people are also getting interested in pairing wine with Asian cuisine, and it's not uncommon to see Chinese restaurants—especially the higher-end ones—create tasting menus designed specifically to go with various wines. Many midrange restaurants and private kitchens allow you to bring your own wine for a corkage fee.

For Cantonese food, tea is traditional, but Hong Kong likes its beer—before, during, or after dinner. It's generally light stuff, like Heineken, the locally brewed San Miguel, or a Chinese lager such as immensely popular Tsing Tao. Craft beers are also starting to take off, and you'll find interesting boutique brews served at several gastro pubs around town. When it's time to hit the karaoke bars or clubs, though, people switch to whiskey and cocktails. With whiskey, it's commonly sipped on the rocks or mixed with sweetened, iced, green tea.

HONG KONG ISLAND

Reviews listed alphabetically within neighborhoods.

WESTERN

$$
ITALIAN
✕ **ABC Kitchen.** Hong Kong is no stranger to Continental cuisine, but ABC is in a league of its own. The "restaurant" is made up of a few stand-alone plastic chairs and tables scattered around Sheung Wan's wet market food court. Despite being sandwiched between a curry stall and Chiu Chow dumpling joint, ABC's owners remain loyal to their classic, European training (the manager and chef both hail from Hong Kong's once-iconic M at the Fringe restaurant), serving dishes such as roasted suckling pig and handcrafted pizzas. If you want wine with your meal, ABC allows BYOB for no corkage fee. Ⓢ *Average main: HK$120* ⊠ *Shop CF7, Food Market, 1 Queen St., Sheung Wan, Western* ☎ *9278–8227* ⊙ *No lunch Sun.* ✛ *1:B2.*

$$$
CANTONESE
Fodor's Choice
★
✕ **Tim's Kitchen.** Some of the homespun dishes at this restaurant require at least a day's advanced ordering but the extra fuss is worth it. One signature dish pairs a meaty crab claw with winter melon—a clean and simple combo that allows the freshness of the ingredients to shine. The fist-size "glassy" king prawn looks unassuming, paired with nothing but a slice of Yunnan ham on a plain, ungarnished plate. Take a bite though, and you'll be amazed at how succulent and delectably creamy it is. Word of warning—some of the more intricate dishes can get pretty pricy. But simpler (and cheaper) options are also available, such as pomelo skin sprinkled with shrimp roe, and stir-fried flat rice noodles with beef. Ⓢ *Average main: HK$300* ⊠ *84–90 Bonham Strand E, Sheung Wan, Western* ☎ *2543–5919* ⊕ *www.timskitchen.com.hk* ✍ *Reservations essential* ⊙ *Closed Sun.* Ⓜ *Sheung Wan* ✛ *1:C2.*

BEST BETS FOR HONG KONG DINING

Fodor's writers and editors have listed their favorite restaurants by price, cuisine, and experience below. You can also search by neighborhood in the following pages.

Fodor's Choice ★

8 ½ Otto e Mezzo, $$$$, p. 156
Bo Innovation, $$$$, p. 168
Café Gray Deluxe, $$$, p. 158
Chicha, $$, p. 159
Dong Lai Shun, $$$, p. 180
Fa Zu Jie, $$$, p. 160
L'Atelier de Joël Robuchon, $$$$, p. 163
Man Sing, $, p. 173
Tim Ho Wan, $, p. 192
Tim's Kitchen, $$, p. 153
Tung Po, $, p. 176
Yardbird, $$, p. 156
Yau Yuan Xiao Jui, $, p. 191

By Price

$

ABC Kitchen, p. 153
Capital Café, p. 168
Mak's Noodles Limited, p. 165
Tim Ho Wan, p. 192
Tung Po, p. 176
Yau Yuan Xiao Jui, p. 191

$$

Din Tai Fung, p. 180
Go Koong, p. 184
Goldfinch Restaurant, p. 173
Liu Yuan Pavilion, p. 170
Tim's Kitchen, p. 153
Wu Kong, p. 175

$$$

Ammo, p. 157
Café Gray Deluxe, p. 158
Mirror Restaurant, p. 170
Socialito, p. 166

$$$$

8 ½ Otto e Mezzo, p. 156
Amber, p. 157
Bo Innovation, p. 168
The Drawing Room, p. 173
L'Atelier de Joël Robuchon, p. 163

By Cuisine

ASIAN

Chuan Alfresco Bar & Restaurant, p. 180
Go Koong, p. 184
Islam Food, p. 190
Thai BBQ 2, p. 192

CANTONESE

The Chairman, p. 158
Hoi King Heen, p. 184
Lung King Heen, p. 165
Tim's Kitchen, p. 153
Tung Po, p. 176
Yung Kee, p. 168

DIM SUM

Dimdim Sum Dimsum Specialty Store, p. 189
Tim Ho Wan, p. 192
Yan Toh Heen, p. 188

FRENCH

Amber, p. 157
Caprice, p. 158
L'Atelier de Joël Robuchon, p. 163
Mirror Restaurant, p. 170
Restaurant Pétrus, p. 166

JAPANESE

Sushi Hiro, p. 175
Sushi Sase, p. 167
Yardbird, p. 156

SICHUAN

Da Ping Huo, p. 159
San Xi Lou, p. 166
Yunyan Sichuan, p. 188

By Experience

BUSINESS DINING

8 ½ Otto e Mezzo, p. 156
Amber, p. 157
Aqua, p. 180
Gaia, p. 162

CHILD-FRIENDLY

Café Deco Bar & Grill, p. 157
Crystal Lotus, p. 178
Top Deck, p. 178

GREAT VIEW

Hutong, p. 184
Inakaya, p. 185
Pearl on the Peak, p. 165
Restaurant Pétrus, p. 166
Tai O Lookout, p. 179

MOST ROMANTIC

Caprice, p. 158
Lucy's, p. 177
Pearl on the Peak, p. 165
The Verandah, p. 178

$$ **✕ Yardbird.** This bustling bi-level eatery is one of the hottest places to
JAPANESE eat. Chef-owner Matt Abergel plates perfectly cooked *yakitori* (Japa-
Fodor's Choice nese-style grilled chicken) as well as a repertoire of salads and small
★ plates designed for sharing. Definitely try the Korean fried cauliflower
(KFC) and the liver mousse served with milk bread and crispy shallots.
Drinking is another important part of the experience so try the house
brand junmai sake or choose from the well-selected Japanese beer and
whiskey list. The only downside here is that the restaurant doesn't take
reservations so arrive early or risk waiting for a table. $ *Average main:*
HK$130 ⊠ *33–35 Bridges St., Sheung Wan, Western* ☎ *2547–9273*
⊕ *www.yardbirdrestaurant.com* ⚲ *Reservations not accepted* ⊗ *No*
lunch. Closed Sun. ✚ *1:C3.*

CENTRAL

One of Hong Kong's busiest areas, Central is particularly crazy at lunch-
time, when office workers crowd the streets and eateries. Most restau-
rants have set lunches—generally good values—with speedy service, so
everyone gets in and out within an hour. At night the norm is either a
formal dinner or a quick bite followed by many drinks, especially in
Central's nightlife center, a warren of cobbled backstreets called Lan
Kwai Fong. Mostly known as a drinking hole with mediocre dining
options, LKF has stepped up its game in the last few years, with some
serious restaurants, most of which are tucked away in commercial
buildings, away from the hustle and bustle of the street-level bars.

For a wider array of choices, head up to SoHo, but be wary of where
you go: a lot of these places are average in terms of food and service
quality. NoHo is a bit more bohemian, with some excellent hidden,
independent culinary gems, especially along Gough Street.

Admiralty, wedged between Central and Wan Chai, is home to large
shopping malls, and much of the food is aimed at meeting the lunch
needs of workers and shoppers. It's also home to several large hotels
and their respective high-end restaurants.

Once a mainstay of the Hong Kong streets, there are now only a little
more than 20 licensed *dai pai dongs*—that is, open-air food stalls spe-
cializing in various types of local dishes. These outdoor eateries are
popular for their dirt-cheap prices, minimal service, and—of course—
their awesome food. There's usually no English menu, so be prepared
to point to the dishes at neighboring tables.

$$$$ **✕ 8½ Otto e Mezzo.** Spearheaded by chef Umberto Bombana (the ex-
ITALIAN Ritz Carlton chef, often lauded as "the best Italian chef in Asia"), this
Fodor's Choice glitzy space delivers everything it promises. The service is hotel grade,
★ the wine list is extensive, and the interior is nothing less than glamor-
ous. Most importantly, the authentic Italian food here is magnificent.
Chef Bombana's famed handmade pastas live up to the hype; the bur-
rata cheese ravioli in black-olive and eggplant sauce being particularly
stellar. Mains are solid—the beef tongue and beef cheek is excellently
executed, but seafood options are even better. If you can't make up your
mind, the degustation menu offers a neat sampling of Bombana's best.
$ *Average main: HK$340* ⊠ *Shop 202, 2nd fl., Alexandra House, 18*

Chater Rd., Central ☎ *2537–8859* ⊕ *www.ottoemezzobombana.com* ⌂ *Reservations essential* ⊘ *Closed Sun.* Ⓜ *Central* ✣ *1:E3.*

$$$ ✕ **agnès b. le pain grillé.** This res-
FRENCH taurant in the IFC mall is the most extravagant of all the pain grillé outlets in the city. It's in the center of the giant agnès b. La Loggia flagship store, right next to the faux al fresco patisserie and coffee

shop. Check in at the reception desk and you'll then be led into the dining salon, which is inspired by an elegant study room. The food is, not surprisingly, classic French cuisine. Seafood dishes are particularly well made, and the bouillabaisse is a hearty, no-fail favorite. Ⓢ *Average main: HK$290* ✉ *Shop 3096–3097, La Loggia, 3rd fl., IFC Mall, 8 Finance St., Central* ☎ *2805–0798* ⊕ *www.agnesb-lepaingrille.com* Ⓜ *Central* ✣ *1:E2.*

$$$$ ✕ **Amber.** When the Landmark Mandarin Oriental hotel opened in
FRENCH 2005, its aim was to be seen as the preeminent hotel on Hong Kong Island. So it made sense that it would house an award-winning flagship restaurant with a similar level of impeccable, modern style. The restaurant and the concept are no longer new, but Chef Richard Ekkebus's menu of creative European dishes still doesn't fail to impress, and guests can look forward to signature creations such as foie gras lollipops, line-caught *amadai* (tilefish) with orange and fennel confit and *bottarga* grated potatoes bouillabaisse, as well as sea urchin set in lobster gelatin with cauliflower, caviar, and seaweed waffle. Ⓢ *Average main: HK$460* ✉ *Landmark Mandarin Oriental Hotel, 15 Queen's Rd., Central* ☎ *2132–0066* ⊕ *www.amberhongkong.com* Ⓜ *Central* ✣ *1:E4.*

$$$ ✕ **Ammo.** Few places in Hong Kong have the kind of stunning garden
ITALIAN views that you'll find at Ammo. In a former ammunition compound (hence the name) that was converted into the Asia Society museum, Ammo's interiors and menus blend the old with the new and East with West, resulting in an impressive and dynamic dining experience. Dishes tout Italian roots, but you'll find plenty of Asian flourishes, as in the slow-cooked egg with toro, sea urchin, and roman zucchini sauce; and burrata cheese ravioli doused in Peking duck ragout. Save room for dessert because the panfried brioche is insanely satisfying. Ⓢ *Average main: HK$200* ✉ *9 Justice Drive, Admiralty, Central* ☎ *2537–9888* ⊕ *www.ammo.com.hk* ⌂ *Reservations essential* ✣ *1:G5.*

$ ✕ **Ball Kee.** The stir-fried noodle dishes here are especially good. Thin
CHINESE noodles are cooked until crispy and topped with strips of pork and bean sprouts. Ⓢ *Average main: HK$58* ✉ *Staveley St. and Wellington St., Central* ☎ *2544–5923* ▬ *No credit cards* ⊘ *No dinner.* ✣ *1:C4.*

$$ ✕ **Café Deco Bar & Grill.** As is often the case where there's a captive audi-
ECLECTIC ence, dining up at the Peak Galleria mall can be unpredictable—and this ☾ huge eatery is no exception. You'll come mostly for the views, though the menu is eclectic enough to keep everyone happy. Menu options

traverse five or six continents and there is also a dessert station. Oysters are good, and the pizzas and pastas are okay, but you should avoid the insipid Southeast Asian fare and overpriced steaks. When you book (and you must), be sure to request a table with a view, as many tables in the place have none, which defeats the purpose of coming here. [$] *Average main: HK$190* ✉ *1st fl., Peak Galleria, 118 Peak Rd., The Peak, Central* ☎ *2849–5111* 🌐 *www.cafedecogroup.com* ✍ *Reservations essential* ✥ *1:C6.*

ABOVE-IT-ALL DINING

Central is the place to catch the tram up to the legendary Victoria Peak. A meal in a restaurant at the city's highest point has to be on everyone's itinerary. The trip is justified many times over on clear days, when the views from the top (and en route) are unparalleled. When the clouds are thick and low, though, you won't be able to see a thing—you'll just hear the sounds of the city beneath you.

$$$ CONTEMPORARY Fodor's Choice ★ 🍴 **Café Gray Deluxe.** Celebrated chef Gray Kunz's restaurant offers expertly prepared modern European fare in a casual and relaxed 49th-floor locale that has stunning views of the city. A fan of fresh, seasonal ingredients, Kunz incorporates local produce into the ever-evolving menu whenever possible, and often adds Asian flavorings to excellent effect. Steak tartare with Kunz ketjap and chips shines among the lineup of stellar "first plates," which also include the signature saffron pasta *fiore* served with tangy tomatoes. The bar has a menu of unique and delicious drinks, so even if you can't stop by for a sit-down meal, it's worth stopping in for a cocktail and small bite. [$] *Average main: HK$330* ✉ *49th fl., The Upper House, Pacific Place, 88 Queensway, Admiralty, Central* ☎ *3968–1106* 🌐 *www.cafegrayhk.com* ✍ *Reservations essential* [M] *Admiralty* ✥ *1:F5.*

$$$$ FRENCH 🍴 **Caprice.** The Four Seasons spared no expense in creating this space, bringing in well-known designers and feng shui masters, and the result is a private dining room that might be one of the most spectacular in the world. Guests can see into the entire open kitchen, while floor-to-ceiling windows offer stunning views of Victoria Harbour and beyond. Head chef Vincent Thierry sets himself apart with the details: the menu changes seasonally, but dishes such as Tourteau crab tiramisu and *langoustine* lasagne with veal sweetbreads are always heavenly. Service is expectedly excellent, and restaurant manager Jeremy Evrard makes the utmost effort to ensure that every guest is well taken care of. [$] *Average main: HK$600* ✉ *Four Seasons Hotel, 8 Finance St., Central* ☎ *3196–8888* 🌐 *www.fourseasons.com* ✍ *Reservations essential* [M] *Central* ✥ *1:E2.*

$$$ CHINESE Fodor's Choice ★ 🍴 **The Chairman.** The restaurant celebrates a return to authentic Cantonese fare. Using only fresh, top-quality ingredients—from locally reared free-range chicken to wild-caught seafood—and sticking with their no-MSG policy, the Chairman focuses on the intrinsic flavors of each ingredient. Appetizers are creative—shredded pig's ear and tripe salad is given an extra crunchy edge with the addition of freshly sliced guava; yellow croaker fish are deep-fried and served with aged balsamic vinegar. And it gets even better with the mains. A particular favorite is the signature soy-sauce chicken, perfumed with 18 different fragrant

Lobster and mozzarella salad served at 8½ Otto e Mezzo

Chinese herbs. Also recommended is the steamed fresh crab, which is steeped in aged ShaoXing wine. [$] *Average main: HK$170* ✉ *18 Kau U Fong, NoHo, Central* ☎ *2555–2202* 🌐 *www.thechairmangroup.com* ✍ *Reservations essential* [M] *Central* ✣ *1:D3.*

$$ PERUVIAN 🍴 **Chicha.** Expect complex, chili-fueled flavors from Hong Kong's first Peruvian restaurant. The menu has multicultural influences, from Chinese-style *lomo saltado* (a beef, scallion, and rice stir-fry) to the Spanish paella-like *marisco jugoso* flavored with an umami sea urchin and citrus reduction. Be sure to order a platter of *anticuchos* (grilled skewers) to share; the cod with ponzu miso and chili aioli is close to addictive. If you want to cap your meal off in true Peruvian fashion, finish with a pisco brandy cocktail at the bar. [$] *Average main: HK$198* ✉ *26 Peel St., Central* ☎ *2561–3336* 🌐 *www.conceptcreations.hk* ✍ *Reservations essential* 🕓 *No lunch Sat. Closed Sun.* ✣ *1:B4.*

$$$ BRITISH 🍴 **Clipper Lounge.** The Mandarin Oriental's Clipper Lounge has long been lauded for having one of the best afternoon tea sets in town. Sandwiches, savories, and miniature cakes cascade down a multitier stand. Classic scones are served with clotted cream and the restaurant's famed rose-petal jam. [$] *Average main: HK$258* ✉ *Mandarin Oriental, 5 Connaught Rd., Central* ☎ *2825–4007* 🌐 *www.mandarinoriental.com* ✣ *1:E3.*

$$ SICHUAN 🍴 **Da Ping Huo.** If you can find the semi-hidden door to this restaurant speakeasy, one of Hong Kong's famed private kitchens, the rewards are great indeed. The experience begins with a multicourse meal (usually consisting of 13 or14 dishes) that takes you on a spicy tour of the Sichuan province and ends with live Chinese opera, courtesy of the chef. The menu varies day to day—whatever the chef feels like preparing—so leave your food phobias and quirks at the door, especially if those phobias

Outdoor dining at a dai pai dong

include a burning mouth: this is some of the spiciest food in town. $ *Average main: HK$200* ⊠ *49 Hollywood Rd., SoHo, Central* ☎ *2559–1317* 🕭 *Reservations essential* ▭ *No credit cards* Ⓜ *Central* ✛ *1:B4.*

$$$
SHANGHAINESE
Fodor's Choice
★

✕ **Fa Zu Jie.** This place is good, really, *really* good. Tucked away in a nondescript building in a hidden alley off Lan Kwai Fong, this reservations-only private kitchen plates up inventive French-inspired Shanghainese dishes that are prepped in a polished open kitchen. The prix-fixe menu is tweaked on a regular basis but you'll probably be treated to trademark items such as drunken quail (cooked in Chinese Hua Diao wine) served with al dente Sanuki udon, and plump scallops slicked in shrimp roe oil. The dining room has only a handful of tables so try to book a few weeks in advance if you can. $ *Average main: HK$538* ⊠ *1st fl., 20A D'Aguilar St., Central* ☎ *3487–1715* 🕭 *Reservations essential* ▭ *No credit cards* 🕓 *No lunch. Closed Sun.* ✛ *1:C5.*

$$$
SPANISH

✕ **FoFo by el Willy.** The Hong Kong outpost of Shanghai's popular el Willy Spanish restaurant is showy, with a snow-white interior decked out with designer chairs and fiberglass animal figurines. On the food side of things, authentic and traditional tapas share menu space with creatively contemporary Spanish dishes. The Iberian ham served with tomato bread, the sautéed prawns with garlic, and gazpacho represent the classics—and they're certainly well executed, but the modern dishes offer much more excitement. Scallop ceviche, for instance, is laid on creamy avocado and topped with crispy shallots, while foie gras is paired with beets and popcorn powder. The paellas are also worth trying, whether steeped in the flavors of Boston lobster or bathed in jet-black squid ink. $ *Average main: HK$250* ⊠ *20th fl., M88, 2–8 Wellington St., Lan Kwai Fong, Central* ☎ *2900–2009* ⊕ *www.fofo.hk* 🕓 *Closed Sun.* Ⓜ *Central* ✛ *1:C5.*

CHINA'S CUISINES

To help you navigate China's many cuisines, we have used the following terms in our restaurant reviews.

Cantonese: A diverse cuisine that roasts and stir-fries, braises and steams. Spices are used in moderation. Notable dishes include fried rice, sweet-and-sour pork, and roasted goose.

Chinese: Catch-all term used for restaurants that serve cuisine from multiple regions of China; pan-Chinese.

Chinese fusion: Any type of Chinese cuisine with international influences.

Chiu chow: Known for its vegetarian and seafood dishes, which are mostly poached, steamed, or braised. Signature dishes include *popiah* (nonfried spring rolls), baby oyster congee, and fish ball noodle soup.

Hunan: Stewing, frying, braising, and smoking are featured cooking methods. Flavors are spicy, incorporating chili peppers, shallots, and garlic, along with dried and preserved condiments. Signature dishes are Mao's braised pork, steamed fish head with shredded chilies, and spicy eggplant in garlic sauce.

Macanese: An eclectic blend of southern Chinese and Portuguese cooking, featuring the use of salted dried fish, coconut milk, turmeric, and other spices. Common dishes are "African" barbecued chicken with spicy piri piri sauce, pork buns, and curried baked chicken.

Mandarin (Beijing): China's capital city, Beijing, features cuisine from all over the country. Dishes from the city typically are snack-size, featuring ingredients like dark soy paste, sesame paste, and sesame oil. Regional specialties include Peking duck, moo shu pork, and quick-fried tripe.

Northern Chinese (inner Mongolia and environs): Staples are lamb and mutton, preserved vegetables, and noodles, steamed breads, pancakes, stuffed buns, and dumplings. Common dishes are cumin-scented lamb, congee porridge with pickles, and Mongolian hotpot.

Sichuan (central province): Famed for bold flavors and spiciness resulting from liberal use of chilies and Sichuan peppercorns. Regional dishes include "dan dan" spicy rice noodles, twice-cooked pork, and tea-smoked duck.

Shanghainese: Cuisine characterized by rich flavors produced by braising and stewing, and the use of alcohol in cooking. Dumplings, noodles, and bread are served more than rice. Signature dishes are baby hairy crabs stir-fried with rice cake slices, steamed buns and dumplings, and "drunken chicken."

Taiwanese: Diverse cuisine owing to its history and subtropical location. Seafood, pork, rice, soy, and fruit form the backbone of the cuisine. Specialties include "three cups chicken" with a sauce made of soya, rice wine, and sugar; oyster omelets; cuttlefish soup; and dried tofu.

Yunnan (southernmost province): This region is known as the "kingdom of plants and animals." Its cuisine is noted for its use of vegetables, fruit, bamboo shoots, and flowers in its spicy preparations. Signature dishes include rice noodle soup with chicken, pork, and fish.

5

$$$ ITALIAN 🍴 **Gaia.** The concept at this trendy restaurant is a re-creation of Rome's Spanish Steps, complete with alfresco seating. The restaurant is particularly popular with the business crowd, many of whom come especially for the excellent antipasti buffet. The authentic pan-Italian fare includes wide *pappardelle* noodles in a Sangiovese-marinated rabbit ragout, beef carpaccio, and signature thin-crust pizzas topped with everything from hot salami and mozzarella cheese to fresh arugula with prosciutto. [$] *Average main: HK$260* ✉ *Ground fl., The Piazza, Grand Millennium Plaza, 181 Queen's Rd., Central* ☎ *2167–8200* 🌐 *www.gaiaristorante.com* [M] *Sheung Wan* ✣ *1:C4.*

$$$$ ITALIAN 🍴 **Gold by Harlan Goldstein.** The menu here is inspired by the multicultural flavors chef Harlan Goldstein grew up with while living in New York. Italian preparations take precedence, but you'll also find things like sea scallop sashimi and crispy falafel served with tahini. The handcrafted pastas are easy favorites, but if you're in the mood to feast, go for the 42-ounce *fiorentina* (steak Florentine-style, designed for two) with a side of black truffle mash. Gold also has a great wine selection, and guests can always enjoy a glass out on the restaurant's open-air terrace. [$] *Average main: HK$300* ✉ *2nd fl., LKF Tower, 33 Wyndham St., Central* ☎ *2869–9986* 🌐 *www.gold-dining.com* 🕒 *Closed Sun.* ✣ *1:C5.*

$$ INDIAN 🍴 **Jashan.** This established Indian restaurant has stepped up its game since it opened, and although you'll still find the well-spiced classics on the menu, the newer dishes have a more contemporary twist, and these are the items that steal the spotlight. Try the *mirchi kebab*—delicious grilled chicken that's been flavored with coriander and chilies and is served with a cooling cilantro dip. We also recommend the *nilgiri halibut* and mackerel medallions cooked in coconut gravy with fennel seeds. The restaurant has a wide range of vegetarian specialties that can impress even devout carnivores. [$] *Average main: HK$142* ✉ *1st fl., Amber Lodge, 23 Hollywood Rd., Central* ☎ *3105–5300, 3105–5311* 🌐 *www.jashan.com.hk* ✣ *1:C5.*

$$$ ECLECTIC 🍴 **Jimmy's Kitchen.** One of the oldest restaurants in Hong Kong, Jimmy's opened in 1928 and continues to serve comfort food from around the world to a loyal clientele in a colonial private-club atmosphere. The handy location just off Queen's Road in Central and a menu that offers a wide selection of both western and Asian dishes including steak, borscht, goulash, bangers and mash, curry, and burgers have made Jimmy's a favorite with both Chinese locals and tourists looking for a taste of home. It's not cheap, but it's a good choice for a night out with friends, especially if your group's cravings are pulling you in different directions. [$] *Average main: HK$260* ✉ *Ground fl., South China Bldg., 1–3 Wyndham St., Central* ☎ *2526–5293* 🌐 *www.jimmys.com* [M] *Central* ✣ *1:C5.*

$$$$ INTERNATIONAL 🍴 **JW's California.** Lobster, fresh fish, and expertly grilled steaks are the main draws at this sleek, yet warm and welcoming flagship restaurant of the JW Marriott Hotel. For our money, we'd say slide up to the sushi bar and leave your fate in the hands of the virtuoso sushi chef, who serves up pricey but artistic plates of sushi and sashimi made with incredibly fresh ingredients. You might also try king crab linguine with

Dessert served at L'Atelier de Joël Robuchon

chorizo, grilled Japanese Wagyu, or roast suckling pig, and finish with the liquid chocolate cake with vanilla-ginger ice cream. $ *Average main: HK$330* ⊠ *5th fl., JW Marriott Hotel, Pacific Place, 88 Queensway, Admiralty, Central* ☎ *2841–3899* ⊕ *www.jwmarriotthk.com* Ⓜ *Admiralty* ✛ *1:F4.*

$$$$ ✕ **Krug Room.** This private dining room is a must-visit for serious epi-
CONTEMPORARY cures. The experience is a bit surreal—guests are led through the hotel's legendary Chinnery Bar to a black door that announces the exclusive Krug Room; within is a table that seats up to 12 diners and gives full view of the kitchen, where chef Uwe Opocensky and his team are busy at work. This is essentially Opocensky's creative workshop: he trained at El Bulli, and he calls his cuisine "progressive gastronomy"—dishes such as the signature "Rain" salad appear like potted plants with edible soil (usually made with arugula or anchovy purée). A meal here isn't cheap; it costs at least HK$2,000—but you get 10 to 14 courses (sometimes more) and a complimentary first glass of bubbly. $ *Average main: HK$1988* ⊠ *1st fl., Mandarin Oriental, 5 Connaught Rd., Central* ☎ *2825–4014* ⊕ *www.mandarinoriental.com* ✍ *Reservations essential* ☽ *No lunch. Closed Sun.* Ⓜ *Central* ✛ *1:E3.*

$$$$ ✕ **L'Atelier de Joël Robuchon.** Joël Robuchon, one of the most iconic chefs
FRENCH in the world, claims that his atelier (or "artist's workshop") is for con-
Fodor's Choice temporary casual dining. Diners sit on barstools around a counter
★ designed like a modern Japanese sushi bar so that everyone can watch the chefs preparing the food in the open kitchen. Though entrées are available, diners typically order small plates for sharing. Everything from the freshly baked bread to desserts is immaculately presented. The quail with foie gras, served with the deservedly famous mashed

potatoes; and the sea urchin in a lobster jelly, topped with cauliflower cream, are all standouts. Those who don't want to splurge on a full meal should try the superb croissants and cakes at the salon one floor down from the restaurant. $ *Average main: HK$500* ✉ *Shop 315 (salon) and 401 (restaurant), The Landmark, 15 Queen's Rd., Central* ☎ *2166–9000* ⊕ *www.robuchon.hk* Ⓜ *Central* ✛ *1:E4.*

$
CHINESE

✕ **Leaf Dessert.** Visit this outdoor stall for authentic Chinese desserts. Sweet soups made with red bean or ground black sesame are served in both hot and chilled versions. Warmed, chewy glutinous rice balls heaped with sugar, crushed peanuts, and desiccated coconut are messy but delicious. $ *Average main: HK$12* ✉ *2 Elgin St., SoHo, Central* ☎ *2544–3795* ▭ *No credit cards* ✛ *1:B4.*

$$$
AMERICAN

✕ **Liberty Exchange Kitchen & Bar.** This two-level restaurant and bar fuses comfort food with fine-dining execution and finesse. It's unabashedly casual, from the stylish young waitstaff decked out in clean white shirts and skinny black ties to the menu dotted with refined yet hearty comfort dishes such as baked mac 'n' cheese and buttermilk fried chicken served with cornbread. The team behind Liberty Exchange also runs a reservations-only kitchen near Lan Kwai Fong called Liberty Private Works, which offers a more personal (and more expensive) fine-dining experience. $ *Average main: HK$250* ✉ *2 Exchange Sq., 8 Connaught Pl., Central* ☎ *2810–8400* ⊕ *www.lex.hk* Ⓜ *Central* ✛ *1:E3.*

$$$
AMERICAN

✕ **Lily & Bloom.** Enjoy city-inspired, American comfort fare at this Prohibition Era–style restaurant and bar. The lower level— Lily—serves raw bar seafood, oyster shooters, late-night bar bites, and artisanal, classic cocktails made with premium spirits. For a more formal dining experience, head upstairs to Bloom and enjoy catchy Cotton Club tunes and hearty dishes such as Iberico pork chop and smoked ribs with braised cabbage and sage marmalade. The kitchen at Lily stays open until late at night, making this a popular snacking pit stop for Central's party crowd. $ *Average main: HK$280* ✉ *5th and 6th fl., LKF Tower, 33 Wyndham St., Central* ☎ *2810–6166* ⊕ *www.lily-bloom.com* ⊗ *No lunch Sat. No dinner Sun.* ✛ *1:C5*

$$
ITALIAN

✕ **Linguini Fini.** The food at this casual, Italian-American restaurant pays tribute to local produce and artisanal cooking methods. Enjoy home-cured salumi and antipasti at the bar downstairs or head up to the main dining room for the handcrafted pastas infused with ingredients such as salted duck egg yolk and dried shrimp. The "white gold bars" are to die for—breaded and deep-fried housemade mozzarella served with tangy marinara sauce. Expect some of the friendliest and most efficient service in town. $ *Average main: HK$180* ✉ *Ground and 1st fl., The L Place, 139 Queen's Rd., Central* ☎ *2857–1333* ⊕ *www.linguinifini. com* ✛ *1:D3.*

$$$$
SEAFOOD

✕ **Lobster Bar and Grill.** The giant tropical-fish tank at the entrance sets the scene, and, as the name suggests, lobster is the featured ingredient on the menu. It's whipped into soups, stuffed into appetizers, and presented in full glory in numerous entrées. The lobster bisque is creamy yet light, with great chunks of meat at the bottom. The seafood platter—half a lobster thermidor, whole grilled langoustine, shrimp, baked oysters, creamy scallops, crab cakes, and black cod—doesn't disappoint. Decorated in blue and gold, with mahogany timbers and leather upholstery, the restaurant has a vibe that is at once formal and cozy: it's great for before- or after-dinner drinks at the bar. [$] *Average main: HK$340* ✉ *Lobby fl., Island Shangri-La, Pacific Place, Supreme Court Rd., Admiralty, Central* ☎ *2820–8560* 🌐 *www.shangri-la.com* [M] *Admiralty* ✥ *1:F4.*

$$$ CHINESE 🍴 **Lung King Heen.** Lung King Heen has made a serious case for being the best Cantonese restaurant in Hong Kong, especially after winning three Michelin stars for three consecutive years. Where other contenders tend to get too caught up in prestige dishes and name-brand chefs, Lung King Heen focuses completely on taste. When you try a steamed lobster-and-scallop dumpling, or a dish of house-made XO sauce that is this divine, you'll be forced to reevaluate your entire notion of Chinese cuisine. [$] *Average main: HK$250* ✉ *4th fl., Four Seasons Hotel, 8 Finance St., Central* ☎ *3196–8880* 🌐 *www.fourseasons.com* ✍ *Reservations essential* [M] *Central* ✥ *1:E2.*

5

$ CHINESE 🍴 **Mak's Noodles Limited.** Mak's may look like any other Hong Kong noodle shop, but this tiny store is one of the best known in town, with a reputation that belies its humble decor. The staff is attentive, and the menu includes a wide range of delicious dishes, such as various sauce-tossed noodles with pork. The real test of a good Cantonese noodle shop, however, is its wontons, and here they're fresh, delicate, and filled with whole shrimp. And don't miss the *sui kau*—a slightly larger and heavier dumpling that has diced mushrooms mixed in to the shrimp filling. [$] *Average main: HK$40* ✉ *77 Wellington St., Central* ☎ *2854–3810* 💳 *No credit cards* [M] *Central* ✥ *1:C4.*

$ MIDDLE EASTERN 🍴 **Mana!.** The guys at Mana! have come up with the concept of "fast slow food"—a convenient and eco-conscious mode of eating that's good for the body and the environment. Utensils and containers are all biodegradable while the menu brims with plant-based dishes prepared from sustainable organic produce sourced from the city's local farms. Enjoy mixed salads, veggie burgers, and good-for-you shakes and juices. The main attraction though are the flatbreads, which are freshly baked in Mana's brick oven. They're spread with *za'atar* (Middle East herbs), then topped with hearty items such as roasted veggies, garlic mayo, or hummus. Saving the planet never tasted so delicious. [$] *Average main: HK$90* ✉ *92 Wellington St., Central* ☎ *2851–1611* 🌐 *www.mana.hk* ✥ *1:C4.*

$$$ ECLECTIC 🍴 **Pearl on the Peak.** Sitting atop Victoria Peak, one of Hong Kong's must-see attractions, the Pearl has a 270-degree view of the glittering city far below through its floor-to-ceiling windows. Though the stunning view alone is reason to come, this lofty place has more than a sensational view—it also serves quite good modern international cuisine. The menu changes seasonally, but most of the seafood dishes will impress. Make sure to book well in advance for windowside tables. For those who just want to enjoy the view, the restaurant has a bar area on the terrace. [$] *Average main: HK$280* ✉ *Shop 2, 1st fl., The Peak Tower, 128 Peak Rd., Central* ☎ *2849–5123* [M] *Admiralty or Central* ✥ *1:C6.*

$ 🍴 **Petite Amanda.** For western treats, head to Petite Amanda at the
BAKERY IFC, opened by model-turned-pastry chef Amanda Strang. The sweets shop sells traditional French cakes and pastries such as the layered hazelnut and chocolate Plaisir Sucré. [$] *Average main: HK$45* ✉ *Shop 2096, 2nd fl., IFC Mall, 8 Finance St., Central* ☎ *2234–7222* 🌐 *www.petiteamanda.com* ✥ *1:E2.*

$$$$ 🍴 **Restaurant Petrus.** Commanding breathtaking views atop the Island
FRENCH Shangri-La, Restaurant Petrus scales the upper Hong Kong heights of prestige, formality, and price. This is one of the city's few flagship hotel restaurants that have not attempted to reinvent themselves as fusion; sometimes traditional French haute cuisine is the way to go. Likewise, the design of the place is in the old-school restaurant-as-ballroom mode. The kitchen has a particularly good way with foie gras, and the wine list is memorable, listing more than 1,500 celebrated labels. The dress here is business casual—no jeans or sneakers. [$] *Average main: HK$500* ✉ *56th fl., Island Shangri-La, Pacific Place, Supreme Court Rd., Admiralty, Central* ☎ *2820–8590* 🌐 *www.shangri-la.com* [M] *Admiralty* ✥ *1:F4.*

$$ 🍴 **San Xi Lou.** This Mid-Levels eatery is known for the high quality of its
CHINESE spicy Sichuan cuisine. The famous Chongqing spicy chicken is heaped with dried red chili peppers for a sensational tingling, mouth-numbing effect. Another unique creation is the homemade silken tofu, which is bathed in a bright red spicy broth speckled with chunks of whitefish, chopped scallions, and crunchy roasted peanuts. Those in town during the cold winter months should go for the yinyang hot pot—the fiery hot side dish is perfect for dunking with thin slices of fat marbled beef and the local favorite, deep-fried fish skin. [$] *Average main: HK$150* ✉ *7th fl., Coda Plaza, 51 Garden Rd., Midlevels, Central* ☎ *2838–8811* [M] *Central* ✥ *1:D5.*

$ 🍴 **Shui Kee.** Fold-up tables and stools are scattered around this small
CHINESE stall, which specializes in cow offal. Tender beef brisket and deep-fried wontons are also popular options. [$] *Average main: HK$28* ✉ *2 Gutzlaff St., Central* ☎ *2541–9769* ▭ *No credit cards* ⏲ *No dinner, closed Sun.* ✥ *1:C4.*

$ 🍴 **Sing Heung Yuen.** This outdoor stall has been in operation for well over
CHINESE 30 years and the canopied tables are pretty much always packed from 8 am to 5:30 pm, when they close up shop. The iconic dishes here are the instant ramen noodles with beef, served in a sweet tomato broth, as well as the toasted, crispy buns drizzled with condensed milk. [$] *Average main: HK$28* ✉ *2 Mei Lun St., NoHo, Central* ☎ *2544–8368* ▭ *No credit cards* ⏲ *No dinner. Closed Sun.* ✥ *1:C3.*

$ 🍴 **Sing Kee.** This is one of the rare dai open-air food stalls in the area
CHINESE that stays open late into the evening. The menu is pretty extensive, and the home-style stir-fries are particularly good. Chewy calamari in spicy salt is a classic favorite. The adventurous should try the soy-sauce goose intestines. [$] *Average main: HK$98* ✉ *9–10 Stanley St., Central* ☎ *2541–5678* ▭ *No credit cards* ✥ *1:C4.*

$$$ 🍴 **Socialito.** One of the hottest entries from the city's recent prolifera-
MEXICAN tion of Latin American restaurants, Socialito is a happening, multipurpose space that flaunts a taquería by the entrance and a slick

dining room inside that transforms into a club when it gets close to midnight. The menu features refined Mexican favorites, from Wagyu beef–filled tacos to tangy, chili-spiked ceviches loaded with fresh seafood, avocado, and tomatoes. And on the drinks side of things, there are expertly prepared specialty cocktails as well as high-grade tequilas to choose from. [$] *Average main: HK$220* ✉ *Shop 2, ground fl., The Centrium, 50 Wyndham St., Central* ☎ *3167–7380* 🌐 *www.socialito.com.hk* 🕒 *Closed Sun.* ✥ *1:C5.*

$$$$ ASIAN 🍴 **St Betty.** Having found success in the UK with establishments such as Wagamama and Hakkasan, restaurateur Alan Yau has returned to his home city with this retro-inspired restaurant concept headed by Australian chef Shane Osborn. The menu combines Osborn's classical culinary training with seasonal Asian ingredients such as daikon, yuzu, and locally caught fish. Meats are done especially well here, and diners tend to wax lyrical about the Sagabuta pork with Japanese sweet corn, as well as the fabulously tender honey-and-soy-glazed short rib of beef. [$] *Average main: HK$398* ✉ *Shop 2075, 2nd fl., IFC Mall, 8 Finance St., Central* ☎ *2979–2100* 🌐 *www.stbetty.com* ✥ *1:E2.*

5

$$$$ JAPANESE 🍴 **Sushi Sase.** Helmed by veteran chef Satoshi Sase (who hails from the much-lauded Sushi Zen in Hokkaido, Japan), this high-caliber Japanese restaurant offers some of the freshest fish in town set against a tranquil and sophisticated setting. Omakase is the way to go here, which means you leave your meal in the hands of the chefs, allowing them to dictate the menu according to the best ingredients of the day. The omakase menu is designed according to the seasons and usually consists of sashimi, appetizers, and a wide array of nigiri sushi. [$] *Average main: HK$1380* ✉ *UG fl., Hilltop Plaza, 49 Hollywood Rd., Central* ☎ *2815–0455, 2815–0477* ✥ *1:B5.*

$ BAKERY 🍴 **Tai Cheong.** Tai Cheong is an ultrapopular bakery that was supposed to shut down for good in 2005, but due to immense public support it reopened shortly after it closed and has since expanded to a multichain company with outlets all across the city. They sell all sorts of packaged and oven-fresh baked goods. The egg tarts, with their buttery crust and custardy-rich centers, are the real scene stealers, but thin and crunchy egg biscuit rolls are also popular. Other local delicacies include sugar-dusted Chinese donuts. [$] *Average main: HK$8* ✉ *35 Lyndhurst Terr., Central* ☎ *2544–3475* ✥ *1:B5.*

$$$$ ECLECTIC 🍴 **TBLS.** Chef-owner Que Vinh Dang plates up refined comfort food at this eatery tucked away under the Mid-Levels Escalators (you'll need a pass code to get into the building; it's given when you make your reservation). There's no à la carte menu, only a six-course set dinner that's updated on a monthly basis, and the menu theme can be inspired by anything, from Vietnamese cuisine to Fourth of July barbeque, so it's a good idea to check what they're serving before you reserve. Dishes are always changing, but there are a few staples, including some form of soup-and-sandwich combo and Dang's delicious ice cream *macaron* cookies. [$] *Average main: HK$500* ✉ *7th fl., 31 Hollywood Rd., Central* ☎ *2544–3433* 🌐 *www.tbls-kitchenstudio.com* ✍ *Reservations essential* 🕒 *No lunch. Closed Sun.* ✥ *1:B5.*

$$ CANTONESE 🍴 **Yung Kee.** Close to Hong Kong's famous nightlife and dining district of Lan Kwai Fong, Yung Kee has become a local institution since it first opened shop as a street-food stall in 1942. The food is authentic Cantonese, served amid riotous decor and writhing gold dragons. Locals come here for roast goose with beautifully crisp skin and tender meat, as well as dim sum. Other excellent dishes include the "cloudy tea" smoked pork, which needs to be reserved a day in advance, and deep-fried prawns with mini crab roe. More adventurous palates may wish to check out the thousand-year-old preserved eggs. [$] *Average main: HK$200* ✉ *32–40 Wellington St, Central* ☎ *2522–1624* 🌐 *www.yungkee.com.hk* [M] *Central* ✥ *1:C5.*

$$$ JAPANESE 🍴 **Zuma.** This funky *izakaya* has been serving good (though pricey) Japanese food since it opened in 2007, following the huge success of its London restaurant. Zuma makes abundant use of wood and stone in design, which gives the space a hip but relaxed feel. Chefs concoct primarily Japanese food with a creative twist in an open kitchen. The sushi and sashimi are fresh and beautifully presented on a slab of ice with chrysanthemum-flower petals sprinkled on top. The dessert platter, which includes a chocolate cake that has a melted chocolate center and exotic Asian fruits, is equally stunning. An outdoor balcony allows diners to take in the surrounding Central night view. [$] *Average main: HK$320* ✉ *5th and 6th fl., The Landmark, 15 Queen's Rd., Central* ☎ *3657–6388* 🌐 *www.zumarestaurant.com* [M] *Central* ✥ *1:E4.*

WAN CHAI, CAUSEWAY BAY, AND BEYOND

WAN CHAI

The range of dining options in Wan Chai is extreme—from five-star luxury to noodle-shop dives open into the wee hours.

$$$$ CHINESE Fodor's Choice ★ 🍴 **Bo Innovation.** The mastermind behind this renowned, Michelin-approved restaurant is Alvin Leung, who dubbed himself the "demon chef" and had the moniker tattooed on his arm. Bo Innovation serves what he calls "X-treme Chinese" cuisine, applying molecular gastronomy, French, and Japanese cooking techniques to traditional Cantonese dishes. The Australian Wagyu strip loin with black-truffle *cheung fun,* or rice roll, is a winner, as is the signature molecular *xiao long bao* (soup dumpling). At dinner you must choose between the eight-course tasting menu or the 12-course chef's menu; à la carte dining is not available. Tables are often full on Friday and Saturday, so book in advance. [$] *Average main: HK$680* ✉ *Shop 13, 2nd fl., J Residence, 60 Johnston Rd., Wan Chai* ☎ *2850–8371* 🌐 *www.boinnovation.com* ✍ *Reservations essential* ⏲ *No lunch Sat. Closed Sun.* [M] *Wan Chai* ✥ *2:B4.*

$ CHINESE 🍴 **Capital Café.** It's a blast from the past at this retro Hong Kong café, done up in period 1980s and early 1990s decor, complete with autographed Cantopop idol posters from that era. The food is old-school as well and you'll find hearty local specialties, such as elbow macaroni with barbecued pork, milk tea, and toasted sandwiches filled with fluffy scrambled eggs. If you come after 3 pm, try the "principal's toast"—it's black truffle paste and cheese smothered on thick pieces of bread. It's delicious indulgence done the cheap and cheerful way. [$] *Average main: HK$25* ✉ *6 Heard St., Wan Chai* ☎ *2666–7766* ▭ *No credit cards* ✥ *2:D3.*

$$ ✕ **Che's Cantonese Restaurant.** Smartly dressed locals in the know head
CHINESE for this casually elegant dim sum specialist, which is in the middle
of the downtown bustle yet well concealed on the fourth floor of an
office building. From the elevator, you'll step into a classy Cantonese
world. It's hard to find a single better dim sum dish than Che's crispy
pork buns, whose sugary baked pastry conceals the brilliant salti-
ness of stewed pork within. Other dim sum to try include panfried
turnip cake and a refreshing dessert of cold pomelo and sago with
mango juice for a calming end to an exciting meal. $ *Average main:
HK$100* ✉ *4th fl., The Broadway, 54–62 Lockhart Rd., Wan Chai*
☎ *2528–1123* Ⓜ *Wan Chai* ✛ *2:B3.*

$$$ ✕ **DiVino Patio.** Located along a stretch of semi-alfresco eateries known
ITALIAN as Brim 28 (named after its waterside location on 28 Harbour Road),
DiVino Patio touts rustic, homestyle Italian fare to match its laid-back
surroundings. The expansive space is designed like a retro grocery store
and diners can purchase gourmet condiments, salumi, and cheeses to
enjoy at home. For eat-in orders, try any of the hand-tossed pizzas, or go
for one of the succulent selections from the rotisserie. The spit-roasted
Vallespluga game hen is exceptional, with tender meat and crispy skin.
The restaurant has an excellent lunchtime deal, in which an antipasti
buffet spread is matched with a rotating choice of mains. $ *Average
main: HK$230* ✉ *Shop 11, 1st fl., Brim 28, Causeway Centre, 28 Har-
bour Rd., Wan Chai* ☎ *2905–1020* ⊕ *www.divinopatio.com* ✛ *2:D2.*

$$$$ ✕ **Dynasty.** Dining on haute Cantonese cuisine at this stunning Chinese
CHINESE restaurant with panoramic views over Victoria Harbour is a memorable
☾ experience. The expert chefs here are famed for adapting family-style
recipes into works of art, and the service is impeccable yet friendly. The
menu changes with the seasons and leans heavily toward fresh seafood,
though the barbecued pork is some of the best in town. With its high
ceilings, old-world charm, and laid-back tempo, Dynasty is one of the
rare top-notch restaurants where you can comfortably linger over a
meal. $ *Average main: HK$320* ✉ *3rd fl., Renaissance Harbour View,
1 Harbour Rd., Wan Chai* ☎ *2802–8888* Ⓜ *Wan Chai* ✛ *2:C2.*

$ ✕ **Kam Fung.** The space is dingy, the tables are cramped, and the staff is
BAKERY brash—but the food makes it all worth it. Kam Fung has been around
for more than five decades, serving traditional Hong Kong café fare
such as crumbly crusted freshly baked egg tarts, and pineapple buns
wedged with a thick slab of butter. Wash everything down with their
famous velvety smooth milk tea after a meal that's cheap, quick, and
absolutely satisfying. $ *Average main: HK$25* ✉ *41 Spring Garden
Lane, Wan Chai* ☎ *2572–0526* ▬ *No credit cards* Ⓜ *Wan Chai* ✛ *2:C4.*

$ ✕ **La Crêperie.** This French-owned spot specializes in authentic, thin
FRENCH Breton crêpes filled with all sorts of sweet or savory fillings. Most of
the clientele are French, which is a good indication of the authentic-
ity of the food. Fillings for these made-fresh-to-order pancakes range
from traditional to fresh and experimental; La Complète buckwheat
galette is loaded with a classic combination of egg, ham, and deliciously gooey melted cheese, while L'Italienne has tomato, mozzarella
cheese, anchovies, and olives. The dessert crêpe selection is just as wide-
ranging. La Crêperie also carries a delicious apple cider—the traditional

Diners gather at the Pawn.

drink of choice for accompanying galettes in Brittany. [$] *Average main: HK$80* ✉ *1st fl., Kui Chi Mansion, 100 Queen's Rd. E, Wan Chai* ☎ *2529–9280* ⏲ *Closed Mon.* [M] *Wan Chai* [$] *Average main: HK$80* ✉ *69 Jervois St., Sheung Wan, Sheung Wan* ☎ *2679–4666* 🌐 *Sheung Wan* ⏲ *Closed Mon.* ✥ *2:B4.*

$$ CHINESE
🍴 **Liu Yuan Pavilion.** Often regarded as one of the best Shanghainese restaurants in town, Liu Yuan's cooking style stays loyal to tradition with a no-fuss mentality that has worked in their favor for years. Easy favorites include sweet strips of crunchy eel, panfried meat buns, and steamed xiao long bao dumplings plumped up with minced pork and broth. Diners also wax lyrical about the house special crispy rice soup and rice crackers smothered in salted egg yolk. Come hungry, since you'll need plenty of room to stomach all of these deliciously carby dishes. [$] *Average main: HK$120* ✉ *3rd fl., The Broadway, 54–62 Lockhart Rd., Wan Chai* ☎ *2804–2000* ✥ *2:B3.*

$$$$ FRENCH
🍴 **Mirror Restaurant.** This dark and intimate restaurant serves top-tier French cuisine crafted by seasoned head chef Jeremy Biasiol and his expert team. Dishes are presented as a prix-fixe multicourse meal that's largely influenced by daily market-fresh ingredients. The menu changes often but everything is solidly executed, whether it's classic roasted frog's legs or more inventive items like brown-crab jelly laced with gazpacho dressing. The restaurant does only one dinner seating per evening, so it's best to call a few weeks in advance to reserve. [$] *Average main: HK$498* ✉ *6th fl., Tiffan Tower, 197–199 Wan Chai Rd., Wan Chai* ☎ *2573–7288* 🌐 *www.themirror.hk* ✍ *Reservations essential* ⏲ *No lunch. Closed Sun.* ✥ *2:D3.*

$$$$ CHINESE 🍴 **One Harbour Road.** It's hard to say what's more impressive at the Grand Hyatt's Cantonese showpiece—the interior design (two terraced indoor levels, the sound of the lily pond's rushing water, and an incredible sense of space and motion), or the view over the harbor from the restaurant's floor-to-ceiling windows. Unlike many harborside establishments, though, you don't need a window seat to catch the view. And the Cantonese cuisine is traditional but excellent—for best results, order from among the rotating seasonal dishes and be sure to ask the sommelier for wine pairing recommendations. [$] *Average main: HK$320* ✉ *7th and 8th fl., Grand Hyatt Hong Kong, 1 Harbour Rd., Wan Chai* ☎ *2584–7722* 🌐 *www.hongkong.grand.hyatt.com* [M] *Wan Chai* ✥ *2:C2.*

$$ BRITISH 🍴 **The Pawn.** Inside a refurbished old heritage pawn shop, the Pawn serves high-end British gastro-pub fare in a truly stunning environment. The first floor "living room" bar and lounge is a great drinking spot, complete with an outdoor terrace and a wide array of beers, cocktails, and whiskeys; head upstairs, though, to the dining room to enjoy the full food potential of the restaurant. The signature fish-and-chips is stellar and is served with their homemade tartar sauce. After your meal, check out the third-floor open-air rooftop terrace and take in the breathtaking views of the busy Wan Chai district. [$] *Average main: HK$200* ✉ *62 Johnston St., Wan Chai* ☎ *2866–3444* 🌐 *www.thepawn.com.hk* [M] *Wan Chai* ✥ *2:C4.*

5

CAUSEWAY BAY

Causeway Bay is one of Hong Kong's busiest shopping districts and has some of the trendiest restaurants in town. It's popular with the younger crowd and is often compared with Tokyo's Shibuya district—and this is also where you'll find some of Hong Kong's best Japanese food, as well as many mid-price eateries. The area behind the giant SOGO department store has some great street snacking options. If you fancy a tall glass of milk tea dotted with black tapioca pearls, this is the place to go, though Causeway also has its fair share of high-end eateries, which are concentrated in the area surrounding Lee Gardens Two, home to many luxury fashion stores.

Some of the most exciting dining options in the area are the upstairs eateries. Hidden away from street view, these venues rely mainly on foodies in the know, but house some of the best eats in the neighborhood.

$ CAFÉ 🍴 **agnès b. café.** The agnès b. café is a great spot to rest your heels after a day of shopping, and enjoy a cup of tea and a slice of cake. Some of the cakes are marked with the brand's iconic "b." logo to reel in the fashionista-foodies. The cheesecake and the zesty lemon tart are excellent, and those looking for a light lunch can also order one of the salads or sandwiches. [$] *Average main: HK$40* ✉ *Shop 1–2A, 2–4 Kingston St., Causeway Bay* ☎ *2577–0370* 🌐 *www.agnesb-delices.com* ✥ *2:G2.*

$ JAPANESE 🍴 **Bang Bang Pan Pan.** The signature dish here is the do-it-yourself *okonomiyaki* (Japanese-style pancake), so you can basically make your own meal. Diners are presented with the basic batter and a choice of raw ingredients, ranging from pork belly, to squid, mushrooms, and kimchi. You mix together the desired ingredients and then place the batter onto a heated grill until cooked through. [$] *Average main: HK$60* ✉ *34 Leighton Rd., Causeway Bay* ☎ *2203–4009* ✥ *2:F3.*

$$ ✕**Bridges.** You may be familiar with mainstream Japanese sushi and
JAPANESE sashimi but Okinawan cooking is something completely different.
Dishes from the Ryukyu Islands carry Chinese and American influ-
ences, and you'll find plenty of *chanpuru* (stir-fry) dishes, as well as
obscure things such as salt and cookie ice cream. The islands are also
credited for their bountiful fresh produce; be sure to try the *umi budo*
"green caviar" sea kelp and the bitter gourd melon. Carnivores, don't
fret—Okinawa's Motobu Wagyu beef and Aguu pork are delicious,
well-marbled versions that work well in everything from grills to shabu
shabu. $ *Average main: HK$140* ⊠ *6th fl., Cubus, 1 Hoi Ping Rd.,
Causeway Bay* ☎ *3428–2131* ✢ *2:F3.*

$ ✕**Café Match Box.** The decor, staff uniforms, and—of course—the food
CHINESE all capture the retro vibe of the 1960s Hong Kong *cha chaan teng*
(local café). Cantonese pop songs from that era play over the sound
system while diners relish bowls of elbow macaroni served in soup
and topped with spam and eggs. Other staples include spaghetti served
in chicken broth with green peas. But the sweets here are what really
stand out. The egg tarts are rich and custardy, and the French toasts
are served with a giant slab of butter. Surely the best item in the
house, though, are the hotcakes topped with bananas, buttered wal-
nuts, and soft-serve ice cream. Credit cards are accepted only in the
evening with a minimum of HK$200. $ *Average main: HK$50* ⊠ *8
Cleveland St., Causeway Bay* ☎ *2868–0363* ⊕ *www.cafematchbox.
com.hk* Ⓜ *Causeway Bay* $ *Average main: HK$50* ⊠ *2 Sun Wui Rd.,
Causeway Bay, Causeway Bay* ☎ *2881–0616* ⊕ *www.cafematchbox.
com.hk* Ⓜ *Causeway Bay* ✢ *2:G3.*

$ ✕**C'est La B.** Indulge your sweet tooth with C'est La B's wide array of
BAKERY gorgeously whimsical cakes and desserts. The sugary creations at this
bakery-café are decidedly extravagant and come with playful, tongue-
in-cheek names such as Better Than Sex (chocolate fudge cake with
caramel crunch, salted caramel, and red sugar lips) and Heaven Can
Wait (chocolate pudding, triple chocolate cake, and dark chocolate
chips). Cakes are available in miniature portions or in larger, celebra-
tion sizes for takeaway orders. C'est La B operates a second branch at
Pacific Place, as well as a takeout-only bakery in Central called Ms B's
Cakery. $ *Average main: HK$50* ⊠ *110–114 Tung Lo Wan Rd., Tai
Hang, Causeway Bay* ☎ *2806–8168* ⊕ *www.msbscakery.hk* ☾ *Closed
Mon.* $ *Average main: HK$50* ⊠ *Shop 202, 2nd fl., Pacific Place, 88
Queensway, Admiralty, Central* ☎ *2536–0173* ⊕ *www.msbscakery.
hk* ✢ *2:H2.*

$ ✕**Chez Shibata.** Dessert fans should check out Chez Shibata just
JAPANESE across the street from the agnès b. café. The pâtisserie combines clas-
sic French recipes with Japanese ingredients and techniques, and the
results are all delicious. Definitely try the signature éclair filled with
caramel and topped with butter and sea salt. Yum! $ *Average main:
HK$42* ⊠ *9 Kingston St., Causeway Bay* ☎ *2886–8962* ⊕ *www.chez-
shibata.com.hk* ✢ *2:G2.*

$ ✕**Dim Sum.** This elegant jewel breaks with tradition and serves dim
CHINESE sum at night as well as during the day. The original menu goes beyond
common Cantonese morsels like *har gau* (steamed shrimp dumplings),

embracing dishes more popular in the north, including chili prawn dumplings, Beijing onion cakes, and steamed buns. Luxury dim sum items, such as abalone dumplings are particularly popular. Lunch reservations are not taken so there's always a long line, especially on weekends. Arrive early, or admire the antique telephones and old Chinese posters while you wait. [$] *Average main: HK$50* ✉ *63 Sing Woo Rd., Happy Valley, Causeway Bay* ☎ *2834–8893* [M] *Causeway Bay.*

$$$$ ITALIAN 🍴 **The Drawing Room.** Within the stylish JIA boutique hotel, the Drawing Room serves contemporary Italian fare in a slick, artfully decorated space. The menu is tweaked on a regular basis depending on the freshest ingredients and the kitchen team's creative culinary whims. Several popular signatures are almost always available though, such as the panfried quail and foie gras, and the inspired trio of Wagyu short rib, beef tenderloin, and ox tongue. Two different tasting menu options are offered every night, but the dishes are also available à la carte. This is a dining hot spot, so reservations are a definite must. [$] *Average main: HK$340* ✉ *1st fl., JIA Boutique Hotel, 1–5 Irving St., Causeway Bay* ☎ *2915–6628* 🌐 *www.thedrawingroom.com.hk* ✍ *Reservations essential* ⏲ *No lunch. Closed Sun.* [M] *Causeway Bay* ✥ *2:G3.*

5

$$ INTERNATIONAL 🍴 **Goldfinch Restaurant.** Travel back to the romantic 1960s as you dine at this retro restaurant. Film buffs might recognize this spot as the backdrop to renowned director Wong Kar-wai's most famous films (*In the Mood for Love, 2046*). Like the decor, the food here has remained largely unchanged since the restaurant's heyday, and you'll find local interpretations of Western dishes such as borscht or cream of mushroom soup and gravy-covered steaks served on sizzling iron plates. Don't come here if you're looking for an authentic steakhouse experience, though: this place is strictly for those who want to relive the nostalgic charm of Hong Kong's swinging era. [$] *Average main: HK$120* ✉ *13–15 Lan Fong Rd., Causeway Bay, Causeway Bay* ☎ *2577–7981* ✥ *2:F3.*

$$ CANTONESE 🍴 **Hotpot Instinct.** Hot pot cooking is immensely popular in Hong Kong, and places like Hotpot Instinct are packed even during the hot and humid summer months. The large menu offers thinly sliced beef, pork, seafood, and a range of house-made fish balls and meatballs, which diners then dip into a boiling vat of broth at their table. [$] *Average main: HK$120* ✉ *52 Tang Lung St., Causeway Bay* ☎ *2573–2844* 🌐 *www.hotpotinstinct.com* ⏲ *No lunch.* ✥ *2:F3.*

$$ JAPANESE 🍴 **Iroha.** Experts in the art of *yakiniku* (grilled meats), Iroha stocks top-quality ingredients for its tabletop grills. Many go for the premium Wagyu beef selection, but seafood choices are also worth trying. The thick-sliced beef tongue is legendary. [$] *Average main: HK$180* ✉ *2nd fl., Jardine Centre, 50 Jardine's Bazaar, Causeway Bay* ☎ *2882–9877* 🌐 *www.iroha.com.hk* ✥ *2:G2.*

$ CHINESE Fodor's Choice ★ 🍴 **Man Sing.** Hong Kong's top foodies swear by the steamed meat cake from this cheap and cheerful roadside eatery—the trademark dish consists of a towering mound of minced fatty pork that's been drizzled in soy sauce and topped with a golden orb of salted egg yolk. But the meat cake is not the only thing that makes this place a worthwhile visit; also try the spicy "saliva" chicken (a classic Sichuan poultry dish named after its complex, mouthwatering flavors), spice-tossed lamb rack, and

Hot pot cooking in action

silken steamed egg with fresh crab. Come early though because it gets extremely packed at peak mealtimes. [$] *Average main: HK$60* ✉ *16 Wun Sha St., Tai Hang, Causeway Bay* ☎ *2576–7272* 💳 *No credit cards* 🕒 *No lunch.* [M] *Tin Hau* ⊕ *2:H3.*

$$$ THAI 🍴 **Mango Tree.** Mango Tree has been receiving rave reviews since their first property opened in Bangkok close to a decade ago. The Hong Kong branch lives up to its mother brand's reputation and boasts a winning formula of designer decor, friendly service, and tasty, refined takes on authentic Thai dishes. Diners can start with an order of grilled pork neck before moving on to one of the spicy and sweet, herb-laden soups or salads. We also recommend the duck and lamb curries, as well as a stir-fried noodle dish to anchor the meal. [$] *Average main: HK$224* ✉ *5th fl., Cubus, 1 Hoi Ping Rd., Causeway Bay* ☎ *2577–0828* 🌐 *www.mangotree.com.hk* ⊕ *2:F3.*

$ JAPANESE 🍴 **Nan Tei.** This izakaya is always buzzing, and the aproned waitstaff serves up plate upon plate of *yakitori* and *kushiyaki* (grilled skewered items) in a raucously jovial atmosphere. Opt for a seat at the bar for a full view of the busy chefs working the grill. The skewered ox tongue is exceptional—succulent, soft, and flavored with just the right pinch of salt. Kushiyaki staples, such as chicken wings and shiitake mushrooms are also excellent. Nightly specials are displayed on a chalkboard. And in true izakaya fashion, Nan Tei offers a well-ranging sake list to accompany the bite-sized noshes. This is a great place for a casual Japanese meal with good food and a couple of drinks. [$] *Average main: HK$95* ✉ *2nd fl., Bigfoot Centre, 38 Yiu Wa St., Causeway Bay* ☎ *3118–2501* 🕒 *No lunch.* [M] *Causeway Bay* ⊕ *2:F3.*

$$$ JAPANESE 🍴 **Sushi Hiro.** *Uni* (sea urchin), *shirako* (blowfish sperm), *o-toro* (the fattiest of fatty tuna) . . . If these words can make you drool, then you should make a beeline for Sushi Hiro, hidden in an office building but quite possibly the best place for raw fish in Hong Kong. The minimalist interior stays faithful to Japanese style, unlike at some more opulent Hong Kong restaurants. But what really draws in the Japanese crowd here is the freshness of the fish, which you can watch being filleted in front of you at the sushi bar. Dinner may get pricey, but the restaurant also does some fantastic lunch deals. [$] *Average main: HK$290* ✉ *10th fl., Henry House, 42 Yun Ping Rd., Causeway Bay* ☎ *2882–8752* 🌐 *www.sushihiro.com.hk* [M] *Causeway Bay* ✥ *2:G3.*

$$ JAPANESE 🍴 **Tonkichi Tonkatsu Seafood.** This restaurant specializes in *tonkatsu*—pork cutlets that are panko-crusted and deep-fried. When it's done right, as here, the pork is crispy on the outside but remains tender and juicy on the inside. The fillet is sliced up and served with an appetizing, tangy tonkatsu sauce, and goes perfectly with a bowl of steamed rice. [$] *Average main: HK$160* ✉ *Shop 412, 4th fl., World Trade Centre, 280 Gloucester Rd., Causeway Bay* ☎ *2577–6617* ✥ *2:F2.*

5

$$ CHINESE 🍴 **Wu Kong.** This chain restaurant serves good Shanghainese fare at reasonable prices. Pigeon in wine sauce is an excellent appetizer, and the honey ham with crispy bean curd skin wrapped in soft bread is delicious and authentic. Be sure to try the trademark tofu dumpling—a unique dish that has mixed greens enveloped in thin sheets of silken bean curd. This requires advanced ordering but is worth the extra effort. We also recommend the Shanghai-style donut on the dessert menu: it's a deep-fried sphere of whipped and fluffy egg whites stuffed with red bean and bananas. The set lunch, which includes an appetizer, main dish, dim sum of your choice, and dessert, is a great value. [$] *Average main: HK$130* ✉ *17th fl., Lee Theatre Plaza, 99 Percival St., Causeway Bay* ☎ *2506–1018* 🌐 *www.wukong.com.hk* [M] *Causeway Bay* ✥ *2:F3.*

$$$ JAPANESE 🍴 **Xenri D'zen.** A hidden gem in this always-bustling neighborhood, Xenri D'zen follows a strict philosophy of seasonal eating that's inspired by Japan's traditional *kaiseki* formal dining, albeit interpreted in a modern manner. [$] *Average main: HK$280* ✉ *3rd fl., Jardine Centre, 50 Jardine's Bazaar, Causeway Bay* ☎ *3523–1955* ✥ *2:F3.*

EASTERN

$ ECLECTIC 🍴 **Chaiwanese.** Despite being hidden away in an industrial warehouse building, this café still draws in the city's artsy, creative types with its relaxed atmosphere and simply prepared breakfast and lunch items. Sandwiches are the big sell here, and you'll find playful creations such as Mumbai curry chicken on rye bread and an Asian-inspired hotdog served on a cottony white roll with Korean pickle mayo and caramelized onions. The baristas brew excellent coffee so enjoy a cup with a slice of their homebaked cakes. Aside from doing food, Chaiwanese doubles as a makeshift art space and hosts exhibits on a semi-regular basis. [$] *Average main: HK$48* ✉ *Unit 1307, 13th fl., Phase 1 Chai Wan Industrial City, 60 Wing Tai Rd., Chai Wan, Eastern* ☎ *3698–0935* 🌐 *www.chaiwanese.com* 💳 *No credit cards* ⏲ *No dinner. Closed Sun.* ✥ *2:H3.*

CLOSE UP

Shark's Fin Soup

It makes sense that soup made from a shark's fin—said to be an aphrodisiac—costs so much. Only the promise of increased virility would lead someone to pay HK$1,000 or more for a bowl of the stuff. It actually consists of cartilage from the great beast's pectal, dorsal, and lower tail fins that has been skinned, dried, and reconstituted in a rich stock form. This cartilage has almost no taste on its own, and is virtually indistinguishable from *tun fun* (cellophane) noodles that are used to create "mock shark's-fin soup."

Selling sharks' fins is a big business, and Hong Kong is said to be responsible for 50% of the global trade. The soup is a fixture at banquets, weddings, and state dinners here. Love potion, elixir, vitality booster, or not, at the very least the dish is high in protein. Recently, however, conservation groups have pointed out that it's also high in mercury. But of even greater concern is the practice of "finning." Since shark meat as a whole isn't valuable, fishermen often clip the fins and dump the rest of the animal back into the sea.

So, is eating shark's-fin soup a not-to-be-missed Hong Kong experience or a morally reprehensible act? Well, we don't need to take sides in the debate to warn you away from it. Let us repeat: the shark's-fin cartilage *has no taste*. This makes it—and bird's-nest soup, that other tasteless Cantonese delicacy—one of the biggest wastes of money in the culinary universe.

$$ SPANISH

🍴 **Tapeo.** This is the second outpost of an über-popular tapas bar (the original one is in SoHo). The Eastern District branch is bigger than the original, and has a fabulous harborside location, which adds to the chill, laid-back vibe. Authentic Spanish tapas, including ham croquettes and sautéed mushrooms with sherry, are perfect for sharing over glasses of wine. The crispy pork belly served with quince aioli is delicious, and hearty paellas have been added to the original menu. [$] *Average main: HK$80* ✉ *Shop GA01–03, 55 Tai Hong St., Sai Wan Ho, Eastern* ☎ *2513–0199* 🌐 *www.conceptcreations.hk* [M] *Sai Wan Ho* ✣ *2:H3.*

$ CHINESE Fodor's Choice ★

🍴 **Tung Po.** Arguably Hong Kong's most famous—if not most perpetually packed—indoor *dai pai dong*, Tung Po has communal tables large enough to fit 18 guests and the restaurant's walls are scribbled with their ever-growing list of specials. The food is Hong Kong cuisine with fusion innovations. Try the spaghetti with cuttlefish, which is flavored with aromatic jet-black fresh squid ink. The seafood dishes and stir-fries are all satisfying, but it's really the atmosphere that makes Tung Po a must-visit. Owner Robby Cheung is one of the most delightful characters in the Hong Kong dining biz. Later in the evening, he'll blast the latest pop songs from the sound system. And if you're lucky, you might just catch him in one of his moonwalking moods. [$] *Average main: HK$70* ✉ *2nd fl., Java Road Cooked Food Centre, 99 Java Rd., North Point, Eastern* ☎ *2880–9399* 💳 *No credit cards* 🕒 *No lunch.* [M] *North Point* ✣ *2:H3.*

SOUTHSIDE

The south side of Hong Kong Island is a string of beaches, rocky coves, and luxury developments; the Repulse Bay complex has some good restaurants, most of which boast alfresco seating so diners can take full advantage of the sea breeze. Stanley Village has a much slower pace of life than the one you see in the city. After exploring the market, historic sights, and beaches, have a leisurely meal at one of the top-notch restaurants scattered around, some of which have harbor views. Also on Southside, Shek O is a tiny seaside village with a few decent open-air restaurants.

$$$
SEAFOOD
✕ **Aberdeen Fish Market Canteen.** If you have a Cantonese-speaking friend, your lunch here will be easier to navigate, but trust us, it's worth the effort. First off, the canteen is housed within the Aberdeen Fish Market, which is a bit of a trek if you're not familiar with the area. Secondly, there's no set menu; you'll have to set a budget with the boss and he'll design your multicourse lunch based on the day's freshest catch. Expect anything from blanched shrimp served with soy sauce to abalone with chili and salt. It's a bit of a hassle and it's not exactly cheap for lunch but if you like seafood, this place is about as good as it gets. $ *Average main: HK$300* ✉ *102 Shek Pai Wan Rd., Aberdeen, Southside* ☎ *2552–7555* ⌕ *Reservations essential* ▭ *No credit cards* ⊘ *No dinner.* ✛ *2:B5.*

$$
INTERNATIONAL
✕ **The Boathouse.** In a gorgeous, three-story building, the cozy Boathouse has a lovely view of the seafront, making it the perfect spot to hang out with friends and family. The menu has a heavy focus on seafood specials, and the bucket of seafood (steamed mussels, prawns, clams, or a combination), served with nicely toasted garlic bread, goes down well with a glass of chilled white wine. Sandwiches and pastas are also good bets for casual dining. $ *Average main: HK$248* ✉ *86–88 Stanley Main St., Stanley, Southside* ☎ *2813–4467* ⊕ *www.cafedecogroup.com* ✛ *2:E6.*

$$$
EUROPEAN
✕ **Lucy's.** Hidden inside the famous Stanley Market, this warm, intimate eatery is rarely uncovered by tourists. You may feel like you've walked into someone's house when you enter the dining room, but Lucy's is a professionally run restaurant offering excellent, home-cooked food. The daily specials are always a good bet, and often include risottos and grilled or roasted meat. Desserts, especially the pecan pudding, are not to be missed. More upscale than most of the beachside restaurants in Stanley, and with lots more character, Lucy's is a perfect end to a relaxed day browsing in the market, and easily your best bet in Stanley. $ *Average main: HK$250* ✉ *64 Stanley Main St., Stanley, Southside* ☎ *2813–9055* ✛ *2:E6.*

$
ASIAN
✕ **Shek O Chinese & Thai Seafood Restaurant.** The seaside village of Shek O, past Stanley, is worth a trip for the large sandy beach and fresh local seafood, and this casual Asian restaurant is an all-time favorite for the quality and variety of food. Come here for simple seaside dining at its best—the menu is extensive, and everything's good and fresh—but prepare for plastic tables and toilets that are best approached with caution. This is a great spot for relaxing and dining with friends or family, at very reasonable prices. $ *Average main: HK$90* ✉ *main intersection, next to bus stop, 303 Shek O Village, Shek O, Southside* ☎ *2809–4426, 2809–2202* ✛ *2:F5.*

$$$
ECLECTIC
☺

✕ **Top Deck.** For a long time the Jumbo Floating Restaurant and Dragon Court were the only places to eat at Aberdeen's famed Jumbo Kingdom, but now there's Top Deck, a classier, less kitschy—though equally pricey—alfresco option on the roof deck of the big boat, beneath a three-story pagoda. It has a vastly better views (and breezes) than the indoor restaurants beneath so if the weather permits, you should sit outdoors. The menu is somewhat haphazard (Thai, Japanese, Indian, Italian, steak) but generally good. The raw bar is the best option if you like seafood. The weekend brunch is also a great way to relax on a lazy Sunday afternoon. $ *Average main: HK$200* ⊠ *Shum Wan Pier Drive, Wong Chuk Hang, Aberdeen, Southside* ☎ *2552–3331* ⊕ *www. cafedecogroup.com* ⊗ *Closed Mon.* ✛ *2:B5.*

$$$$
EUROPEAN

✕ **The Verandah.** You will not forget an evening at the Verandah. From the well-spaced, candlelit tables overlooking the bay to the menu of delicious classics (French onion soup, baked milk-fed veal, slow-cooked duck breast) and excellent, unobtrusive service, this is an unabashedly colonial experience that delivers with finesse at every turn. A live pianist sets the scene for romance, while slow-moving ceiling fans add to that hazy feeling that time is standing still. The food doesn't disappoint, and the wine list is more reasonably priced than you might expect. Note that sleeveless shirts and shorts aren't allowed for men during dinner. $ *Average main: HK$330* ⊠ *1st fl., The Repulse Bay, 109 Repulse Bay Rd., Repulse Bay, Southside* ☎ *2292–2822* ⊕ *www.therepulsebay.com* ⊗ *Closed Mon and Tue.* ✛ *2:D5.*

LANTAU ISLAND

You'll wind up on Lantau Island if you're visiting Disneyland Hong Kong. There are several restaurants within the Disneyland park itself, none of them distinguished, but good if you're traveling with children. The best restaurants are in the hotels. You can reach Lantau by ferry or by one of the many airport-bound buses. But the easiest way to reach the island is by MTR. The Tung Chung line connects from Central and transfers straight to the Disneyland Resort.

$$$
CHINESE
☺

✕ **Crystal Lotus.** The first thing you'll notice here is the most Disney-ish touch: a computer-animated koi pond, where electronic fish dart out of the way as you walk by. Once inside the crystal-studded space, your focus will turn to the food, and the pan-Chinese menu has dishes like barbecue fillets of eel glazed with Osmanthus honey, seafood fried rice, and double-boiled pear topped with mandarin peel. Kids will get a kick out of the "character dim sum" such as barbecue pork buns shaped like the three little pigs, and seafood pancakes bearing the likeness of Mickey Mouse—though these are available only during weekends and public holidays. If you wind up in Disneyland, this is by far the best way to dine (unless the kids demand a character meal at the Enchanted Garden in the hotel's lower level). $ *Average main: HK$240* ⊠ *Lobby fl., Hong Kong Disneyland Hotel, Lantau Island* ☎ *3510–6000* ⊕ *park. hongkongdisneyland.com* Ⓜ *Disneyland Resort* ✛ *3:C2.*

A food stall near the Ladies' Market in Kowloon.

$ **✕ Tai O Lookout.** If you've made your way out to Tai O, the Lookout is
CHINESE a great place to enjoy a leisurely afternoon tea or dinner. Formerly the
✿ Tai O Police Station, the bulding has been lovingly refurbished histori-
cal building and the restored colonial décor inside, includes wooden
furnishings donated by Pedder Building's former China Tee Club.
The menu doesn't provide a lot of choices but be sure to try the Tai
O-inspired items such as the fried rice and pork chop bun. **$** *Average
main: HK$60* ✉ *2nd fl., Tai O Heritage Hotel, Shek Tsai Po St, Tai O,
Lantau Island* ☎ *2985–8383* ⊕ *www.taioheritagehotel.com* ✛ *3:A2.*

KOWLOON PENINSULA

Parts of Kowloon are among the most densely populated areas on the
planet and support a corresponding abundance of restaurants. Many
hotels, planted here for the view of Hong Kong Island (spectacular at
night), also have excellent restaurants, though they're uniformly expensive. Some of the best food in Kowloon is served in backstreet eateries,
where immigrants from Vietnam, Thailand, and elsewhere in Asia keep
their native cooking skills sharp.

TSIM SHA TSUI

Tsim Sha Tsui is a foodie's paradise. The high density of hotels here—
from the legendary Peninsula Hotel to the chic and modern Mira
Hotel—means that there is no shortage of luxury dining options.
This district also has several large shopping malls, all filled with restaurants, some better than others. The area is also known for its

authentic Korean and Indian cuisine. For the best local eats though, head to neighboring Yau Ma Tei, especially the Jordan Road area, and to Mong Kok. The eateries here tend to be cramped and noisy, but it's worth exploring for those who want to immerse themselves in the city's local culture.

$$$
ECLECTIC

✕**Aqua.** This trendy restaurant and bar is in the penthouse of the One Peking Road building, and you might hear it referred to by many different names (Aqua Tokyo, Aqua Roma, Aqua Spirit). The menu brings together the East and the West—the Japanese kitchen plates up fresh sashimi, tempura, and innovative sushi and maki rolls, while the restaurant's Italian side offers risottos and pastas. The Japanese offerings usually fare better than the Italian ones, but the thing really worth going to Aqua for is the superb view of the Hong Kong skyline. You might want to just stop in for a drink—the bar stays open until 2 am. $ *Average main: HK$270* ✉ *29th and 30th fl., 1 Peking Rd., Tsim Sha Tsui* ☎ *3427–2288* ⊕ *www.aqua.com.hk* Ⓜ *Tsim Sha Tsui* ✛ *3:D6.*

$$
JAPANESE

✕**Chuan Alfresco Bar & Restaurant.** Come here for two things: the spacious outdoor terrace and the tasty barbecued skewers. The owners have ample grilling street cred, having first opened a Sichuan-style kushiyaki store that became a smash success with the foodie crowd. The menu here focuses on premium ingredients such as fresh seafood and marbled meats. We recommend the grilled razorclams and scallops topped with minced garlic and scallions. Deep-fried chicken cartilage and onsen eggs served in crispy bean curd sheets are also delicious. All dishes here are designed to be alcohol-friendly so remember to order one of the house cocktails from the bar. $ *Average main: HK$110* ✉ *5th fl., The Lamma Tower, 12–12A Hau Fook St., Tsim Sha Tsui, Kowloon* ☎ *2311–0123* ⊗ *No lunch. Closed Sun.* ✛ *3:F4.*

$$
TAIWANESE

✕**Din Tai Fung.** Originally from Taiwan, this global restaurant chain is most famous for their expertly made dumplings. And they're serious about their craft—each dumpling is made from a specified amount of dough and kneaded to a uniform thinness to ensure maximum quality control. The signature steamed xiao long bao dumplings arrive piping hot at the table, filled with delectable fatty pork and slurpfuls of flavorful broth. Anyone with a sweet tooth should try the taro-paste dumpling. The excellent food is paired with VIP treatment from the friendly staff, making Din Tai Fung completely worthy of its immense popularity. $ *Average main: HK$110* ✉ *Shop 130, 3rd fl., Silvercord, 30 Canton Rd., Tsim Sha Tsui* ☎ *2730–6928* ⊕ *www.dintaifung.com. hk* Ⓜ *Tsim Sha Tsui* ✛ *3:E5.*

$$$
CHINESE

Fodor's Choice
★

✕**Dong Lai Shun.** This Northern Chinese restaurant is known for its mutton hot pot, but it's the oxtail in black vinegar sauce that will really win you over. The generous pot arrives with tender meat and bits of cartilage immersed in a sweet and tangy sauce that's close to addictive. Be sure to finish the carrots and potatoes sitting at the bottom of the pot. Dong Lai Shun also offers a host of other great dishes, including traditional Peking duck and tea-leaf-smoked eggs boasting creamy, yolky centers. $ *Average main: HK$200* ✉ *2nd fl., The Royal Garden, 69 Mody Rd., Tsim Sha Tsui* ☎ *2733–2020* ⊕ *www.rghk.com.hk* ✛ *3:G5.*

$$$ JAPANESE 🍴 **Farm Kitchen Vegi.** This Japanese-owned restaurant offers all-you-can-eat indulgence with healthy food as the main focus. At a fixed price and without having to visit a buffet table, guests can enjoy free-flow portions of any of the menu items, most of which are prepped with organic vegetables using low-fat and low-grease cooking methods. Tuna, tofu, and avocado salad; roasted sea urchin risotto; and deep-fried cream croquette plumped up with crab and soybeans are just a few of things that are worth gorging on. The restaurant also does a selection of sushi and sashimi and hearty meat dishes such as Japanese-style hamburger steak. Dinner is just under HK$300 per adult, which is extremely reasonable for the quality (and health benefits) of the food you're getting. [$] *Average main: HK$298* ✉ *2nd fl., The Cameron, 33 Cameron Rd., Tsim Sha Tsui* ☎ *2721–1800* 🌐 *www.vegihongkong.com* ✣ *3:F4.*

$$$$ ECLECTIC 🍴 **Felix.** It's not for the faint of stomach, this Philippe Starck–designed, preposterously fashionable scene atop the Peninsula hotel, where the floor-to-ceiling walls have breathtaking views of Hong Kong. The dinner menu is artistic, and while rooted in French cooking, includes bright Asian touches as demonstrated by items such as the citrus-and-yuzu-pepper-crusted Boston lobster with tomato-veal sauce. The food here is generally good, but expect it to be quite pricey. Many people come just for cocktails—or to try out the most celebrated pissoir in Asia, whose views across Tsim Sha Tsui are superior to those in the restaurant itself. Note that sleeveless shirts and shorts are not allowed for men. [$] *Average main: HK$480* ✉ *28th fl., The Peninsula Hong Kong, 19–21 Salisbury Rd., Tsim Sha Tsui* ☎ *2315–3188* 🌐 *www.hongkong.peninsula.com* ✍ *Reservations essential* ⏲ *No lunch.* [M] *Tsim Sha Tsui* ✣ *3:E6.*

$$$ SCANDINAVIAN 🍴 **FINDS.** The name stands for Finland, Iceland, Norway, Denmark, and Sweden, and these Nordic countries are where the restaurant draws its inspiration from. Finnish chef Jaakko Sorsa explores the flavors of his home country with dishes such as cold-smoked salmon and venison tenderloin filled with porcini mushrooms. The menu expands from there to cover other parts of Scandinavia; be sure to try the Norwegian cod fish cakes and the Daim parfait—a crunchy, sticky, layered dessert based on a popular Swedish chocolate bar. Another reason to love FINDS? The restaurant is a firm supporter of eco-conscious eating, and you'll find seafood specials on the menu that have been sustainably sourced. [$] *Average main: HK$283* ✉ *1st fl., The Luxe Manor, 39 Kimberley Rd., Tsim Sha Tsui* ☎ *2522–9318* 🌐 *www.finds.com.hk* ✣ *3:F4.*

$$ INDIAN 🍴 **Gaylord.** Opened in the early 1970s, this was one of the first Indian restaurants on the Hong Kong dining scene, and the atmosphere is still intimate and fun, especially with the live musical performances. The food is packed with authentic spices and there's an extensive menu for vegetarians. The chowpatty chaat is a winning combination of potatoes, chickpeas, and crisp wafers in a spicy dressing, and the chicken tikka masala here is almost legendary. Lamb dishes are also done well, especially those in fragrant curry sauce, perfect for scooping up with bits of naan bread, or for spooning over plates of fragrant basmati rice. The restaurant also offers several set and buffet lunch and dinner menus at excellent value. [$] *Average main: HK$120* ✉ *1st fl., Ashley Centre, 23–25 Ashley Rd., Tsim Sha Tsui* ☎ *2376–1001* 🌐 *www.chiram.com.hk* [M] *Tsim Sha Tsui* ✣ *3:E5.*

The Dim Sum Experience

Dim sum restaurants have always been associated with noise, so don't be dissuaded by the boisterous throngs of locals gathered around large round tables. At one time big metal carts filled with bamboo baskets were pushed around the restaurant by ladies who would shout out the names of the dishes and stamp a mark onto a table's check when it ordered a basket of this or that. This is still the typical dim sum experience outside of China, but in Hong Kong most restaurants require you to order off a form, creating a more sedate and efficient dining experience. Thankfully, many places offer English-translated order forms or menus, although you should ask your waiter about daily specials that might not appear in translation, as those are often some of the most exciting dim sum options. And never forget that most basic principle of Hong Kong ordering: simply point to something you see at a nearby table.

Although dim sum comes in small portions, it's still intended for sharing between three or four people. When all is said and done, a group can expect to try about 10 or 12 dishes, but don't order more than one of any single item. Most dim sum restaurants prepare between 15 and 100 varieties of the more than 2,000 kinds of dim sum in the Cantonese repertoire, daily. These can be dumplings, buns, crepes, cakes, pastries, or rice; they can be filled with beef, shrimp, pork, chicken, bean paste, or vegetables; and they can be bamboo-steamed, panfried, baked, or deep-fried. More esoteric offerings vary vastly from place to place. Abandon any squeamish tendencies and try at least one or two unusual plates, like duck web (foot) in abalone sauce, tripe, liver dumplings, or dried pork bellies.

You'll be able to find dim sum from before dawn to around 5 or 6 pm, but it's most popular for breakfast (from about 7:30 to 10 am) and lunch (from about 11:30 am to 2:30 pm). Dim sum is served everywhere from local teahouses to high-concept restaurants, but it's often best at casually elegant, blandly decorated midrange spots that cater to Chinese families.

The following is a guide to some of our favorite common dim sum items, but don't let it narrow your mind. It's almost impossible to find a bite of dim sum that's anything less than delicious, and the more unique house specialties can often be the best.

BUNS
■ **Cha siu so:** baked barbecued pork pastry buns; they're less common than the steamed cha siu bao, but arguably even better.

■ **Cha siu bao:** steamed barbecued pork buns are an absolute must. With the combination of soft and chewy textures and sweet and salty tastes, you might forget to remove the paper underneath before eating.

DUMPLINGS
■ **Har gau:** steamed dumplings with a light translucent wrap that conceals shrimp and bamboo shoots.

■ **Siu mai:** steamed pork dumplings are the most common dumplings, and you'll find them everywhere, easily recognizable by their bright yellow wrappers; some are stuffed with shrimp.

MEATS

■ **Ngau yuk yuan:** steamed beef balls, like meatballs, placed on top of thin bean-curd skins; not the most flavorful option, but a good one for kids or picky eaters.

■ **Pie gwat:** bite-size pieces of succulent pork spare ribs in a black-bean and chili-pepper sauce.

RICE CREATIONS

■ **Ha cheong fun:** shrimp-filled rice rolls, whose dough is made in a rice-noodle style; the thick, flat rice rolls are drowned in soy sauce. Other versions include ngau yuk cheong fun (beef filled) and cha siu cheong fun (barbecued pork filled; if available, these are not to be missed).

■ **Ja leung:** similar to cheong fun but filled with a crunchy, deep-fried pastry. The rice-noodle dough is sometimes dotted with chopped scallions. These are also served with soy sauce but should also be dunked in sweet sauce and peanut paste.

■ **Ho yip fan:** delicious sticky rice, which is usually cooked with chopped Chinese mushrooms, Chinese preserved sausage, and dried shrimp, and wrapped and steamed in a lotus leaf to keep it moist (don't eat the leaf).

DON'T BE AFRAID OF . . .

■ **Woo tao go:** a glutinous panfried taro cake, sweet enough for dessert but eaten as a savory dish, with delicate undertones that come from preserved Chinese sausage, preserved pork belly, and dried shrimp. Another version of this is *lau bak go*, which is made with turnip instead of taro.

■ **Foong jow:** marinated chicken feet, whose smooth, soft texture is unlike any other. Once you get past the idea that you're sucking the cartilage off a foot, the sensation is wonderful.

■ **Gam cheen to:** cow's stomach served with chunks of daikon and doused in an addictive black-bean sauce with chili.

SWEETS

■ **Dan taht:** tarts with a custard filling, generally served for dessert.

■ **Mong gwor bo deen:** mango pudding that has a consistently glassy texture. The pudding itself is not too sweet and needs to be eaten with condensed milk.

■ **Ma lai go:** This soft and spongy steamed cake is served warm and is popular for its eggy, custardy aroma.

5

Aqua's expansive windows allow for breathtaking views of the Hong Kong skyline.

$$ Go Koong. Go Koong is one of the best Korean restaurants in town. The menu covers extensive ground, from raw meats and seafood that are cooked sizzling on the tabletop grill, to kimchi stews and thick pancakes studded with shrimp, squid, and scallions. The complimentary *banchans* (Korean appetizers) are a feast in themselves, with over ten different items available every day. Order the smoked duck-breast salad to start before moving on to more substantial fare such as the tender beef ribs steamed in whole pumpkin. If you still have room at the end of the meal, remember to try the *patbingsoo*—a giant bowl of crunchy shaved ice laced with sweetened red beans and fresh fruit. $ *Average main: HK$200 ⊠ Shop 202, 2nd fl., Toyomall, 94 Granville Rd., Tsim Sha Tsui* ☎ *2311-0901* Ⓜ *Tsim Sha Tsui* ✛ *3:G4.*

KOREAN

$$ Hoi King Heen. If you're looking for stellar Cantonese cuisine, this is the place for you. Chef Leung Fai-hung and his team plate up a range of modern classics using the freshest ingredients and influenced by their reverence for natural, umami flavors. There are excellent—and expensive—dishes on the menu such as double-boiled bird's nest and braised abalone, but the humbler dishes like braised short ribs with papaya and Hakka-style pork and peanut-filled dumplings really steal the show. Hoi King Heen is a great dinner destination, and the lunchtime dim sum menu is also worth checking out, too. $ *Average main: HK$180* ⊠ *B2nd fl., InterContinental Grand Stanford, 70 Mody Rd., Tsim Sha Tsui* ☎ *2731-2883* ✛ *3:G4.*

CHINESE

$$$ Hutong. It's not hard to see why Hutong is one of the hottest tables in Hong Kong: it has some of the most imaginative food in town, yet it's completely Chinese. Meanwhile, its spot at the top of the dramatic One Peking Road Tower overlooks the entire festival of lights that is

CHINESE

the Hong Kong island skyline. Best among the sensational selection of northern Chinese creations are crispy, deboned lamb ribs, whose crackling skin conceals a deep, tender gaminess. More subtle dishes include the abalone carpaccio in spring onion oil, and delicate scallops with fresh pomelo. Hutong is a good choice for a memorable meal in Hong Kong. Make sure to reserve well in advance. $ *Average main: HK$354* ✉ *28th fl., 1 Peking Rd., Tsim Sha Tsui* ☎ *3428–8342* ⊕ *www.aqua. com.hk* ⌨ *Reservations essential* Ⓜ *Tsim Sha Tsui* ✛ *3:D6.*

$$$$
JAPANESE
✗ **Inakaya.** On the 101st floor of the ICC building, Inakaya flaunts a jaw-dropping, bird's-eye view of the city below, but the interior of the restaurant is equally extravagant—the highlight is the specialized *roba-tayaki* (the Japanese equivalent to barbecue) room, which has a long counter decorated with baskets of fresh ingredients. Choose your prey and the chefs will grill your meat/fish/vegetables to order and serve it the traditional way, on long wooden paddles. Because robatayaki is served in bite-sized morsels, prices can add up but it's a fun and unique experience. If you don't want to splurge on grilled goods, Inakaya also offers other *washoku* (Japanese cuisines) such as sushi and traditional, multicourse *kaiseki* meals. $ *Average main: HK$500* ✉ *Shop A, 101st fl., ICC, 1 Austin Rd West, Tsim Sha Tsui* ☎ *2972–2666* ⊗ *No lunch Fri and Sat.* ✛ *3:D3.*

$$$
ITALIAN
✗ **Osteria.** Osteria flies under the radar but the restaurant does excellent, home-style Italian fare in a sophisticated yet relaxed and inviting environment. The traditional cuisine has won over many homesick Italian expats. The pizzas and pastas are done with respect to classic, authentic recipes without being tired; the recommended spaghetti *mancini* is a satisfyingly hearty dish loaded with fresh seafood and tomatoes. Starters also hold their own—the beef carpaccio is tender and flavorful, and the other favorite starter, Ligurian octopus salad, is a balance of delectable chewiness and delightful herby freshness from the basil pesto. $ *Average main: HK$290* ✉ *Holiday Inn Golden Mile, 50 Nathan Rd., Tsim Sha Tsui* ☎ *2315–1010* Ⓜ *Tsim Sha Tsui* ✛ *3:E5.*

$$$$
SEAFOOD
✗ **Oyster & Wine Bar.** Against the romantic backdrop of Hong Kong's twinkling harbor, this is the top spot in town for oyster lovers. More than 20 varieties are flown in daily and displayed around the horseshoe oyster bar, ready for shucking. Staff cheerfully explain the characteristics of the available mollusks and guide you to ones to suit your taste. Also on the menu is an excellent oyster chowder with a hint of dry Vermouth, as well as clams, mussels, crab, and pan-fried cod. The Dungeness crab cake is another standout, made with sweet and succulently delicious crabmeat. Wine aficionados are also spoiled for choice here, with the extensive wine selection that lines the walls. $ *Average main: HK$390* ✉ *18 fl., Sheraton Hong Kong Hotel & Towers, 20 Nathan Rd., Tsim Sha Tsui* ☎ *2369–1111* ⊗ *No lunch except Sun.* Ⓜ *Tsim Sha Tsui* ✛ *3:F6.*

$$$$
ITALIAN
✗ **Sabatini.** Run by the Sabatini family (who have restaurants in Rome, Japan, and Singapore), this small corner of Italy with sponge-painted walls and wooden furnishings has a cult following among those who crave authentic Italian cuisine. Linguine Sabatini, the house specialty, is prepared according to an original Roman recipe in a

fresh-tomato-and-garlic marinara sauce, served with an array of seafood. For dessert, try the famed, homemade tiramisu or the refreshing wild-berry pudding. [$] *Average main: HK$400* ✉ *3rd fl., The Royal Garden, 69 Mody Rd., Tsim Sha Tsui* ☎ *2733–2000* 🌐 *www.rghk.com.hk* ✍ *Reservations essential* [M] *Tsim Sha Tsui* ✥ *3:G5.*

$$ CHINESE 🍴 **Spring Deer.** The pastel blue and green interior and the waiters in bland uniforms make this Peking duck specialist look like something from 1950s Beijing. The crowd, too, is hilariously old-school, which only adds to the experience. You'll see locals with noodle dishes, stir-fried wok meat dishes, and so forth, but the Peking duck is the show-stopper—it might be the best in town. Even the peanuts for snacking, which are boiled to a delectable softness, go above and beyond the call of duty. This place is extremely popular, so it's best to book your table at least a week in advance. [$] *Average main: HK$160* ✉ *1st fl., 42 Mody Rd., Tsim Sha Tsui* ☎ *2366–4012, 2366–5839* ✍ *Reservations essential* [M] *Tsim Sha Tsui* ✥ *3:F5.*

$$$$ STEAKHOUSE 🍴 **The Steak House winebar + grill.** This restaurant with its lively, informal din, salad buffet, and gleaming harbor views serves the best steak in the city. You can choose from among 10 steak knives and a dozen mustards and rock salts—gimmicky, but fun—but the main event is of course the meat: Wagyu steaks from Japan and Australia are grain-fed for more than a year (400 days), and the results are shockingly tender, buttery, and flavorful. The restaurant also has its own dry-aged beef. Other delicious cuts are flown in from the United States; and all of it is lovingly seared on a charcoal grill. There isn't a jacket-and-tie policy but note that shorts are not allowed. [$] *Average main: HK$528* ✉ *Lower fl., InterContinental Hong Kong, 18 Salisbury Rd., Tsim Sha Tsui* ☎ *2313–2323* 🌐 *hongkong-ic.intercontinental.com* ✍ *Reservations essential* 🕓 *No lunch except Sun.* [M] *Tsim Sha Tsui* ✥ *3:F6.*

$$$$ EUROPEAN 🍴 **St. George.** Hullett House—the former marine police headquarters turned into a boutique hotel—was designed with maxed-out luxury in mind, so it's to be expected that its signature fine-dining restaurant would be a no-expenses-spared venture. The restaurant is decked out in colonial era–inspired duds, complete with chandeliers and comfy leather sofas. But while the decor pays homage to days gone by, the cuisine—designed by executive chef Philippe Orrico (who trained with Pierre Gagnaire)—is modern, creative, and totally inspired. Guests can look forward to things like crispy 63-degree eggs served with crabmeat velouté, sweet potato purée, and wild mushrooms. Two tasting menus are also available (four or eight courses), for those who want the full St. George experience. [$] *Average main: HK$350* ✉ *Hullett House, 1881 Heritage, 2A Canton Rd., Tsim Sha Tsui* ☎ *3988–0220* 🌐 *www.hulletthouse.com* ✍ *Reservations essential* 🕓 *Closed Sun.* [M] *Tsim Sha Tsui* ✥ *3:E6.*

$ ASIAN 🍴 **Sun Kee.** This little café might not be the easiest of places to locate, being tucked away in an old complex filled mainly with second-hand camera and wristwatch stores, but it has a cult following, with photos of local celebrity patrons adorning almost every inch of wall space. Most customers come for one thing—the instant noodles blanketed in a rich and creamy melted cheese sauce. These coiled noodles go best

A Spot of Tea

Legend has it that the first cup dates from 2737 BC, when *Camellia sinensis* leaves fell into water being boiled for Emperor Shenong. He loved the result, tea was born, and so were many traditions.

Historically, when a girl accepted a marriage proposal she drank tea, a gesture symbolizing fidelity (tea plants die if uprooted). Betrothal gifts were known as "tea gifts," engagements as "accepting tea," and marriages as "eating tea." Traditionally the bride and groom kneel before their parents, offering cups of tea in thanks.

Serving tea is a sign of respect. Young people proffer it to their parents or grandparents; subordinates do the same for their bosses. Pouring tea also signifies submission, so it's a way to say you're sorry. When you're served tea, show your thanks by tapping the table with your index and middle fingers.

Even modern medicine acknowledges that tea's powerful antioxidants reduce the risk of cancer and heart disease. It's also thought to be such a good source of fluoride that Mao Zedong eschewed toothpaste for a green-tea rinse.

TEA TYPES

Pu'er tea, which is known here as *Bo Lei*, is the beverage of choice at dim sum places. In fact, another way to say dim sum is *yum cha*, meaning "drink tea."

Afternoon tea is another local fixation—neighborhood joints with Formica tables, grumpy waiters, and often, menus written only Chinese. Most people go for *nai cha* made with evaporated milk. A really good cup is smooth, sweet, and hung with drops of fat. An even richer version, *cha chow*, is made with condensed milk. If *yuen yueng* (yin yang, half milk tea and half instant coffee) sounds a bit much, *ling-mun cha* (lemon tea) is also on hand. Don't forget to order peanut-buttered toast or *dan-taht* (custard tarts).

The bubble (or *boba*) tea craze may have died down a bit, but you'll still find plenty street stalls selling the popular Taiwanese drink. These cold brews contain pearly balls of tapioca or coconut jelly. There's also been a return to traditional teas with chains such as Chinese Urban Healing Tea, which serves healthy blends in MTR stations all over town.

FLAGSTAFF HOUSE MUSEUM OF TEA WARE

All that's good about British colonial architecture is exemplified in the simple white facade, wooden monsoon shutters, and colonnaded verandas of Flagstaff House Museum of Tea Ware. More than 600 pieces of delicate antique tea ware from the Tang (618–907) through the Qing (1644–1911) dynasties fill rooms that once housed the commander of the British forces.

The best place to put your tea theory into practice is the **LockCha Tea House** (☎ 2801–7177) in the K.S. Lo Gallery annex of Flagstaff House. It is half shop, half teahouse, so you can sample brews before you buy. ▥ TIP➔ The Hong Kong Tourist Board runs tea appreciation classes at LockCha Tea House—phone the shop to book a place. ✉ *Hong Kong Park, 10 Cotton Tree Dr., Central* ☎ *2801–7177* ⊕ *www.lockcha. com* ◷ *Wed.–Mon. 10–10* Ⓜ *Admiralty MTR, Exit C1.*

with tender slices of grilled pork neck meat on top of the sauce. It's not exactly healthy eating but definitely satisfying. [$] *Average main: HK$34* ✉ *Shop 13, ground fl., Champagne Court, 16–20 Kimberley Rd., Tsim Sha Tsui* ☎ *2722–4555* ▭ *No credit cards* [M] *Tsim Sha Tsui* ✣ *3:F4.*

$ ECLECTIC 🍴 **Tai Ping Koon.** This is one of the oldest restaurants in Hong Kong, and also one of the first places to serve "soy sauce" Hong Kong–styled western cuisine. The decor, staff, and menu seem to have remained unchanged since day one, adding to the nostalgic charm of the place. Steaks are served to dramatic effect on sizzling iron plates and brought to the table by waiters clad in waistcoats. Other menu highlights include the baked Portuguese chicken, the near-perfect stir-fried rice noodles with beef (a classic Hong Kong dish), chicken wings doused in "swiss sauce" (which has no real Swiss associations), and the enormous baked soufflé that takes 20 minutes to prepare and at least three people to devour. [$] *Average main: HK$90* ✉ *40 Granville Rd., Tsim Sha Tsui* ☎ *2721–3559* 🌐 *taipingkoon.com* [M] *Tsim Sha Tsui* ✣ *3:F4.*

$$$$ EUROPEAN 🍴 **Whisk.** At the Mira Hotel's flagship restaurant, seasonal ingredients are turned into creative European dishes designed to impress. Steamed Bretagne lobster is dressed with a blended cucumber and coriander-jalapeño sauce that lends brightness to the dish. There's also the famed crispy suckling pig—a layer of melt-in-the-mouth, fatty meat covered in a sheet of deliciously crispy skin—this is one pig worth trying. Be sure to save room for the flaky apple tart. For diners wanting to sample the best of Whisk's offerings, opt for the five-to-seven-course set dinner menus (HK$820–HK$1,280), which are inspired by the cooking traditions of various European countries. [$] *Average main: HK$410* ✉ *5th fl., The Mira Hotel, 118 Nathan Rd., Tsim Sha Tsui* ☎ *2315–5999* 🌐 *www.themirahotel.com* [M] *Tsim Sha Tsui* ✣ *3:E4.*

$$$$ CHINESE 🍴 **Yan Toh Heen.** This Cantonese restaurant in the InterContinental Hong Kong sets formal elegance against expansive harbor views, and the food is at the top of its class. Exquisite is hardly the word for the place settings, all handcrafted with green jade. Dim sum is done well and if you're looking for more extravagant dishes, there's a vast selection of seafood that includes fresh fish, red coral crab, cherrystone clam, and sea whelk. The menu also has a full vegetarian section, showcasing delicious and nutritious dishes created by Chef Lau Yiu Fai. Note that sleeveless shirts and shorts are not allowed on men. [$] *Average main: HK$600* ✉ *Lower fl., InterContinental Hong Kong, 18 Salisbury Rd., Tsim Sha Tsui* ☎ *2313–2323* 🌐 *hongkong-ic.intercontinental.com* ✍ *Reservations essential* [M] *Tsim Sha Tsui* ✣ *3:F6.*

$$ CHINESE 🍴 **Yunyan Sichuan.** This is one of Hong Kong's most popular Sichaun restaurants. Veteran chef Kenny Chan is generous with the chili spices in dishes such as his famed crispy chicken with red chilies and Sichuan peppercorns. The poached sliced Mandarin fish with crispy soybeans is another classic. For something with a little less heat but still equally delicious, go for the roasted duck, which is marinated in sweet honey and stuffed with bean sprouts, shallots, and sliced meats and then roasted to crispiness. [$] *Average main: HK$170* ✉ *Shop 4A, 4th fl., Miramar Shopping Centre, 132–134 Nathan Rd., Tsim Sha Tsui* ☎ *2375–0800* 🌐 *www.yunyan.hk* [M] *Tsim Sha Tsui* ✣ *3:E4.*

Moon cakes served at Yan Toh Heen

YAU MA TEI, MONG KOK, AND NORTHERN KOWLOON

Yau Ma Tei and Mong Kok have some of the best cheap eats in town, especially the area of Yau Ma Tei around Jordan Road, which is known as Jordan. Jordan has a large Nepalese population in this neighborhood, so look out for excellent authentic Nepalese and Indian food.

These areas may not seem like the most tourist-friendly of places (non-English menus, impatient waiters, etc.), you're more likely to score an interesting meal here than anywhere else.

YAU MA TEI

Yau Ma Tei's famed Temple Street is a good place to start. The street hides dai pai dongs and wallet-friendly noodle shops amid the many DVD shops and souvenir stores.

$ CHINESE 🍴 **Dimdim Sum Dimsum Specialty Store.** Hidden away near the old Jordan pier, this little sit-down restaurant has excellent dim sum without the insane queues that plague its more famous competitors. That's not to say that it doesn't get packed during mealtimes; thankfully, the venue stays open until 1 am, so you can sneak in for a late-night dinner when the crowds have dissipated. While they do all the classics, it's the new-fangled house creations that are really worth trying. We love the crispy shrimp rice-flour rolls, which are designed to be eaten with a drizzle of soy sauce. They also do pan-fried black pepper steak dumplings and golden pastries filled with a combination of apples and cha siu pork. [$] *Average main: HK$18* ✉ *23 Man Ying St., Jordan, Yau Ma Tei* ☎ *2771–7766* 💳 *No credit cards* ✥ *3:D2.*

$ CANTONESE 🍴 **Hing Kee Restaurant.** You can enjoy cheap and cheerful local specialties at this crowded, open-air-stall-style eatery. The kitchen does particularly well with wok-tossed stir-fries laced with pungent black-bean sauce or spicy chili salt. Hing Kee is also known for its claypot dishes, which are especially comforting during the colder winter months. [$] *Average main: HK$68* ✉ *15–19 Temple St., Yau Ma Tei* ☎ *2384–3647* ▭ *No credit cards* ⏲ *No lunch.* ✥ *3:E1.*

$ CHINESE 🍴 **Islam Food.** This halal restaurant may not be the prettiest restaurant you've ever seen, and you should expect to wait a while for a table (lines get extremely crazy during peak meal hours), but we promise that the pan-fried beef patties (translated as "veal goulash" on the menu) here are well worth the pilgrimage. The browned pastry packets arrive at the table piping hot and bursting with tender, minced beef. Good luck trying to stop at just one, but other excellent dishes include the delicious lamb brisket curry, the pan-fried mutton dumplings, and the hot and sour soup. [$] *Average main: HK$35* ✉ *1 Lung Kong Rd., Kowloon City* ☎ *2382–2822, 2382–8928* ▭ *No credit cards* [$] *Average main: HK$35* ✉ *33–35 Tak Ku Ling Rd., Kowloon City* ☎ *2382–1882* 🌐 *www.islamfood.com.hk* ✥ *3:H1.*

$$ CHINESE 🍴 **Ko Lau Wan Hotpot and Seafood Restaurant.** Anyone seeking an authentic hot-pot experience need look no farther than Ko Lau Wan. Locals flock here for the tender beef and seafood that you cook at your table in a piping-hot pot of broth (the soup selection is quite extensive, but the satay broth and the fish stock with crab are particularly tasty). The owner runs his own fish farm in the New Territories so there's no wonder the cuttlefish, shrimp balls, sea urchin, amberjack, and abalone are all so tantalizingly fresh. The adventurous should try the geoduck, a giant clam popular among Hong Kongers, which can be eaten raw with soy sauce and wasabi or slightly cooked in soup. [$] *Average main: HK$180* ✉ *1st fl., 21–23 Hillwood Rd., Jordan, Yau Ma Tei* ☎ *3520–3800* ⏲ *No lunch.* [M] *Jordan* ✥ *3:F3.*

$ VIETNAMESE 🍴 **Lo Chiu Vietnamese Restaurant.** The Spartan interior may not impress but pay no heed, because you're here for the hearty authentic Vietnamese food. Deep-fried shrimp paste on sugarcane is sweet and juicy and be sure to order the signature grilled king prawns. Take your time and try not to burn your tongue on the sizzling hot and wonderfully flavorsome lemongrass chicken wings. There is also a good variety of noodles and vermicelli served in soup or with fish sauce. A bottle of imported beer is just the thing to wash it all down. [$] *Average main: HK$80* ✉ *10–12 Hillwood Rd., Jordan, Yau Ma Tei* ☎ *2314–7966, 2314–7933* [M] *Jordan* ✥ *3:F3.*

$ NEPALESE 🍴 **Manakamana Restaurant.** For a dose of Indian and Nepalese food, head to Manakamana. The restaurant serves the essentials—like brightly colored curries with herbs and spices, and meat-filled steamed *momo* dumplings—complete with an awesome atmosphere, Nepalese music, and a decent selection of South Asian beers. [$] *Average main: HK$35* ✉ *165 Temple St., Jordan, Jordan* ☎ *2385–2070* ▭ *No credit cards* ✥ *3:E2.*

$ CAFÉ 🍴 **Mido Café.** This old-school *cha* chaan teng (local café) has a nostalgic charm: the decor hasn't changed much since the '60s and though prices have gone up with time, the food still draws in legions of loyal fans. Try the famous baked pork chop rice or enjoy a slice of crispy French toast with a cup of milk tea. $ *Average main: HK$36* ⊠ *63 Temple St., Yau Ma Tei* ☎ *2384–6402* ▬ *No credit cards* ✛ *3:E1*.

$ ✕ **Pâtisserie Tony Wong.** Opened by one of Hong Kong's best-known pastry chefs, this takeaway bakery offers a gorgeous collection of classic and original French-style gâteaux. The most famous creation here is the Rose—an elaborate layered cake decorated with edible chocolate petals. If you don't want to splurge on this signature creation (or if it sells out by the time you get there), consider some of the other equally tasty treats such as the green tea opera, raspberry napoleon, or chocolate truffle cake. $ *Average main: HK$42* ⊠ *74 Fuk Lo Tsun Rd., Kowloon City* ☎ *2382–6639* ⊕ *www.patisserietonywong.com* ✛ *3:H1*.

BAKERY

$ ✕ **Si Sun.** One of the pioneers of American fast-food-style dining in Hong Kong, Si Sun still looks and feels like an eatery from the swinging 60s. The plastic fixtures have stayed the same over the last few decades and the menu doesn't seem to have changed much either. Burgers are geared toward local tastes and freshly grilled beef patties are sandwiched simpley between two soft Garden brand buns with ketchup and mayo. Add cheese or a fried egg and your meal will still be less than 20 bucks. Si Sun also offers pork and fish fillet burgers, as well as a few rice and noodles dishes. $ *Average main: HK$20* ⊠ *1A Whampoa St., Hung Hom, Kowloon City* ☎ *2362–1279* ▬ *No credit cards* Ⓜ *Hong Hom* ✛ *3:H3*.

AMERICAN

$ ✕ **Tan Ngan Lo.** Chinese herbal teas are served by the bowl at this Temple Street institution. Some of the bittersweet beverages may not be to everyone's taste but most of them—such as the five-flower tea—have beneficial medicinal properties and are especially refreshing on a hot day. $ *Average main: HK$12* ⊠ *151 Temple St., Yau Ma Tei* ☎ *2384–3744* ▬ *No credit cards* ✛ *3:E2*.

CHINESE

$ ✕ **Yau Yuan Xiao Jui.** This tiny storefront may look like any other noodle joint, but its humble appearance belies its culinary prowess. The restaurant plates up authentic Shaanxi snacks, which can be best described as some of the heartiest and delicious chow that China has to offer. The handmade dumplings are amazing, especially if they're fattened up with lamb and umami scallion oil. Then there's the signature *biang biang mien*, which translate into (extremely) long and wide al dente noodle sheets designed to be anointed with chili oil, scallions, and marinated spare ribs. Definitely check this place out. $ *Average main: HK$28* ⊠ *Shop 3, ground fl., Keybond Commercial Building, 38 Ferry St., Jordan, Yau Ma Tei* ☎ *5300–2682* ▬ *No credit cards* ⊘ *Closed Tue.* ✛ *3:D2*.

CHINESE
Fodor's Choice
★

MONG KOK

For the best street snacks in town, look no further than Mong Kok, where you'll find curry fish balls, among other snacks. The Tung Choi Street vicinity is especially rich in eateries of this type, selling everything from regional specialties like spicy Chongqing noodles to curry fish balls on bamboo skewers and fragrant egg waffles.

$ ✕ **100 Bites.** The miniature cakes here sit like jewels behind the pastry case. You'll find a colorful assortment that includes everything from lemon-mint mousse gâteaux to a dome-shaped white-chocolate mousse cake filled with raspberry and black currant purée. Our favorite

BAKERY

creations are the ones that use Asian ingredients such as green tea and yuzu. [$] *Average main: HK$35* ✉ *Shop 21–25, 10th fl., Langham Place Mall, 8 Argyle St., Mong Kok* ☎ *2191–6638* ✣ *3:D1.*

$ CHINESE 🍴 **Delicious Food.** The street stalls of Hong Kong are filled with interesting snacks of all shapes and sorts. The intrepid should trek over to Delicious Food for their infamous stinky tofu. [$] *Average main: HK$8* ✉ *30–32 Nullah Rd., Mong Kok* ☎ *2142–7468* 💳 *No credit cards* [M] *Prince Edward* ✣ *3:E1.*

WORD OF MOUTH

"Tim Ho Wan is awesome! We went there a few months ago and the wait is super long (get there early in the morning to get your number if you hope to wait less than two hours) but it's very delicious. Pork buns are their specialty."

—katrinab

$ CHINESE 🍴 **Fei Jie Snacks Stall.** Dundas Street in Mong Kok is filled with street eats. The Fei Jie Snacks Stall is one of the best, with its dizzying selection of skewered choices—from chewy squid, pig intestine (best eaten with a squirt of mustard), and duck gizzard. [$] *Average main: HK$8* ✉ *55 Dundas St., Mong Kok* 💳 *No credit cards* ✣ *3:E1.*

$ BAKERY 🍴 **Lee Keung Kee.** Egg waffles are a local specialty in Hong Kong, and Lee Keung Kee offers a delicious rendition. The waffles here are crisp on the outside but soft and cottony on the inside. [$] *Average main: HK$15* ✉ *53–55 Dundas St., Mong Kok* ✣ *3:E1.*

$ THAI 🍴 **Thai BBQ 2.** The Thai food here is truly excellent and about as authentic you can get in Hong Kong. It's a point-and-order kind of restaurant, since some of the best items are the ones that aren't on the menu. One of these is the *moo kata:* various raw meats and offal, cooked on a raised, dome-shape charcoal-powered grill, which is surrounded by a mote of boiling broth. The meat juices trickle down from the grill to flavor the broth, which can also be used to cook the meats or accompanying greens, mushrooms, and vermicelli. Call a day ahead if you want to try this dish. [$] *Average main: HK$70* ✉ *17 Nam Kok Rd., Kowloon City, Northern Kowloon* ☎ *2718–6219* 💳 *No credit cards* ⏲ *No lunch.* ✣ *3:H1.*

$ CHINESE Fodor's Choice ★ 🍴 **Tim Ho Wan.** Don't let the undiscerning storefront fool you—Tim Ho Wan is an award-winning eatery that serves some of the city's best dim sum. Opened by a former Four Seasons Hotel chef, this humble Mong Kok eatery makes all of its shrimp dumplings, rice rolls, baked cha siu buns, and such, fresh to order. It's top-quality food at dirt-cheap prices. But be warned—the shop is small, and its popularity is immense, so go at off hours between 2:30 pm and 5 pm, or you might find yourself waiting up to half an hour for a seat. There are Tim Ho Wan branches in Sham Shui Po, North Point, and Central, but this Mong Kok flagship remains the most popular. [$] *Average main: HK$15* ✉ *2–8 Kwong Wah St., Mong Kok* ☎ *2332–2896* 💳 *No credit cards* [M] *Mong Kok* ✣ *3:E1.*

$ CHINESE 🍴 **Yee Shun Milk Company.** Expect to wait in line if you want to try the famed milk desserts from Yee Shun Milk Company. The velvety-smooth, double-boiled milk pudding is rich and comforting. The ginger-flavored milk pudding has a nice spicy kick, making it the perfect stomach warmer—a must-try if you're visiting Hong Kong in the wintertime. Chocolate and coffee puddings are also available. *$ Average main: HK$25 ✉ 63 Pilkem St., Jordan ☎ 2730–2799 ▭ No credit cards ✣ 3:F3.*

KOWLOON BAY

$ CHINESE ✕ **Siu Shun Village Cuisine.** This is one of the few restaurants in town specializing in authentic Shunde cuisine (Shunde is an area in the Pearl River Delta). A collection of tanks at the front of the restaurant display various types of freshwater fish, which can be ordered steamed, fried, baked, or sautéed. Steamed fish in broth is one of the best ways to enjoy the freshwater selection. Sautéed fresh milk is one of Shunde's most renowned dishes—at Siu Shun, it's made with fresh soy milk, egg whites, fresh prawns, and *conpoy* (dried scallops). Don't skip dessert—the double-boiled sweetened milk is reminiscent of a rich, custardy pudding and is a perfectly comforting closure. *$ Average main: HK$80 ✉ Shop 6, 7th fl., MegaBox, 38 Wang Chiu Rd., Kowloon Bay, Kowloon City ☎ 2798–9738 ⊕ www.siushun.com Ⓜ Kowloon Bay ✣ 3:H1.*

5

THE NEW TERRITORIES

Sai Kung in the New Territories is worth a visit, if only for a meal. The many restaurants lining the main street and the giant fish tanks with the dizzying selection of fresh fish, crabs, prawns, clams, and oysters are a sight to behold. Point to your catch of choice and have the kitchen cook it up in any way your stomach desires (stir-fried with spicy salt is the no-fail way to go).

$ SRI LANKAN ✕ **AJ's Sri Lankan Cuisine.** Sai Kung may be best known for its local seafood joints, but we'll happily shine a light on the city's only Sri Lankan restaurant. Housed in a quaint, cottagelike structure, AJ's rolls out regional delicacies from the South Asian island country—if you haven't tried it before, Sri Lankan cuisine shares similarities with its neighboring countries though there are some distinct differences in the use of spices and cooking techniques. Definitely order the *pittu*—a mound of coconut-perfumed rice meal that marries particularly well with AJ's vegetarian curries. We're also fans of any string hopper (shredded, steamed rice flour dough) dish that's tossed in a wok with diced meats and spices. *$ Average main: HK$88 ✉ 14 Sai Kung Hoi Pong St., Sai Kung, New Territories ☎ 2792–2555 ⊕ www.aj.srilankan.hk ⏲ No lunch Mon. ✣ 3:F1.*

$ CHINESE ✕ **Honeymoon Dessert.** Though it's expanded into a multistore chain across the city, Honeymoon Dessert's first ever store in Sai Kung still draws droves of loyal and new fans alike. The store sells homemade traditional Chinese desserts such as black sesame sweet soup and the refreshing mango pomelo sweet soup with sago. They also do newfangled items, including glutinous rice dumplings dusted with desiccated coconut and filled with fresh mango. In the summertime, don't miss out on the wide selection of cooling grass jelly items. *$ Average main: HK$35 ✉ 9–10 ABC Po Tung Rd., Sai Kung, New Territories ☎ 2792–4991 ⊕ www.honeymoon-dessert.com ▭ No credit cards Ⓜ Hang Hau ✣ 3:F1.*

$$
INTERNATIONAL
⟳

✕ **Jaspa's.** The food at Jaspa's is delicious and filling, perfect after a day walking in the hills or enjoying the water and sun, and the international menu is wide-ranging enough to satisfy all tastes. The chicken fajitas arrive on your table sizzling hot; grilled snapper with Asian herbs and parmesan-crusted rack of lamb are also delicious. Enjoy your meal indoors or opt for a table on the alfresco terrace. ⓢ *Average main: HK$190* ✉ *13 Sha Tsui Path, Sai Kung, New Territories* ☎ *2792–6388* ⊕ *www.casteloconcepts.com* Ⓜ *Hang Hau* ✛ *3:F1.*

$$
SEAFOOD

✕ **Loaf on.** Off of Sai Kung's main drag of restaurants, this hidden gem stands out as one of the finer seafood joints for those in the know. Unlike its big and boisterous competitors, this tiny store has no flashy fish tanks displayed outside and the tables are extremely limited, so it's best to book in advance. The food, however, is truly a cut above the rest. Try the fish soup—a milky white broth that's brimming with umami sweetness. There's also the famous deep-fried abalone dusted in chili and salt. Aside from seafood, Loaf On also serves an amazing deep-fried tofu dish that's crisp and golden on the outside and silken, soft, and supple in the center. ⓢ *Average main: HK$120* ✉ *49 See Cheung St., Sai Kung, New Territories* ☎ *2792–9966* ⌷ *Reservations essential* ✛ *3:F1.*

$$$
CHINESE

✕ **Sha Tin 18.** If you're exploring the Sha Tin neighborhood, consider visiting Sha Tin 18 for a pan-Chinese feast. The restaurant is equipped with several open kitchens, each with its own culinary specialty. Northern Chinese dishes are best, and you'll find a range of homespun noodles and dumplings, but the traditional Peking duck, which is roasted in house and served as three separate courses, is also excellent. If you're dropping by for lunch, the extensive dim sum menu should keep you well sated. Save room for dessert, though, because the selection—which includes candied kumquat crème brûlée and milk tea ice cream—is definitely more innovative than your average Chinese eatery. ⓢ *Average main: HK$238* ✉ *4th fl., Hyatt Regency Hong Kong, 18 Chak Cheung St., Sha Tin, New Territories* ☎ *3723–1234* ⊕ *www.hongkong.shatin.hyatt.com* ✛ *3:F1.*

$$$
SEAFOOD

✕ **Tung Kee Seafood Restaurant.** Lobsters, clams, abalone, crabs, prawns, fish, and everything else from the deep blue sea is here for the tasting on Sai Kung's picturesque harbor. Crustaceans and fish are quickly cooked by steaming and wok-frying, but are first presented whole, leaving no doubt as to the freshness of your food. A quick look inside the tank is like a lesson in marine biology. Pick your favorites, and leave the rest to the chef. Then just prepare yourself for a feast *de la mer.* ⓢ *Average main: HK$220* ✉ *96–102 Man Nin St., Sai Kung, New Territories* ☎ *2792–7453* ⊕ *www.tungkee.com.hk* Ⓜ *Hang Hau* ✛ *3:F1.*

Hong Kong Dining and Lodging Atlas

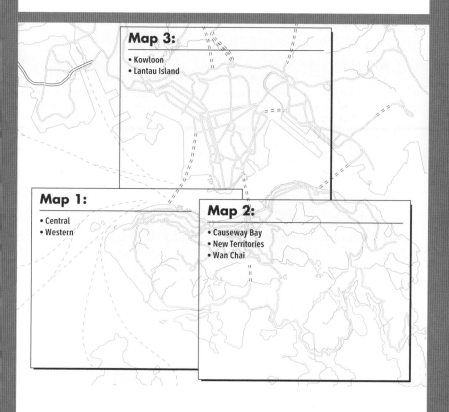

Map 3:
- Kowloon
- Lantau Island

Map 1:
- Central
- Western

Map 2:
- Causeway Bay
- New Territories
- Wan Chai

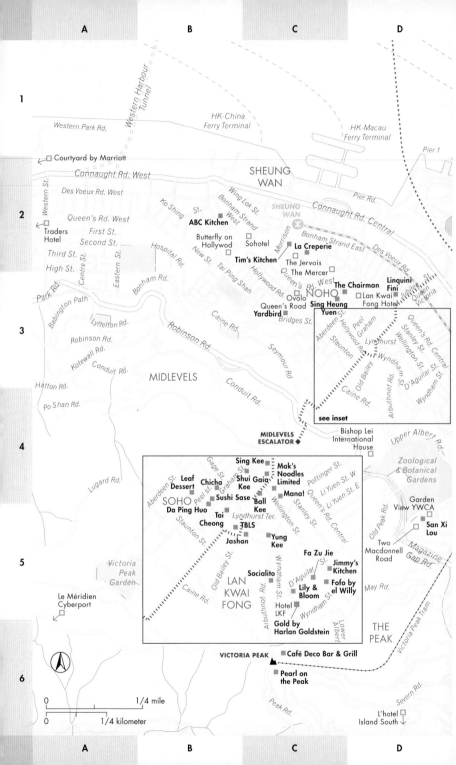

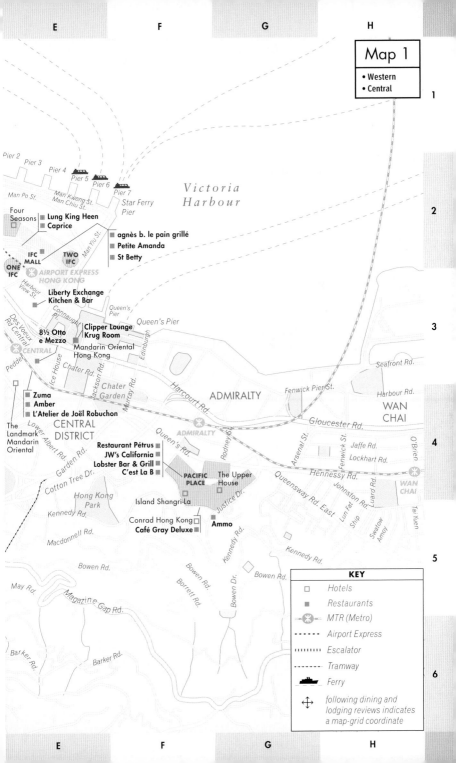

Map 1

- Western
- Central

E   F   G   H

1

Pier 2 Pier 3

Pier 4 Pier 5 Pier 6 Pier 7

Man Po St. Man Kwong St. Star Ferry
Man Chiu St. Pier

Victoria Harbour

2

Four Seasons ☐ ■ **Lung King Heen**
■ **Caprice**

■ **agnès b. le pain grillé**
Man Yiu St. ■ **Petite Amanda**
■ **St Betty**

IFC ■ TWO
MALL IFC
ONE ✷
IFC AIRPORT EXPRESS
HONG KONG

Harbour View St. ■ **Liberty Exchange**
Kitchen & Bar

Connaught Queen's
Pier

Queen's Pier

3

8½ Otto
e Mezzo ■ **Clipper Lounge**
Krug Room

Ice House Mandarin Oriental
Hong Kong

Pedder

✷ CENTRAL

Edinburgh

Seafront Rd.

Chater Rd. Chater
Garden Harcourt Rd.

ADMIRALTY

Fenwick Pier St.

Harbour Rd.

■ **Zuma**
■ **Amber**
■ **L'Atelier de Joël Robuchon**

WAN CHAI

Murray Rd. Jackson Rd. Lower Albert Rd.

CENTRAL
DISTRICT

✷ ADMIRALTY

Gloucester Rd.

4

The Landmark
Mandarin Oriental

Garden Rd.

Queen's Rd. Rodney St.

■ **Restaurant Pétrus**
■ **JW's California**
■ **Lobster Bar & Grill**
■ **C'est La B**

PACIFIC
PLACE The Upper
House

Arsenal St. Fenwick St. Jaffe Rd.
Lockhart Rd. O'Brien

WAN
CHAI

Hennessy Rd.

Tai Yuen

Cotton Tree Dr.

Hong Kong
Park

Kennedy Rd.

Island Shangri-La

Justice Dr.

Conrad Hong Kong ■ **Ammo**
■ **Café Gray Deluxe**

Queensway Rd. East

Johnston Rd. Lun Fat Ship Swatow Amoy

Macdonnell Rd.

5

Bowen Rd. Bowen Rd. Kennedy Rd.

Bowen Rd.

May Rd. Magazine Gap Rd. Borrett Rd. Bowen Dr. Bowen Rd.

KEY

☐ *Hotels*
■ *Restaurants*
✷ *MTR (Metro)*
- - - - *Airport Express*
⋅⋅⋅⋅⋅⋅ *Escalator*
⋯⋯⋯ *Tramway*
▬ *Ferry*
⊕ *following dining and*
lodging reviews indicates
a map-grid coordinate

6

Barker Rd. Barker Rd.

E   F   G   H

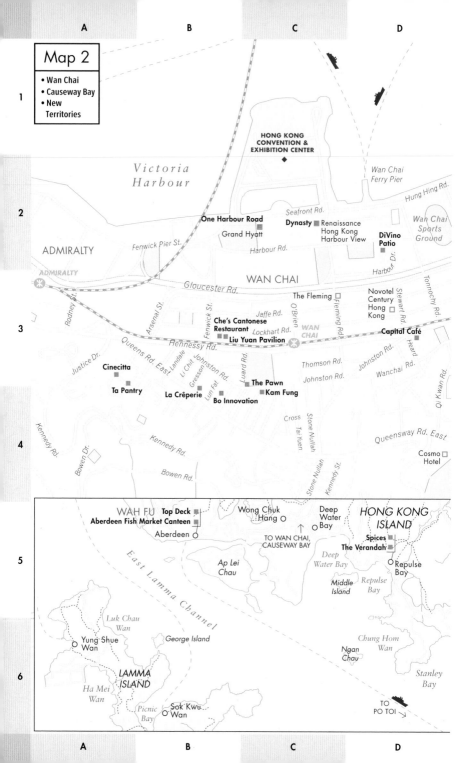

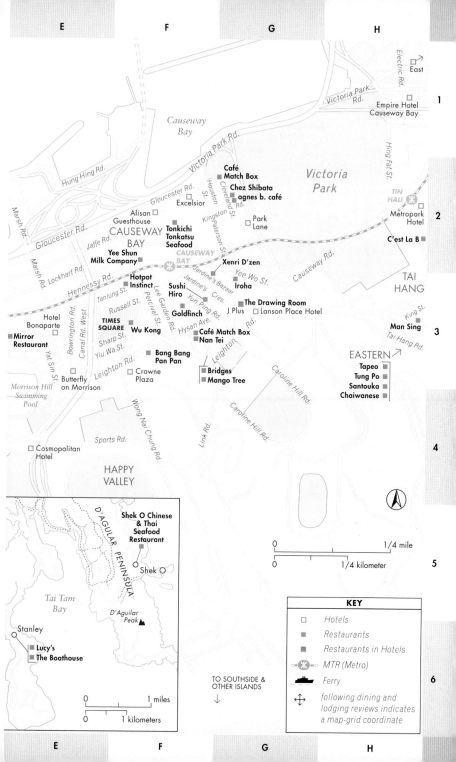

E   F   G   H

Causeway Bay

East

Victoria Park Rd.

Electric Rd.

Empire Hotel
Causeway Bay

1

Hung Hing Rd.

Gloucester Rd.

Café
Match Box

Chez Shibata
agnes b. café

Excelsior

*Victoria
Park*

TIN
HAU

Metropark
Hotel

2

Marsh Rd.

Gloucester Rd.

Alisan
Guesthouse

CAUSEWAY
BAY

Houston St.

Cleveland St.

Park
Lane

Kingston St.

Paterson St.

C'est La B

Marsh Rd.

Jaffe Rd.

Tonkichi
Tonkatsu
Seafood

CAUSEWAY
BAY

Causeway Rd.

TAI
HANG

Lockhart Rd.

Yee Shun
Milk Company

Xenri D'zen

Jardine's Bazaar

Yee Wo St.

Iroha

Hennessy Rd.

Hotpot
Instinct

Jardine's Cres.

Sushi
Hiro

Yun Ping Rd.

King St.

Man Sing

3

Tanlung St.

Lee Garden Rd.

Percival St.

Russell St.

Goldfinch

J Plus

The Drawing Room

Lanson Place Hotel

Tai Hang Rd.

Hotel
Bonaparte

TIMES
SQUARE

Wu Kong

Hysan Ave.

Café Match Box
Nan Tei

EASTERN

Mirror
Restaurant

Bowrington Rd.

Canal Rd. West

Sharp St.

Yiu Wa St.

Bang Bang
Pan Pan

Leighton Rd.

Bridges
Mango Tree

Caroline Hill Rd.

Tapeo
Tung Po
Santouka
Chaiwanese

Yat Sin St.

Leighton Rd.

Butterfly
on Morrison

Crowne
Plaza

Link Rd.

*Morrison Hill
Swimming
Pool*

Sports Rd.

Caroline Hill Rd.

4

Cosmopolitan
Hotel

**HAPPY
VALLEY**

Wong Nai Chung Rd.

D'AGUILAR PENINSULA

Shek O Chinese
& Thai
Seafood
Restaurant

Shek O

*Tai Tam
Bay*

D'Aguilar
Peak

0   1/4 mile

0   1/4 kilometer

5

Stanley

Lucy's
The Boathouse

0   1 miles

0   1 kilometers

KEY

☐   *Hotels*

■   *Restaurants*

■   *Restaurants in Hotels*

✪   *MTR (Metro)*

⛴   *Ferry*

✛   *following dining and
lodging reviews indicates
a map-grid coordinate*

TO SOUTHSIDE &
OTHER ISLANDS
↓

6

E   F   G   H

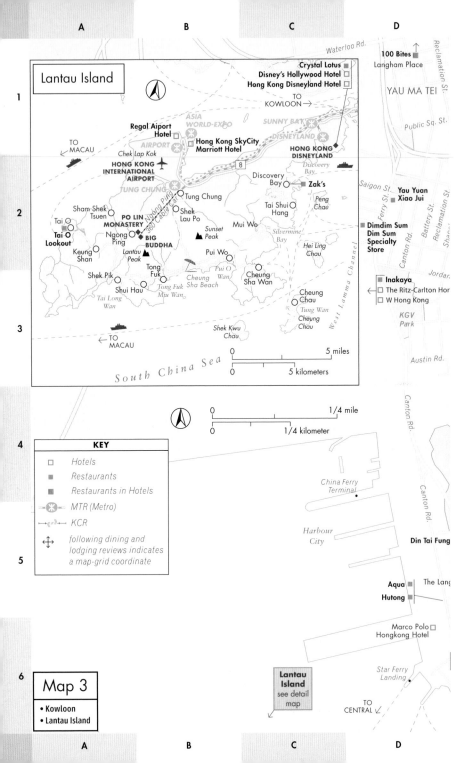

Lantau Island

A   **B**   **C**   **D**

Waterloo Rd.

Crystal Lotus ■
100 Bites ■ Langham Place
Disney's Hollywood Hotel □
Hong Kong Disneyland Hotel □

YAU MA TEI

TO
KOWLOON →

Public Sq. St.

ASIA
WORLD-EXPO

**Regal Aiport
Hotel** □

AIRPORT

**Hong Kong SkyCity
Marriott Hotel** □

SUNNY BAY

DISNEYLAND

**HONG KONG
DISNEYLAND** ◆

Chek Lap Kok

← TO
MACAU

**HONG KONG
INTERNATIONAL
AIRPORT** ✈

8

Discovery
Bay ○

Discovery
Bay

Zak's ■

Saigon St.

TUNG CHUNG

Tung Chung

Tai Shui ○
Hang

Yau Yuan
Xiao Jui

Ferry St.

Battery St.

Reclamation St.

Sham Shek ○
Tsuen

Shek ○
Lau Po

Peng
Chau

Mui Wo

Tai ○
O

**Tai O
Lookout** ■

**PO LIN
MONASTERY**

Ngong ○
Ping

**BIG
BUDDHA** ◆

Sunset
Peak ▲

Silvermine
Bay

Hei Ling
Chau

■ **Dimdim Sum
Dim Sum
Specialty
Store**

Canton Rd.

Jordan

Keung ○
Shan

Lantau
Peak ▲

Pui Wo ○

■ **Inakaya**
□ The Ritz-Carlton Hor
□ W Hong Kong

Shek Pik

Tong ○
Fuk

Pui O
Wan

Cheung ○
Sha Wan

KGV
Park

Shui Hau

Cheung
Sha Beach

Tong Fuk
Miu Wan

Cheung ○
Chau

Austin Rd.

Tai Long
Wan

Cheung
Chau

Tung Wan

Shek Kwu ○
Chau

TO
← MACAU

South China Sea

0   5 miles

0   5 kilometers

0   1/4 mile

0   1/4 kilometer

**China Ferry
Terminal** •

Canton Rd.

Din Tai Fung

KEY

□	*Hotels*
■	*Restaurants*
■	*Restaurants in Hotels*
✳	*MTR (Metro)*
⊢•⊣	*KCR*
⬌	*following dining and lodging reviews indicates a map-grid coordinate*

**Harbour
City**

Aqua ■
Hutong ■

The Lang

Marco Polo □
Hongkong Hotel

Map 3

• Kowloon
• Lantau Island

**Lantau
Island**
see detail
map

*Star Ferry
Landing* •

TO
CENTRAL ↙

A   **B**   **C**   **D**

1   2   3   4   5   6

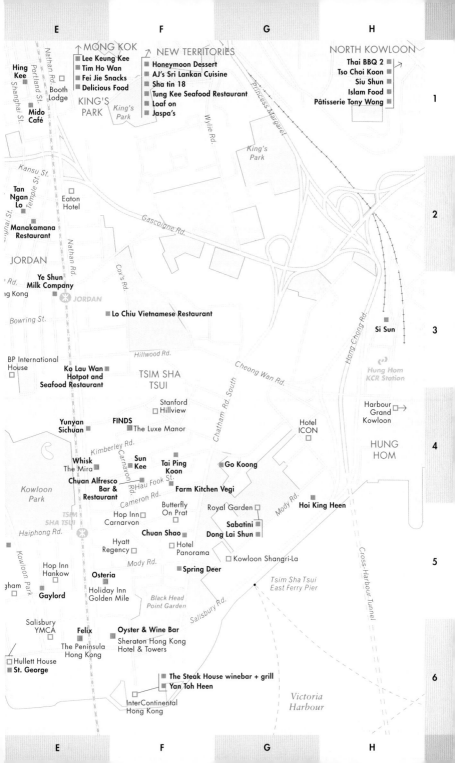

E

F

G

H

↑ MONG KOK

↗ NEW TERRITORIES

NORTH KOWLOON

Hing Kee

■ Lee Keung Kee
■ Tim Ho Wan
■ Fei Jie Snacks
■ Delicious Food

■ Honeymoon Dessert
■ AJ's Sri Lankan Cuisine
■ Sha tin 18
■ Tung Kee Seafood Restaurant
■ Loaf on
■ Jaspa's

Thai BBQ 2 ■
Tso Choi Koon ■
Siu Shun ■
Islam Food ■
Pâtisserie Tony Wong ■

Booth Lodge

KING'S PARK

King's Park

1

Mido Café

Nathan Rd.

Portland St.

Shanghai St.

Princess Margaret

King's Park

Kansu St.

Temple St.

Tan Ngan Lo

Eaton Hotel

Gascoigne Rd.

2

Manakamana Restaurant

Nathan Rd.

Cox's Rd.

Hong Chong Rd.

JORDAN

...ng Rd.

Ye Shun Milk Company

✗ JORDAN

Si Sun

3

ng Kong

Bowring St.

Lo Chiu Vietnamese Restaurant

Wylie Rd.

Cheong Wan Rd.

Hung Hom KCR Station

BP International House

Hillwood Rd.

Ko Lau Wan Hotpot and Seafood Restaurant

TSIM SHA TSUI

Harbour Grand Kowloon

4

Yunyan Sichuan

FINDS

Stanford Hillview

The Luxe Manor

Hotel ICON

HUNG HOM

Kimberley Rd.

Whisk

The Mira

Sun Kee

Tai Ping Koon

Go Koong

Hoi King Heen

Carnarvon Rd.

Chuan Alfresco Bar & Restaurant

Hau Fook St.

Farm Kitchen Vegi

Kowloon Park

Cameron Rd.

Hop Inn Carnarvon

Butterfly On Prat

Royal Garden

Sabatini

Mody Rd.

Chatham Rd. South

Hyatt Regency

Chuan Shao

Dong Lai Shun

Haiphong Rd.

TSIM SHA TSUI ✗

Hotel Panorama

Kowloon Shangri-La

5

Hop Inn Hankow

Mody Rd.

Spring Deer

Tsim Sha Tsui East Ferry Pier

Kowloon Park

Osteria

Black Head Point Garden

Cross-Harbour Tunnel

...gham

Gaylord

Holiday Inn Golden Mile

Salisbury Rd.

Salisbury YMCA

Felix

Oyster & Wine Bar

6

The Peninsula Hong Kong

Sheraton Hong Kong Hotel & Towers

Hullett House
St. George

The Steak House winebar + grill
Yan Toh Heen

Victoria Harbour

InterContinental Hong Kong

E

F

G

H

Where to Stay

WORD OF MOUTH

"People kill too many neurons debating HK Island vs Kowloon. For every person who says 'Don't stay in Kowloon,' I can find 0.8 to 1.2 persons who will tell you they love Kowloon. Seriously, one should look for the best hotel for your budget on the days you want. And location and transportation are important, for both sides of the harbor."

—rkkwan

Updated by
Jason Spotts

Whether you're a business traveler or a casual tourist, you'll inevitably be caught up with the manic pace of life in Hong Kong. Luckily, hotels are constantly increasing their efforts to provide their guests with a restful haven, often bundling spectacular views of the famous skyline and harbor with chic luxury, snazzy amenities, and soothing ambience.

From budget guesthouses to gleaming towers, you're sure to find a style and site to fit your needs. Prices tend to reflect quality of service and amenities as well as location, so it's worth the effort to examine neighborhoods closely when making your choice—you may end up paying the same to stay exactly where you want to be as you would to be off the beaten path.

The rock stars of Hong Kong's hotel industry are perfectly situated around Victoria Harbour, offering unobstructed harbor views, sumptuous spas, and reputable service to compete for the patronage of business-suited jet-setters, status-sensitive mainland tourists, and any visitor willing to splurge for uncompromised luxury. Farther up the hills on both Kowloon and Hong Kong Island, cozy hotels have blossomed over the past five years and seduce travelers who simply want a safe and practical place to crash in a trendy locale.

Travelers familiar with European cities might be surprised by the lack of provenance among Hong Kong hotels—the 80-plus-year-old Peninsula passes as the venerable old timer in this brashly new city where most hotels are perched in modern towers. And the scene keeps changing: Hong Kong's continued growth as a top tourist destination and business capital means that when it comes to choice of lodging, the next big thing is always around the corner. The Ritz-Carlton, Hong Kong, recently hit the heights when it began hosting guests on the 102nd through 118th floors of the ICC tower in Kowloon, suggesting that on the Hong Kong hotel scene the sky really is the limit.

PLANNING

CHECKING IN

Typical check-in and checkout times are 2 pm and noon, respectively, although most hotels will be flexible if they are not fully booked and if you make a request in advance. Many major hotel chains have privilege clubs that allow their members to extend their checkout times until the evening, and some hotels now offer completely flexible checkout times, with checkout based on when you check in, rather than a set time. Some hotels also offer you the opportunity to check out online, so you can simply pack up and leave.

CHILDREN

Many hotels allow children under a certain age to stay in their parents' room at no extra charge, and most offer a babysitting service. The hotels that are especially accommodating to those traveling with children are marked with the ☾ symbol. Remember that many Hong Kong hotels have swimming pools, an attraction that in itself can satisfy young travelers.

EXECUTIVE PRIVILEGE

Most high-end hotels have a VIP executive floor or lounge, and these tend to come with sweeping panoramic views. Complimentary breakfast (not a regular feature in most Hong Kong hotels) and cocktails are usually served in these clubs, while business facilities tend to include Wi-Fi, laser printing, special dedicated concierges, and sometimes a mini-conference room. Entry to these clubs and lounges is based on the type of room you book, although some hotels allow guests staying in less expensive rooms to pay an additional fee for executive privileges.

FACILITIES

Unless stated otherwise in the review, hotels are equipped with elevators and all guest rooms have air-conditioning, TV, telephone, and private bathrooms. Note that bathrooms with showers but no bathtubs are the norm in smaller hotels so be sure to check if you want a tub. All hotels have designated no-smoking rooms or floors. Many also have designated "special access" rooms for guests in wheelchairs.

Note that the majority of hotels, even the budget ones, now come with in-room Wi-Fi, although some hotels (ironically, often the more expensive ones) charge a fee; almost all hotels now offer free Wi-Fi in public areas. Most moderately priced hotels will offer up-to-date technologies such as plasma screens, entertainment on demand, iPod docks, and sometimes even cell phones. Most hotels are conveniently situated near the MTR subway system and those that are not will often provide free shuttle service to the nearest station, as well as to popular downtown destinations.

LODGING STRATEGY

The 60-plus selections here represent the best this city has to offer. Scan "Best Bets" on the following pages for top recommendations by price and experience. Reviews are arranged alphabetically within neighborhood.

PRICES

Prices vary depending on season and occupancy. Most hotels offer their best rates and special offers on their websites. Many hotels offer discounts for longer stays or advance purchase, or for that matter, last-minute booking. Hong Kong's high seasons are generally May through June and October through November, though rates also go up during certain holiday periods and for events such as the Hong Kong Sevens rugby tournament in March. While many hotels put on lavish breakfast buffets, breakfast is usually extra and not included in basic room rates.

RESERVATIONS

Most hotels have reliable online booking systems but phone reservations are also accepted, and receptionists speak English.

Specify arrival and departure dates, number of guests, room type (standard, deluxe, suite), and any specific preferences. Make sure to find out what is, and what is not, included in the room rate, such as breakfast, in-room Wi-Fi, and local calls. A credit-card deposit is generally required to secure reservations.

Flights from the United States often arrive in the evening, so it's a good idea to inform the hotel when you plan to arrive. Some hotels will not otherwise hold a booking after 6 pm.

ROOMS WITH A VIEW

It's no secret that the prime waterfront properties have the best views in Hong Kong. On the Kowloon side, hotels in Tsim Sha Tsui and West Kowloon generally have the most compelling skyline views across Victoria Harbour. Because of the curvature of the bay, hotels in Causeway Bay and North Point can also have an equally exhilarating view down the coast of Hong Kong Island as well as of Kowloon. Remember that silence speaks loudly; if the hotel doesn't advertise views, no matter how hip it is, it probably has none. And while more low-profile small hotels are cleverly designing their rooms to optimize limited square footage, nothing opens up a room like a far-reaching view, be it harbor (preferably) or city (high-rise horizons).

USING THE MAPS

Throughout the chapter, you'll see mapping symbols and coordinates (✛ 3:F2) after property names or reviews. To locate the property on a map, turn to the Hong Kong Dining and Lodging Atlas at the end of the Where to Eat chapter. The first number after the ✛ symbol indicates the map number. Following that is the property's coordinate on the map grid.

WHERE SHOULD I STAY?

	NEIGHBORHOOD VIBE	PROS	CONS
Western	A sprawling neighborhood with hidden alleyways, antique shops, Chinese medicine markets, and temples.	Western is akin to the residential extension of Central, with less traffic and similarly spectacular views. Most accessible on foot, and a leisurely tram ride from Central during off-peak hours.	May require steep footwork if your destination is not near the main road, where the trams and MTR run. Even taxis have difficulty navigating many narrow, one-way streets.
Central	A dense international finance center full of banks, shopping malls, and footbridges above traffic. High up the escalators, Mid-Levels is an exclusive residential getaway.	Home to major luxury brands' flagship stores, as well as grand hotels, fine restaurants, and the famous nightlife area, Lan Kwai Fong. Mid-Levels offers quiet views from above the fray.	Congested streets by day, crowded bars by night. Mid-Levels Escalators run uphill only after morning rush hour.
Wan Chai, Causeway Bay, and Beyond	Wan Chai hosts a strip of street-level bars in addition to the designer Star Street area. Causeway Bay is the haven of hip young locals who come to eat, shop, and hang out in upstairs cafés.	Wan Chai has stylish restaurants, the convention center, and some performing-arts venues. Causeway Bay, home to Victoria Park, is conveniently situated with hotels in all price ranges.	The Wan Chai bar strip can get seedy, while Causeway Bay is extremely crowded on weekends. Eastern is mostly for business or residents.
Southside	Lower building density means more space and fewer people, with a fishing-village atmosphere around Aberdeen.	Proximity to great beaches on Hong Kong Island, as well as to Stanley Market and Cyberport.	Be prepared for a lot of car and bus rides along winding roads, often in slow traffic.
Lantau Island	Hong Kong's largest island hosts disparate attractions: an international airport, an outlet shopping mall, natural scenery, Hong Kong Disneyland, and AsiaWorld-Expo.	MTR end-of-the-line town Tung Chung is the point of access to the Ngong Ping scenic cable-car ride and Citygate outlet shopping. Some may prefer a more resortlike setting inside Disneyland.	Inconvenient for exploring the rest of Hong Kong, as even Tung Chung is a half-hour MTR ride out from Central.
Kowloon	The "wild" side of Hong Kong (at least according to Islanders) culminating in the commercial centers of Mong Kok and Tsim Sha Tsui.	Shopping paradise indeed, for both malls and markets. The TST promenade, including the touristy Avenue of Stars, offers postcard views of the Hong Kong skyline.	Kowloon is not everyone's idea of a holiday—outside residential areas the streets (even pedestrian) are generally noisy, crowded, and congested.

6

BEST BETS FOR HONG KONG LODGING

Fodor's offers a selective listing of quality lodgings at every price range, from the city's best budget guesthouses to its most sophisticated luxury hotels. We've compiled our top recommendations by price and experience.

HONG KONG ISLAND

Reviews listed alphabetically within neighborhood.

WESTERN

The steep, narrow streets of Western District, navigated by old-fashioned trams, are a natural setting for new, small hotels catering to those who favor local flavor over opulence. Hotels in Sheung Wan combine transport convenience with an abundance of neighborhood character, while hotels farther out on the main drive focus on sleek efficiency and minimalist style. However, getting here usually means passing through high-traffic Central or navigating congested streets, steps, and alleyways.

$ HOTEL **Butterfly on Hollywood.** A charming location alone is reason enough to stay in one of these snug but stylishly contemporary rooms in a cozy neighborhood full of antique shops, galleries, cafés, and up-and-coming restaurants. **Pros:** excellent location for wandering; a 10-minute walk from the hub of Hong Kong nightlife; free Wi-Fi throughout. **Cons:** cramped lobby and few hotel facilities; no views. $ *Rooms from: HK$1040* ⊠ *263 Hollywood Rd., Sheung Wan, Western* ☎ *2850–8899* ⊕ *www.butterflyhk. com* ⟿ *142 rooms* ¡○¡ *No meals* Ⓜ *Sheung Wan* ✛ *1:B2.*

$$$ HOTEL **Courtyard by Marriott Hong Kong.** Tidily presented and comfortably no-frills rooms are close to Western Tunnel and especially convenient for those with business in Kowloon. **Pros:** business-friendly; close to Sheung Wan Ferry Terminal and Western Tunnel; nice views of Kowloon West from upper floors. **Cons:** few dining options in hotel or immediate area; rooms on lower floors look out over a lot of traffic; fitness center but no pool. $ *Rooms from: HK$2900* ⊠ *167 Connaught Rd. West, Western* ☎ *3717-8888* ⊕ *www.marriott.com/hotels/travel/hkgcy-courtyard-hong-kong* ⟿ *245 rooms* ¡○¡ *No meals* Ⓜ *Western* ✛ *1:A2.*

$$ HOTEL **The Mercer.** Spacious junior suites with kitchenettes (about two-thirds of the accommodations) are the best choice in this needlelike spire, where all rooms come with lots of light, airy views, and soothing contemporary styling. **Pros:** a fun neighborhood to explore; good Japanese restaurant on the ground floor; open-air pool (tiny). **Cons:** cramped lobby; surrounding area can get congested with traffic; glass-walled bathrooms are not popular with all guests. $ *Rooms from: HK$1980* ⊠ *29 Jervois St., Sheung Wan* ☎ *2922–9988* ⊕ *www.themercer.com.hk* ⟿ *55 rooms* ¡○¡ *Breakfast* Ⓜ *Sheung Wan* ✛ *1:C2.*

$ HOTEL **Sohotel.** It's a toss-up whether the rooms here should be considered basic and no-frills or minimally sleek, but they are extremely functional and nicely tucked away in a colorful neighborhood of galleries and local shops. **Pros:** free Wi-Fi and local calls; subway and Macau Ferry Terminal nearby. **Cons:** few in-hotel facilities; some rooms are tiny. $ *Rooms from: HK$1500* ⊠ *139 Bonham Strand, Sheung Wan* ☎ *852/2851–8818* ⊕ *www.sohotel.com.hk* ⟿ *37 rooms* ¡○¡ *No meals* Ⓜ *Sheung Wan* ✛ *1:C2.*

$$ HOTEL **Traders Hotel.** Most guest quarters, soothingly decorated in simple shades of beige and white, come with cushioned seats set into bay windows that are perfect for reading while taking in the city and harbor

6

views—which you may have plenty of time to do, since the surrounding area is quiet at night. **Pros:** rooftop pool and a gym with a view; free shuttle bus to locations around Hong Kong; short walk to the galleries and antique shops around Hollywood Road. **Cons:** a long walk to the nearest subway station. $ *Rooms from: HK$1900* ✉ *508 Queen's Road W., Western* ☎ *2974–1234* ⊕ *www.shangri-la.com/hongkong/traders* ↙ *283 rooms* ❍| *No meals* Ⓜ *Western* ✢ *1:A2.*

CENTRAL

As Hong Kong's financial hub, Central has attracted many fine restaurants, luxury shops, and swank hotels where deals are hatched, closed, and celebrated. Prepare to pay top prices for uncompromising service amid glamorous skyline views. Just up the hill, Lan Kwai Fong nightlife beckons with rowdy release; farther up the escalators, the Mid-Levels offers peaceful respite. Admiralty is a busy traffic-hub extension of Central that climbs into the gentrified heights of Pacific Place, above shopping malls and embassies, to more remote palatial hotel offerings with panoramic views.

$ | HOTEL | Fodor's Choice | ★ **Bishop Lei International House.** If you've ever dreamed of living a life of privilege in the Mid-Levels without having to pay through the nose for it, this is your chance—all the better if you go for a slightly pricier harbor-view room. **Pros:** unique perch near escalators, saving you countless steps up and down to SoHo and Central; good value. **Cons:** escalator runs only upward after 10 am so lots of steps down in the morning. $ *Rooms from: HK$1400* ✉ *4 Robinson Rd., Mid-levels* ☎ *852/2868–0828* ⊕ *www.bishopleihtl.com.hk* ↙ *227 rooms* Ⓜ *Central* ✢ *1:D4.*

$$$$ | HOTEL | ⟳ **Conrad Hong Kong.** A gleaming-white, oval-shaped tower rising from the Pacific Place complex offers dramatic views of the harbor and the Peak, along with super convenience for shopping and transport to other parts of Hong Kong. **Pros:** open-air pool area is dramatically backed by towering skyscrapers; elevator whisks guests down to Pacific Place shopping mall. **Cons:** not the most distinctive property in this popular neighborhood for upscale hotels. $ *Rooms from: HK$4700* ✉ *Pacific Place, 88 Queensway, Admiralty, Central* ☎ *2521–3838* ⊕ *www.conrad.com.hk* ↙ *512 rooms* ❍| *No meals* Ⓜ *Admiralty* ✢ *1:F5.*

$$$$ | HOTEL | Fodor's Choice | ★ **Four Seasons Hotel Hong Kong.** Few comforts are neglected, with amenities ranging from sumptuous Chinese-accented furnishings to all sorts of high-tech gadgetry, but the main features are the knockout views of the harbor and Victoria Peak through walls of glass. **Pros:** elite service and attention to detail; outstanding 24-hour business center. **Cons:** breakfast not included in high rates; some views are better than others. $ *Rooms from: HK$4500* ✉ *International Finance Centre, 8 Finance St., Central* ☎ *3196–8888* ⊕ *www.fourseasons.com/hongkong* ↙ *399 rooms* ❍| *No meals* Ⓜ *Central* ✢ *1:E2.*

$$ | HOTEL | **The Garden View – YWCA.** Rooms in this attractive, cylindrical, high-rise guesthouse overlook the peaceful Hong Kong Zoological and Botanical Gardens and are clean, well designed, and affordable. **Pros:** nice park views; value for money; kitchenettes in some suites; walking distance to Central. **Cons:** traffic can get bad during rush hours; limited

amenities. $ *Rooms from: HK$1950* ⊠ *1 MacDonnell Rd., Mid-Levels* ☎ *2877–3737* ⊕ *hotel.ywca.org.hk* ↪ *141 rooms* ⦿ *No meals* Ⓜ *Central* ✛ *1:D5.*

$$$
HOTEL
Ⓣ **Hotel LKF.** Enthusiastic partygoers can roll out of bed and land in a bar— one is on the hotel rooftop, others are in the same tower, and dozens of others are on the surrounding Lan Kwai Fong bar strips. **Pros:** at the towering center of Hong Kong's nightlife; pet-friendly; long-stay discounts. **Cons:** noise through the walls; rowdy neighborhood streets; as expensive as some elite hotels while offering far fewer amenities. $ *Rooms from: HK$3000* ⊠ *33 Wyndham St., Lan Kwai Fong, Central* ☎ *3518–9688* ⊕ *www.hotel-lkf.com.hk* ↪ *95 rooms* ⦿ *No meals* Ⓜ *Central.*

$$$$
HOTEL
Ⓣ **Island Shangri-La.** A city icon towering above Pacific Place drips with old-world charm and offers spacious and luxurious accommodations with an Asian twist, along with fine dining and impeccable service. **Pros:** grand lobby; beautiful pool deck with a great close-up view of the skyline; elevator access to Pacific Place Mall. **Cons:** no real spa. $ *Rooms from: HK$4500* ⊠ *Pacific Place, Supreme Court Rd., Admiralty, Central* ☎ *2877–3838* ⊕ *www.shangri-la.com/island* ↪ *565 rooms* ⦿ *No meals* Ⓜ *Admiralty* ✛ *1:F4.*

$$
HOTEL
Ⓣ **Lan Kwai Fong Hotel.** The scent of lemongrass and cozy feel of an old Hong Kong apartment building extend to the small but beautiful rooms enlarged by bay windows and plunging views of the surrounding cityscape. **Pros:** hotel and neighborhood have lots of character. **Cons:** narrow roads surrounding the hotel are often congested. $ *Rooms from: HK$2200* ⊠ *3 Kau U Fong, SoHo, Central* ☎ *3650–0000* ⊕ *www.lankwaifonghotel.com.hk* ↪ *162 rooms* ⦿ *No meals* Ⓜ *Sheung Wan* ✛ *1:D3.*

$$$$
HOTEL
Fodor's Choice
★
Ⓣ **The Landmark Mandarin Oriental.** Some of the city's most beautifully designed and spacious rooms are equipped with massive, circular spa-style bathtubs, the centerpieces of huge, view-filled bathrooms. **Pros:** you can't get more central in Central; beautiful rooms. **Cons:** relatively small lobby; no harbor views. $ *Rooms from: HK$4500* ⊠ *15 Queen's Rd. Central, The Landmark, Central* ☎ *2132–0188* ⊕ *www.mandarinoriental.com/landmark* ↪ *113 rooms* ⦿ *No meals* Ⓜ *Central* ✛ *1:D1.*

$$$$
HOTEL
Fodor's Choice
★
Ⓣ **Mandarin Oriental Hong Kong.** Hong Kong's most famous hotel has lost none of its opulence, colonial charm, and shine over the past 50 years and is still known for spacious and luxurious accommodation and impeccable service. **Pros:** spacious, open, and beautifully designed rooms; old-world ambience at its finest; exquisite spa. **Cons:** in-room Wi-Fi isn't free. $ *Rooms from: HK$4500* ⊠ *5 Connaught Rd., Central* ☎ *2522–0111* ⊕ *www.mandarinoriental.com/hongkong* ↪ *501 rooms* ⦿ *No meals* Ⓜ *Central* ✛ *1:E3.*

$$$$
HOTEL
Fodor's Choice
★
Ⓣ **The Upper House.** Even standard rooms in this haven of stylish luxury are suites—tranquil havens of design and indulgence that feature huge windowside bathtubs, walk-in rain showers, personal iPod touch with everything on it, free mini-bars, and high-end wine fridges. **Pros:** high design and filled with work of contemporary Asian artists; feels worlds away from Central below; incredible personalized service. **Cons:** no spa or pool; can be difficult to get a taxi. $ *Rooms from: HK$4600* ⊠ *Pacific Place, 88 Queensway, Admiralty, Central* ☎ *2918–1838* ⊕ *www.upperhouse.com* ↪ *117 rooms* ⦿ *No meals* Ⓜ *Admiralty* ✛ *1:G4.*

6

The Upper House exterior.

Harbour view from a suite at The Upper House

WAN CHAI, CAUSEWAY BAY, AND EASTERN

Wan Chai, the neighborhood made famous in *The World of Suzie Wong*, still has nightlife (and red-light activity), in addition to 24-hour noodle joints and hip new wine bars. Hotels around the Hong Kong Convention and Exhibition Centre may offer great views, but nights can get noisy around Lockhart Road. Causeway Bay is the choice of the young and trendy in search of food and fashion, but is overcrowded with pedestrians around Times Square on the weekends. This part of Hong Kong also includes the recreational green spaces of Victoria Park and the Happy Valley Racecourse. Outlying Eastern is strictly about business.

WAN CHAI

$$
HOTEL
The Fleming. A fresh face in a neighborhood known for sleazy clubs and bars offers views of the bustling streets below from clean rooms decorated in subdued earth tones, and provides some nice amenities, too, including free wine in the evenings. **Pros:** free DVD library; Wan Chai location is discretely removed from the sleazier nightlife. **Cons:** standard rooms come with only double beds. $ *Rooms from: HK$1600* ✉ *41 Fleming Rd., Wan Chai* ☎ *3607–2288* ⊕ *www.thefleming.com.hk* ⟿ *66 rooms* ⦿| *No meals* Ⓜ *Wan Chai* ✛ *2:C3.*

$$$$
☾
Grand Hyatt Hong Kong. A direct connection to the Hong Kong Convention and Exhibition Centre makes this a business-first hotel, but leisure travelers also enjoy the elegant rooms, with sweeping harbor views and accented by curving wooden desks and black marble. **Pros:** excellent service; extensive sports facilities; Plateau spa is a beautiful sanctuary. **Cons:** quiet outside the hotel at night but complimentary taxi service available. $ *Rooms from: HK$5200* ✉ *1 Harbour Rd., Wan Chai* ☎ *2588–1234* ⊕ *www.hongkong.grand.hyatt.com* ⟿ *549 rooms* ⦿| *Breakfast* Ⓜ *Wan Chai* ✛ *2:C2.*

$$
HOTEL
Novotel Century Hong Kong. Decent harbor views from some rooms compensate for sparse furnishings and the lack of any design sense, while a decent business center is handy for those with work to do. **Pros:** near the subway, Wan Chai bars and clubs, and Hong Kong Convention and Exhibition Centre; well priced for what you get. **Cons:** flat, lifeless rooms; can get crowded with tour groups. $ *Rooms from: HK$1800* ✉ *238 Jaffe Rd., Wan Chai* ☎ *2598–8888* ⊕ *www.novotelhongkongcentury.com* ⟿ *511 rooms* ⦿| *Breakfast* Ⓜ *Wan Chai* ✛ *2:D3.*

$$$
HOTEL
☾
Renaissance Hong Kong Harbour View Hotel. These modest guest rooms in the Hong Kong Convention and Exhibition Centre complex are simply outfitted with attractive modern decor, and many have harbor views. **Pros:** harborside recreational garden. **Cons:** a little walk away from the subway but near the Star Ferry. $ *Rooms from: HK$2800* ✉ *1 Harbour Rd., Wan Chai* ☎ *2802–8888* ⊕ *www.renaissancehotels.com/hkghv* ⟿ *857 rooms* ⦿| *No meals* Ⓜ *Wan Chai* ✛ *2:C2.*

CAUSEWAY BAY

$
B&B/INN
Fodor'sChoice
★
Alisan Guest House. Some of these no-frills rooms nestled into an old apartment building in Causeway Bay have nice views of the yachts just across Gloucester Road, and all offer cleanliness, safety, and friendly hospitality at a budget price. **Pros:** friendly, English-speaking staff; pride in cleanliness; good location; free Wi-Fi. **Cons:** small rooms and windows;

surcharge to pay with credit card (pay with cash or via PayPal instead). [$] *Rooms from: HK$380* ✉ *Flat A, 5/F, Hoi To Court, 275 Gloucester Rd., Causeway Bay* ☎ *2838–0762* 🌐 *www.alisanguesthouse.com* 🛏 *30 rooms* 🍴 *No meals* [M] *Causeway Bay* ✥ *2:F2.*

> **WORD OF MOUTH**
>
> "There are also hotels in Causeway Bay, the far eastern section of Wan Chai. I am not a huge fan of this area for a first-time tourist, as there are no major tourist sights in the area, so you will spend time getting to sights (and then back to your hotel to collect luggage, etc). If you are here *exclusively* for clothes shopping, then Causeway Bay is a good location."
>
> —Cicerone

$ 🏨 **Butterfly on Morrison.** Standard rooms are small and housed on lower floors with no views, so consider upgrading to a larger room on the upper floors where the surrounding skyline and even Happy Valley Racecourse form a dramatic backdrop. **Pros:** chic contemporary-style rooms with decent neighborhood views from some. **Cons:** few in-hotel facilities. [$] *Rooms from: HK$1200* ✉ *39 Morrison Hill Rd., Causeway Bay* ☎ *3962–8333* 🌐 *www.butterflyhk.com* 🛏 *93 rooms* 🍴 *No meals* [M] *Causeway Bay* ✥ *2:E4.*

$$ HOTEL 🏨 **Cosmo Hotel.** The Cosmopolitan's little next-door neighbor appeals to guests who enjoy trendy, contemporary design as well as the allure of the popular ground floor Nooch Bar, with its lush, red velvet booths and lavish cocktails. **Pros:** cheerful rooms in one of three mood colors—orange, green, or yellow; 24-hour check-in and checkout; guests can use facilities of the Cosmopolitan next door. **Cons:** surrounded by busy streets. [$] *Rooms from: HK$1600* ✉ *375–377 Queen's Rd. E, Wan Chai* ☎ *3552–8388* 🌐 *www.cosmohotel.com.hk* 🛏 *142 rooms* 🍴 *No meals* [M] *Causeway Bay* ✥ *2:D4.*

$ HOTEL 👶 🏨 **Cosmopolitan Hotel.** Kid-friendly services extend to family-sized rooms that sleep up to five and even suites filled with stuffed animals and electronic games, while adults enjoy a choice of 11 pillows and many other personal touches. **Pros:** great shuttle service; packages to Ocean Park and other kid-friendly amenities; good in-house restaurant and bar; extremely reasonable rates. **Cons:** surrounded by insanely busy streets with little pedestrian appeal. [$] *Rooms from: HK$800* ✉ *387–397 Queen's Rd. E, Wan Chai* ☎ *3552–1111* 🌐 *www.cosmopolitanhotel.com.hk* 🛏 *454 rooms* [M] *Causeway Bay* ✥ *2:E4.*

$$ HOTEL 🏨 **Crowne Plaza Hong Kong.** A tall, black tower overlooking Happy Valley and the hills through floor-to-ceiling double-glazed windows features sleek executive rooms equipped with surround-sound DVD systems and 42-inch flat screens; suites afford especially panoramic views through three walls of windows. **Pros:** great outdoor pool has a nice view; short walk from Times Square and other attractions. **Cons:** racing fans get better track views at nearby Cosmopolitan. [$] *Rooms from: HK$2400* ✉ *8 Leighton Rd., Causeway Bay* ☎ *3980–3980* 🌐 *www.cphongkong.com* 🛏 *263 rooms* 🍴 *No meals* [M] *Causeway Bay* ✥ *2:F4.*

$$ HOTEL 🏨 **Empire Hotel Hong Kong, Causeway Bay.** A quiet locale just east of Victoria Park is enhanced by soothingly decorated guest rooms, where the amenities include posh glass-walled showers. **Pros:** quiet neighborhood;

beautiful west-looking views. **Cons:** small rooms and windows; no pool or gym; situated away from the action. $ *Rooms from: HK$1900* ⊠ *8 Wing Hing St., Causeway Bay* ☎ *3692–2333* ⊕ *www.empirehotel.com. hk* ⇨ *280 rooms* ⦿| *No meals* Ⓜ *Tin Hau* ⧐ *2:H1*.

$$$ ⌂ **Excelsior.** Some rooms are spacious with splendid views of the bay
HOTEL while other rooms are smaller with close-up street views, but all have a light, contemporary design and are moderately priced compared with other high-end hotels (especially in the center of Causeway Bay). **Pros:** excellent location to explore bustling Causeway Bay. **Cons:** no pool; faces one of the most congested main roads in the city. $ *Rooms from: HK$2500* ⊠ *281 Gloucester Rd., Causeway Bay* ☎ *2894–8888* ⊕ *www. mandarinoriental.com/excelsior* ⇨ *884 rooms* ⦿| *Breakfast* Ⓜ *Causeway Bay* ⧐ *2:F2*.

$$ ⌂ **J Plus.** Designer Philippe Starck's incredible ability to blend seem-
HOTEL ingly unblendable themes makes every corner an exercise in eye candy,
Fodor's Choice but it isn't all style over substance: each white-swathed room is like a
★ mini suite, full of cozy corners that combine old Hong Kong, Alice in Wonderland, and everyday practicalities. **Pros:** great value for money; a design geek's dream; complimentary breakfast; kitchenettes; laundry facilities. **Cons:** no views. $ *Rooms from: HK$1700* ⊠ *1–5 Irving St., Causeway Bay* ☎ *3196–9000* ⊕ *www.jplushongkong.com* ⇨ *56 rooms* ⦿| *Breakfast* Ⓜ *Causeway Bay* ⧐ *2:G3*.

$$$ ⌂ **Lanson Place Hotel.** The understated, striking design promotes a sense
HOTEL of calm, from the relaxing lounge/library to guest quarters that feel like exclusive apartments and come with kitchenettes and cleverly designed living areas. **Pros:** attractive, distinctive surroundings; business center, gym, and many other amenities. **Cons:** no harbor views; no substantial dining. $ *Rooms from: HK$2600* ⊠ *133 Leighton Rd., Causeway Bay* ☎ *3477–6888* ⊕ *hongkong.lansonplace.com* ⇨ *194 rooms* ⦿| *Breakfast* Ⓜ *Causeway Bay* ⧐ *2:G3*.

$ ⌂ **Metropark Hotel Causeway Bay.** The views of the skyline and adja-
HOTEL cent Victoria Park are beautiful, whether enjoyed from the simple but effectively designed modern rooms with all the basics or the pleasant rooftop pool. **Pros:** spectacular views for less; across from Victoria Park. **Cons:** limited hotel facilities; small lobby; few in-room ameni-ties. $ *Rooms from: HK$1200* ⊠ *148 Tung Lo Wan Rd., Causeway Bay* ☎ *2600–1000* ⊕ *www.metroparkhotel.com* ⇨ *266 rooms* ⦿| *No meals* Ⓜ *Tin Hau* ⧐ *2:H2*.

$$ ⌂ **Park Lane.** Guest rooms are as airy as the views at this elegant landmark
HOTEL overlooking Victoria Park, with glass-topped furnishings and glass walls that accent the open outlooks over greenery, the harbor, and the skyline. **Pros:** sprawling views; close to Causeway Bay shopping. **Cons:** often crowded; no pool; showing its age in places. $ *Rooms from: HK$1700* ⊠ *310 Gloucester Rd., Causeway Bay* ☎ *2293–8888* ⊕ *www.parklane. com.hk* ⇨ *809 rooms* ⦿| *No meals* Ⓜ *Causeway Bay* ⧐ *2:G2*.

EASTERN

$$ ⌂ **East.** Regulars, many of whom are business travelers, appreciate being
HOTEL comfortably away from the Island's bustling madness while enjoying such perks as the comfortably soothing guest rooms, rooftop deck, and tranquil spa. **Pros:** free Wi-Fi; beautiful rooftop lounge and deck;

6

The reception area at J Plus.

A guest room at J Plus.

good fitness center. **Cons:** quiet residential surroundings; little nearby nightlife. $ *Rooms from: HK$1800* ✉ *29 Taikoo Shing Rd., Tai Koo, Eastern* ☏ *3968–3968* ⊕ *www.east-hongkong.com* ☏ *344 rooms* ❍ *No meals* Ⓜ *Tai Koo* ✛ *2:H1.*

KOWLOON

If you enjoy rubbing elbows with the locals in chatty all-day noodle stalls just as much as shuffling through touristy pedestrian night markets and malls, Kowloon is the place to be. Postcard skyline views abound from harborfront hotels in Tsim Sha Tsui, a 10-minute ferry ride away from Hong Kong Island, with a calmer atmosphere heading eastward toward Hung Hom.

TSIM SHA TSUI

The southern tip of the Kowloon peninsula is the birthplace of the Golden Mile, and upholding its reputation is the territory's greatest density of luxury hotels around the southern end of Nathan Road. Postcard skyline views from posh suites overlooking Victoria Harbour provide an oasis of serenity above the bustling and boisterous neighborhood below.

6

$ 🏨 **BP International House.** These small and no-frills rooms in a modern
HOTEL   tower on the north side of Kowloon Park come with a bonus: views over an extensive swath of greenery or the harbor; quarters vary in size considerably, so be sure to ask for a spacious room. **Pros:** coffee shop, restaurant, and lounge on premises; self-service coin laundry. **Cons:** can get crowded with business and tour groups; modest with few amenities. $ *Rooms from: HK$1200* ✉ *8 Austin Rd., Tsim Sha Tsui* ☏ *2376–1111* ⊕ *www.bpih.com.hk* ☏ *529 rooms* ❍ *No meals* Ⓜ *Tsim Sha Tsui* ✛ *3:E4.*

$$ 🏨 **Butterfly on Prat.** Pleasant rooms done in soothing earth tones and
HOTEL   natural wood are a restful retreat from oft-rowdy Prat Avenue, overflowing with restaurants, bars, and clubs—meaning guests don't have to venture far to explore Hong Kong nightlife. **Pros:** friendly staff; colorful, practical rooms; 24-hour gym; fridge, microwave, and electric kettles in rooms. **Cons:** very limited views; rowdy neighborhood; no restaurant and few amenities. $ *Rooms from: HK$1600* ✉ *21 Prat Ave., Tsim Sha Tsui* ☏ *3962–8888* ⊕ *www.butterflyhk.com* ☏ *122 rooms* ❍ *No meals* Ⓜ *Tsim Sha Tsui* ✛ *3:F5.*

$$ 🏨 **Harbour Grand Kowloon.** For many guests, a long list of amenities
HOTEL   makes up for an isolated-from-action locale: most of the large, comfortable, contemporary rooms have harbor views, and the year-round outdoor pool, spa, gym, and array of lounges and restaurants are spectacular. **Pros:** harborfront location on the peaceful side of the promenade; extensive business center. **Cons:** isolated location in residential neighborhood; no easy subway access. $ *Rooms from: HK$1550* ✉ *Whampoa Garden, 20 Tak Fung St., Hung Hom, Tsim Sha Tsui* ☏ *2621–3188* ⊕ *www.harbourgrand.com/kowloon* ☏ *554 rooms* ❍ *No meals* Ⓜ *Hung Hom* ✛ *3:H4.*

$$
HOTEL

Holiday Inn Golden Mile. Most views from the basic, medium-size rooms involve an up-close look at your neighbors, but being in the heart of Tsim Sha Tsui is the main attraction, along with such perks as a refreshing outdoor pool area with sauna and steam rooms. **Pros:** multiple dining options include a Cantonese restaurant, German deli, Italian restaurant, and popular buffet. **Cons:** no views; can get crowded with groups. $ *Rooms from: HK$1800 ⌧ 50 Nathan Rd., Tsim Sha Tsui ☎ 2369–3111 ⊕ holidayinn. com/hongkong-gldn ⤳ 614 rooms* ⫢ *No meals* Ⓜ *Tsim Sha Tsui ✛ 3:F5.*

$
HOTEL
Fodor's Choice
★

Hop Inn Carnarvon. One of the city's most charming and personable budget locations exudes loads of character in tidy, comfortable rooms that are clean, well-organized, and individually decorated with lots of color by local artists. **Pros:** fun, beautifully original decor for budget lodgings; friendly staff; ultra-cool common room and outside deck; private bathrooms. **Cons:** if you bring a guest back who stays past 1 am, you will be charged an extra 50 percent on your room rate; not too many amenities, but the price is right. $ *Rooms from: HK$650 ⌧ 9/F James S. Lee Mansion, 33–35 Carnarvon Road, Tsim Sha Tsui ☎ 2881–7331 ⊕ www.hopinn.hk ⤳ 27 rooms* ⫢ *No meals* Ⓜ *Tsim Sha Tsui ✛ 3:F5.*

$
HOTEL

Hop Inn Hankow. Much like the affiliated ⇨ *Hop Inn Carnarvon*, this appealing guest house is a budget traveler's dream, with loads of personality in the guest rooms designed by local artists. **Pros:** friendly service and amazing personality for budget lodgings; private bathrooms. **Cons:** no common hangout areas; comically small elevator. $ *Rooms from: HK$400 ⌧ 2/F, Hanyee Building, Flat A, Tsim Sha Tsui ☎ 2881–7331 ⊕ www.hopinn.hk ⤳ 9 rooms* ⫢ *No meals* Ⓜ *Tsim Sha Tsui ✛ 3:E5.*

$$
Fodor's Choice
★

Hotel ICON. Here's a stunning design statement, from the vertical garden hanging above the lobby café to the stylish, panoramic lounge on the top floor—in between are gorgeous, view-filled guest rooms outfitted with cozy woods and natural fabrics and all the high-tech amenities. **Pros:** a designer's dream; dedication to guest experience; tranquil feel with no tour groups allowed. **Cons:** surrounding area is thick with crowds at times. $ *Rooms from: HK$2000 ⌧ 17 Science Museum Rd., Tsim Sha Tsui ☎ 3400–1000 ⊕ www.hotel-icon.com ⤳ 262 rooms* ⫢ *No meals* Ⓜ *Tsim Sha Tsui East ✛ 3:G4.*

$
HOTEL

Hotel Panorama. True to the name, each of the contemporary-style guest rooms is on a corner, allowing breathtaking harbor and city views through floor-to-ceiling windows. **Pros:** sophisticated experience in an old neighborhood; pet-friendly; executive lounge and other facilities geared to business travelers. **Cons:** no spa or pool; even non-smoking rooms may smell of smoke. $ *Rooms from: HK$1400 ⌧ 8A Hart Ave., Tsim Sha Tsui ☎ 3550–0388 ⊕ www.hotelpanorama.com.hk ⤳ 324 rooms* ⫢ *No meals* Ⓜ *Tsim Sha Tsui ✛ 3:F5.*

$$$$
HOTEL

Hullett House. Ten huge suites occupy a former colonial police headquarters from 1881 and each recreates a different era of Hong Kong history with bold, artistic flair showcasing Asian and colonial styles—while pampering guests with 21st-century technology and luxury. **Pros:** historic surroundings; several restaurants and bars on the ground floor. **Cons:** public areas can get crowded. $ *Rooms from: HK$4500 ⌧ 2A Canton Rd., Tsim Sha Tsui ☎ 3988–0000 ⊕ www.hulletthouse.com ⤳ 10 suites* ⫢ *Breakfast* Ⓜ *Tsim Sha Tsui ✛ 3:E6.*

The sushi bar at the InterContinental Hong Kong.

Aerial view of the Peninsula lobby.

$$ HOTEL 🏨 **Hyatt Regency Hong Kong, Tsim Sha Tsui.** Boxed in location by high-rises, only the upper-floor rooms have memorable views, but all are cozy retreats done in olive and brown tones with burgundy armchairs and classic photos of Hong Kong on the walls. **Pros:** close to the action and Minden Street bar scene; good dining options. **Cons:** busy shopping-mall surroundings; limited views. [$] *Rooms from: HK$2200* ✉ *18 Hanoi Rd., Tsim Sha Tsui* ☎ *2311–1234* 🌐 *www.hongkong.tsimshatsui.hyatt.com* 🛏 *381 rooms* 🍴 *No meals* [M] *Tsim Sha Tsui* ✛ *3:F5.*

$$$ HOTEL Fodor's Choice ★ 🏨 **InterContinental Hong Kong.** A location at the tip of the Kowloon peninsula ensures panoramic, front-row harbor views from most of the contemporary rooms, designed with Asian accents that include deep, sunken tubs in the marbled bathrooms. **Pros:** exceptional views; modern design; extravagant spa. **Cons:** the Avenue of Stars just outside is one the most crowded tourist scenes in Hong Kong. [$] *Rooms from: HK$3000* ✉ *18 Salisbury Rd., Tsim Sha Tsui* ☎ *2721–1211* 🌐 *www.hongkong-ic.intercontinental.com* 🛏 *495 rooms* [M] *Tsim Sha Tsui* ✛ *3:F6.*

$$$$ HOTEL 🏨 **Kowloon Shangri-La.** You might feel like a '70s tycoon amid murals, fountains, and crystal chandeliers in the lobby, and the feeling extends to the spacious rooms decorated in warm colors with armchairs, rich wooden furniture, bay windows, and nice marbled bathrooms. **Pros:** warm hospitality; attention to detail; quality Chinese restaurant; excellent business facilities. **Cons:** less exciting garden views on lower floors. [$] *Rooms from: HK$4100* ✉ *64 Mody Rd., Tsim Sha Tsui* ☎ *2721–2111* 🌐 *www.shangri-la.com/kowloon* 🛏 *688 rooms* 🍴 *No meals* [M] *Tsim Sha Tsui East* ✛ *3:G5.*

$$ HOTEL 🏨 **The Langham.** Attractive luxury is apparent everywhere, from the opulent lobby to warmly decorated guest rooms done in a soothing, English-country style, many with such touches as separate sitting areas and marble bathrooms with deep tubs and walk-in showers. **Pros:** one of the better buffet breakfasts in Hong Kong (included in some room rates); excellent dining options. **Cons:** limited city views; surrounded by heavy traffic. [$] *Rooms from: HK$1900* ✉ *8 Peking Rd., Tsim Sha Tsui* ☎ *2375–1133* 🌐 *www.hongkong.langhamhotels.com* 🛏 *495 rooms* 🍴 *No meals* [M] *Tsim Sha Tsui* ✛ *3:E5.*

$$$ 🏨 **The Luxe Manor.** In the absence of views, rooms are a show in themselves, with audacious design themes (gold, frilly picture frames around flat-screen TVs) that don't sacrifice comfort and luxury. **Pros:** a trippy experience for the eyes; close proximity to more mellow nightlife and easy shopping. **Cons:** no views; lobby feels deserted at times. [$] *Rooms from: HK$2800* ✉ *39 Kimberley Rd., Tsim Sha Tsui* ☎ *3763–8880* 🌐 *www.theluxemanor.com* 🛏 *159 rooms* 🍴 *No meals* [M] *Tsim Sha Tsui* ✛ *3:F4.*

$$$ HOTEL 🏨 **Marco Polo Hongkong Hotel.** Spacious rooms with sweeping views of Hong Kong Island are near the shopping hub along Canton Road and linked to Harbour City's immense shopping complex. **Pros:** westward views; convenient to Star Ferry and other transports. **Cons:** full in late March during the Hong Kong Rugby Sevens tournament; boisterous crowds during Oktoberfest. [$] *Rooms from: HK$2600* ✉ *Harbour City, Canton Rd., Tsim Sha Tsui* ☎ *2113–0088* 🌐 *www.marcopolohotels.com* 🛏 *665 rooms* 🍴 *Some meals* [M] *Tsim Sha Tsui* ✛ *3:D6.*

$$
HOTEL
The Mira. Streamlined-sleek guest rooms have touches of modern buzz everywhere (glass-pod showers, laptop safes, fully ready mobile phones), but the excellent service and guest-friendly facilities make this much more than a hip showplace. **Pros:** hip, seen-and-be-seen vibe; good in-house dining; great spa with pool. **Cons:** lobby can be a little too active at times. $ *Rooms from: HK$2100* ⊠ *118 Nathan Rd., Tsim Sha Tsui* ☎ *2368–1111* ⊕ *www.themirahotel.com* ⊶ *492 rooms* ⏍*No meals* Ⓜ *Tsim Sha Tsui* ✛ *3:E4.*

$$$$
HOTEL
Fodor's Choice
★
The Peninsula Hong Kong. Even in a city with so many world-class hotels, the Peninsula manages to stand above the rest, an oasis of old-world glamour, with high-ceiling apartmentlike suites in the old wing and newer rooms in the upper wing, where Kowloon and harbor views make you feel like you own Hong Kong. **Pros:** state-of-the-art room facilities; impeccable service; tons of character; world-class dining, facilities, and entertainment. **Cons:** price; a bit rarified for some tastes. $ *Rooms from: HK$5600* ⊠ *Salisbury Rd, Tsim Sha Tsui* ☎ *2920–2888* ⊕ *www.peninsula.com* ⊶ *354 rooms* ⏍*Some meals* Ⓜ *Tsim Sha Tsui* ✛ *3:E6.*

$$
HOTEL
Royal Garden. A comfortable business hotel built around a towering garden atrium happens to be a particularly good place for world-class dining, with four notable restaurants on-site, though the spacious, sleek, and soothing guest rooms do not have views. **Pros:** illuminated rooftop tennis court; inspired pool facilities; distinguished restaurants. **Cons:** no views from rooms; busy lobby. $ *Rooms from: HK$1550* ⊠ *69 Mody Rd., Tsim Sha Tsui* ☎ *2721–5215* ⊕ *www.rghk.com.hk* ⊶ *417 rooms* Ⓜ *Tsim Sha Tsui East* ✛ *3:G5.*

$
HOTEL
☾
Salisbury YMCA. Little wonder this upscale YMCA is a popular budget choice: it sits next to the mighty Peninsula and across from the city's three biggest museums on Tsim Sha Tsui's harborfront, and most rooms have at least partial harbor views. **Pros:** prime views at modest prices; pool and fitness activities to occupy the whole family. **Cons:** busy lobby. $ *Rooms from: HK$1100* ⊠ *41 Salisbury Rd., Tsim Sha Tsui* ☎ *2268–7000* ⊕ *www.ymcahk.org.hk* ⊶ *363 rooms* ⏍*No meals* Ⓜ *Tsim Sha Tsui* ✛ *3:E6.*

$$
HOTEL
Sheraton Hong Kong Hotel & Towers. Such perks as good dining and the chance to sip champagne in a bubbling rooftop Jacuzzi enhance the warm and modern guest rooms, many with city and harbor views. **Pros:** beautiful art-filled lobby and public spaces; pleasant, contemporary room decor; excellent business and fitness facilities. **Cons:** at the dense and congested southern end of Nathan Road. $ *Rooms from: HK$2200* ⊠ *20 Nathan Rd., Tsim Sha Tsui* ☎ *2369–1111* ⊕ *www.sheraton.com/hongkong* ⊶ *782 rooms* ⏍*No meals* Ⓜ *Tsim Sha Tsui* ✛ *3:E6.*

6

$ HOTEL **Stanford Hillview Hotel.** Straightforward and relatively no-frills rooms are set above busy Tsim Sha Tsui on a hillside below the Hong Kong Observatory, providing a nice retreat and pleasant views. **Pros:** quiet; stately renovated building; excellent all-day buffet in the Hillview Cafe. **Cons:** small, simple rooms. [$] *Rooms from: HK$1200* ✉ *Observatory Rd., Knutsford Terrace, Tsim Sha Tsui* ☎ *2722–7822* 🌐 *www.stanfordhillview.com* 🛏 *177 rooms* 🍴 *No meals* [M] *Tsim Sha Tsui* ⊕ *3:F4.*

YAU MA TEI, MONG KOK, AND NORTHERN KOWLOON

As you venture up and off Kowloon's central artery of Nathan Road through Yau Ma Tei, accommodations tend to be older and cheaper until you reach the grand hotels dominating the shopping malls in Mong Kok. Northern Kowloon, centered around the classier Elements shopping mall and ICC tower, is the high-end up-and-coming exception.

YAU MA TEI

$ HOTEL **Booth Lodge.** At this surprisingly pleasant budget retreat, operated by the Salvation Army for the past quarter of a century, everything is bright and clean, from the walls to the starched sheets on the firm double beds in the Spartan but large rooms. **Pros:** clean but no-frills lodgings at a bargain price. **Cons:** noisy vehicle and foot traffic on the main street. [$] *Rooms from: HK$1200* ✉ *11 Wing Sing Lane, Yau Ma Tei* ☎ *2771–9266* 🌐 *boothlodge.salvation.org.hk* 🛏 *60 rooms* 🍴 *No meals* [M] *Yau Ma Tei* ⊕ *3:E1.*

$ HOTEL **Eaton Hotel.** Rooms above a theater and shopping complex come in a variety of welcoming styles, from an East-meets-West decor in some to airy, bright, functional contemporary design in others—all are set up for maximum comfort and relaxation. **Pros:** comfortable rooms in a relatively convenient location. **Cons:** Nathan Road can be overwhelming with the traffic and noise. [$] *Rooms from: HK$1200* ✉ *380 Nathan Rd., Yau Ma Tei* ☎ *2782–1818* 🌐 *hongkong.eatonhotels.com* 🛏 *465 rooms* 🍴 *No meals* [M] *Yau Ma Tei* ⊕ *3:E2.*

MONG KOK

$$ HOTEL 👶 **Langham Place.** At this sleek glass-and-steel box that transformed a once sleazy block, whimsical sculptures of Mao's Red Guards greet you at the entrance, and luxurious guest rooms feature floor-to-ceiling windows, mirrored walls, mood lighting, and glass-walled marble bathrooms. **Pros:** great spa and pool; loads of shopping at adjoining high-end mall; good choice of in-house bars and restaurants. **Cons:** very busy surroundings; parts of colorful neighborhood are a bit rough. [$] *Rooms from: HK$1600* ✉ *555 Shanghai St., Mong Kok* ☎ *3552–3388* 🌐 *hongkong.langhamplacehotels.com* 🛏 *665 rooms* 🍴 *No meals* [M] *Mong Kok* ⊕ *3:D1.*

NORTHERN KOWLOON

$$$$ HOTEL 👶 Fodor's Choice ★ **The Ritz-Carlton, Hong Kong.** From the world's highest hotel, perching on the 102nd through the 118th floors of the ICC skyscraper in West Kowloon, every large and luxurious guest room enjoys a stupendous vantage point. **Pros:** earth-shattering views; top-class service and amenities. **Cons:** extremely pricey; surrounding Kowloon area

Modern décor within the W Hong Kong

The W Hong Kong stands tall in Kowloon.

lacks nightlife. [$] *Rooms from: HK$6800* ✉ *International Commerce Center, 1 Austin Rd. W, Northern Kowloon* ☎ *2263–2263* 🌐 *www.ritzcarlton.com/en/Properties/HongKong* 🛏 *312 rooms* 🍴 *No meals* [M] *West Kowloon* ✥ *3:D3.*

$$$ HOTEL Fodor's Choice ★ **W Hong Kong.** A hip, young vibe prevails, but guest rooms are veritable urban oases—soundproof and spacious, alternately colorful or sleek on even and odd floors, with mood lighting, surround audiovisual systems, big mirrors, and even bigger views of the harbor. **Pros:** friendly service; spacious and colorful rooms; panoramic views; exciting bars and restaurants. **Cons:** noisy atmosphere outside rooms; removed shopping-mall location. [$] *Rooms from: HK$2700* ✉ *1 Austin Rd. W, Kowloon Station, Northern Kowloon* ☎ *3717–2222* 🌐 *www.whotels.com/hongkong* 🛏 *393 rooms* 🍴 *No meals* [M] *West Kowloon* ✥ *3:D3.*

SOUTHSIDE

Southside feels relatively far removed from the more frequented northern coast of Hong Kong Island, due to less direct transport routes. The area's only major hotel is situated within Cyberport, which was initially launched in 2004 as a high-tech business hub. Today the complex also includes residential, commercial, and even educational facilities, but it's still pretty lifeless at night. On the upside, it's only a short drive to popular south-coast destinations such as Aberdeen, Ocean Park, Repulse Bay beach, and Stanley Market.

$$ HOTEL **L'hotel Island South.** These towering 37 floors offer clean and modern rooms, and though the surroundings are industrial, water and lush greenery views, along with an outdoor pool and casual ambience throughout, provide a nice getaway feel. **Pros:** south coast views; close to Southside attractions; free shuttle service to city center. **Cons:** Aberdeen tunnel traffic; almost zero nightlife nearby. [$] *Rooms from: HK$1900* ✉ *55 Wong Chuk Hang Rd., Aberdeen* ☎ *3968–8888* 🌐 *www.lhotelislandsouth.com* 🛏 *432 rooms* 🍴 *No meals* [M] *Aberdeen* ✥ *1:D6.*

$$ HOTEL **Le Méridien Cyberport.** Though most guests belong to the convention crowd gathering at nearby Cyberport, bright and spacious guest rooms break out of the business mode with a hip vibe and generously sized windows for sea gazing; corner suites enjoy especially sensational sea views. **Pros:** vast sunset views over bay and sea; five restaurants; outdoor pool; glass-and-chrome bathrooms with walk-in showers. **Cons:** isolated location on south side of island. [$] *Rooms from: HK$1600* ✉ *100 Cyberport Rd., Pok Fu Lam* ☎ *2980–7788* 🌐 *www.lemeridien.com/hongkong* 🛏 *170 rooms* 🍴 *No meals* [M] *Pok Fu Lam* ✥ *1:A6.*

LANTAU ISLAND

The main advantage to staying on Lantau Island is its proximity to the airport and SkyPier for late-night arrivals or early-morning departures, or to AsiaWorld-Expo, if you're here on business. Most visitors come to Lantau by MTR as a day trip; popular attractions include Disneyland, the Ngong Ping cable-car ride, the Great Buddha, scenic hikes and beaches, and outlet shopping at Citygate mall. For the more adventurous, the island is also home to remote fishing villages, reached

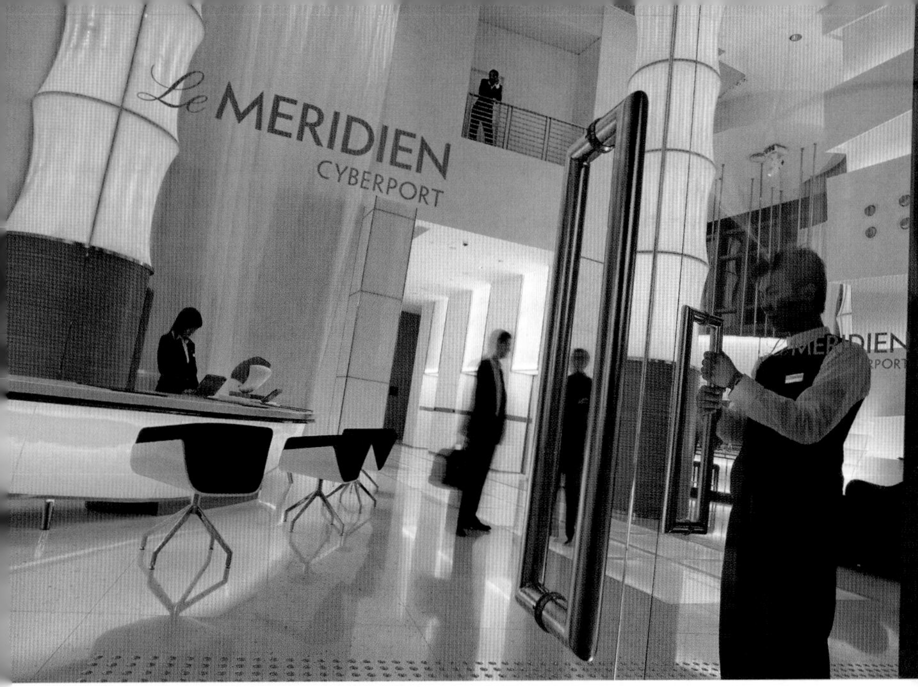

A look inside Le Meridien Cyberport.

by ferry and roads less traveled. Gentrified Discovery Bay beach, easily accessible by ferry from Central, hosts Dragon Boat races every spring.

$$ RESORT 👪 🏨 **Disney's Hollywood Hotel.** This being Disneyland, the focus is on kids—from Chef Mickey restaurants to the piano-shaped pool to well-stocked playrooms—but adults might enjoy the theme of silver-screen glamour that extends to art-deco styling in the cocktail lounge and the small but comfortable guest rooms. **Pros:** good value; a children's paradise; Discovery Bay restaurants are just minutes away; near airport. **Cons:** cut off from other Hong Kong attractions; corniness factor; generic theme-park ambience. [$] *Rooms from: HK$2100* ✉ *Hong Kong Disneyland Resort, Lantau Island* ☎ *3510–5000* 🌐 *www.hongkongdisneyland.com* 🛏 *600 rooms* 🍴 *No meals* [M] *Lantau* ✥ *3:C1.*

$$$ RESORT 👪 🏨 **Hong Kong Disneyland Hotel.** Modeled in Victorian style after the Grand Floridian at Florida's Disney resort, this hugely popular resort is beautifully done, from the spacious rooms with balconies overlooking the sea to kids' activities hosted by Disney characters. **Pros:** great for kids; handy to airport. **Cons:** cut off from the rest of Hong Kong; can seem crowded at times. [$] *Rooms from: HK$2900* ✉ *Hong Kong Disneyland Resort, Lantau Island* ☎ *3510–6000* 🌐 *www.hongkongdisneyland.com* 🛏 *400 rooms* 🍴 *Breakfast* [M] *Lantau* ✥ *3:C1.*

$ HOTEL 🏨 **Hong Kong SkyCity Marriott Hotel.** Perks at this standard-issue airport hotel are views of the picturesque Nine Eagles golf course or the bay, a footbridge that conveniently crosses the highway to AsiaWorld-Expo, and free shuttle service to and from Disneyland and Citygate shopping mall in Tung Chung. **Pros:** comfortable if generic ambience; spacious rooms good for families. **Cons:** tiny spa; low-ceilinged indoor pool area;

Lodging Alternatives

Almost every hotel will offer you a special rate for longer-term stays of a week or more—and some, like The Upper House, J Plus, and Lanson Place Hotel in Causeway Bay are especially equipped for residential guests. But if you prefer a more hands-off atmosphere, consider renting a serviced apartment. The following properties, which are all licensed to accommodate tenants for both short-term and long-term stays, were chosen for their compelling locations, amenities, and cozy but comfortable interiors. However, as most of these are inhabited year-round by monthly renting expatriates, it's best to call and discuss dates, rates, and conditions well in advance.

The Jervois. A bright new ode of contemporary design in Sheung Wan provides one or two-bedroom suites for long- or short-term stays while offering some of the most comfortable lodgings around. $ *Rooms from: HK$2200 ⊠ 89 Jervois St., Sheung Wan ☎ 3994–9000 ⊕ www.thejervois.com.*

Ovolo Queen's Road. Ovolo specializes in serviced apartments in Central and Western District, but only this Queen's Road location rents studios by the day. $ *Rooms from: HK$2080 ⊠ 286 Queen's Rd. Central, Central ☎ 2910–0700 ⊕ www.ovologroup.com* M *Sheung Wan.*

Shama Causeway Bay. These 110 flats range from studios to two-bedroom suites directly across from the Times Square shopping mall. $ *Rooms from: HK$1280 ⊠ 8 Russell St., Causeway Bay ☎ 3100–8555 ⊕ www.shama.com ⤶ 110 apartments* M *Causeway Bay.*

Two Macdonnell Road. Offering sweeping views of the Hong Kong Zoological and Botanical Gardens and beyond from its Mid-Levels perch, this property offers six different apartment layouts, ranging from studios to two-bedroom suites. $ *Rooms from: HK$2800 ⊠ 2 Macdonnell Rd., Mid-Levels ☎ 2132–2132 ⊕ www.twomr.com.hk* M *Central.*

beware of boy-band groupies camping out before a concert at AsiaWorld-Expo. $ *Rooms from: HK$1400 ⊠ 1 Sky City Rd. E, Hong Kong International Airport, Lantau ☎ 3969–1888 ⊕ www.skycitymarriott.com ⤶ 658 rooms* ⦿ *No meals* M *Asia World Expo ✛ 3:B1.*

$$
HOTEL **Regal Airport Hotel.** One of the world's largest airport hotels is more than just a place to sleep before the next flight—rooms have terrific views of planes landing from afar or overlook the swimming pool, and the spa has pleasant alfresco areas for relaxation. **Pros:** direct airport access via indoor moving walkway; refreshing pool and spa facilities. **Cons:** far removed from Hong Kong sights. $ *Rooms from: HK$1700 ⊠ 9 Cheong Tat Rd., Hong Kong International Airport, Lantau ☎ 2286–8888 ⊕ www.regalhotel.com ⤶ 1,171 rooms* ⦿ *No meals* M *Airport ✛ 3:B1.*

Nightlife

WORD OF MOUTH

"A trip on Aqua Luna includes a drink and some hors d'oeuvres. The wooden junk is lovely and goes back and forth and around the harbour. It takes about an hour and is a good thing to do at sunset or in the afternoon."

—Cicerone

Updated by
Samantha
Leese

A riot of neon, heralding frenetic after-hours action, announces Hong Kong's nightlife districts. Clubs and bars fill to capacity, evening markets pack in shoppers looking for bargains, restaurants welcome diners, cinemas pop corn as fast as they can, and theaters and concert halls prepare for full houses.

The neighborhoods of Wan Chai, Lan Kwai Fong, and SoHo are packed with bars, pubs, and nightclubs that cater to everyone from the hippest trendsetters to bankers ready to spend their bonuses and more laid-back crowds out for a pint. Partying in Hong Kong is a way of life; it starts at the beginning of the week with a drink or two after work, progressing to serious barhopping and clubbing on the weekends. Wednesday is a big night out here, too. Work hard, play harder is the motto in Hong Kong, and people follow it seriously.

Because each district has so much to offer, and since they're all quite close to each other, it's perfectly normal to pop into two or three bars before heading to a nightclub. At the other end of the spectrum, the city's arts and culture scene is equally lively, with innovative music, dance, and theater. Small independent productions as well as large-scale concerts take to the stage across the territory every weekend. You simply cannot go home without a Hong Kong nightlife story to tell.

PLANNING AND TIPS

BETTER SAFE THAN SORRY

All premises licensed to serve alcohol are supposedly subject to stringent fire, safety, and sanitary controls, although at times this is hard to believe, given the overcrowding at the hippest places. Think twice before succumbing to the city's raunchier hideaways. If you stumble into one, check out cover and table charges *before* you get too comfortable. If you don't have a table, pay for each round of drinks as it's served (by cash rather than credit card).

Hong Kong is a surprisingly safe place, but as in many destinations, the art of the out-of-towner rip-off has been perfected. If you're unsure, visit places signposted as approved by the Hong Kong Tourism Board (HKTB).

DANCING

Nightclubs range from down-to-earth dives with boisterous cover bands to hermetically sealed hip-hop dungeons packed with models and millionaires. The venues listed here tend to be smaller and more intimate than their high-octane megaplex cousins. Cover charges, if levied, can be steep, from HK$120 to HK$250, but often include a drink or two. Information and tickets for international DJ events can be found at ⊕ *www.hkclubbing.com* or ⊕ *www.hiphongkong.com.* Some bars and restaurants also hold weekly or monthly club nights, where music ranges from blues to house.

HOSTESS CLUBS

Many hostess clubs found in Hong Kong are clubs in name only. Some of these are multimillion-dollar operations with plush interiors and hundreds of hostess-companions working for them. Hostess clubs are a stage for showgirls and tycoons, designed to sweeten lucrative deals and lubricate business relationships. Expect to see exhibitions of arguably tasteless extravagance as patrons pay up to HK$1,000 per hour for the privilege of drinking in the company of attractive women. Between minimum drink charges, drinks for the hostesses, tips, and the possibility of spending upwards of five figures on a bottle of wine, you're looking at an HK$100,000-plus tab, a sum that does not faze the regulars. Indeed, legend has it that the biggest security problem faced by bouncers is breaking up fights over who gets to pay the bill.

The better clubs are on a par with music lounges in deluxe hotels, though they cost a little more. Dance floors are often large, with live bands and a lineup of both pop and cabaret singers. Their happy hours start in the afternoon, when many have a sort of tea-dance ambience, and continue through to mid-evening. Peak hours are 10 pm to 4 am.

Many so-called hostess clubs, however, are in fact fronts for prostitution. In Wan Chai, for instance, hostess clubs—too many to mention by name—are dotted among regular bars. Most if not all of them are sad little places full of leering men watching girls with vacant expressions, dressed in leotards, performing halfhearted pole dances. These houses of prostitution are not the same as establishments such as the upmarket Club BBoss in Tsim Sha Tsui.

HOURS

Twenty-four-hour liquor licenses are common, so strict closing times are not. Bars start closing around 2 am, clubs around 4 am, with some seeing in the sunrise. Happy hours are from midafternoon to 8 or 9 pm on weekdays. Closing times listed refer to Friday, Saturday, and the eves of public holidays; you can expect things to wind down an hour or two earlier midweek. Bars are typically open nightly, but nightclubs are closed or quiet on Sunday and Monday.

HOW TO GET HOME AFTER THE PARTY

The clean and reliable subway (MTR) shuts down at around 1 am, depending on your location. Taxis are your only way home after that. They are relatively cheap and can easily be flagged down on the street; when the light on the car roof is on, it's available for hire. If the cab has an "out of service" sign over its round "for hire" neon sign on the dashboard, it means it's a cross-harbor taxi. Fares start at HK$20.

MEMBERS ONLY

Many bars and clubs have a "members-only" policy, but don't let this deter you. It's mostly a way of prioritizing the guest list on busy nights. It can also mean that you're required to pay a cover charge, usually in the region of HK$150 to HK$200, including a drink on the house.

MUG OR MARTINI GLASS

From champagne decadence to sports bars lined with peanut shells, each of Hong Kong's districts has its own distinct nighttime personality. Even on a single street, dress codes and drink prices can vacillate wildly. The bar- and pub-lined streets of Lan Kwai Fong, Wan Chai, and Kowloon are a fairly casual affair, though shorts and flip-flops will limit your options. A beer or a mixed drink will cost from HK$50 to HK$80.

The Central, SoHo, and Wyndham Street areas are home to classy bars and glamorous nightclubs where a cosmopolitan mix of high rollers and partiers comes out to play. Drinks are expensive; a fresh-fruit martini will set you back more than HK$100. If you're prepared to pay a steep minimum for bottle service (HK$1,000 to HK$10,000 depending on the club), you can reserve a table for your party at some of these swanky establishments. Door trolls abound, so dress up to get in and blend in—shorts, flip-flops, and sneakers are definite no-nos.

NIGHTLIFE SAVVY

HK magazine is distributed free each Friday. Listings authority *Time Out Hong Kong* costs HK$18 and is published every other Wednesday. Another good source of nightlife and cultural information is the daily English-language newspaper the *South China Morning Post.*

URBTIX. Tickets for most big cultural events are on sale through citywide branches of URBTIX. ☎ *2111–5999* ⊕ *www.urbtix.hk.*

HK Ticketing. HK Ticketing sells tickets to many shows. ☎ *3128–8288* ⊕ *www.hkticketing.com.*

HONG KONG ISLAND

WESTERN

BARS

Club 71. This bohemian diamond-in-the-rough was named in tribute to July 1, 2003, when half a million Hong Kongers successfully rallied against looming threats to their freedom of speech. Tucked away on a terrace down a market side street, the quirky, unpretentious bar is a mainstay of artists, journalists, and left-wing politicians. The outdoor

HONG KONG'S TOP FIVE NIGHTLIFE SPOTS

dragon-i: The door's clipboard-wielding glamazons will not make entry easy, but this remains the kingpin of the big Central clubs, and second home to the city's extravagant elite.

Felix: Aqua Spirit may be trendier, but Philippe Starck–designed Felix, at the Peninsula, is an institution. The best view of the skyline is marketing currency in Kowloon, and this penthouse bar really matches its claim.

The Pawn: Modern panache and history's charm combine to make this one of the most unique establishments in town. Order a bottle of

wine and settle onto one of the vintage couches in the ever-popular "living room."

Socialito: A recent addition to the Wyndham Street nexus and right next door to Solas (below), this casual taqueria—slash—hidden nightclub was one of 2012's favorite new openings. Never underestimate a skirt-steak taco as the perfect midnight pick-me-up.

Solas: Stronghold of Wyndham Street's after-dark action, Solas is great if you're looking for somewhere loud and lively to meet new people over well-mixed drinks.

area closes around midnight. ⊠ *B/F, 67 Hollywood Rd., Sheung Wan, Western* ☎ *2858–7071* ⊘ *Closes 2 am* Ⓜ *Central.*

GAY AND LESBIAN SPOTS

Volume Beat. A friendly, mixed crowd of gays, lesbians, and their friends enjoys free entry and the club's open-door policy. New Arrivals Wednesdays are a staple of the scene, welcoming tourists and newbies and attracting locals with free vodka between 7 and 9 pm. Weekends are reliably hyper, with dance anthems filling the floor till the wee hours. Regular events include '70s and '80s retro nights and quiz nights. ⊠ *Ground fl., 62 Jervois St., Sheung Wan, Western* ☎ *2857–7683* ⊘ *Closes late* Ⓜ *Sheung Wan.*

CENTRAL

On weekends the streets of Lan Kwai Fong are liberated from traffic, and the swilling hordes from both sides of the street merge into one heaving organism. A five-minute walk uphill is SoHo. Back in the '90s it took local businesses some effort to convince district councilors that the sometimes vice-associated moniker (which in this case stands for South of Hollywood Road) was a good idea, but Hong Kong is now proud of this *très* chic area, a warren of streets stuffed with commensurately priced restaurants, bars, and late-night boutiques. Midway between Lan Kwai Fong's madness and SoHo's bohemian glamour is Wyndham Street, home to an array of sophisticated bars, nightclubs, and restaurants, and strict domain of the over-25s.

BARS

Armani Privé. The Armani brand has made its mark on Chater House, between the IFC and Lan Kwai Fong, bringing a taste of Milan to Hong Kong. One of their latest ventures is this lounge club, an update

Lan Kwai Fong

A curious, L-shape cobblestone lane in Central is the pulsating center of nightlife and dining in Hong Kong. Lan Kwai Fong, or just "the Fong," is a spot that really shines after the sun sets. You can start with a predinner drink at any number of bars, then enjoy some of the territory's finest dining before stopping at a nightclub to dance the night away.

For such a small area, Lan Kwai Fong has an incredibly broad range of nightlife to offer, with dozens of bars, restaurants, and clubs within just a few blocks. Since most of the ground-floor establishments spill out onto the pavement, there's an audible buzz about the place, lending it a festive air that's unmatched elsewhere in Hong Kong. Whether it's corporate financiers celebrating their latest million-dollar deals at La Dolce Vita or more humble office workers having drinks with their buddies at Le Jardin, there's a place here to suit everyone.

The same "something for everyone" motto extends to the plethora of upmarket restaurants in Lan Kwai Fong. From Asia, there are Chinese, Thai, Japanese, and Vietnamese restaurants, while European food can be found at French and Italian establishments. If your wallet's feeling a little light from your latest shopping expedition, take heed of the excited waiters waving to potential customers along Wing Wah Lane (affectionately known as Rat Alley). Here you'll find rowdy Indian, Thai, and Malaysian restaurants that serve piping-hot dishes at reasonable prices.

Lan Kwai Fong used to be a hawkers' neighborhood before World War II. Its modern success is largely due to Canadian expatriate Allan Zeman, an eccentric figure who has been dubbed the "King of Lan Kwai Fong" by the local media. He opened his first North American–style restaurant here 20 years ago; today he not only owns dozens of other restaurants and bars, but also the buildings they're in. He claims to have about 100 restaurants, and although he doesn't actually own them all, he acts as the landlord for most of them. The Fong restaurants are now simply a hobby for Zeman, whose business empire includes everything from property development to fashion.

New Year's Eve (December 31) is undoubtedly the busiest time for Lan Kwai Fong. Thousands of people line the tiny area to celebrate and party. You'll notice a strong police presence moving the human traffic through the streets and keeping an eye out for any troublemakers. This is mainly to prevent another tragedy such as the one in the early 1990s when 21 people were crushed to death as a massive throng went out of control as they ushered in a new year. Now when large crowds are anticipated—usually New Year's Eve, Christmas Eve, and also Halloween—the police carefully monitor the number of people entering the area.

Call it progress or a type of survival-of-the-strongest evolution, but this trendy neighborhood has seen as many establishments open as close down. New spots are constantly in development, or old places under refurbishment. Regardless of the changes, Lan Kwai Fong is always alive with scores of people and places to be merry.

—Eva Chui Loiterton

Partiers vie for elbow room on Lan Kwai Fong, Central's nightlife hub.

of the previous Armani Bar. The big draw here is a wide, gorgeous deck with skyscraper views, chic outdoor seating, and an impressive list of classic cocktails. Go into the bar and turn right up the stairs. ✉ *2/F, Chater House, 8 Connaught Rd., Central* ☎ *3583–2828* ⊕ *www. armaniprive-hk.com* ⊙ *Closes 4 am.*

The Blck Brd. This whisky bar (pronounced "blackbird") has become the go-to watering hole for a more creative crowd. The design is bachelor-pad chic, with exposed brick walls, Chesterfield sofas on gray, tiled floors, and an outdoor terrace with long wood tables and potted palm trees. Take the elevator up to the sixth floor of 8 Lyndhurst Terrace, a building worth noting for its variety of bars and restaurants. ✉ *6th fl., 8 Lyndhurst Terrace, Central* ☎ *2545–8555* ⊕ *www.theblckbrd.com* ⊙ *Closes 2 am.*

The Cutty Sark. Named after the legendary British tea clipper in homage to Hong Kong's colonial history, this small pub in SoHo is a cozy, reliable spot with a nautical theme. It's a good place for a pint on weekend afternoons too, when locals gather around the streetside tables with their dogs. ✉ *20 Elgin St., SoHo, Central* ☎ *2868–1250* ⊙ *Closes 2am.*

Goccia. Beautiful people both young and not-so-young flock to this Italian bar (with a restaurant upstairs), and it's packed wall-to-wall most nights. *Goccia*—which means "drop" in Italian—occupies a long room on the ground floor. If it had a VIP table it would be one by the open front facing the street, where you can see and be seen. ✉ *73 Wyndham St., Central* ☎ *2167–8181* ⊕ *www.divinogroup.com* ⊙ *Closes 3 am* Ⓜ *Central.*

La Dolce Vita. Crowds at this Lan Kwai Fong mainstay, beneath its sister restaurant **Post 97** and next to its other sibling **Club 97,** often spill onto the pavement. One of the first modern bars to pop up when the area gained popularity, La Dolce Vita has a sleek interior and is a popular stomping ground for the moneyed masses. ⊠ *9 Lan Kwai Fong, Lan Kwai Fong, Central* ☎ *2186–1888* ⊘ *Closes 3 am* Ⓜ *Central.*

Le Jardin. For an otherworldly, cosmopolitan vibe, check out this casual bar with a terrace overlooking the gregarious outdoor dining lane known locally as Rat Alley. Walk through the dining area and up a flight of steps. It's a little tricky to find, but the leafy, fairy-lit setting is worth it. ⊠ *1st fl., 10 Wing Wah Lane, Lan Kwai Fong, Central* ☎ *2877–1100* ⊘ *Closes 4 am* Ⓜ *Central.*

Lux. This two-story bistro and bar recently enjoyed a face-lift. Decorated in lush red and deep wooden tones, the busy street-level bar is separated from the restaurant by an internal staircase. Upstairs, the cuisine is modern European, with signature dishes including roasted lobster spaghetti, while downstairs the cocktail menu has 20 different kinds of martinis. The daily happy hour is popular with the after-work crowd and runs from 5 to 9 pm. ⊠ *Upper ground fl. and 1st fl., The Plaza, 21 D'Aguilar St., Lan Kwai Fong, Central* ☎ *2868–9538* ⊕ *www. luxhongkong.com* ⊘ *Closes 4 am.*

MO Bar. This plush bar in the Landmark Mandarin Oriental is where the banking set goes to relax. You'll pay top dollar for the signature drinks (up to HK$200), but the striking interior makes it worthwhile. A huge, red-light circle dominates an entire wall, the "O" being a Chinese symbol of shared experience. ⊠ *The Landmark Mandarin Oriental, 15 Queen's Rd. Central, Central* ☎ *2132–0077* ⊕ *www.mandarinoriental. com* ⊘ *Closes 2 am* Ⓜ *Central.*

RED Bar. Although its shopping mall location, outdoor terrace self-service policy, and incongruous affiliation with the next-door gym may not seem appealing, once you arrive, you'll throw all your preconceived notions into the harbor. On the roof of IFC Mall, RED has breathtaking views of the city, making it a great place to grab an early dinner and relax with a cocktail while watching the sunset. ⊠ *Level 4, Two IFC, 8 Finance St., Central* ☎ *8129–8882* ⊕ *www.pure-red.com* ⊘ *Closes 2 am* Ⓜ *Hong Kong.*

Sevva. With a view onto Central's glittering valley of skyscrapers, this cool and elegant rooftop bar is always busy on Friday and Saturday nights. If you're feeling indulgent, come for dessert (the cakes are among the city's best) and stay for cocktails. Most of Sevva's well-heeled clientele prefer to drink outside on the spacious, slatted terrace, but there are couches inside too. A dress code of smart casual applies. ⊠ *25th fl., Prince's Bldg., 10 Chater Rd., Central* ☎ *2537–1388* ⊕ *www.sevva.hk* ⊘ *Closes 2 am* Ⓜ *Central.*

Fodor's Choice ★   **Solas.** Positioned a floor below super-club dragon-i, this red-lit, always crowded bar is Wyndham Street's party central. Expect a mostly expat crowd of twenty- and thirtysomethings, who come straight from work on weekdays. To avoid the excited crush on Wednesday's ladies night and on weekends, head for the booths along the walls and leave before

CLOSE UP

Art Spaces

Fringe Club. The pioneer of Hong Kong's alternative arts scene has been staging excellent independent theater, music, and art productions since opening in 1983. The distinctive brown-and-white-stripe colonial structure was built as a cold-storage warehouse in 1892. It was derelict when the Fringe moved in, and the painstaking renovation has earned awards. Light pours through huge windows into the street-level Anita Chan Lai-ling Gallery, with its small, well-curated exhibitions.

The Fotogalerie, upstairs, showcases photography and serves food and drinks. Downstairs, meat and cheese were once sold in the space that now houses the Fringe Theatre. The lighting box of the smaller Fringe Studio was once a refrigeration unit, built to preserve not food but winter clothes from summer mildew. Fringe productions are sometimes in Cantonese, so check the program carefully. All are closed Sunday. ⊠ *2 Lower Albert Rd., Central* ☎ *2521–7251 general inquiries, 3128–8288 Hong Kong Ticketing box office* ⊕ *www.hkfringe.com.hk* 🎭 *Galleries free* Ⓜ *Central*.

Hong Kong Arts Centre. A hodgepodge of activities takes place in this deceptively bleak concrete tower, financed with horse-racing profits donated by the Hong Kong Jockey Club. The split-level Pao galleries house year-round exhibitions of art and crafts. Thematic cycles of art-house flicks run in the basement of agnès b. CINEMA! Community theater groups are behind much of the fare at the Shouson Theatre and smaller McAulay Studio, though international drama and dance troupes sometimes appear. Quality is hit-and-miss, so check newspaper reviews for advice. From Wan Chai MTR, cross the footbridge to Immigration Tower, then dogleg left through the open plaza until you hit Harbour Road: the center is on the left. ⊠ *2 Harbour Rd., Wan Chai* ☎ *2582–0200* ⊕ *www.hkac.org.hk* 🎭 *Free* Ⓜ *Wan Chai*.

Ma Tau Kok Cattle Depot. A former slaughterhouse in industrial To Kwa Wan has become a happening hub of independent art. It's divvied up into spaces run by different groups. The easiest way to get here is by taxi from Tsim Sha Tsui (around HK$55) or from Lok Fu MTR (around HK$40). Look out for specific events held here, such as Hong Kong's annual ArtWalk (April), for a taste of the site's full potential. In July 1997—as Hong Kong was handed back to China—a group of young local artists formed the **Artists' Commune** (Unit 12, 2104–3322, www.artist-commune.com, free) whose massive loftlike premises showcase offbeat works. Expect funky, well-curated pickings at **1aspace** (Unit 14, 2529–0087, www.oneaspace.org.hk), a cool, sleek gallery. Both are open Tuesday–Sunday 2–8 with free admission. ⊠ *63 Ma Tau Kok Rd., To Kwa Wan, Kowloon*.

—Victoria Patience

7

the DJ starts to spin at around 11 pm. ⊠ *60 Wyndham St., SoHo, Central* ☎ *3162–3710* ⊕ *www.solas.com.hk* ☉ *Closes late* Ⓜ *Central.*

Staunton's Wine Bar & Cafe. Adjacent to Hong Kong's famous outdoor escalator is this popular bistro-style café and bar. It's the perfect place to people-watch, whether from the balcony or the steps, where you can hang out on foam picnic mats. You can come for a drink at night or coffee during the day. It's also a Sunday-morning favorite for nursing hangovers over brunch. ⊠ *10–12 Staunton St., SoHo, Central* ☎ *2973–6611* ⊕ *www.stauntonsgroup.com* ☉ *Closes 3 am* Ⓜ *Central.*

DISCOS AND NIGHTCLUBS

Azure. Head skyward to this cosmopolitan, bi-level club at the top of the 30-story Hotel LKF. The downstairs lounge is a sophisticated space with pool tables, couches, and a soundtrack of ambient tunes. Upstairs, take in a 270-degree panorama of the harbor from the smoker's terrace, or dance to funky-house music inside. ⊠ *29th fl., Hotel LKF, 33 Wyndham St., Central* ☎ *3518–9330* ⊕ *www.azure.hk* ☉ *Closes 3 am* Ⓜ *Central.*

Fodor'sChoice ★ **dragon-i.** This hotspot has been around for a decade and lost none of its popularity, which is rare for a nightclub in Hong Kong. Have a drink on the deck by the doorway or step inside the rich, red playroom, which doubles as a Chinese restaurant at lunchtime and in the early evening. It's the domain of the city's young, rich, and beautiful (if not necessarily classy) and attracts a busy roster of international acts and DJs. The club's notorious Models' Night takes place on Wednesdays. ⊠ *The Centrium, 60 Wyndham St., Central* ☎ *3110–1222* ⊕ *www.dragon-i.com.hk* ☉ *Closes 3 am* Ⓜ *Central.*

Drop. This pint-size gem is where celebrities party—usually until sunrise—when they're in town. Hidden down an alley beside a late-night food stand, Droplet, its location only adds an air of exclusivity to the speakeasy feel. Excellent fresh-fruit martinis are its forte. Drop has two incarnations: after-dinner cocktail lounge before midnight, and impenetrable fortress later on, so arrive early to avoid disappointment. Happy hour is from 6 pm to 10 pm, Tuesday through Friday. ⊠ *Basement, On Lok Mansion, 39–43 Hollywood Rd., entrance off Cochrane St., Central* ☎ *2543–8856* ☉ *Closes 6 am* Ⓜ *Central.*

Fly. This midsize club attracts a younger crowd than many of its competitors, making it one of Central's rowdier nightlife spots. Popular with the 18-to-35s on Wednesday through Saturday nights, Fly's music tends to be more varied than the commercial fare at other clubs, encouraging visits from a lively mix of local and international talent. ⊠ *24–30 Ice House St., Central* ☎ *2810–9902* ⊕ *www.clubfly.com.hk* ☉ *Closes late.*

Fodor'sChoice ★ **Socialito.** One of a number of trendy Latin American joints to open in the city's Central and Western districts, Socialito offers more than just tacos and tequila. Behind the stylized canteen doors of the storefront is an exotic hidden nightclub, which trumps its predecessor Privé with panache. ⊠ *G/F, The Centrium, 50 Wyndham St., Central* ☎ *3167–7380* ☉ *Closes 2 am.*

Varga Lounge. Named after the Peruvian painter of pinup girls, this *New York Times*–recommended bar is a colorful, eclectic little spot for a cocktail. Large groups can take over the 2nd-floor lounge, with its bright walls and fun, 1950s-inspired art. Downstairs, the bar opens onto the street and snacks can be brought in from other outlets in SoHo. ✉ *36 Staunton St., SoHo, Central* ☎ *2104–9697* ⊕ *www. vargaloungehk.com* ⊘ *Closes 3 am.*

Volar. By midnight the line outside this club is more like a scrimmage. The maze of low-ceilinged basement rooms hosts a young, hip crowd and a genuinely eclectic mix of music, from electro-house to hip-hop and rock-and-roll mash-ups. Head to the lounge area, featuring gem-studded carousel horses, for a slightly more low-key vibe. ✉ *Basement, 38–44 D'Aguilar St., Lan Kwai Fong, Central* ☎ *2810–1510* ⊕ *www. volar.com.hk* ⊘ *Closes late* Ⓜ *Central.*

Midnight & Co. This tiny space is the den of local DJ talent, and one of only a few clubs in Central that play underground electronic tunes. As such, it has garnered a band of fiercely loyal regulars, who have frequented the venue since its early, darker days as Yumla and can make the casual visitor feel out of place. Even with a cover charge of up to HK$200 on weekends, the place can get packed, but if you're there for the music it's worth it. ✉ *Lower basement, Harilela House, 79 Wyndham St., Central* ☎ *2147–2012* ⊕ *www.midnight.hk* ⊘ *Closed Sun.–Mon.* Ⓜ *Central.*

GAY AND LESBIAN SPOTS

Propaganda. Off a quaint but steep cobblestone street is a popular gay nightclub with an art-deco bar area that hosts quite the flirt-fest, while the sunken dance floor has poles on either side for go-go boys to flaunt their wares. It's pretty empty during the week, and the crowds arrive well after midnight on weekends. The entrance is in an alleyway, Ezra Lane, which runs parallel to Hollywood Road and is best accessed from Pottinger Street. Happy hour is Tuesday to Thursday, 10 pm to 1:30 am. ✉ *Basement, 1 Hollywood Rd., Central* ☎ *2868–1316* ⊘ *Closes 5 am* Ⓜ *Central.*

MUSIC CLUBS

Fodor's Choice ★ **Fringe Club.** The arts-minded mingle in this historic redbrick building that also houses the members-only Foreign Correspondents' Club, next door. The Fringe is the headquarters for Hong Kong's alternative arts scene, and stages regular live music events at the recently opened Cabaret Theater. The outdoor roof bar or Fotogalerie, with its potted plants and fairy lights, is laid-back and serves reasonably priced drinks. ✉ *2 Lower Albert Rd., Central* ☎ *2521–7251* ⊕ *www.hkfringe.com.hk* ⊘ *Closes 2 am.*

Grappa's Cellar. This cavernous basement restaurant clears its tables regularly for some of the best live music gigs in town. Whether the performers are visiting indie bands or homegrown Dixieland jazz talent, the huge dance floor and rowdy second-level bar make it difficult not to have fun. Swing kings Stray Katz Big Band play on the first Saturday of each month at 8 pm. City magazines like *HK* and *Time Out* sometimes host sponsored multiband events here, so look out for these year-round. ✉ *Basement, Jardine House, 1 Connaught Pl., Central* ☎ *2521–2322* ⊘ *Closes midnight; last orders 11 pm* Ⓜ *Central.*

7

Late-Night Bites

The Flying Pan. Nix that looming hangover with a greasy fry-up before you hit the sack. The Flying Pan is a popular 24-hour breakfast diner, equally busy at 3 am and 3 pm on weekends. Eggs any style come with your two picks from a huge list of sides including grits, blintzes, baked beans, and fruit salad. The truly greedy can order a Kitchen Sink, which is a taste of everything. ⊠ *Ground fl., 9 Old Bailey St., Central* ☎ *2140–6333* ⊕ *www.the-flying-pan.com* ⊠ *3rd fl., 81–85 Lockhart Rd., Wan Chai* ☎ *2528–9997.*

Hay Hay Kitchen. A brightly lit oasis on Lockhart Road, this busy restaurant serves fast Cantonese food, similar to Tsui Wah (⇨ *see below*). Hay Hay is best known for its Hong Kong–style noodles and rice plates. The *char siu*

hor fun (barbecue pork noodles in soup) is a popular late-night dish. Pay at the cashier on your way out. ⊠ *Hay Wah Bldg., 72–86 Lockhart Rd., Wan Chai* ☎ *2143–6183* ⊗ *Closes 4 am.*

Tsui Wah. While locals head to Tsui Wah, a large, three-story Chinese restaurant, at any time of the day, the late-night crowds are the happiest. Service is quick and there's a huge menu of typical Chinese fare such as fried rice and noodles as well as western dishes such as steak and pasta. It's noisy and bright, but the crowds just keep on coming. You may even find the odd celebrity chowing down on beef brisket noodles at 2 am. ⊠ *15–19 Wellington St., Central* ☎ *2525–6338* ⊕ *www.tsuiwah.com* Ⓜ *Central.*

—Eva Chui Loiterton

PUBS

Fodor'sChoice ★ **Globe.** This gastropub and perennial British expat hangout in a large, trendy SoHo space brings the feel of southwest London with it. You can book the sectioned off "chill-out" area to watch live sports coverage with a private party. Good luck trying to get the proprietors to turn on the World Series or the Super Bowl, though. Soccer and rugby reign supreme here, and you'll have to share the TV. ⊠ *45–53 Graham St., SoHo, Central* ☎ *2543–1941* ⊕ *www.theglobe.com.hk* ⊗ *Closes 2 am* Ⓜ *Central.*

The Keg. As its name implies, beer and more beer is the beverage of choice at this small pub. It is designed to resemble the inside of a keg, with interiors finished in wood, copper, and polished steel. Large wooden barrels serve as tables, and the floors are covered with discarded peanut shells. Sports coverage rules the TV screens. ⊠ *52 D'Aguilar St., Lan Kwai Fong, Central* ☎ *2810–0369* ⊗ *Closes 3 am* Ⓜ *Central.*

WINE BAR

Tastings. Oenophiles will discover like minds at this vanguard of the city's blossoming (and very serious) wine scene. Tucked in an alley off Wellington Street, the bar stocks more than 160 wines. A rotating 40 are available for sampling through an Enomatic wine dispenser, which the sommeliers use to draw from rare wines without uncorking the entire bottle. Head toward the door's blue glow to find the place. Enjoy the spread of fine cheeses and Italian antipasti before the tasting begins. ⊠ *Basement, 27 and 29 Wellington St., Central* ☎ *2523–6282* ⊕ *tastings.hk* ⊗ *Closes 2 am* Ⓜ *Central.*

The Globe offers a bit of Britain in SoHo.

WAN CHAI

Wan Chai is the pungent night flower of the nocturnal scene, where the way of life served as inspiration for the novel *The World of Suzie Wong*. It now shares the streets with hip wine bars, salsa nights, old men's pubs, and after-parties that continue past sunrise. The seedy "hostess bars" in this neighborhood are easy to spot and avoid, with curtained entrances guarded by old ladies on stools and suggestive names in neon. But some things never change: the busiest nights are still when there's a navy ship in the harbor on an R&R stopover. Wednesday's ladies' night, with free or half-price drinks, is also a big draw.

BARS

Mes Amis. In the heart of Wan Chai, on the corner of Lockhart and Luard roads, Mes Amis is a friendly, high-ceilinged bar that also serves food. Its corner setting and open bifold doors mean that none of the action outside is missed, and vice versa: the perpetual crowd inside is on display to those on the street. Happy hour is all day until 9 pm, until 10 pm on weekends. ⊠ *83–85 Lockhart Rd., Wan Chai* ☎ *2527–6680* ⊕ *www.mesamis.com.hk* ☉ *Closes 4 am* Ⓜ *Wan Chai.*

1/5 nuevo. Popular tapas lounge and cocktail bar 1/5 nuevo occupies a prime spot in Wan Chai's ever-growing Star Street neighborhood. High-flyers, financiers, and expats populate this sleek hangout. ⊠ *9 Star St., Wan Chai* ☎ *2529–2300* ☉ *Closes 2 am* Ⓜ *Wan Chai.*

Fodor's Choice ★ **The Pawn.** In a district plagued by controversial redevelopment, this attractive historic building, a former pawnshop, has been preserved with minimal fuss. The stylish interior is outfitted with retro furniture,

LES PECHES

Though Central has a relatively open gay scene, Hong Kong's lesbians are notoriously low profile. For newcomers, Les Peches Lounge is an oasis of sorts: a monthly get-together, open to lesbians, bisexual women, and their friends, with a good mix of ages and ethnic backgrounds. Les Peches takes place on the first Tuesday of every month at LaKage (✉ 3/F Cosmos Bldg., 8–11 Lan Kwai Fong ✉ lespechesinfo@yahoo.com Ⓜ Central) from 8:30 pm to 2 am; the HK$100 cover includes one drink. Past themes have included wine tasting, belly dancing, fashion shows, drag kings, and palm reading. Les Peches Club is a higher-octane monthly event, held at the same venue from 10 pm to 3:30 am. Advance tickets are available via email for HK$160, or HK$180 at the door.

while carefully selected items from its less salubrious days give the space a decadent, vintage feel. The long balcony overlooking the iconic Hong Kong tramway is a great place for spying on bustling everyday life below. Upstairs is the restaurant, serving quality gastro-pub fare. ✉ 62 Johnston Rd., Wan Chai ☎ 2866–3444 ⊕ www.thepawn.com.hk ⊙ Closes 2 am Ⓜ Wan Chai.

Wooloomooloo. This sleek rooftop bar, named after the Australian aboriginal word for "young male kangaroo," provides a respite from the Wan Chai crowds. The downstairs steak house had its original branch in Lan Kwai Fong and has done well enough to open three more branches in Hong Kong. Here it's the alfresco bar that's the real draw. The breezy terrace and a panoramic view over Happy Valley have made it a favorite. ✉ 31st fl., 256 Hennessy Rd., entrance on 211 Johnson Rd., Wan Chai ☎ 2893–6960 ⊕ www.wooloo-mooloo.com ⊙ 6 pm–late Ⓜ Wan Chai.

DISCOS AND NIGHTCLUBS

Dusk Till Dawn. Loud, energetic cover bands get the dance floor jumping on Wednesday to Saturday nights. Popular with expats, it can be seedy, but patrons are usually having too much fun to notice or care. ✉ 76–84 Jaffe Rd., Wan Chai ☎ 2528–4689 ⊙ Closes 6 am Ⓜ Wan Chai.

Joe Bananas. This disco and bar has a reputation for all-night partying and general good times. People dressed too casually are strictly excluded: no shorts, sneakers, or T-shirts (the only exception is the Rugby Sevens weekend, when even Joe can't turn away the thirsty swarm). Arrive before 11 pm to avoid the line. ✉ 23 Luard Rd., Wan Chai ☎ 2529–1811 ⊕ www.joebananas.com ⊙ Closes 4 am Ⓜ Wan Chai.

PUBS

Carnegie's. Named after the Scotsman and steel baron Andrew Carnegie, whose family sailed to America in the late 1800s, this rock-and-roll bar lives up to its name. Although Carnegie himself probably didn't imagine bar-top dancing to classic rock tunes at an establishment bearing his name, the Scottish owners feel that the spirit of his love of music lives on regardless. ✉ 53–55 Lockhart Rd., Wan Chai ☎ 2866–6289 ⊕ www. carnegies.net/hongkong ⊙ Closes 2 am Ⓜ Wan Chai.

CLOSE UP

Chinese Opera

For a unique evening out, nab tickets to a Chinese Opera performance.

7

There are 10 **Cantonese opera** troupes headquartered in Hong Kong, as well as many amateur singing groups. Some put on performances of "street opera" in, for example, the Temple Street Night Market almost every night, while others perform at temple fairs, in City Hall, or in playgrounds under the auspices of the Urban Council. Those unfamiliar with Chinese opera might find the sights and sounds of this highly complex and sophisticated art form a little strange. Every gesture has its own meaning; in fact, there are 50 gestures for the hand alone.

Props attached to the costumes are similarly intricate and are used in exceptional ways. For example, the principal female often has 5-foot-long pheasant-feather tails attached to her headdress; she shows anger by dropping the head and shaking it in a circular fashion so that the feathers move in a perfect circle. Surprise is shown by what's called "nodding the feathers." You can also "dance with the feathers" to show a mixture of anger and determination. Orchestral music punctuates the singing. It's best to attend with someone who can translate the gestures for you; or you can learn more at the Cantonese Opera Halls in the Hong Kong Heritage Museum.

The highly stylized **Peking opera** employs higher-pitched voices than Cantonese opera. Peking opera is an older form, more respected for its classical traditions; the meticulous training of the several troupes visiting Hong Kong from the People's Republic of China each year is well regarded. They perform in City Hall or at special temple ceremonies. You can get the latest programs from the Hong Kong Cultural Centre.

—Eva Chui Loiterton

The Canny Man. In the basement of the nondescript Wharney Guang Dong Hotel on Wan Chai's heaving Lockhart Road is an oasis of relative calm, with a dart board, a pool table, and live sports coverage, as well as a full menu that includes Haggis balls. It's Hong Kong's only old-school Scottish pub, decked out in timber and red-tartan furnishings. The bar serves an impressive collection of 180 single malts and 28 artisan beers, alongside a roster of guest ales that changes regularly. ⊠ *Basement, Wharney Guang Dong Hotel, 57–73 Lockhart Rd., Wan Chai* ☎ *2861–1935* ⊕ *thecannyman.com* ⊗ *Closes 2 am* Ⓜ *Wan Chai.*

ARTFUL DATES

Hong Kong Arts Festival (February and March).
Hong Kong Arts Festival (February and March): Past visitors have included Mikhail Baryshnikov, Pina Bausch, and José Carreras. The focus is on performing arts.
⊕ *www.hk.artsfestival.org.*

Hong Kong International Film Festival (March and April).
Asian cinema accounts for many of the 280-plus new films shown at this festival, which includes citywide exhibitions and parties.
⊕ *www.hkiff.org.hk.*

CAUSEWAY BAY

BARS

ToTT's and Roof Terrace. Also known as Talk of the Town, this restaurant and bar takes up the 34th floor of one of Hong Kong's legendary hotels and has enjoyed many face-lifts since its heyday in the 1980s. Today, it is best known for its Sunday brunch buffet, where live jazz and free-flowing champagne complement daytime views of Victoria Harbour. At night, a classic cocktail on the outdoor terrace is one of the area's classier offerings. ⊠ *34th fl., The Excelsior, 281 Gloucester Rd., Causeway Bay* ☎ *2837–6786* ⊕ *www.mandarinoriental.com/excelsior* ⊗ *Closes 2 am* Ⓜ *Causeway Bay.*

PUBS

East End Brewery. Deep in the veritable beer desert of Hysan Avenue lies a pub with the refreshing motto "Let No Man Thirst For Want Of Real Ale" displayed on its wall. Here, you will find dozens of brews, accompanied by live sports coverage and a reassuring ocean of peanut shells underfoot. ⊠ *Sunning Plaza, 10 Hysan Ave., Causeway Bay* ☎ *2577–9119* ⊕ *www.elgrande.com.hk* ⊗ *Closes 2 am* Ⓜ *Causeway Bay.*

KOWLOON

Central and Wan Chai are undoubtedly the king and queen of nightlife in Hong Kong. If you're staying in a hotel, however, or having dinner across the water in Kowloon, Ashley Road and Knutsford Terrace, both in Tsim Sha Tsui, still make for a fun night out. If cocktails on the water, with a view of the harbor sounds like your kind of thing, check out the *Aqua Luna.*

Rock out at Carnegie's, a pub in Wan Chai.

TSIM SHA TSUI
BARS

All Night Long. The classier cousin to Wan Chai's bawdy Dusk Till Dawn, this Knutsford Terrace staple hosts a talented Filipino cover band, which mainly works hits from the '80s and '90s. Drinks are a little overpriced, but acoustics are supported by an impressive sound system and a loud sing-along from the crowd is standard. Spanish-style artwork adorns the red and yellow walls. ⊠ *9 Knutsford Terr., Tsim Sha Tsui* ☎ *2367–9487* ☽ *Closes 5 am* Ⓜ *Tsim Sha Tsui.*

Aqua Luna. As the city's last traditionally crafted vessel, or junk, *Aqua Luna*'s dramatic appearance and red sails make her easy to spot. Step off dry land from either pier, in Kowloon or Central, order a G&T, and take in the shimmering harbor sights for 45 minutes, with snack menus and plush seating. The HK$190 price tag includes one drink. The ferry runs every hour from 5:30 pm daily. ▥**TIP**➜ Catch the more expensive 7:30 cruise to watch the city's nightly Symphony of Lights show from the harbor. ⊠ *Cultural Center Pier No. 1, Tsim Sha Tsui, Kowloon* ☎ *2116–8821* ⊕ *www.aqua.com.hk* ☽ *Last sail 10:30 pm, Tsim Sha Tsui; 10:45 pm, Central* ⊠ *Pier No. 1, Tsim Sha Tsui, Kowloon* ⊠ *Pier No. 9, Central* Ⓜ *Central.*

Fodor's Choice
★

Aqua Spirit. Inside One Peking, an impressive curvaceous skyscraper, this very cool bar is on the mezzanine level of the top floor. The high ceilings and raking glass walls offer up unrivaled views of Hong Kong Island and the harbor filled with ferries and ships. ⊠ *29th fl. and 30th fl., One Peking, 1 Peking Rd., Tsim Sha Tsui* ☎ *3427–2288* ⊕ *www. aqua.com.hk* ☽ *Closes 2 am* Ⓜ *Tsim Sha Tsui.*

CLOSE UP

Performance Places

City Hall. From Isaac Stern, Yo-Yo Ma, and the New York Philharmonic to the Bee Gees; from the Royal Danish Ballet to the People's Liberation Army Comrade Dance Troupe, the offerings here are varied, but consistently excellent. Two buildings make up the chunky '60s complex, divided by a World War II memorial garden and shrine. The 1,500-seat concert hall and a smaller theater are in the low-rise block, as is Maxim's City Palace, a massive clattering restaurant with really good dim sum. The high-rise building has an exhibition space and a smaller recital hall, as well as a public library and marriage registry office. Performances are usually held Friday and Saturday at 8 pm. ⊠ *5 Edinburgh Pl., Central* ☎ *2921–2840, 2734–9009 Urbtix box office* ⊕ *www.lcsd.gov.hk* ⊙ *Daily 9 am–11 pm; box office daily 10–9:30* Ⓜ *Central.*

Hong Kong Academy for Performing Arts. Many of Hong Kong's most talented performers studied at this academy's schools of drama, music, dance, television, and film. It also has five theaters and a gallery. Large-scale productions are staged in the Lyric Theatre and the smaller Drama Theatre; offerings are often in the round at the tiny Studio Theatre. The two concert halls host choice classical or traditional Chinese music performances. ▮**TIP→** When the weather's good, inquire about shows in the garden amphitheater. ⊠ *1 Gloucester Rd., Wan Chai* ☎ *2584–8580* ⊕ *www.hkapa.edu* ⊙ *Box office Mon.–Sat. noon–6 pm; on performance nights, the box office remains open until 30 minutes after the last performance starts* Ⓜ *Wan Chai.*

Hong Kong Cultural Centre. The center's two-tier oval concert hall, which seats 2,000 and is fitted with an adjustable acoustic canopy and curtains, houses an 8,000-pipe Austrian organ, one of the world's largest. The Grand Theatre often hosts visiting Broadway musicals, opera, and ballet productions, while cozier plays take place in the Studio Theatre. The Hong Kong Philharmonic Orchestra performs here, too (⊕ *www. hkpo.com*). Exhibitions are occasionally mounted in the atrium. ⊠ *10 Salisbury Rd., Tsim Sha Tsui, Kowloon* ☎ *2734–2009, 2734–2820 Program Enquiries* ⊕ *www.hkculturalcentre. gov.hk* ⊙ *Daily 9–11; box office daily 10–9:30* Ⓜ *Tsim Sha Tsui.*

Kwai Tsing Theatre. It might be in the sticks, but it's a major player in the cultural scene. Sunlight pours into the atrium through a curving glass facade that looks onto a plaza where performances are often held. Inside, the 900-seat theater provides a much-needed middle ground between the massive spaces and tiny studio theaters at other venues. And if the likes of Philip Glass and the Royal Shakespeare Company can schlep out here, 25 minutes by MTR from Central, to perform, you can certainly get out here to watch. ⊠ *12 Hing Ning Rd., Kwai Chung, New Territories* ☎ *2408–0128, 2406–7505 Booking Enquiries* ⊕ *www.lcsd.gov.hk/ktt* ⊙ *Daily 9 am–11 pm; box office daily 10–9:30 pm* Ⓜ *Kwai Fong.*

—Victoria Patience

Drinks come with a spectacular view of Hong Kong at Felix, high up in the Peninsula Hotel.

Bahama Mama's. You'll find tropical rhythms at the Caribbean-inspired bar, where world music plays and the kitsch props include a surfboard over the bar and the silhouette of a curvaceous woman showering behind a screen over the restroom entrance. ⊠ *4–5 Knutsford Terr., Tsim Sha Tsui* ☎ *2368–2121* ☉ *Closes 4 am* Ⓜ *Tsim Sha Tsui.*

Dada. This bar in the eccentric Luxe Manor hotel is a tribute to anarchic surrealism and works hard to be weird in an early 20th-century way. A side gallery boasts two original etchings by Salvador Dalí. References to the artist and other greats like Magritte abound. A dark and spacious bar area is anchored by a central counter, from which cast resin ponies sprout and bottles of absinthe glimmer. ⊠ *2nd fl., 39 Kimberly Rd., Tsim Sha Tsui* ☎ *3763–8778* ⊕ *www.dadalounge.com.hk* ☉ *Closes 2 am* Ⓜ *Tsim Sha Tsui.*

Fodor's Choice ★ **Felix.** High up in the Peninsula Hotel, this bar is immensely popular with visitors; it not only has a brilliant view of the island, but the interior was designed by the visionary Philippe Starck. Don't forget to check out the padded mini-disco room. Another memorable feature, the urinals in the men's restroom are situated right by glass windows overlooking the city. ⊠ *28th fl., Peninsula Hong Kong, Salisbury Rd., Tsim Sha Tsui* ☎ *2920–2888* ⊕ *www.peninsula.com* ☉ *Closes 2 am* Ⓜ *Tsim Sha Tsui.*

The Lobby. You'll feel well taken care of at the Peninsula's classic colonial lobby bar. Society watchers linger here; sit to the right of the hotel entrance to observe the crème de la crème. ⊠ *Peninsula Hotel, Salisbury Rd., Tsim Sha Tsui* ☎ *2920–2888* ⊕ *www.peninsula.com* ☉ *Closes 1 am.*

PUBS

Delaney's. Both branches of Hong Kong's pioneer Irish pub have interiors that were shipped here from the Emerald Isle, and the mood is as authentic as the furnishings. Guinness and Delaney's ale (a specialty microbrew) are on tap, there are corner snugs (small private rooms) and an Irish menu. The crowd includes some genuine Irish regulars; get ready for spontaneous outbursts of fiddling and other Celtic traditions. Happy hour runs from 5 to 9 pm daily in Kowloon, noon to 9 pm in Wanchai. ⊠ *Basement fl., 71–77 Peking Rd., Tsim Sha Tsui* ☎ *2301–3980* ⊕ *www.delaneys.com.hk* Ⓜ *Tsim Sha Tsui* ⊠ *Ground fl. and 1st fl., One Capital Place, 18 Luard Rd., Wan Chai* ☎ *2804–2880* ☉ *Closes 3 am* Ⓜ *Wan Chai.*

Ned Kelly's Last Stand. Come to this boisterous Australian watering hole, named for the continent's notorious bushranger, for pub meals and an exuberant Dixieland jazz and comedy outfit. They are popular among visitors and expats from Down Under and often lead the crowd in a rowdy singalong. The band plays from 9:30 pm to 1 am nightly. Arrive early for decent seats. ⊠ *11A Ashley Rd., Tsim Sha Tsui* ☎ *2376–0562* ☉ *Closes 2 am* Ⓜ *Tsim Sha Tsui.*

NORTHERN KOWLOON

BARS

Woobar. On the sixth floor of the W Hotel is a sprawling bar originally designed to feel like a stylized living room. It was reimagined recently as Woobar, a fashionable space in keeping with the hotel's "chic and fun" aesthetic. On Wednesdays from 8 to 10:30, pay HK$238 for free-flowing wine and a selection of cheese. Two-for-one drinks are on offer weekday evenings from 5 to 8. The lychee martinis are excellent. ⊠ *W Hong Kong, 1 Austin Rd. W, Kowloon Station, Northern Kowloon* ☎ *3717–2222* ⊕ *www.woobarhongkong.com* ☉ *Closes 1 am* Ⓜ *Kowloon.*

Side Trip to Macau

WORD OF MOUTH

"There's a day's worth of walking around hilly narrow streets of ancient housing to various fortifications, churches, and a hill-top museum on Macau's history, which is well-done. The Portuguese [influence has] quite a different type of charm from Hong Kong . . ."

— PeterN_H

WELCOME TO MACAU

TOP REASONS TO GO

★ **Discover the Ruins of São Paulo.** The church façade, all that remains of a former center of learning, is a symbol of Macau.

★ **Take a seat in Senado Square.** A bench here is the perfect perch from which to watch Macau's comings and goings while admiring the colonial surroundings.

★ **Explore the A-Ma Temple.** It's steeped in Macau's culture and history. Search for the Lucky Money Pool, then wash your hands in the blessed water before heading to the casinos.

★ **Place Your Bets.** Even if you don't gamble, take a peek inside the Lisboa, a classic Macau landmark, or the newer and splashier Venetian, a sprawling complex where singing gondoliers glide down indoor canals and luxury shopping abounds.

★ **Spaaahhh.** Macau's spas have ultra-indulgent treatments and world-class facilities—with prices to match. But for many, the pampering is well worth the expense.

1 Downtown Macau. You'll experience authentic Macau in squares, along cobblestone streets, and in European-style sidewalk cafés, as well as in Buddhist temples, with their red lanterns and fragrant joss sticks. In this exotic place where two worlds collide, don't be surprised to find a pink colonial Portuguese building housing a Chinese herbal medicine shop.

2 Taipa Island. Although the Portuguese presence on Macau dates from the mid-1500s, Taipa wasn't occupied until the mid-1800s. The island remained a garrison and a pastoral retreat until the 1970s, when it was linked to Macau by bridge. Today some parts retain a village feel, while others are crowded with soul-less high-rises.

3 Cotai. The 3-km (2-mile) causeway that once separated Coloane from Taipa has been bridged by a massive land-reclamation and development project that includes casinos and hotels, resorts, and shopping malls.

GUANDONG PROVINCE (CHINA)

A Ma Temple

GUANDONG PROVINCE (CHINA)

CHINA

GETTING ORIENTED

Macau, a Special Administrative Region (SAR) of the People's Republic of China, is on the western bank of the Pearl River Delta, about an hour from Hong Kong by hydrofoil. It consists of the Macau Peninsula and Taipa and Coloane islands. The Cotai area, a glitzy, Vegas-like strip of hotels and casinos that began development in 2006, lies between Taipa and Coloane and virtually merges the two. Most people visit Macau to gamble, eat cheap seafood, and shop. But don't overlook its time-less charms and unique culture, born from centuries of both Portuguese and Chinese influence.

4 Coloane Island.
The larger island remains less populated and more intimate than Taipa, and few tourists venture this far south. It's also known for its parks, beaches, and golf links, as well as unchanged Portuguese architecture and cobblestone streets.

TO ZHUHAI

Macau Island

Av. do Almante Lacerda

Rua Nova da Meia Praia

Av. de Moraes

ins of Paolo

Reservoir

Macau Ferry Terminal

Outer Harbour

Av. Almeida Ribeiro

boa

Macau-Taipa Bridge

Friendship Bridge

ZHUJIANG KOU

Taipa Island

Taipa Ferry Terminal

2

Macau International Airport

Venetian

Avenida de Cotai

3

Lotus Bridge

Taipa-Coloane Causeway

4

Coloane Island

Hác-Sá Beach

Estrada de Cheoc Van

Cheoc Van Beach

8

Updated by
Kate Springer

Enter the desperate, smoky atmosphere of a Chinese casino, where frumpy players bet an average of five times more than the typical Vegas gambler. Sit down next to grandmothers who smoke like chimneys while playing baccarat—the local game of choice—with visiting high rollers. Then step out of the climate-controlled chill and into tropical air that embraces you like a warm, balmy hug. Welcome to Macau.

The many contrasts in this tiny enclave of 555,000 people serve as reminders of how different cultures have embraced one another's traditions for hundreds of years. Though Macau's population is 95% ethnic Chinese, there are still vibrant pockets of Portuguese and Filipino expats. And some of the thousands of Eurasians—who consider themselves neither Portuguese nor Chinese, but something in between—can trace the intermarriage of their ancestors back a century or two.

Macau's old town, while dominated by the buildings, squares, and cobblestone alleyways of colonial Portugal, is tinged with eastern influences as well. In Macau you can spend an afternoon exploring Buddhist temples before feasting on a dinner of *bacalhau com natas* (dried codfish with a cream sauce), grilled African chicken (spicy chicken in a coconut-peanut broth—a classic Macanese dish), Chinese lobster with scallions, or fiery prawns infused with Indian and Malaysian flavors. Wash everything down with *vinho verde*, the crisp young wine from northern Portugal, and top it all off with a traditional Portuguese *pastel de nata* (egg-custard tart) and dark, thick espresso.

PLANNING

THE BASICS

The Macau Government Tourist Office (MGTO) is well managed.

To enter Macau, Americans and Canadians need only a valid passport for stays of up to 30 days, while EU citizens can stay for 90.

The Macanese *pataca* (MOP) has a fixed exchange rate of MOP$1.032 to HK$1 and roughly MOP$8 to US$1. Patacas come in 10, 20, 50, 100, 500, and 1,000 MOP banknotes plus 1, 2, and 5 MOP coins. A pataca is divided into 100 *avos,* which come in 10-, 20-, and 50-avo coins. Hong Kong dollars are accepted in Macau on a 1:1 basis.

Contacts Macau Government Tourist Office (*MGTO*). ✉ *335–341, Alameda Dr. Carlos d'Assumpção* ☎ *853/2833–3000 in Macau, 8238–8680 in Hong Kong* ⊕ *www.macautourism.gov.mo.*

LANGUAGE

Chinese and Portuguese are Macau's official languages. Cantonese and Mandarin are widely spoken. English is unreliable outside tourist areas. It's best to print your destination in Chinese characters for taxi drivers.

GETTING TO MACAU

AIR TRAVEL

International flights (from Asia) come into Macau, but there are no planes from Hong Kong. Fifteen-minute helicopter flights fly between Hong Kong's Shun Tak Centre and the Macau Ferry Terminal on Sky Shuttle; they leave every 30 minutes from 9 am to 11 pm daily. Prices are HK$3,700 Monday to Thursday with an HK$200 surcharge on Friday, Saturday, Sunday, and holidays. Reservations are essential.

Contacts Sky Shuttle ☎ *853/2872–7288 Macau Terminal, 2108–9898 Shun Tak Centre* ⊕ *www.skyshuttlehk.com.* **Macau International Airport** ☎ *853/2886–1111* ⊕ *www.macau-airport.com/en.*

FERRY TRAVEL

Ferries run between Hong Kong and Macau every 15 minutes with a reduced schedule from midnight to 7 am. Prices for economy/ordinary and super/deluxe run HK$151–HK$291. VIP cabins begin at HK$1,164 (four seats) to HK$1,746 (six seats). Weekday traffic is usually light, so you can buy tickets right before departure. Weekend tickets often sell out, so make reservations. You can book tickets up to 90 days in advance with China Travel Service (⊕ *www.ctshk.com*) agencies or directly with CotaiJet or TurboJET by phone or online. Booking by phone requires a Visa card. You must pick up tickets at the terminal at least a half hour before departure.

Most ferries leave from Hong Kong's Shun Tak Centre Sheung Wan MTR station in Central, though limited service is available from First Ferry at Kowloon's Tsim Sha Tsui terminal. In Macau most ferries disembark from the main Macau Ferry Terminal, but CotaiJet services the terminal on Taipa Island. The trip takes one hour each way. Buses, taxis, and free shuttles to most casinos and hotels await on the Macau side.

Contacts CotaiJet ☎ *853/2885–0595 in Macau, 2359–9990 in Hong Kong* ⊕ *cotaijet.com.mo.* **First Ferry** ☎ *2131–8181* ⊕ *www.nwff.com.hk.* **TurboJET** ☎ *2859–3333 information* ⊕ *www.turbojet.com.hk/en.*

8

GETTING AROUND MACAU

BUS TRAVEL

Public buses are clean and affordable; trips to anywhere in the Macau Peninsula cost MOP$3.20. Service to Taipa Island is MOP$4.20, service to Coloane is MOP$5, and the trip to Hác Sá is MOP$6.40. Buses run 6:30 am–midnight and require exact change upon boarding. But you can get downtown for free, via casino shuttles, from the official Border Gate crossing just outside mainland China, from the airport, and from the Macau Ferry Terminal.

CAR TRAVEL

As in Hong Kong, driving in Macau is on the left-hand side of the road. Road signs are in Chinese and Portuguese only. Rental cars with Avis are available at the Grand Lapa Hotel. Regular cars start at MOP$700 on weekdays and MOP$850 on weekends. Book three to four days in advance for weekend rentals.

Contact Avis ☎ *853/2833–6789 in Macau, 2882–2927 in Hong Kong* ⊕ *www.avis.com.*

TAXI TRAVEL

Taxis are inexpensive but not plentiful in Macau. The best places to catch a cab are the major casinos—the Wynn, Lisboas, Sands, and Venetian. Carry a bilingual map or ask the concierge at your hotel to write the name of your destination in Chinese. All taxis are metered, air-conditioned, and reasonably comfortable. The base charge is MOP$15 for the first 1.6 km (1 mile) and MOP$1.50 per additional 230 meters. Trips between Coloane and either the Macau Peninsula or Taipa incur respective surcharges of MOP$5 and MOP$2. Drivers don't expect a tip.

TOURS

Depending on your mind-set, you can join a group tour of Macau or make one to order.

Cotai Travel. Cotai Travel hosts daily tours from 9 am to 1 pm that include the Taipa Houses-Museum, Senado Square, and the A-Ma Temple for MOP$400 per person. ⊠ *Shop 1028, Venetian Macao-Resort-Hotel* ☎ *853/8118–2933.*

Book at least one day in advance from one of many travel agents in Hong Kong. Browse your options at the travel counters of the main ferry terminals in either Macau or Hong Kong, or check ⊕ *www. macautourism.gov.mo* for a list of authorized travel agencies in Macau; some offer tours in multiple languages.

Estoril Tours. Estoril Tours will customize a private group tour, from bungee-jumping off the Macau Tower to wandering through Coloane Village or a day visiting museums. ⊠ *Shop 3711A, 3rd fl., Shun Tak Centre, 200 Connaught Rd., Central, Hong Kong, Hong Kong–China* ☎ *2559–1028* ⊕ *www.estoril.com.mo.*

EXPLORING MACAU

Macau is a small place, where on a good day you can drive from one end to the other in 30 minutes. This makes walking the ideal way to explore winding city streets, nature trails, and long stretches of beach. Most of Macau's population lives on the peninsula attached to mainland China. The region's most famous sights are here—Senado Square, the Ruins of St. Paul's, A-Ma Temple—as are most of the luxury hotels and casinos. As in the older sections of Hong Kong, cramped older buildings stand comfortably next to gleaming new structures.

DOWNTOWN MACAU

Chances are you'll arrive at the Macau Ferry Terminal after sailing from Hong Kong. There's not much to see around the terminal itself, so hop into one of the many waiting casino or hotel shuttles (free) and head straight downtown, less than 10 minutes away. From there it's a short walk to the city's historic center, along the short stretch of road named Avenida Almeida Ribeiro, more commonly known as San Ma Lo, which is Macau's commercial and cultural heart.

TOP ATTRACTIONS

Fodor'sChoice **Fortaleza da Guia.** This fort built between 1622 and 1638 on Macau's
★ highest hill was key to protecting the Portuguese from invaders. You can walk the steep, winding road up to the fortress or take a five-minute cable-car ride from the entrance of Flora Garden on Avenida Sidónio Pais. Once inside, notice the gleaming white Guia Lighthouse (you can't go up, but you can get a good look at the exterior) that's lit every night. Next to it is the Guia Chapel, built by Clarist nuns to provide soldiers with religious services. Restoration work in 1998 uncovered elaborate frescoes mixing western and Chinese themes. They're best seen when the morning or afternoon sun floods the chapel, which is no longer used for services. ⊠ *Guia Hill, Downtown* ☎ *853/8399–6699* ⌑ *Free* ☽ *Daily 9–5:30.*

Igreja de São Domingos (*St. Dominic's Church*). The cream-and-white interior of one of Macau's most beautiful churches takes on a heavenly golden glow when illuminated for services. St. Dominic's was originally a convent founded by Spanish Dominican friars in 1587. In 1822 China's first Portuguese newspaper, *The China Bee,* was published here, and the church became a repository for sacred art in 1834 when convents were banned in Portugal. ■ **TIP➔ Admission to all churches and temples is free, though donations are suggested.** ⊠ *Largo de São Domingos, Downtown* ☽ *Daily 8–6.*

Fodor'sChoice **Largo do Senado** (*Senado Square*). The charming hub of Macau for cen-
★ turies, open only to pedestrians and paved in shiny black-and-white tiles, is lined with neoclassical-style colonial buildings painted in bright pastels. The **Edifício do Leal Senado** (Senate Building) that gives the square its name was built in 1784 as a municipal chamber and continues to be used by the government today. An elegant meeting room on the first floor opens onto a magnificent library based on one in the Mafra Convent in Portugal, with books neatly stacked on two levels of

8

A Casino Crawl in Macau

These days, casinos are as much a part of the character of Macau as its cobblestone streets. Don't expect dusty, down-to-earth caverns, though. This neon-clad city is all glam and glitz, chandeliers and sommeliers. Win or lose, checking out casinos is all part of the fun of being in Macau, and this itinerary includes some cultural sights, too.

PLANNING

Where to stay: MGM Macau, Wynn Macau, Altira Macau

Where to eat and drink: Margaret's Café e Nata, Portas Do Sol, Il Teatro, Robuchon au Dôme, 38 Lounge

Where to play: The Lisboa, The Grand Lisboa, Wynn Macau, Altira Macau

What to see: Senado Square, Ruins of St. Paul's Cathedral, Grand Prix Museum, Macau Canidrome, House of Dancing Water

ITINERARY

1. Margaret's Café e Nata. Start the day with a warm, flaky egg tart.

2. Largo do Senado. You almost have to go home with the obligatory Ruins of St. Paul's Cathedral photo. Saunter through Senado Square for a quick hit of history.

3. Wynn Macau. Break from the maddening crowds and head to this swish address. With thick, beige drapes and plush furniture, the casino offers VIP treatment.

4. Hotel Lisboa. The infamous basement corridors and sparkling gaming floors of the Lisboa sister hotels are just a few blocks from the Wynn.

5. Portas do Sol. Spend any remaining change you have left on dim sum. The pork buns and soup dumplings won't disappoint.

6. Grand Prix Museum. A bit farther north, you'll find colorful Formula 3 cars and memorabilia, as well as Macau's Wine Museum next door.

7. Cotai Strip. Fast and furious in its own right, Cotai is constantly expanding. Despite a stream of incoming resort-cum-casino complexes, the Venetian remains the highlight with 2,000 slot machines and 550 gaming tables.

8. House of Dancing Water. Snag tickets to the city's most mesmerizing show, staged in the City of Dreams Complex.

9. Robuchon au Dôme: If you hit the jackpot, head to this French dining room for an unforgettable meal—and price tag.

(option) 9. 38 Lounge. Those ending the day with thinner wallets may opt for tapas and cocktails on the top floor of Altira hotel. Views are free.

10. Macau Canidrome. The greyhound racetrack operates every evening except Wednesdays and Fridays. You won't find ersatz frescoes in this doghouse.

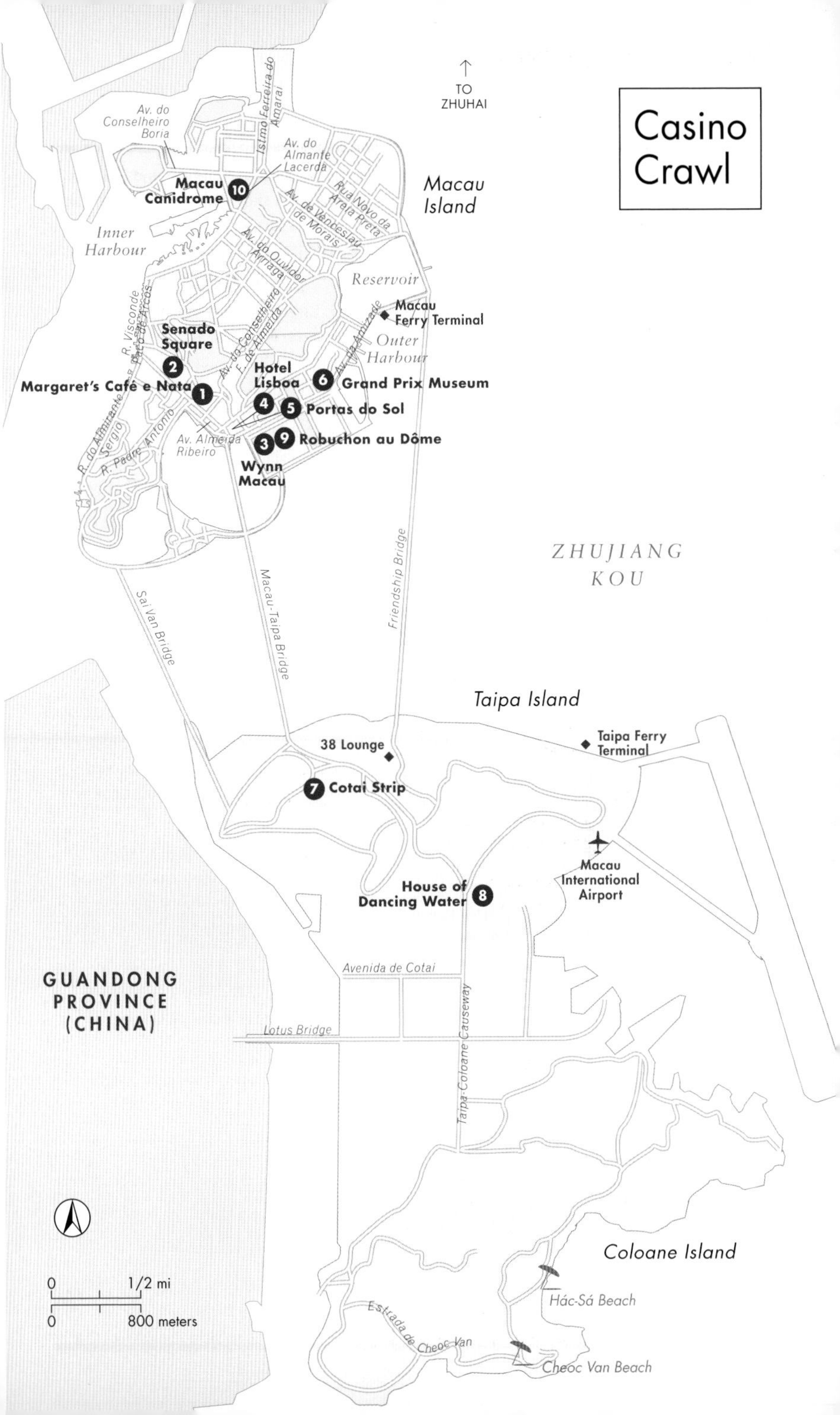
Casino Crawl
TO ZHUHAI
Macau Island
Inner Harbour
Av. do Conselheiro Boria
Istmo Ferreira do Amaral
Av. do Almante Lacerda
Rua Novo da Areia Preta
Av. de Venceslau de Morais
Av. do Ouvidor Arriaga
Av. do Conselheiro F. de Almeida
Reservoir
Macau Ferry Terminal
Outer Harbour
Av. da Amizade
R. Visconde Paço de Arcos
R. do Almirante Sergio
R. Padre Antonio
Av. Almeida Ribeiro
10 Macau Canidrome
2 Senado Square
1 Margaret's Café e Nata
Hotel Lisboa
4
5 Portas do Sol
6 Grand Prix Museum
3 9 Robuchon au Dôme
Wynn Macau
ZHUJIANG KOU
Sai Van Bridge
Macau-Taipa Bridge
Friendship Bridge
Taipa Island
38 Lounge
Taipa Ferry Terminal
7 Cotai Strip
8 House of Dancing Water
Macau International Airport
Avenida de Cotai
Lotus Bridge
Taipa-Coloane Causeway
GUANDONG PROVINCE (CHINA)
Coloane Island
Hác-Sá Beach
Estrada de Cheoc Van
Cheoc Van Beach
0 1/2 mi
0 800 meters

Exploring Macau's Culture

Macau's historical reputation may have been eclipsed by an ever-expanding matrix of casinos, but this former Portuguese colony has much to offer in the way of heritage and beauty. From the cobblestone streets to colonial facades, museums to Moorish architecture, fortresses to street food, Macau remains a city of color, character, and top-notch cuisine.

PLANNING

Where to stay: Pousada de Sao Tiago, Altira Macau, Wynn Macau

Where to eat and drink: A Lorcha, Margaret's Café e Nata, Fernando's, MacauSoul

What to see: Senado Square, Ruins of St. Paul, Guia Lighthouse, A-Ma Temple, Moorish Barracks

ITINERARY

1. Leitaria i Son. Sip on fresh juices while munching on an egg tart at Literati, one of Senado Square's most beloved cafés.

2. Largo do Senado. See everything or just the standouts, which include the House of Holy Mercy, St. Dominic's Church, The Cathedral and, of course, the Ruins of St. Paul's Cathedral, and neighboring Na Tcha temple.

3. Macau Museum and Fortress. Head inside to see how Macau has evolved.

4. Margaret's Café e Nata. Heading northeast along Avenida da Amizade, pop in for a quick lunch. Choose from flaky egg tarts, pastries, and made-to-order sandwiches.

5. Guia Hill Lighthouse and Fortress. Take the short cable car ride up Guia Hill, or lace up your sneakers and hike past quirky shrubs manicured to resemble dragons.

6. Largo do Barra. Anchoring Barra Square, the A-Ma Temple was built in 1488 for the goddess of the sea. This tiered Taoist temple is one of the oldest in Macau. Next door, find The Mandarin's House—a complex showcasing traditional Guangdong architecture—and the Maritime Museum.

7. Pousada de São Tiago. If you're feeling peckish, stop by The Terrace for a tipple or high tea.

8. Penha Hill. From there, head straight for the dominating facade of Bishop's Palace and the Chapel of Our Lady Penha.

9. Moorish Barracks. Originally housing a regiment from Goa to bolster local police, this neoclassical and Moghul complex has stood since 1874.

10. A Lorcha. Just off of Barra Square, the ever-popular Macanese eatery serves up hearty favorites in a friendly atmosphere. Best to make reservations.

11. Macau Soul. Digest over Portuguese wine and live music at this jazzy venue.

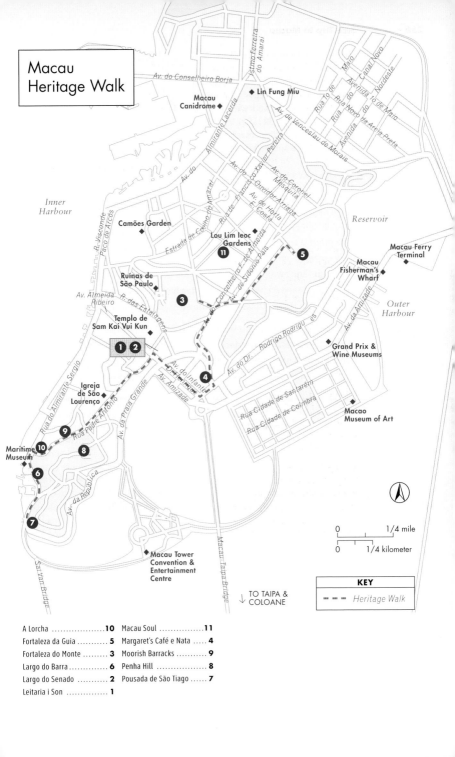

Macau
Heritage Walk

Inner
Harbour

Av. do Conselheiro Borja

◆ Lin Fung Miu

Macau
Canidrome ◆

Reservoir

Camões Garden

Lou Lim Ieoc
Gardens
⑪

⑤

Macau Ferry
Terminal

Macau
Fisherman's
Wharf ◆

Ruínas de
São Paulo

③

Templo de
Sam Kai Vui Kun

① ②

Outer
Harbour

Grand Prix &
Wine Museums ◆

④

Igreja
de São
Lourenço

Macao
Museum of Art ◆

⑨

Maritime ⑩
Museum ◆
⑥

⑧

⑦

Macau Tower
◆ Convention &
Entertainment
Centre

↓ TO TAIPA &
COLOANE

0   1/4 mile

0   1/4 kilometer

KEY
- - - - *Heritage Walk*

shelves reaching to the ceiling, and art and historical exhibitions are frequently hosted in the beautiful foyer and garden. Alleys adjacent to the square are packed with restaurants and shops. ■■TIP➔ Visit on a weekday to avoid the crowds, and try to come back at night, when locals of all ages gather to chat and the square is beautifully lit. ⊠ *Downtown.*

WORLD HERITAGE

"The Historic Centre of Macau" is listed as a UNESCO World Heritage Site. The term "center" is misleading, as the site is really a collection of churches, buildings, and neighborhoods that colorfully illustrate Macau's 400-year history. Included in it are China's oldest examples of western architecture and the region's most extensive concentration of missionary churches.

Margaret's Café e Nata. Not far off the main drag but somewhat hidden down an alleyway, Margaret's Café e Nata offers a cool—albeit increasingly crowded—place to sit, outside under fans and awnings, with some of the best custard tarts in town, plus fresh juices, sandwiches, homemade tea blends, and pizza slices. ⊠ *Rua Comandante Mata e Oliveira, Downtown* ☎ *853/2871-0032.*

Leitaria i Son. Look for the small cow sign marking the out-of-the-ordinary Leitaria i Son milk bar. The decor is cafeteria-style and spartan, but the bar whips up frothy glasses of fresh milk from its dairy and blends them with all manner of juices: papaya, coconut, apricot, and more. ⊠ *Largo do Senado 7, Downtown* ☎ *853/2857-3638.*

Macau Canidrome. The greyhound track looks rundown and quaint compared to the bigger Jockey Club and glitzy casinos, but it offers a true taste of Macau in a popular neighborhood near the China border crossing. The Canidrome opened in 1932; it tends to attract a steady crowd of older gamblers several times a week for the slower-pace, lower-stakes gambling rush of betting on fast dogs chasing an electronic rabbit. Check out the parade of race dogs before each race. You can sit on benches in the open-air stadium, at tables in the air-conditioned restaurant, or in an upstairs box seat. ⊠ *Av. do Artur Tamagnini Barbosa at Av. General Castelo Branco, Downtown* ☎ *853/2833–3399, 853/2826–1188 to place bets* ⊕ *www.macauyydog.com* ⊠ *Public stands MOP$10, private box seats MOP$120* ⊙ *Mon., Tues., Thurs., and weekends 6 pm–11:45 pm; first race at 7:30.*

Fodors Choice ★ **Macau Tower Convention & Entertainment Centre.** Rising above peaceful San Van Lake, the 335-meter (1,100-foot) freestanding tower recalls Sky Tower, a similar structure in New Zealand—and it should, as both were designed by New Zealand architect Gordon Moller. The Macau Tower offers a variety of thrills, including the Mast Climb, which challenges the daring and strong of heart and body with a two-hour climb on steel rungs 105 meters (344 feet) up the tower's mast for incomparable views of Macau and China. Other thrills include the Skywalk X, an open-air stroll around the tower's exterior—without handrails; the SkyJump, an assisted, decelerated 233-meter (765-foot) descent; and the world's

Pedestrian-only Largo do Senado preserves the Portuguese influence that shaped Macau for centuries.

highest bungee jump. More subdued attractions inside the tower are a mainstream movie theater and a revolving lunch, high tea, and dinner buffet at the 360-degree Café. ✉ *Largo da Torre de Macau, Downtown* ☎ *853/2893–3339* ⊕ *www.macautower.com.mo* ✉ *MOP$688 for Skywalk X to MOP$2,488 for the Mast Climb; photos extra.* ☉ *Observation deck, weekdays 10–9, weekends and holidays 9–9.*

Fodor's Choice
★
Ruínas de São Paulo (*Ruins of St. Paul's Church*). Only the magnificent, towering facade, with its intricate carvings and bronze statues, remains from the original Church of Mater Dei, built between 1602 and 1640 and destroyed by fire in 1835. The church, an adjacent college, and Mount Fortress, all Jesuit constructions, once formed East Asia's first western-style university. The ruins are now the widely adopted symbol of Macau, a tourist attraction with snack bars and antiques and other shops at the foot of the site. The small **Museum of Sacred Art and Crypt** tucked behind the facade of São Paulo holds statues, crucifixes, and the bones of Japanese and Vietnamese martyrs. There are also some intriguing Asian interpretations of Christian images, including samurai angels and a Chinese Virgin and Child. ✉ *Top end of Rua de São Paulo, Downtown* ☎ *853/8399–6699* ✉ *Free* ☉ *Ruins, daily 8–5; museum, daily 9–6.*

Santa Casa da Misericordia. Founded in 1569 by Dom Belchior Carneiro, Macau's first bishop, the Holy House of Mercy is the China coast's oldest Christian charity, and it continues to take care of the poor with soup kitchens and health clinics, as well as providing housing for the elderly. The exterior, with its imposing white facade, is neoclassical, but the interior is done in a contrasting opulent, modern style. A reception room on the second floor contains paintings of benefactress Marta Merop. ⊠ *2 Travessa da Misericordia, Downtown* 🕾 *853/2857–3938* 🖀 *MOP$5* ⊗ *Mon.–Sat. 10–1 and 2:30–5:30.*

Fodor's Choice
★

Templo de A-Ma. One of Macau's most picturesque temples is thought to be Macau's oldest building. Properly Ma Kok Temple but known to locals as simply A-Ma, the structure originated during the Ming Dynasty (1368–1644) and was influenced by Confucianism, Taoism, and Buddhism, as well as local religions. Vivid red calligraphy on large boulders tells the story of the goddess A-Ma (also known as Tin Hau), the patron of fishermen. A small gate opens onto prayer halls, pavilions, and caves carved directly into the hillside. ⊠ *Rua de São Tiago da Barra, Largo da Barra, Downtown* ⊗ *Daily 7–6.*

Templo de Na Tcha. This small Chinese temple was built in 1888, during the Macauan plague, in the hope that it would appeal to a mythical Chinese character who granted wishes and could save lives. The **Troço das Antigas Muralhas de Defesa** (Section of the Old City Walls), all that remains of Macau's original defensive barrier, borders the left side of the temple. These crumbling yellow walls were built in 1569 and illustrate the durability of *chunambo*, a local material made from compacted layers of clay, soil, sand, straw, crushed rocks, and oyster shells. ⊠ *Top end of Rua de São Paulo, Downtown.*

WORTH NOTING

Camões Garden. Macau's most popular park is frequented from dawn to dusk by tai chi enthusiasts, lovers, students, and men huddled over Chinese chessboards with their caged songbirds nearby. The gardens, which were developed in the 18th century, are named after Luís de Camões, Portugal's greatest poet, who was banished to Macau for several years during the 16th century. A rocky niche shelters a bronze bust of the poet in the park's most famous and picturesque spot, Camões Grotto. At the grotto's entrance a bronze sculpture honors the friendship between Portugal and China. A wall of stone slabs is inscribed with poems by various contemporary writers, praising Camões and Macau. In **Casa Garden,** a smaller park alongside Camões Garden, the grounds of a merchant's estate are lovingly landscaped with a variety of flora and bordered with a brick pathway. A central pond is stocked with lily pads and lotus flowers. ⊠ *13 Praça Luis de Camões, Downtown* ⊗ *Daily 6 am–10 pm.*

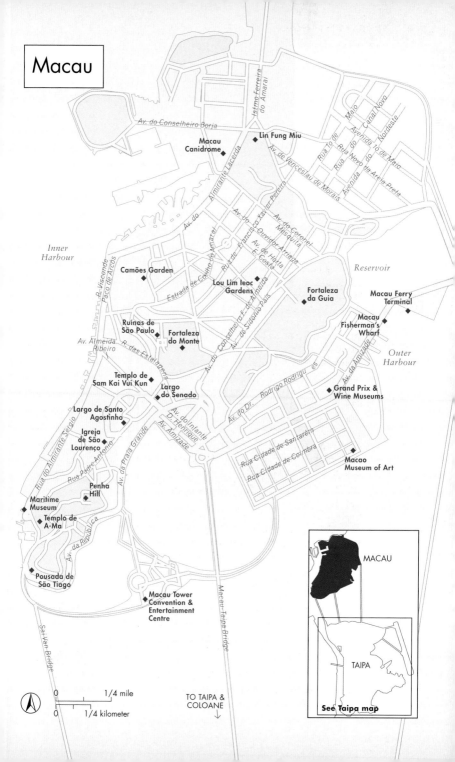

Macau

Inner
Harbour

Av. do Conselheiro Borja

Istmo Ferreira do Amaral

Macau
Canidrome

Lin Fung Miu

Av. de Venceslau de Morais

Rua do Maio
Canal Novo
Avenida 10 de Maio
Rua 10 de Maio
Rua Novo da Areia Preta
Avenida do Nordeste

Av. do Almirante Lacerda

Av. do Coronel Mesquita

Av. do Ouvidor Arriaga

Rua de Francisco Xavier Pereira

Av. de Horta E. Costa

Reservoir

Camões Garden

Lou Lim Ieoc
Gardens

Estrada de Cacho do Amaral

Rua de Coelho do Amaral

Av. do Conselheiro F. de Almeida

Av. de Sidónio Pais

Fortaleza
da Guia

Macau Ferry
Terminal

Ruínas de
São Paulo

Fortaleza
do Monte

R. das Estalagens

Av. Almeida
Ribeiro

Macau
Fisherman's
Wharf

Av. da Amizade

Outer
Harbour

Templo de
Sam Kai Vui Kun

Largo
do Senado

Av. do Dr. Rodrigo Rodrigues

Grand Prix &
Wine Museums

Largo de Santo
Agostinho

Igreja
de São
Lourenço

Av. do Infante
D. Henrique

Av. da Amizade

Rua do Almirante Sergio

Rua da Prata Grande

Rua Padre Antonio

Rua Cidade de Santarém

Rua Cidade de Colmbra

Macao
Museum of Art

Penha
Hill

Maritime
Museum

Templo de
A-Ma

Av. da República

Pousada de
São Tiago

Macau Tower
Convention &
Entertainment
Centre

Macau-Taipa Bridge

Sai Van Bridge

0   1/4 mile
0   1/4 kilometer

TO TAIPA &
COLOANE
↓

MACAU

TAIPA

See Taipa map

DID YOU KNOW?

The Macau Tower, modeled on Sky Tower in Auckland, offers thrills just like its Down Under counterpart. Do the Mast Climb up the side of the tower to reach Macau's highest point. Nowhere else in the world can you scale a freestanding building to its top. You can also walk around the outside of the outer rim of the tower on the Skywalk X or bungee-jump from 233 meters (765 feet) up.

Fortaleza do Monte (*Mount Fortress*). On the hill overlooking the ruins of São Paulo and affording great peninsular views, this renovated fort was built by the Jesuits in the early 17th century. In 1622 it was the site of Macau's most legendary battle, when a priest's lucky cannon shot hit an invading Dutch ship's powder supply, saving the day. The interior buildings were destroyed by fire in 1835, but the outer walls remain, along with several large cannons and artillery pieces. Exhibits at the adjoining **Macau Museum** (daily 10–6, MOP$15) take you through the territory's history, from its origins to modern development. ⊠ *Monte Hill, Downtown* ☎ *853/2835–7911* ⊕ *www.macaumuseum. gov.mo* ◪ *Free* ◷ *Daily 6 am–7 pm.*

Grand Prix Museum. Inaugurated in 1993 to celebrate the 40th anniversary of the Macau Grand Prix, this museum tells the stories of the best drivers from every year, but the highlights are the actual race cars on display. More than 20 Formula vehicles are exhibited in the hall, of which the centerpiece is the red-and-white Formula Three car driven by the late champion Aryton Senna. ⊠ *431 Rua Luis Gonzaga Gomes, Downtown* ☎ *853/8798–4108* ◪ *Free* ◷ *Wed.–Mon. 10–9.*

Igreja de São Lourenço (*Church of St. Lawrence*). One of Macau's three oldest churches, the Church of St. Lawrence was founded by Jesuits in 1560 and has been lovingly rebuilt several times. Its present appearance dates to 1846. It overlooks the South China Sea amid pleasant, palm-shaded gardens. Families of Portuguese sailors used to gather on the front steps to pray for the sailors' safe return; hence its Chinese name, Feng Shun Tang (Hall of the Soothing Winds). Focal points of its breathtaking interior are the elegant wood carvings, a baroque altar, and crystal chandeliers. ⊠ *Rua de São Lourenço, Downtown* ☎ *8399–6699* ◷ *Mon.–Fri. 10–4, Sat. 10–1.*

Largo de Santo Agostinho. Built in the pattern of traditional Portuguese squares, St. Augustine Square is paved with black-and-white tiles laid out in mosaic wave patterns and lined with leafy overhanging trees and lots of wooden benches. It's easy to feel as if you're in a European village, far from South China. One of the square's main structures is the **Teatro Dom Pedro V,** a European-style hall with an inviting green-and-white facade built in 1859. It's an important cultural landmark for Macanese and was regularly used until World War II, when it fell into disrepair. The 300-seat venue once again hosts concerts and recitals—especially during the annual Macau International Music Festival—as well as important public events, the only times you can go inside. It does, however, have a garden that's open daily, and admission is free. **Igreja de Santo Agostinho (Church of St. Augustine),** to one side of the square, dates from 1591, and has a grand, weathered exterior and a drafty interior with a high wood-beam ceiling (open daily 10–6). There's a magnificent stone altar with a statue of Christ on his knees, bearing the cross, with small crucifixes in silhouette on the hill behind him. The statue, called Our Lord of Passos, is carried in a procession through the streets of downtown on the first day of Lent. ⊠ *Off R. Central, Downtown.*

8

Lin Fung Miu. Built in 1592, the Temple of the Lotus honors several Buddhist and Taoist deities, including Tin Hau (goddess of the sea), Kun Iam (goddess of mercy), and Kwan Tai (god of war and wealth). The front of the temple is embellished with magnificent clay bas-reliefs of renowned figures from Chinese history and mythology. Inside are several halls, shrines, and courtyards. The temple is best known as a lodging place for Mandarins traveling from Guangzhou. Its most famous guest was Commissioner Lin Zexu, whose confiscation and destruction of British opium in 1839 was largely responsible for the First Opium War. ⊠ *Av. do Almirante Lacerda, Downtown* ۞ *Daily dawn–dusk.*

Lou Lim Ieoc Gardens. These beautiful gardens were built in the 19th century by a Chinese merchant named Lou Kau. Rock formations, water, vegetation, pavilions, and sunlight were all carefully considered, and the balanced landscapes are the hallmark of Suzhou garden style. The government took possession and restored the grounds in the mid 1970s, so that today you can enjoy tranquil walks among delicate flowering bushes framed with bamboo groves and artificial hills. A large auditorium frequently hosts concerts and other events, most notably recitals during the annual Macau International Music Festival. Adjacent to the gardens, a European-style edifice contains the **Macau Tea Culture House,** a small museum with exhibits on the tea culture of Macau and China (Tues.–Sun. 9–7, free). ⊠ *Estrada de Adolfo Loureiro, at Av. do Conselheiro Ferreira de Almeida, Downtown* ☎ *853/2835–6622* ᠍ *Free* ۞ *Daily 6 am–9 pm.*

Macao Museum of Art. The large, boxy museum is as well known for its curving, rectangular framed roof as it is for its calligraphy, painting, copperware, and international film collections. It's Macau's only art museum, and has five floors of eastern and western works, as well as important examples of ancient indigenous pottery found at Hác-Sá Beach on nearby Coloane Island. ⊠ *Macao Cultural Centre, Av. Xian Xing Hai, Outer Harbour* ☎ *853/8791–9814* ⊕ *www.mam.gov.mo* ᠍ *MOP$5 (free Sun.)* ۞ *Tues.–Sun. 10–7.*

۞ **Macau Fisherman's Wharf.** This sprawling complex of rides, games, and other minor attractions has an appealing Old World aura. The centerpiece is the Roman Amphitheatre, which hosts outdoor performances, but the main draws are the lively themed restaurants on the west side, such as AfriKana, serving up Macau's best African brews and barbecues. Come for the food, and stay after dark, as Fisherman's Wharf is most active at night. ⊠ *Av. da Amizade, at Av. Dr. Sun Yat-Sen, Downtown* ☎ *853/8299–3300* ⊕ *www.fishermanswharf.com.mo* ᠍ *Admission free, games MOP$1–MOP$32* ۞ *Open 24 hours.*

Maritime Museum. This handsome white building across from the A-Ma temple looks like a ship, with jutting white slats and porthole windows, and is a great place to spend an interesting hour brushing up on seafaring history. A row of fountains out front soothes you almost as much as the calm, cool interior. Multimedia exhibits cover fishermen, merchants, and explorers from Portugal, South China, and Japan. Look for compasses, telescopes, and sections of ships. There's even a small

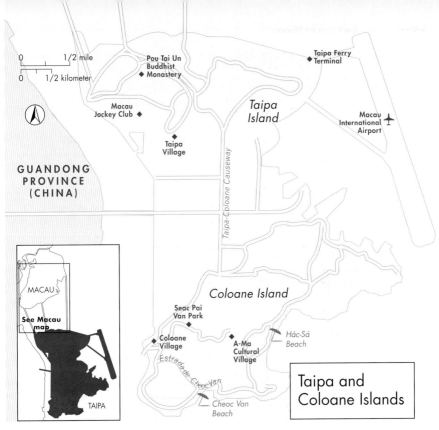

Taipa and Coloane Islands

aquarium gallery with local sealife. Try your hand at astronomic navigation—which sailors have used for thousands of years—by looking up at the top floor's nifty celestial dome ceiling. ☒ *1 Largo do Pagode da Barra, Inner Harbour* ☏ *853/2859–5481* ⊕ *www.museumaritimo. gov.mo* ☒ *MOP$10 ($5 Sun.)* ☽ *Wed.–Mon. 10–5:30.*

Templo de Sam Kai Vui Kun. Built in 1750, this temple is dedicated to Kuan Tai, the bearded, fierce-looking god of war and wealth in Chinese mythology. Statues of him and his two sons sit on an altar. A steady stream of people comes to pray and ask for support before they go wage battle in the casinos. May and June see festivals honoring Kuan Tai throughout Macau. ☒ *Rua Sui do Mercado de São Domingos, Downtown* ☽ *Daily 8–6.*

Wine Museum. In the same building as the Grand Prix Museum, this museum has more than 1,100 wines on display; some are almost 200 years old. You'll learn about production techniques and the importance of vinho (wine) in Portuguese culture. Several varieties are on hand for impromptu tastings. ☒ *431 Rua Luis Gonzaga Gomes, Downtown* ☏ *853/8798–4188* ☒ *Free* ☽ *Wed.–Mon. 10–9.*

A BIT OF HISTORY

In 1557 the Portuguese took over Macau as the first European colony in East Asia. Macau was known as "A Ma Gao" in honor of the patron goddess of sailors, A-Ma. The Portuguese adapted this Chinese name to "Macau," and for more than a century the port thrived as the main intermediary in the trade between Asia and the rest of the world. Ships from Italy, Portugal, and Spain came here to buy and sell Chinese silks and tea, Japanese crafts, Indian spices, African ivory, and Brazilian gold.

In addition to international trade, Macau became an outpost for western religions. St Francis Xavier successfully converted large numbers of Japanese and Chinese to Christianity and used Macau as a base of operations. In the 1500s and 1600s many churches were built, including an ambitious Christian college. Today in Macau this religious legacy can be seen in the array of well-preserved churches.

Macau's age of prosperity ended in the 1800s, when the Dutch and British gained control of most trading routes to East Asia. After the British victory over China in the 1814 Opium War, the huge, deep-water port of Hong Kong was established, and Macau was relegated to a quiet, sleepy port town. Macau did, however, remain important to Chinese refugees of World War I and World War II and the Cultural Revolution. With the widespread introduction of legalized gambling in the 1960s, Macau became a freewheeling place, where gambling, espionage, and crime reigned in the long shadow of modern, wealthy Hong Kong.

Today textile, furniture, electronics, and other exports join a world-class tourism industry in making Macau prosperous. Just before the 1999 handover to the Chinese government, the Portuguese administration launched a staggering number of public works. A huge international airport was built on a reclaimed island, and two new bridges were built to connect Macau's two islands. Recent years also saw the construction of two artificial lakes in the Outer Harbour along the Praia Grande and another in Cotai. These projects and the continuing developments have transformed Macau into a location of choice for casinos and luxury resorts.

TAIPA ISLAND

The island directly south of peninsular Macau was once two small islands that were, over time, joined by deposits from the Pearl River Delta. Taipa is connected to peninsular Macau by three long bridges. Macau's two universities, horse-racing track, scenic hiking trails, and international airport are all here.

Like downtown Macau, Taipa has been greatly developed in the past few years, yet it retains a visual balance between old Macau charm and modern sleekness. Try to visit on a weekend, so you can shop for clothing and crafts in the traditional flea market that's held every Sunday from morning to evening in Taipa Village.

Pou Tai Un Buddhist Monastery. The region's largest temple is part of a functioning monastery with several dozen monks. The classically designed structure has an ornate main prayer hall and central pavilions with sculptures, fish ponds, and banyan trees. Monks tend the vegetable plots that supply the popular on-site vegetarian restaurant. ⊠ *Estrada Lou Lim Leok, Taipa* ☎ *853/2881–1007* 🔲 *Free* ☉ *Daily 9–5.*

Taipai Houses-Museum. These five sea-green houses are interesting examples of Porto-Chinese architecture and were originally residences of wealthy local merchants. They now house changing art exhibitions. Paths lead into the beautiful adjoining **Carmel Garden,** where palm trees provide welcome shade. Within the garden stands the brilliant white-and-yellow **Nossa Senhora do Carmo** (Church of Our Lady of Carmel), built in 1885 and featuring a handsome single-belfry tower. ⊠ *Av. da Praia, Carmo Zone, Taipa* ☎ *853/2882–7103* 🔲 *Museum MOP$5, free Sun.; garden free* ☉ *Museum Tues.–Sun. 10–6; garden daily, 24 hours.*

Fodor'sChoice
★ **Taipa Village.** The narrow, winding streets are packed with restaurants, bakeries, shops, temples, and other buildings with traditional South Chinese and Portuguese design elements. The aptly named Rua do Cunha (Food Street) has many great Chinese, Macanese, Portuguese, and Thai restaurants. Several shops sell homemade Macanese snacks, including steamed milk pudding, almond cakes, beef jerky, and coconut candy. ⊠ *Macau, Macau–China.*

OUTDOOR ACTIVITIES

Whether you prefer a leisurely walk though a park or conquering steep hills on foot or by bike, Taipa Island has the region's best trails. The rewards for heading up Taipa Grande and Taipa Pequena, the island's two largest hills, are majestic views. The Taipa Grande trail starts at Estrada Colonel Nicolau de Mesquita, near the United Chinese Cemetery. The Taipa Pequena trail starts at Estrada Lou Lim Ieoc (Lou Lim Ieoc Gardens) behind the Regency Hotel. Be sure to wear rugged hiking shoes, use bug repellent, and, if possible, bring a mobile phone for emergency calls. The most popular place to rent bicycles is the shop at the bus stop outside the Civic and Municipal Affairs Bureau in Taipa Village on Largo Camões, where you can also find trail maps.

COLOANE ISLAND

Centuries ago, Coloane was a wild place, where pirates hid in rocky caves and coves, awaiting their chance to strike at cargo ships on the Pearl River. Early in the 20th century the local government sponsored a huge planting program to transform Coloane from a barren place to a green one. The results were spectacular—and enduring. Today this island is idyllic, with green hills and clean sandy beaches. The most popular is Hác-Sá; translated from the Chinese, hác-sá means "black sand," although the sands of the area's biggest beach are actually a deep gray.

Once connected to Taipa Island by a thin isthmus, Coloane is now almost completely fused with Taipa via the huge Cotai reclaimed land project, where the "Strip" was completed in 2010. Regardless of the recent development boom, Coloane remains the destination of choice for anyone seeking natural beauty and tranquility.

READY, SET, GO!

Grand Prix racing, which began in Macau in 1954, is the region's most glamorous annual sporting event. During the third or fourth weekend of November the city is pierced with the sound of supercharged engines testing the 6.2-km (3.8-mile) Guia Circuit, which follows city roads along the Outer Harbour to Guia Hill and around the reservoir. The route is as challenging as that of Monaco, with rapid gear changes demanded at the right-angle Statue Corner, the Doña Maria bend, and the Melco hairpin. Cars achieve speeds of 275 kph (171 mph) on the straightaways, with the lap record approaching two minutes, 10 seconds. The premier event is the Formula 3 Macau Grand Prix, but there are also races for motorcycles and production cars. If you plan to visit Macau during this time, beware of the logistical disruption that results from the race, including rerouting of main roads and lack of hotel vacancies.

TOP ATTRACTIONS

A-Ma Cultural Village. A huge complex built in a traditional Qing Dynasty style pays homage to Macau's namesake, the goddess of the sea. The vibrancy and color of the details in the bell and drum towers, the tiled roofs, and the carved marble altars are truly awe-inspiring. It's as if you've been transported back to the height of the Qing Empire and can now see temples in their true state of greatness. Other remarkable details include the striking rows of stairs leading to Tian Hou Palace at the entrance. Each row features painstakingly detailed marble and stone carvings of auspicious Chinese symbols: a roaring tiger, double lions, five cranes, the double phoenix, and a splendid imperial dragon. The grounds here also have a recreational fishing zone and an arboretum with more than 100 species of local and exotic flora.

Behind A-Ma Cultural Village is the 560-foot-tall **Coloane Hill,** crowned by a gleaming white-marble statue of A-Ma (commemorating the year of Macau's handover), soaring 65 feet and visible from miles away. You can make the short hike up to the top or take one of the shuttle buses that leave from the foot of the hill every 30 minutes. ⊠ *Off Estrada de Seac Pai Van, Coloane Island South* ☉ *Daily 8–6.*

Fodor's Choice
★

Coloane Village. Quiet, relaxed Coloane Village is home to traditional Mediterranean-style houses painted in pastels, as well as the baroque-style Chapel of St. Francis Xavier and the Taoist Tam Kung Temple. The narrow alleys reveal surprises at every turn; you may well encounter fishermen repairing their junks or a baptism at the chapel. At the village's heart is a small square adorned with a fountain with a bronze Cupid. The surrounding Macanese and Chinese open-air restaurants are among the region's best; some are the unheralded favorites of chefs visiting from Hong Kong and elsewhere in Asia. ⊠ *Macau, Macau–China.*

Rickshaws await the gamblers leaving the Casino Lisboa, the gambling den that started it all.

CASINOS

In February 2006 Macau surpassed Las Vegas in gambling revenue. By June 2008 Macau's casinos were turning over 2.6 times the revenue of their Vegas Strip counterparts. Small wonder that international casino groups have swarmed the region, and they continue to drive Macau's explosive double-digit growth.

From the late 1960s until 2001, Macau native Dr. Stanley Ho owned all the casinos, becoming one of the world's wealthiest people. One of the first steps the Chinese government took after the 1999 handover was to break up Dr. Ho's monopoly and award casino licenses to several consortiums from Las Vegas. The grand plan to transform Macau from a quiet town that offered gambling into one of the world's top gaming destinations has become a reality.

THE SCENE

Gambling is lightly regulated, so there are only a few things to remember. No one under age 18 is allowed into casinos. Most casinos use Hong Kong dollars in their gaming and not Macau patacas, but you can easily exchange currencies at cashiers. High- and no-limit VIP rooms are available on request, where minimum bets range from HK$50,000 to HK$100,000 per hand. You can get cash from credit cards and ATMs 24 hours a day, and every casino has a program to extend additional credit to frequent visitors. Most casinos don't have strict dress codes outside of their VIP rooms, but men are better off not wearing shorts or sleeveless shirts. Minimum bets for most tables are higher than those in Las Vegas, but there are lower limits for slots and video gambling.

The players here may not look sophisticated, but don't be fooled. Many of Macau's gamblers are truly hard-core. Average bets are in the hundreds per hand, and many people gamble until they're completely exhausted or completely broke, usually the latter.

Macau is also famous for gambling's sister industries of pawnshops, loan sharks, seedy saunas, and prostitution. This underbelly is hidden, though. You won't encounter such things unless you seek them out.

ASIA'S VEGAS

Sheldon Anderson, CEO of the Las Vegas Sands, spearheaded a $13 billion venture to transform the Cotai area into "Asia's Las Vegas." The huge Venetian Macao-Resort-Hotel has already made its mark, along with Hilton, InterContinental Hotels Group, Four Seasons, Sheraton, and St. Regis. The Cotai area now boasts more than 20 luxury properties; more than 6,000 gaming tables; 29,000 hotel rooms; and 4,000,000 square feet of retail space.

THE CASINOS

Gone are the days of Macau's dark and dingy underground gaming parlors. Stanley Ho no longer has an iron grip on the gambling scene. Over the past few years American-style casinos have been mushrooming like mad, primarily in Macau's NAPE (zona Nova de Aterros do Porto Exterior), or New Reclamation Area, in the Outer Harbour district between the main ferry terminal and the historic center. The foreign exports are most likely to please both casual tourists and serious players for their variety of gaming and other entertainment, relatively clean and well-lit atmosphere, free 24/7 accessibility, and overall glamour-resort experience.

DOWNTOWN

Casino Lisboa. Welcome to the casino that started it all. Opened in 1965 by Dr. Stanley Ho, this iconic Macau gaming den is replete with ancient jade ships in the halls, gilded staircases, and more baccarat tables than you can shake a craps stick at. It's great for a few rounds of *dai-siu*— dice bets over cups of iced green tea. Most of the gamblers are from neighboring Guangdong province, and Cantonese is the lingua franca. Other popular pastimes at this storied casino revolve around international fine-dining venues and colorful coffee shops, if you care to wander around a maze of marbled floors and low ceilings. ⊠ *Av. de Lisboa, Downtown* ☎ *853/2888–3888* ⊕ *www.hotelisboa.com.*

Galaxy Macau Complex. It's impossible to miss the six 24-karat gold cupolas of the Galaxy complex towering over the northwestern end of the Cotai Strip. This 2,200-room palatial resort is home to three hotels—Banyan Tree Macau, Galaxy Hotel, and Hotel Okura Macau— as well as the world's largest wave pool, a cinema, video arcade, and nightly laser show. Smack in the center is a brightly lit casino floor packed with gaming tables, surrounded by high-end shopping and restaurants where you can actually hear yourself think. ⊠ *Estrada da Baia de Nossa Senhora da Esperanca, Cotai* ☎ *853/2888–0888* ⊕ *www. galaxymacau.com.*

The opulent Wynn Macau is both luxurious and family-friendly.

Galaxy StarWorld. As you enter the StarWorld empire you're greeted by tall girls in high heels, while a mariachi band serenades you from across the lobby. The gaming floors are small and have a couple of Chinese-style diners if you get peckish, but the cool Whisky Bar *(⇨ After Dark)* on the 16th floor of the adjacent hotel is an atmospheric place to either begin or wind down your evening. The neon-blue building is just across from the Wynn and down the block from the MGM Grand. Live lobby entertainment and local holiday attractions add a kitschy, friendly feel. ⊠ *Av. da Amizade, Downtown* ☎ *853/2838–3838* ⊕ *www.starworldmacau.com.*

Grand Lisboa. With more than 300 tables and about 750 slot machines, the main gaming floor is anchored with a glowing egg statue and a leggy Paris cabaret show every 15 minutes. The second floor features craps and sports betting, and has a great bar. The Grand also has a variety of dining choices, from the baroque Don Alfonso 1890 to the Round-the-Clock Coffee Shop between the first and second gaming floors. If the slots have been kind, head up to the Grand Lisboa's crown jewel — the three-Michelin-starred Robuchon au Dôme on the 43rd floor. ⊠ *2–4 Av. de Lisboa, Downtown* ☎ *853/2838–2828* ⊕ *www.grandlisboa.com.*

MGM Macau. A stylish part of Macau's gambling scene offers lavish lounges, Dale Chihuly glass sculptures, Portuguese-inspired architecture, and fine dining. The gambling floor itself is popular with high rollers from Hong Kong, including business tycoons who are just in for a few days, and one of the owners, Pansy Ho (like her brother Lawrence Ho), is the daughter of Macau's "gambling godfather," Dr.

Stanley Ho. She is a high-octane business professional in her own right and a woman's classy touch shows up in this place's glitz-and-glam energy and high-society appeal. ⊠ *Av. Dr. Sun Yat Sen, Downtown* ☎ *853/8802–8888* ⊕ *www.mgmmacau.com.*

Fodor'sChoice **Sands Macao.** The Sands Macao was the largest casino on earth until
★ its sibling, the Venetian, stole the spotlight. It's the first casino you'll see on the peninsula even before debarking from the ferry. Past the sparkling 50-ton chandelier over the entrance, the grand gaming floor is anchored with a live cabaret stage above an open bar and under a giant screen. Several tiers are tastefully linked with escalators leading to the high-stakes tables upstairs. The friendly atmosphere and handy location, just across from Fisherman's Wharf and near the bar street in NAPE, makes this place a good choice for a warm-up to your night out. ⊠ *203 Largo de Monte Carlo, Downtown* ☎ *853/2888–3333* ⊕ *www.sands.com.mo.*

Fodor'sChoice **Wynn Macau.** Listen for theme songs such as "Diamonds are Forever,"
★ "Luck Be a Lady," or "Money, Money" as Wynn's outdoor Performance Lake dazzles you with flames and fountain jets of whipping water every 15 minutes from 11 am to midnight. Inside the "open hand" structure of Steve Wynn's Macau resort, the indoor Rotunda Tree of Prosperity also wows guests with feng shui glitz. Wynn's expansive, brightly lit gaming floor, fine dining, buffet meals, luxury shops, deluxe spa, and trendy suites make this one of the more swish resorts in Macau. ⊠ *Rua Cidade de Sintra, Downtown* ☎ *853/2888–9966* ⊕ *www.wynnmacau.com.*

MACAU INNER HARBOUR

Ponte 16. In the swinging seaside days of the 1950s, Macau's western port, or Ponte 16, is where all the action was. When the eastern port opened in the mid-1960s, the area fell into decay, but with the 2008 opening of Ponte 16, this legendary Latin Quarter has seen new momentum. The resort-casino has attracted Hong Kong and Taiwanese pop stars, mainland mass-market gamblers, and VIPs from Beijing and Shanghai. Probably because of the relatively isolated location, the atmosphere tends to be casual, and you can expect a winning combination of gorgeous views of the Inner Harbour as well as 109 gaming tables and 300 slot machines. ⊠ *4th fl., Rua do Visconde Paço de Arcos, Inner Harbour* ☎ *853/8861–8888* ⊕ *www.ponte16.com.mo.*

TAIPA

Fodor'sChoice **Altira Macau.** Touting itself as Macau's first "six-star" integrated resort,
★ the Altira is indeed stellar. The only classy casino on the island of Taipa faces the glow of casinos to the north on the peninsula and offers swank, '70s-style gaming floors decked out in browns and taupes with mod-style chandeliers. The selection of game play is abundant, from baccarat to straight-up slots to posh VIP gaming rooms. The VIP resort suites, fine-dining, and elegantly discreet 38 Lounge on the roof add to the overall ambience. ⊠ *Av. de Kwong Tung, Taipa* ☎ *853/2886–8888* ⊕ *www.altiramacau.com.*

Transport yourself to Renaissance Italy at the Venetian Macao-Resort-Hotel.

COTAI

City of Dreams. The underwater theme is immediately apparent, with giant screens flashing images of mermaids swimming to and fro. Cotai's glitzy entertainment complex boasts a 420,000-square-foot casino with 400 gaming tables and 1,300 gaming machines, and more than 20 cafés, restaurants, and bars. Kids will love the free multimedia show "Dragon's Treasure," as well as the Kids' City playground. "House of Dancing Water," an aquatic-based spectacle that cost HK$2 billion to mount, is the main event. Once you're tired out, you can elect to stay at one of the three attached hotels: Grand Hyatt, Hard Rock Hotel, and Crown Towers. ⊠ *Estrada do Istmo, Cotai* ☎ *8868–6688* ⊕ *www.cityofdreamsmacau.com.*

Sands Cotai Central. Across the street from the Venetian, is this huge, new hotel and shopping and casino complex: the jungle-themed shopping center is flanked by the Holiday Inn Macao, the Conrad Macao, and the Sheraton Macao Hotel. The whole thing is perhaps the most child-friendly of the resort complexes, with budget-friendly prices, children's pools, and an array of colorful family suites. The enormous 3,863-room Sheraton—the largest in the world—even offers free popcorn and games near reception. ⊠ *Estrada da Baía de N. Senhora da Esperança, Downtown* ☎ *853/2886–6688* ⊕ *www.sandscotaicentral.com.*

Fodor'sChoice
★

Venetian Macao-Resort-Hotel. The Macau Venetian is twice the size of its namesake in Las Vegas, offering gambling, shopping, eating, and sleeping, along with faux-Renaissance decoration, built-in canals plied by crooning gondoliers, live carnival acts, plenty of sheer spectacle, and more than a touch of pretension. The 534,000-square-foot gaming floor has some 2,000 slot machines and more than 550 tables of casino favorites. The sprawling property also includes nearly 3,000 suites, a 15,000-seat arena, and the multi-purpose Venetian Theater. It's no wonder the Venetian is the must-see megacomplex that everyone's talking about. ✉ *Estrada da Baía de N. Senhora da Esperança, Cotai* ☎ *853/2882–8888* 🌐 *www.venetianmacao.com.*

WHERE TO EAT

Macau's medley of Portuguese and Cantonese cuisine—spicy and creamy Macanese interpretations of traditional Cantonese dishes such as baked prawns, braised abalone, and seafood stews—has made the peninsula one of Asia's top fine-dining destinations for decades.

Now, thanks to the spate of new casino-hotels, Macau has also become an exciting world-class culinary frontier. But Macau dining isn't all highbrow. Near the Largo do Senado, in the villages of Taipa or Coloane, wander the back alleys for *zhu-bao-bao,* a slab of fried pork on a toasted bun served with milk tea, or the signature *pasteis de nata* (custard tart): simple and delicious, and classic Macau.

Long-renowned restaurants such as Fernando's and Litoral are staying the course. So, too, are Cantonese restaurants such as Fat Siu Lau, particularly well known among Hong Kong residents who travel to Macau just for dim sum, weekend brunches, and seafood feasts at more affordable prices and made from higher-quality ingredients.

PLANNING

Expect to shell out MOP$90 to MOP$200 per person per meal without wine, though you can always go to a hole-in-the-wall noodle shop for MOP$25–MOP$30. Budget MOP$500 per person for an unforgettable dinner. A 10% service charge is added automatically, but, depending on the service quality, it's common for customers to round up the total. While major credit cards are accepted at most restaurants, cash is preferred at the smaller eateries.

Despite the surge in upscale dining accompanying casino development in Macau, the pace is still siesta style, with serious lunches lasting a few hours. The hotels serve breakfast early, but corner coffee shops start serving ham and cheese on croissants with espresso by around 11 am. Cocktails begin at around 6:30, and dinner at around 8.

DOWNTOWN MACAU

$$ PORTUGUESE

🍴 **Afonso III.** After four years at the Hyatt Regency, Chef Afonso Carrao Pereira decided to open his own place and cook the way his grandmother did. The result is his modest café in the heart of downtown near Senado Square, with an intimate space downstairs of dark wood and stucco, and a more expansive upstairs. The food consists of simple, hearty, traditional dishes served in huge portions, mostly to Portuguese expatriates and Macanese locals. Your best bets are the daily specials, which invariably include *bacalhau* (Portuguese salted codfish), braised pork, or beef stew probably better than any other you'll taste in Macau. The wine list is extensive, and comes in generous goblets or by the bottle. [$] *Average main: MOP$150* ✉ *11A Rua Central, Downtown* ☎ *853/2858–6272* 💳 *No credit cards* ⏲ *Closed Sun.*

$$$ FRENCH 🍴 **Aux Beaux Arts.** A 1930s-style Parisian brasserie in the MGM Grand is one of the trendiest restaurants in Macau. Chinese diners are particularly fond of its fresh, catch-of-the-day seafood—the lobster is especially choice. So, too, are the French mains, such as beef tartare with french fries. Oysters and caviar are also exclusive, at prices reaching MOP$2,950 for 50 grams. In-house sommeliers are at hand to pair the latest wines with dishes. With tan wood, private booths, and a terrace, the decor is as much old French Concession Shanghai as it is old Paris. Either way, the place has raised the bar for Macau's restaurant scene. [$] *Average main: MOP$300* ✉ *MGM Grand, Av. Dr. Sun Yat Sen, Downtown* ☎ *853/8802–3888* 🌐 *www.mgmmacau.com* 🕒 *Closed Mon.*

LOVE OF VINHO

Wine lovers should take full advantage of Macau's intimate love of vinho. Some restaurants have wine lists as thick as phone books. Most places list at least a couple of bottles of delicious Portuguese wine—usually a hearty red from the Dão region or a slightly sparkling vinho verde from the north.

$$ PORTUGUESE 🍴 **Clube Militar de Macau (The Macau Military Club).** Founded in 1870 as a private military club, the stately pink-and-white structure was restored in 1995 and reopened as a restaurant. The languid Old World atmosphere perfectly complements the extensive list of traditional Portuguese dishes, such as *bacalhau dourado* ("golden cod," a specialty of fried cod and potatoes), African chicken, and *arroz de marisco* (flavored rice and seafood). Leave room for dessert—the options include Portuguese sweet rice pudding with mango, warm chestnut tart, and coconut ice cream with caramelized pineapple. [$] *Average main: MOP$150* ✉ *975 Av. da Praia Grande, Downtown* ☎ *853/2871–4000* 🌐 *www.clubemilitardemacau.net.*

$ PORTUGUESE Fodor's Choice ★ 🍴 **Dom Galo.** "Quirky" springs to mind when describing the colorful decor, with plastic monkey puppets and funky chicken toys hanging from the ceilings. A wide clientele includes graphic designers, gambling-compliance lawyers, and 10-year-old Cantonese kids celebrating birthdays. The owner is Portuguese and the food is usually spot-on, with *insalada de polvo* (octopus salad), king prawns, and steak fries served with a tangy mushroom sauce among the stand-outs. Pitchers of sangria are essential with any meal here. So, too, are reservations, as this place is increasingly popular with tourists. [$] *Average main: MOP$100* ✉ *Av. Sir Andars Ljung Stedt, Downtown* ☎ *853/2875–1383* ✍ *Reservations essential.*

$$ CANTONESE Fodor's Choice ★ 🍴 **Fat Siu Lau.** Well known to both locals and visitors from Hong Kong, Fat Siu Lau has kept its customers coming back since 1903 with delicious Macanese favorites and modern creations. Try ordering whatever you see the chatty Cantonese stuffing themselves with at the surrounding tables, and you won't be disappointed. Your meal might well consist of whole curry crab, grilled prawns in a butter garlic sauce, and the famous roasted pigeon dressed in a secret marinade. Fat Siu Lau 2 is on Macau Lan Kwai Fong Street, and the newer Fat Siu Lau 3 is near the Venetian—both offer the same great food. [$] *Average main: MOP$125* ✉ *64 Rua da Felicidade, Downtown* ☎ *853/2857–3580* 🌐 *www.fatsiulau.com.mo* ✍ *Reservations essential.*

$$$$
ITALIAN
✗ **Il Teatro.** With its dedicated view of the Wynn's Performance Lake show, and the flashing glows of the Lisboa casinos providing ambience, one of the most romantic restaurants in Macau hosts Hong Kong pop stars and jet-setting millionaires from Malaysia. Popular among the impeccable southern Italian delights are tenderloin carpaccio and cioppino starters and sweet potato and pancetta gnocchi, accompanied by chilled wine from an exhaustive list. Desserts range from crispy cannoli to homemade sorbets and ice cream imported straight from Italy. Window seats in particular are at a premium, and are best reserved three weeks in advance. The dress code is "casual elegance," which means long pants, closed-toe shoes, and no open shirts for men; this is not the place for children under five. $ *Average main: MOP$350* ✉ *Wynn Macau, Rua da Sintra, Downtown* ☎ *853/8986–3663* ⊕ *www.wynnmacau.com* ◷ *No lunch; closed Mon.*

> ### A COLONIAL FEAST
>
> The Macanese like hearty Portuguese fare. Most restaurants serve the beloved bacalhau (salt cod) baked, boiled, grilled, deep-fried with potato, or stewed with onion, garlic, and eggs. Other dishes include sardines, sausages, and *caldo verde* (vegetable soup). Giant prawns in a curry sauce recall the cuisine of Goa, India—another Portuguese colony. Indeed, there are dishes drawn from throughout the colonial empire, including Brazilian *feijoada* (a stew of beans, pork, and vegetables) and Mozambique chicken, baked or grilled and seasoned with piri-piri chili, tangy spices, and coconut.

$
CAFÉ
✗ **Pastelaria Koi Kei.** Walking toward the Ruins of St. Paul's, you will likely be accosted by salespeople forcing Macanese snacks into your hands, and enticement to step into one of the street's *pastelarias* (pastry shops), serving traditional almond cakes, ginger candy, beef jerky, and egg rolls. Have a taste or two—competition is fierce, and one of the oldest and best is Pastelaria Koi Kei. Hong Kong residents regularly haul the distinctive tan bags, heavy with snacks—and in particular, the Portuguese custards—back home for friends and relatives. Other branches are on nearby Rua de São Paulo and on Rua do Cunha in Taipa. Cash is preferred. $ *Average main: MOP$35* ✉ *70–72 Rua Felicidade, Downtown* ☎ *853/2893–8102* ⊕ *www.koikei.com.*

$$$
SHANGHAINESE
✗ **Portas do Sol.** Despite the Portuguese name, specialties are exquisite dim sum and Chinese cuisine. Tiny, sweet Shanghainese pork buns, turnip cakes, steamed rice-flour crepes, and soup dumplings are some of the traditional fare, and there are some innovative new creations that look like miniature jewels on the plate. For dessert you can choose from a wide variety of Chinese sweets, including a fish-shaped chilled mango and coconut pudding, double-boiled papaya with snow fungus (a tasteless mushroom that becomes gelatinous when cooked), and deep-fried sweet milk with longan fruit. Reservations are a good idea on weekends, as this place fills up with Hong Kong and mainland visitors. $ *Average main: MOP$250* ✉ *Hotel Lisboa, Av. da Amizade, Downtown* ☎ *853/8803–3100* ⊕ *www.hotelisboa.com* ✍ *Reservations essential* ◷ *No lunch.*

8

$$
PORTUGUESE

✕ **Praia Grande.** Mediterranean beauty is in evidence inside and outside, with a gleaming white facade opening into a dining room with graceful arches, terra-cotta floors, and wrought-iron furniture. The menu is creative, with dishes ranging from Portuguese dim sum, African chicken, mussels in white wine, and pork and clams *cataplana* (in a stew of onions, tomatoes, and wine). Guitarists serenade you in the evenings. $ *Average main: MOP$130* ✉ *10A Praça Lobo d'Avila, Av. da Praia Grande, Downtown* ☎ *853/2897–3022.*

$$$$
FRENCH

✕ **Robuchon au Dôme.** A slice of Paris overlooking the heart of Macau, this three-Michelin-starred restaurant on the 43rd floor of the Grand Lisboa is a must if you just hit it big in the casino. In the ornate interior, with rich velvets and dark woods, a crystal chandelier twinkles from above and signature dishes are a heavenly mille-feuille of tomato and crabmeat, duck breast with fruit and foie gras, and lamb served with creamy potato puree. But Robuchon's 12-course tasting menus, including two desserts, are the best way to experience the gastronomic offerings. The wine list is as thick as an encyclopedia. $ *Average main: MOP$750* ✉ *Grand Lisboa, Av. de Lisboa, Downtown* ☎ *853/8803–7878* ⊕ *www.grandlisboahotel.com* ⌂ *Reservations essential.*

MACAU OUTER HARBOUR

$
AFRICAN

✕ **AfriKana Bar.** Macau's historical contacts with Africa, especially Angola and Mozambique, come into sharp focus in one of the few places on the peninsula where you can eat roasted coconut chicken under a thatched roof. Scores of Portuguese-speaking residents who were born in Portugal's African colonies come here for parties or cultural events. The eight thatched pavilions feature resilient colors, from dark blues to mustard yellows to sandy reds. $ *Average main: MOP$75* ✉ *Fisherman's Wharf, Outer Harbour* ☎ *853/8299–3678* ☺ *No lunch.*

MACAU INNER HARBOUR

$$
PORTUGUESE
Fodor's Choice
★

✕ **A Lorcha.** Vastly popular A Lorcha (the name means "wooden ship") celebrates the heritage of Macau as an important port with a maritime theme for the menu. Don't miss the signature dish, Clams Lorcha Style, with tomato, beer, and garlic. Other classics include *feijoada* (Brazilian pork-and-bean stew), steamed crab, and perfectly smoky and juicy fire-roasted chicken. Save room for *serradura* (aka Macau sawdust pudding, made from biscuits and vanilla whipped cream). Watch for racers during the Grand Prix, as the Macanese owner Adriano is a fervent Formula fan. $ *Average main: MOP$140* ✉ *289 Rua do Almirante Sérgio, Inner Harbour* ☎ *853/2831–3193* ⌂ *Reservations essential* ☺ *Closed Tues.*

$$
MACANESE

✕ **Litoral.** In tastefully decorated environs with whitewashed walls and dark-wood beams, one of the most popular local restaurants serves authentic Macanese dishes that are simple, straightforward, and deliciously satisfying. Must-try dishes include the tamarind pork with shrimp paste, as well as codfish baked with potato and garlic, and a Portuguese vegetable cream soup. For dessert, try the *bebinca de leite*, a coconut-milk custard, or the traditional egg pudding, *pudim abade de priscos*. Variously priced set menus are also available, and reservations

Make sure to sample one (or more) of Lord Stow's sought after tarts.

are recommended on weekends. $ *Average main: MOP$180* ✉ *261 Rua do Almirante Sergio, Inner Harbour* ☎ *853/2896–7878* ⊕ *www. restaurante-litoral.com.*

$ ✕ **Lord Stow's Bakery.** Originally a modest, traditional bakery opened by

BAKERY a young Englishman named Andrew Stow in 1989, Lord Stow's Bakery

Fodor's Choice is now a culinary landmark in Coloane, just off the town square. Locals

★ sit on nearby benches munching the signature hot and flaky *pasteis de nata* (custard tarts) straight from the oven. Inside the little shop, breads, muffins, cookies, flapjacks, and other homemade goods are on offer, but be sure to walk out with at least one tart. The neighboring Lord Stow's Café (*853/2888–2174*) has sit-down meals as does the outpost in the Venetian (*853/2886–6889*). $ *Average main: MOP$40* ✉ *1 Rua da Tassara, Coloane Village Sq.* ☎ *853/2888–2534* ⊕ *www. lordstow.com.*

COLOANE

$$ ✕ **Restaurante Espaço Lisboa.** Portuguese-owned and with a Portuguese

PORTUGUESE chef, this is a favorite among local Portuguese, occupying a converted two-story house with a small but pleasant outdoor balcony overlooking Coloane Village. Menu highlights include codfish cakes, savory duck rice, monkfish rice, boiled bacalhau with cabbage, sausage flambé, steak topped with ham and fried egg, and smoked ham imported from Portugal. Take your pick from an extensive list of hearty Portuguese wines, and finish the meal with homemade mango ice cream with a cherry flambé. $ *Average main: MOP$200* ✉ *8 Rua das Gaivotas, Coloane Island West* ☎ *853/2888–2226* ⊗ *No lunch.*

$$ PORTUGUESE Fodor's Choice ★ 🍴 **Restaurante Fernando.** Everyone in Hong Kong and Macau knows about Fernando's, but the vine-covered entrance close to Hác-Sá Beach is difficult to spot. The open-air dining pavilion and bar have attracted beachgoers for years now, and the enterprising Fernando has built a legendary reputation for his Portuguese fare. The menu focuses on seafood paired with homegrown vegetables, and diners choose from among the bottles of Portuguese reds on display rather than from a wine list or opt for the beloved sangria. The informal nature of the restaurant fits in with the satisfying, home-style food such as grilled fish, baked chicken, and huge bowlfuls of spicy clams, all eaten with your fingers and washed down with crisp vinho verde. [$] *Average main: MOP$150* ✉ *Hác-Sá Beach 9, Coloane Island South* ☎ *853/2888–2531* 🌐 *www.fernando-restaurant.com* ✍ *Reservations not accepted* 💳 *No credit cards.*

WHERE TO STAY

Since late 2006, an influx of luxury hotels has transformed Macau into a posh place to stay. The musty three-stars are still out there, but the five-stars are generally worth the splurge. For a true Macau experience, try staying in *pousadas,* restored historic buildings that have been converted into intimate hotels with limited facilities but lots of character.

PLANNING

When choosing a hotel, consider the surroundings. In pulsating downtown Macau (or in the Outer Harbour, connected to Downtown via frequent casino shuttles), historic and cultural sites, casinos, and restaurants are all within walking distance. Hotels in more residential Taipa, just a short bus or taxi ride away, often have incomparable sea and bright-lights views. And if you spring for the Altira, you can enjoy the many top-rate facilities within walking distance of Taipa Village. Cotai offers one-stop sleeping, shopping, eating, and gambling. Outside the resorts it's still a construction field, with new, glitzy hotels opening frequently. The peaceful Inner Harbour has excellent sea views, but for true otherworldly quiet, head to Coloane, where you can hit the beach and hiking trails.

For discounted rates in the grand hotels, book a package through a Hong Kong travel agency. Or an agent at the Macau hydrofoil terminal can book you a room at a three- to five-star hotel, subject to availability, for a discount price. Macau hotels are busiest during the Grand Prix (third week of November) and all official Chinese holidays. Book at least a couple of weeks in advance at these times. Year-round, weekends fill up fast and walk-ins can be prohibitively expensive. Visit on a weekday to avoid crowds and inflated prices.

DOWNTOWN MACAU

$$ HOTEL 🏨 **Hotel Lisboa.** In Macau's infamous landmark, redolent with history and intrigue, labyrinthine hallways and salons display jade and artworks, and an ostentatiously gilded staircase leads to luxurious guestrooms with hardwood floors and Jacuzzi baths. [$] *Rooms from: MOP$1850* ✉ *2–4 Av. de Lisboa, Downtown* ☎ *853/2888–3888* 🌐 *www.hotelisboa.com* 🛏 *950 rooms, 50 suites.*

MGM Macau

Westin Resort

$ HOTEL 🏨 **Hotel Sintra.** What these budget lodgings lack in luxury they make up for with lots of pluses: the location, minutes away from Senado Square, is great; the cozy, carpeted rooms are decorated in soothing brown-and-cream color schemes; and the staff is smartly dressed and helpful. **Pros:** in the heart of downtown; simple but tasteful decor. **Cons:** small rooms; small casino. [$] *Rooms from: MOP$680* ✉ *Av. de Dom João IV, Downtown* ☎ *853/2871–0111, 800/969–145 in Hong Kong* 🌐 *www.hotelsintra.com* 🛏 *240 rooms, 9 suites* 🍴 *No meals.*

$$ HOTEL Fodor's Choice ★ 🏨 **MGM Macau.** Rooms are everything you'd expect in the way of comfort and elegance from a luxury accommodation, with decor adhering to a muted cream, brown, and beige color palette, but it's the classy world around them that distinguishes this hotel from the rest. **Pros:** tasteful architecture; fine artwork; refined dining and lounge options. **Cons:** inseparable from the casino, which can get smoky and loud; high-traffic location. [$] *Rooms from: MOP$1788* ✉ *Av. Dr. Sun Yat Sen, Downtown* ☎ *853/8802–8888* 🌐 *mgmmacau.com* 🛏 *468 rooms, 99 suites, 15 villas.*

$ B&B/INN 🏨 **Pousada de Mong-Há.** A training hotel run by students of the Institute for Tourism Studies offers exemplary accommodation and service and spacious rooms nicely decorated with hand-stitched carpets. **Pros:** historic charm; hillside walks and views. **Cons:** half-hour walk north from city center; no pool. [$] *Rooms from: MOP$700* ✉ *Colina de Mong-Há, Downtown* ☎ *853/2851–5222* 🌐 *www.ift.edu.mo/pousada* 🛏 *20 rooms and suites* 🍴 *Breakfast.*

$$$ HOTEL 🏨 **StarWorld Hotel.** Luminous open "studio" suites have high ceilings, Jacuzzi tubs, and panoramic bay windows, and even the deluxe rooms, with their high-quality bedding and dark wood furniture, make you feel like you're somewhere special. **Pros:** celestially designed suites; live entertainment in the lobby and lounge bar. **Cons:** high energy at all hours; in a heavy-traffic area. [$] *Rooms from: MOP$2380* ✉ *Av. da Amizade, Downtown* ☎ *853/2838–3838* 🌐 *www.starworldmacau.com* 🛏 *465 rooms, 40 suites* 🍴 *No meals.*

$$$ HOTEL 🏨 **Wynn Macau.** If you just can't get enough of the Wynn's Performance Lake, all rooms have floor-to-ceiling windows, many with a plunging view of the fire-and-water spectacle, as well as of the peaceful Nam Van Lake. **Pros:** exclusive VIP club space; Nam Van and Performance Lake views. **Cons:** light pollution from neighboring casinos; lowest rooms on 5th floor. [$] *Rooms from: MOP$1888* ✉ *Rua Cidade de Sintra, Downtown* ☎ *853/2888–9966, 800/966–963 in Hong Kong* 🌐 *www.wynnmacau.com* 🛏 *460 rooms, 134 suites* 🍴 *No meals.*

MACAU OUTER HARBOUR

$$ HOTEL 🏨 **Rocks Hotel.** The posh-yet-quaint five-story Rocks Hotel is decorated in English Victorian style, and each room and suite is individually decorated. **Pros:** distinctive decor; low-key fine dining. **Cons:** no pool or spa; inside an amusement park. [$] *Rooms from: MOP$1800* ✉ *Macau Fisherman's Wharf, Outer Harbour* ☎ *853/2878–2782, 800/962–863 in Hong Kong* 🌐 *www.rockshotel.com.mo* 🛏 *66 rooms, 6 suites* 🍴 *No meals.*

$$ HOTEL 🏨 **Sands Macao.** The Sands is nothing if not luxurious, with spacious rooms that have deep, soft carpets, large beds, and huge marble bathrooms with Jacuzzis. **Pros:** heated outdoor pool; across the street from

Fisherman's Wharf. **Cons:** not as new as the Venetian; near lots of vehicle traffic. [$] *Rooms from: MOP$1698* ⊠ *203 Largo de Monte Carlo, Outer Harbour* ☎ *853/2888–3388* ⊕ *www.sands.com.mo* ⤳ *238 suites, 51 VIP suites.*

MACAU INNER HARBOUR

$$$$
B&B/INN
Fodor's Choice
★

Pousada de São Tiago. This romantic lodging's origins as a 17th-century fortress permeate every corner, from the tunnel-like entrance to 12 modern luxury suites, each with Jacuzzi bathrooms and large balconies for room-service breakfast. **Pros:** all the modern comfort of a luxury hotel; complimentary minibar and Wi-Fi; intimate, sunset views of the Inner Harbour. **Cons:** small pool; limited facilities; you'll need to call a taxi to go out and, even then, it's hit or miss. [$] *Rooms from: HK$3000* ⊠ *Fortaleza de São Tiago da Barra, Av. da República, Inner Harbour* ☎ *853/2837–8111* ⊕ *www.saotiago.com.mo* ⤳ *12 suites.*

TAIPA

$$$
HOTEL
Fodor's Choice
★

Altira. Towering over northern Taipa, the Altira offers stunning sea views of the Macau Peninsula from each and every room, each one like a suite, with a dedicated lounge, walk-in wardrobe, and circular stone bath. **Pros:** panoramic-view pool; open-air rooftop bar. **Cons:** may sometimes be noisy from nearby construction; still a taxi (or shuttle) ride from the peninsula. [$] *Rooms from: MOP$1888* ⊠ *Av. de Kwong Tung, Taipa* ☎ *853/2886–8888* ⊕ *www.altiramacau.com* ⤳ *284 rooms, 24 suites, 8 villas.*

COLOANE

$$
RESORT
☾
Fodor's Choice
★

Westin Resort. This is where you truly get away from it all: built into the side of a cliff, every room faces the ocean, and the vast private terraces are ideal for alfresco dining and afternoon naps. **Pros:** green surroundings on Hác-Sá Beach; golf-club access; fun for kids. **Cons:** isolated location; limited access. [$] *Rooms from: MOP$1150* ⊠ *1918 Estrada de Hác Sá, Coloane Island South* ☎ *853/2887–1111, 800/228–3000 in Hong Kong* ⊕ *www.starwoodhotels.com/westin* ⤳ *200 rooms, 8 suites.*

NIGHTLIFE

Old movies, countless novels, and gossip through the years have portrayed Macau's nightlife as a combustible mix of drugs, wild gambling, violent crime, and ladies of the night. Up until the 1999 handover back to mainland China, this image of Macau was mostly accurate, and did much to drive away tourists. These days you can enjoy live music and cocktails in elegant surroundings at an ever-growing range of hotels and casinos.

DOWNTOWN MACAU

LOUNGES AND PUBS

Bar Cristal. An antique French chandelier from the 19th century is the centerpiece of the opulent interior, designed to look like a life-size jewelry box. Sip on cocktails or sample one of the many champagnes in stock. ⊠ *G/F, Encore at Wynn Macau, Rua Cidade de Sintra, Downtown* ☎ *853/8986–3663* ⊕ *www.wynnmacau.com.*

Fodor's Choice **MacauSoul.** This quiet wine bar in a bright pink building with pine-green
★ shutters is just steps away from the ruins of St. Paul's Cathedral. The
two English expats who manage the place have put together a wine
list of more than 430 Portuguese varieties, as well as British cheese
plates, charcuterie boards, homemade hummus, and memorable sour-
dough bread. Stay for the live music that turns up after dinner on
select dates. Best to call ahead for details. ⊠ *31A Rua de Sao Paulo,
Travessa da Paixao, Downtown* ☎ *853/2836-5182* ⊕ *www.macausoul.
com* ☾ *Closed Wed.*

Whisky Bar. Depending on the time of day or night, this bar on the 16th
floor of the StarWorld Hotel provides either upbeat cabaret entertainment or a cool moment of respite from the clinking casinos all around.
Happy hour is daily from 5 to 8, and the Star Band starts playing nightly
at 10:30. In addition to a full selection of the usual hard stuff, the bar
has 100 different kinds of whisky, including the ultra-rare Macallan
1946. ⊠ *StarWorld Hotel, Av. da Amizade, Downtown* ☎ *853/8290–
8698* ⊕ *www.starworldmacau.com.*

MACAU OUTER HARBOUR

LOUNGES AND PUBS

Macau's Lan Kwai Fong. A modest collection of bars lines a small stretch
of street in NAPE, within sight of the huge golden Guan Yin statue in
Macau's Outer Harbour. Although it takes its name from the legendary bar area in Hong Kong, in reality this is a bunch of nice, quiet bars
where you can meet with friends or watch sports on a big-screen TV.
A large number of expats come to this area to relax and drink in the
evenings, but don't expect the wild times and thumping music you might
find in the original LKF in Hong Kong. ⊠ *Edifício Vista Magnifica
Court, Av. Dr. Sun Yat-Sen, Outer Harbour.*

TAIPA

LOUNGES AND PUBS

38 Lounge. When you're finally done with the casinos and ready to look
down on the rest of the world, hop over to Taipa and take the Altira
elevator straight up to this lofty spot just around the corner from the
lobby. Sip cocktails under the stars on the outdoor terrace, where tapas
are served from 2 pm to 2 am. Indoors, a live band plays from 9 pm
to 2 am most evenings. ⊠ *38th fl., Altira Macau, Av. De Kwong Tung,
Taipa* ☎ *853/8803–6868* ⊕ *www.altiramacau.com.*

SHOWS

Acrobatic Dancing Adagio. Cirque du Soleil may have come and gone,
but the Venetian still offers some of the most mind-bending performances. A worthy substitute, the captivating Acrobatic Dancing Adagio captures the arch of a love story with graceful lifts and swoops
from two of Russia's top performers. ⊠ *Venetian Macao, Estrada de
Baía de Nossa Senhora da Esperança, Cotai* ☎ *853/2882–8800* ⊕ *www.
venetianmacao.com.*

The House of Dancing Water. Brought to Macau by Franco Dragone, former star director at Cirque du Soleil, The House of Dancing Water
aquatic show is the star at the City of Dreams complex. This 90-minute
aquatic spectacle harnesses 3.7 million gallons of water—think five

Olympic-sized swimming pools—to weave elaborate stunts, dives, and explosions into a love story. Tickets cost MOP$480, and it's best to book ahead. ⊠ *Estrada do Istmo, Cotai* ☎ *853/8868–6688* ⊕ *www. dragone.be.*

SHOPPING AND SPAS

Macau, like Hong Kong, is a free port for most items, so prices for electronics, jewelry, and clothing are lower here than they are in other international cities. But the shopping experience is completely different in Macau than it is in Hong Kong, with a low-key atmosphere, small crowds, and compact areas. It is a hub for traditional Chinese arts, crafts, and even some antiques (but be aware that there are many high-quality reproductions in the mix, too). Macau's major shopping district is along its main street in the downtown area, Avenida Almeida Ribeiro, more commonly known by its Chinese name, **San Ma Lo**; there are also shops downtown on **Rua Dos Mercadores** and its side streets; in **Cinco de Outubro**; and on the **Rua do Campo.**

You can see craftspeople at work making the "new antiques," particularly on the side streets of Tercena and Estalagens and the alleyways in front of the ruins of St. Paul's. Commonly sold pieces include lacquer screens, Chinese pottery, and huge wooden chests carved from solid mahogany, camphor wood, and redwood.

Major shopping areas for clothes and shoes include the small shops on **Rua do Campo** and around **Rua dos Mercadores** in the downtown area. There are also bustling street markets downtown that sell clothes on **São Domingos** (off Largo do Senado), **Rua Cinco de Outubro**, and **Rua da Palha.**

Jewelry shops across from casinos in the downtown area sell luxury watches, pendants, and rings, some of which have been pawned by desperate gamblers. Prices are generally more reasonable than in Hong Kong. For gold purchase, head to trusted Hong Kong stalwarts **Chow Tai Fook** and **Chow Sang Sang**, which have locations throughout Macau and are known for transparent pricing and knowledgeable staff with good English.

Most of Macau's shops operate year-round with a short break in late January for Chinese New Year and are open from 10 am to 8 pm and later on weekends. While most shops accept all major credit cards, specialty discount shops usually ask for cash, and street vendors accept only cash. For most street vendors and some smaller stores, some friendly bargaining is expected; ask for the "best price," which ideally produces instant discounts of 10%–20%. The shopping mantra here is "bargain hard, bargain often."

Macau is well known for its casinos and restaurants, but it's also rapidly gaining a reputation for its luxury spa and sauna facilities, offering a huge range of treatments. Almost every luxury hotel has its own spa, with special packages and offers for hotel guests. Many visitors opt for spa treatments at luxury hotels, but Macau's independent spas have become a major force, offering equally exquisite

The spa at Grand Lapa scrubs and rubs customers into relaxation.

service at lower prices than hotels. All spas offer services for couples, and provide a great opportunity to relax in a peaceful space with someone special. Treatments begin at around MOP$300 and up for 60 minutes of service. The following are some of the more impressive spa facilities available:

DOWNTOWN MACAU

DEPARTMENT STORE

New Yaohan. Originally a Japanese-owned department store, this failing shop was taken over by Macau entrepreneur Stanley Ho several years ago and transformed into a popular shopping destination for locals. "Macau's only department store" offers a good mix of shops selling household goods, clothing, jewelry, and beauty products. It also has an extensive food court, a well-stocked supermarket, and a large bakery. ⊠ *Av. Comercial de Macau, Downtown* ☎ *853/2872–5338* ⊕ *www. newyaohan.com.*

SPAS

Nirvana Spa. In a quiet area of town near the Nam Van Lake, the Asian-inspired Nirvana has rooms decorated in Chinese, Thai, Balinese, Indian, Macau, and various other eastern themes. Therapists from Thailand and the Philippines are trained in deep-tissue, ayurvedic, herbal, shiatsu, and aromatherapy massages. ⊠ *Ground fl., China Law Bldg., 403 Av. da Praia Grande, Downtown* ☎ *853/2833–1521* ⊕ *www. nirvanaspamacau.com.*

The Spa at the Mandarin Oriental Grand Lapa Macau. The largest and best-known spa in town takes advantage of the Grand Lapa's sumptuous Mediterranean architecture and lets in lots of natural sunlight for a bright and airy spa experience. On offer are numerous Chinese, European, Thai, and Japanese treatments. A signature 2½-hour, four-part Macanese Sangría Ritual includes a full body scrub using fresh grapes, sangria bath in a private outdoor Jacuzzi, and grape-seed-oil massage, for MOP$1,720. Reserve ahead. ⊠ *Grand Lapa, 956–1110 Av. da Amizade, Outer Harbour* ☎ *853/8793–4824* ⊕ *www.mandarinoriental. com/grandlapa/spa.*

COTAI

MALL

The Grand Canal Shoppes. The Venetian's vision of a gentrified megamall comes complete with cobblestone walkways, arched bridges, and working canals manned by singing gondoliers (rides are MOP$118). All the big-name brands and luxury shops in fashion, accessories, gifts, services, and sporting goods are among the more than 330 retailers; it also has a spa, 30 restaurants, and an international food court. Don't be surprised to see wandering stilt walkers, violinists, and juggling jesters, especially around St. Mark's Square, which hosts four daily live performances. The mall connects with the Shoppes at Four Seasons, adding even more exclusive luxury shops to the arcade. ⊠ *Venetian Macao, Av. Xian Xing Hai, Cotai* ☎ *853/2882–8888* ⊕ *www. thegrandcanalshoppes.com.mo.*

8

Travel Smart
Hong Kong

WORD OF MOUTH

"Arrival into HK airport. HUGE lines at customs
. . . but I had remembered that last time we
discovered that there is another section that is
to the right of where the crowds of people are
heading. The section is just on the other side of
the huge columns. And guess what? I was right
(YAY for me!)"

—kooba

GETTING HERE AND AROUND

Visitors can choose from many public transportation options in Hong Kong, and they are all generally clean, safe, and cheap. The first step is to get an Octopus stored-value card from any MTR or Airport Express Station; this is a good alternative to carrying around exact change and can be used on all public transportation. The initial cost of an Octopus Card is HK$150, and you will have HK$100 available for your use right away. The remaining HK$50 is a refundable deposit that provides a buffer in case you go beyond the card's value. You can top up the card at ticket counters or Add Value machines at any MTR station, or at convenience stores, supermarkets, or fast-food chains. These retail outlets also accept the card as a mode of payment, as do many other places, including coffee chains, clothing stores, and vending machines.

When boarding a bus or entering a subway, simply look for the rectangular yellow sensor (on top of the MTR turnstiles or next to the fare-box on buses and minibuses) and place the card on it until you hear a beep. The sensors are sensitive enough to scan through wallets and bags, so you don't need to take your card out. Once your card has been read, the remaining balance appears on the sensor screen.

Before you leave Hong Kong, you can refund your Octopus Card at MTR stations, and you will receive the balance plus the HK$50 deposit. However, if you return your card less than three months after it's been issued, you'll have to pay a refund processing fee of HK$9.

Information Octopus Cards ☎ *2266–2222* ⊕ *www.octopus.com.hk.*

▌ AIR TRAVEL

Flying time to Hong Kong is around 16 hours nonstop from Newark/New York, 15½ hours nonstop from Los Angeles, or 14 hours nonstop from San Francisco.

Airlines and Airports Airline and Airport Links.com. Airline and Airport Links.com has links to many of the world's airlines and airports. ⊕ *www.airlineandairportlinks.com.*

Airline Security Issues Transportation Security Agency ⊕ *www.tsa.gov/public.*

AIRPORTS

Modern, easy to navigate, and full of amenities, Hong Kong International Airport (HKG)—also known as Chek Lap Kok, after its location—is a traveler's dream. Terminal 1, the third-largest terminal in the world, services the departures for most major airlines, as well as all arriving flights. The newer but smaller Terminal 2 handles all other airlines, including budget carriers.

Given the size of Terminal 1, it's advisable to check in early, at least two hours before departure (although check-in counters usually close 50 minutes before departure). Some boarding gates are quite far from immigrations, and you will need to take a short train ride to reach them. Most major airlines let you use the In-Town Check-in service at the Hong Kong or Kowloon Airport Express stations anywhere from 24 hours to 90 minutes before your flight (confirm with your airline first), and you can check luggage as well, saving you the bother of lugging bags out to the airport.

Once you're at the airport, there are multiple options for meals and refreshments, from fast-food outlets and cafés to restaurants and bars. Many open as early as 6 am and close as late as midnight. Beyond immigrations in Terminal 1, you'll find a few places that are open 24 hours, including Café de Coral and

McDonald's on Level 7 of the Departures East Hall and the Starbucks at Departures Central Concourse, Level 6, and Departures Check-in Hall, Level 7.

You can also do some last-minute shopping in both terminals, although most luxury brands can be found only in Terminal 1. Travelers who would rather find a place to relax before their flight can do so in one of the four fee-for-use lounges. Three of the lounges are in Terminal 1, while the Plaza Premium Lounge is located at the Arrivals Hall between the two terminals. These 24-hour lounges have rest areas, showers, massages, Internet access, TV, reading materials, and hot meals. A 10-hour package costs HK$700, and shorter stays are correspondingly cheaper.

There are also free resting lounges (without showers and other perks) and miniature gardens with comfortable seating at the Departure Level near Gates 21, 26, 34, 41, and 61. You can also access free public Wi-Fi or use one of the 56 computers available at 28 different locations in Terminal 1. There are also three nondenominational prayer rooms in the airport, two of which are open 24 hours.

When arriving in Hong Kong, you'll be asked to fill out an immigrations form. An immigrations officer will collect the arrivals slip, and you will have to keep the departure slip to show immigrations when you leave Hong Kong. Airport tax is normally included in your ticket price. If it's not, a fee of HK$120 is payable on departure from the country. It's levied only on those 12 years and older and is waived for all transit and transfer passengers who arrive and leave on the same day.

Airport Information Hong Kong International Airport ☎ *2181–8888* ⊕ *www.hongkongairport.com.* **Plaza Premium Lounge** ☎ *2261–0888* ⊕ *www.plaza-network.com.*

GROUND TRANSPORTATION

The Airport Express train service is the quickest and most convenient way to and from the airport. Gleaming, high-speed trains whisk you to Kowloon in 21 minutes and Central in 24 minutes. Trains run daily every 10 minutes between 5:54 am and 11:28 pm and every 12 minutes between 11:28 pm and 12:58 am. The last train from the airport departs at 12:48 am. The trains have Wi-Fi, plenty of luggage space, legroom, and comfortable seating with video screens on the backs of the passenger seats showing tourist information and the latest news. Although this is the most expensive public transport option, the speed and dependability justify the extra cost.

The Airport Express station is connected to the MTR's AsiaWorld-Expo, Tsing Yi, Kowloon, and Hong Kong (Central) stations. Excluding the AsiaWorld stop, all stations connect to the MTR. One-way or same-day return fare to or from Central is HK$100; to and from Kowloon, HK$90. Round-trip tickets valid for one month cost HK$180 for Central and HK$160 for Kowloon. The Airport Express Travel Pass is an option if you are planning a very short stay, as it allows you unlimited travel on the MTR for 72 hours after activation; the HK$220 pass includes a single airport journey and the HK$300 pass includes an airport round-trip.

Tickets are cheaper if purchased online or through a travel agent. The Airport Express also provides its customers with free porter service, and shuttle buses run every 12 or 20 minutes between major hotels and the Hong Kong and Kowloon stations—there are seven routes, and a list of stops is displayed prominently at the boarding area. Service begins at 6:12 am and ends at 11:12 pm. To board, you must show your Airport Express ticket and airline ticket/boarding pass.

GROUND TRANSPORTATION TO CENTRAL		
Transport Mode	Time	Cost
Airport Express	24 mins	HK$100
Citybus Line A (Cityflyer)	50 mins	HK$40
Citybus Line E (Regular)	70 mins	HK$21
Coach	45 mins	HK$150
Limo	45 mins	HK$750
Taxi	45 mins	HK$280
Tung Chung (S1 bus) + MTR (train)	10 mins +36 mins	HK$3.50 + HK$22.50

Citybus runs five buses ("A" precedes the bus number) from the airport to popular destinations. They make fewer stops than regular buses (which have an "E" before their numbers) do, so the fare is higher. Two useful routes are the A11, serving Central, Admiralty, Wan Chai, and Causeway Bay and ending in North Point; and the A21, going to Tsim Sha Tsui, Jordan, and Mong Kok. The A11's operating hours are from 6:10 am to 12:30 am, while the A21 runs from 6 am to 12 am. Should you arrive in Hong Kong outside of these hours, you can take the N11 or the N21, which are overnight buses serving the same routes. The buses are comfortable and provide free Wi-Fi. There is adequate space for luggage, and the onboard announcements are in Cantonese, Putonghua, and English, so you won't miss your stop.

Several small shuttle buses with an "S" before their numbers run to the nearby Tung Chung MTR station, where you can get the MTR to Central and Kowloon. MTR trains run parallel to the Airport Express route, but they cost much less (HK$22.50 from the airport to Central). However, you won't have the same amenities, and travel time is longer as the trains make more stops.

Taxis from the airport are reliable and plentiful. Trips to Hong Kong Island destinations cost around HK$280, while those to Kowloon are around HK$230. There is also a HK$5 charge per piece of luggage stored in the trunk. Trans-Island runs the Airport Hotelink coach service, which stops at 45 hotels on Hong Kong Island and Kowloon. The coaches depart every 30–60 minutes for HK$150 to destinations on Hong Kong Island, HK$130 to those in Kowloon. Parklane Limousine Service's coaches run at 30-minute intervals, with fares for Hong Kong Island at HK$140 and Kowloon at HK$130. Parklane also offers Mercedes-Benz limousine transfers for HK$550–HK$850, depending on the destination and type of car.

GROUND TRANSPORTATION TO TSIM SHA TSUI		
Transport Mode	Time	Cost
Airport Express	19 mins	HK$90
Citybus Line A (Cityflyer)	45 mins	HK$33
Citybus Line E (Regular)	60 mins	HK$14
Coach	35 mins	HK$130
Limo	35 mins	HK700
Taxi	35 mins	HK$230
Tung Chung (S1 bus) + MTR (train)	10 mins + 38 mins	HK$3.50 + HK$17

Contacts Airport Express ☎ 2881–8888 for MTR hotline ⊕ www.mtr.com.hk. **Citybus** ☎ 2873–0818 ⊕ www.nwstbus. com.hk. **Parklane Limousine** ☎ 2730–0662 ⊕ www.hongkonglimo.com. **Trans-Island Limousine Service** ☎ 3193–9333 ⊕ www.trans-island.com.hk.

FLIGHTS

Cathay Pacific is Hong Kong's flagship carrier. It maintains high standards, with friendly service, good food, an extensive in-flight entertainment system, and an excellent track record for safety. Cathay has nonstop flights from both Los Angeles and San Francisco on the West Coast and from New York–JFK on the East Coast, with connecting services to many other U.S. cities. Singapore Airlines is also another highly rated airline with flights to Hong Kong from multiple American cities, including daily flights from San Francisco. However, these are not nonstop, as the routing usually includes a stopover and/or change in Singapore.

If you are on a tight budget, Air China and China Airlines offer lower-cost flights between New York and Los Angeles and Hong Kong, although the savings are reflected in the service and amenities. Several other airlines also offer service from the United States to Hong Kong, usually with connections in Asia.

If you're planning to travel to three or four Asian destinations, you might want to consider a One World's Visit Asia Pass, which provides travel throughout Southeast Asia via a consortium of airlines. Cities are grouped into zones, and there's a flat rate for each zone. The pass doesn't cover flights from the United States, Europe, or Australia and New Zealand, however. Inquire through American Airlines, Cathay Pacific, or any other One World member.

Airlines Air China ☎ 800/882–8122 in U.S. ⊕ www.airchina.us. **Cathay Pacific Airways** ☎ 800/233–2742 in U.S., 800/268–6868 in Canada, 2747–1888 in Hong Kong ⊕ www.cathay-usa.com. **China Airlines** ☎ 800/227–5118 in U.S., 2868–2299 in Hong Kong ⊕ www.china-airlines.com. **Singapore Airlines** ☎ 800/742–3333 in U.S., 800/663–3046 in Canada, 0208/961–6993 in U.K., 13–10–11 in Australia, 2520–2233 in Hong Kong ⊕ www.singaporeair.com. **Visit Asia Pass** ⊕ www.oneworld.com.

▌ BOAT AND FERRY TRAVEL

With fabulous views of both sides of Victoria Harbour, the Star Ferry is so much more than just a boat. It's an iconic Hong Kong landmark in its own right, and has been running across the harbor since 1888. Double-bowed, green-and-white vessels connect Central and Wan Chai with Kowloon in less than 10 minutes, daily from 6:30 am to 11:30 pm. The ride costs HK$2.50 on the upper deck on weekdays and HK$3.40 on weekends and public holidays, making it the cheapest scenic harbor tour in town. You can use your Octopus Card or cash to pay the fare.

There are also regular ferry services to outlying islands, such as Lantau, Lamma, and Cheung Chau. Ordinary ferries are cheaper but slower, while fast ferries travel at twice the speed for twice the price. You can look up schedules online or pick up printed copies at the Hong Kong Tourist Board (HKTB) info center at the Tsim Sha Tsui Star Ferry Concourse, call the HKTB Visitor Hotline, or simply ask for a schedule at the ferry ticket counters.

(⇨ For information about ferry service to Macau, see Chapter 8, Macau.)

FERRY TRAVEL

Line/Route	Frequency	Travel Time	Fare
DBTPL Central– Discovery Bay (Lantau)	20–30 mins	25 mins	HK$34– HK$48.20
NWFF Central– Cheung Chau	30 mins	35–60 mins	HK$12.60– HK$35.30
NWFF Central– Mui Wo (Lantau)	40 mins	35–55 mins	HK$14.50– HK$40.80
Star Ferry Central– Tsim Sha Tsui	6–12 mins	7 mins	HK$2.50– HK$3.40
Star Ferry Wan Chai– Tsim Sha Tsui	10–14 mins	8 mins	HK$2.50– HK$3.40

Information Discovery Bay Transportation Services Limited ☎ 2238–1188 ⊕ www.discoverybay.com.hk. HKTB Visitor Hotline ☎ 2508–1234. New World First Ferry ☎ 2131–8181 ⊕ www.nwff.com.hk. Star Ferry ☎ 2367–7065 ⊕ www.starferry.com.hk.

▮ BUS TRAVEL

An efficient network of double-decker buses covers most of Hong Kong, often with stops at locations that are not accessible via MTR. Figuring out routes, however, may be a bit daunting for tourists. Drivers don't usually speak English, and routes listed at bus stops may be confusing. Your best bet is to look up your destination on Google Maps, which will display nearby bus and minibus stops. Click on the bus icon to display the bus numbers, as well as the bus company that runs the service. You can then check the route numbers at the bus company's website to see which bus to take. Citybus and New World First Bus share a common

website, as do Kowloon Motor Bus and Long Win Bus Company.

More intrepid visitors who enjoy thrill rides can take a chance on a minibus. These cream-colored vehicles seat 16 people and rattle through the city at breakneck speeds. Routes and prices are prominently displayed in front. While convenient and faster than buses, mini-buses are risky if you aren't sure of your destination. There are designated stops, but minibus drivers will also pick up and drop off passengers at other points along the way. To get off, you'll have to shout out to the driver and hold on tight as he screeches to a halt.

FARES

Double-decker bus fares range from HK$2.50 to HK$48; minibus fares from HK$2 to HK$20. The best way to pay is by Octopus Card. Otherwise, you'll need to give exact change. Some minibuses, particularly the overnight ones, accept only cash, but they do give you change.

Bus Information Citybus ☎ 2873–0818 ⊕ www.nwstbus.com.hk. Kowloon Motor Bus ☎ 2745–4466 ⊕ www.kmb.com.hk. Long Win Bus Company ☎ 2745–4466 ⊕ www.kmb.com.hk. New World First Bus ☎ 2136–8888 ⊕ www.nwstbus.com.hk.

▮ CAR TRAVEL

Frankly, you'd be mad to rent a car on Hong Kong Island or in Kowloon. Maniac drivers, traffic jams, and next-to-no parking make driving here severely stress-inducing, and gasoline costs up to twice what it does in the United States. So why bother, when public transportation is excellent and taxis inexpensive? If you must have your own wheels, consider hiring a driver. Most top-end hotels can arrange this; the Peninsula in Kowloon and the Island Shangri-La even have their own fleets of chauffeur-driven Rolls-Royces and Mercedes available for hourly hire by guests. Avis can also provide chauffeur services along with car rentals.

If you're determined to drive yourself, your driver's license is valid in Hong Kong for up to a year if you're 18 to 70 years old (those over 70 must pass a physical examination before driving). You'll need an International Driver's Permit (HK$80) for longer stays. Check the AAA and Hong Kong Transport Department websites for more info.

The cheapest option for car rentals is Hawk Rent-a-Car, which has lots of models and prices; there are special rates for weekends and longer-term rentals. Rental rates begin at HK$450 per day and HK$3,700 per week for an economy car with air-conditioning, automatic transmission, and unlimited mileage. Parklane Limousine has a fleet of more than 100 Mercedes-Benzes with hourly rates for chauffeur services.

Information Hawk Rent-a-Car ☎ 2516–9822 ⊕ www.hawkrentacar.com.hk. **Parklane Limousine** ☎ 2730–0662 ⊕ www.hongkonglimo.com.

PARKING

There's next to no on-street parking in Central and Tsim Sha Tsui, and the extremely vigilant Hong Kong traffic police hand out copious parking tickets.

Most people use multistory or mall parking garages, which cost up to HK$22 per hour in prime locations. However, some malls will subsidize parking if you make purchases at their shops or eat in one of their restaurants. Be sure to have the receipt validated by the staff before leaving.

RULES OF THE ROAD

Driving is on the left-hand side of the road in Hong Kong. Wearing a seat belt is mandatory in the front and back of private cars, and the standard speed limit is 50 kph (30 mph) unless road signs state otherwise. The Hong Kong Police spend a lot of time setting up photographic speed traps and giving out juicy fines. Using handheld cell phones while driving is forbidden. You can't make a right turn on a red light, and you should scrupulously obey lane markings regarding turns.

Drunk driving is taken very seriously: the legal limit is 50 mg of alcohol per 100 ml of blood (or 22 micrograms of alcohol per 100 ml of breath), and there are penalties of up to HK$25,000 and three years in prison for those who disobey. You can get highly detailed information on Hong Kong's road rules on the Transport Department's website.

Road Rules Hong Kong Government **Transport Department** ☎ 2804–2600 hotline ⊕ www.td.gov.hk.

▌CRUISE TRAVEL

Star Cruises has trips through Southeast Asia that start from, or call at, Hong Kong. The crème de la crème of cruisers, Cunard, docks in Hong Kong on its round-the-world trips. Princess Cruises has a wide variety of packages that call at Hong Kong and many other Asian destinations. Holland America has two-week Asian cruises as well as round-the-world options. Be sure to check out last-minute special offers from all these lines.

Cruise Lines Cunard ☎ 800/728–6273 ⊕ www.cunard.com. **Holland America** ☎ 877/932–4259 in U.S. ⊕ www.hollandamerica.com. **Princess Cruises** ☎ 800/774–6237 in U.S. ⊕ www.princess.com. **Star Cruises** ☎ 2317–7711 Hong Kong ⊕ www.starcruises.com.

▌SUBWAY TRAVEL

By far the best way to get around Hong Kong is on the Mass Transit Railway (MTR). Since merging with the former Kowloon-Canton Railway (KCR) in late 2007, the MTR network now provides all subway and train services in Hong Kong. The trains are among the cleanest in the world; there is hardly any litter to be found. Eating or drinking on the trains or in the paid areas is prohibited, with fines of HK$2,000.

Entrances, platforms, and exits are clearly marked and signposted, and all MTR areas are air-conditioned and Wi-Fi enabled.

Most stations have wheelchair access, and all have convenience stores and other shops or services. Fourteen MTR stations have free Wi-Fi, as well as computer terminals with free Internet access.

The MTR is known for its safety, even late at night. Glass screens have been installed between the edges of platforms and tracks, preventing falls and other mishaps. Emergency stop buttons and help lines are easy to access and ensure instant response from the MTR staff.

Trains run every 2 to 8 minutes during peak times between 6 am and 1 am daily. The five major lines are color-coded for convenience. The Island line (blue line) runs along the north coast of Hong Kong Island; the Tsuen Wan line (red line) goes from Central under the harbor to Tsim Sha Tsui, then up to the western New Territories. Mong Kok links Tsim Sha Tsui to eastern New Kowloon via the Kwun Tong line (green line). Also serving this area is the Tseung Kwan O line (purple line), which crosses back over the harbor to Quarry Bay and North Point. Finally, the Tung Chung line (yellow line) connects Central and West Kowloon to Tung Chung on Lantau, near the airport.

FARES AND SCHEDULES

You can buy tickets from ticket machines (using coins or notes) or from English-speaking staff behind glass-windowed customer-service counters near the turnstile entrances. Fares range from HK$3.70 to HK$42.50, depending how far you travel. You can check on the MTR website or download an app to see how much a journey will cost. There are no monthly or weekly passes, but if you plan to make more than a few trips on public transport during your stay, it's worth getting a rechargeable Octopus Card (⇨ *above*). It saves time lining up for tickets and fussing for change, gives you a discounted fare on each trip, and can also be used for small purchases around Hong Kong.

Another alternative is the Tourist Day Pass. For HK$55, this pass allows you unlimited travel on the MTR, excluding the Airport Express, for one day only. However, you cannot use the pass on other public transport or to purchase items.

Information HKTB Visitor Hotline ☎ 2508–1234. MTR ☎ 2881–8888 ⊕ *www.mtr.com.hk.*

▌ TAXI TRAVEL

While there are some 18,000 taxis in Hong Kong, heavy daytime traffic in Central, Causeway Bay, and Tsim Sha Tsui means they aren't the best option for getting around the city quickly. They're more useful outside these areas, or after dark, especially after the MTR closes. Drivers usually know the terrain well, but, as many don't speak English, having your destination written in Chinese is a good idea. You can hail cabs on the street, provided you're in a stopping area (i.e., not marked by double yellow lines). The white "taxi" sign is lit when the cab is available. Not all taxis will drive from Hong Kong Island to Kowloon (or vice versa). You can usually identify cross-harbor taxis by the red, plastic "No service" sign on their dashboards; you'll find cross-harbor taxi ranks at the Star Ferry terminal and elsewhere around town. Note that it's sometimes hard to find a taxi around 4 pm, when the drivers switch shifts.

Taxis operating in urban Hong Kong are red. Fares for red taxis start at HK$20 for the first 2 km (1½ mile), then HK$1.50 for each .2 km (.1 mile) or minute of waiting time (so fares add up fast in bumper-to-bumper traffic). After the fare reaches HK$72.5, you're charged HK$1 for each .2 km or minute of waiting time.

There's a surcharge of HK$5 for each piece of luggage you put in the trunk. The Cross-Harbour Tunnel, Eastern Harbour Crossing, and Western Harbour Crossing all incur surcharges of the toll plus HK$10 or HK$15 return toll. The surcharge for crossing the Tsing Ma Bridge over to Lantau is HK$30. Passengers must pay the toll amount for other tunnels and roads.

In the New Territories taxis are green; on Lantau they're blue. Fares are lower than in urban areas, but while red urban taxis may travel into rural zones, rural green and blue taxis can't cross into urban zones.

Passengers are required by law to wear a seat belt when available. Most locals don't tip; however, if you round up the fare by a few Hong Kong dollars you're sure to earn yourself a winning smile from your underpaid and overworked driver. Taxis are usually reliable, but if you have a problem, note the taxi's license number, which is usually on the dashboard, and call the Transport Complaints Unit. If you've left an item behind in your taxi, you can call the Road Co-op Lost Property hotline.

In urban areas it's as easy and safe to hail a cab on the street as it is to call one. There are hundreds of taxi companies, so it's usually best to get your hotel or restaurant to call a company it works with. Note that there's a HK$5 surcharge for phone bookings.

Contacts Hong Kong Kowloon Taxi & Lorry Owners Association Ltd. ☎ 2572–0097. **Kowloon Taxi Owners Association (red taxi booking)** ☎ 2760–0411.

Complaints Transport Complaints Unit ☎ 2889–9999. **Lost Property on Taxis Hotline (24 hours)** ☎ 1872–920. **Road Co-op Lost Property** ☎ 1872–920.

TRAIN TRAVEL

Since the former Kowloon–Canton Railway (KCR) merged with the MTR subway system in 2007, all trains now run under the MTR name (⇨ By Subway, above). The ultra-efficient train network connects Kowloon to the eastern and western New Territories. Trains run every 5–8 minutes, and connections to the subway are relatively quick. This is a commuter service and, like the subway, has sparkling-clean trains and stations—smoking and eating are forbidden in both.

The train network has three main lines. The East Rail line begins at Hung Hom, with notable stops at Mong Kok, Kowloon Tong, Sha Tin, Racecourse, Chinese University, and Tai Po on its way to Lo Wu at the mainland Chinese border. East Rail is the fastest way to get to Shenzhen—it's a 40-minute trip from Hung Hom to Lo Wu. The Hung Hom train station terminus connects via a series of walkways with East Tsim Sha Tsui; you can also transfer to the subway at Kowloon Tong.

The short Ma On Shan Rail service starts at Tai Wai and has eight stops in the northeastern New Territories.

West Rail starts at East Tsim Sha Tsui, moves on to Tsim Sha Tsui for a possible connection to the subway, then extends westward through 10 more stops to Tuen Mun, in the New Territories. Here West Rail connects with the local Light Rail Transit, an above-ground train serving mainly residential and industrial areas in the western New Territories.

Fares range from HK$3.10 to HK$42.50; you can pay by Octopus Card or buy tickets from sales counters or ticket machines.

TRAM TRAVEL

PEAK TRAM

It's Hong Kong's greatest misnomer—the Peak Tram is actually a funicular railway. Since 1888 it's been rattling the 1,365 feet up the hill from Mid-Levels to the Victoria Peak tram terminus. As well as a sizable adrenaline rush due to the steepness of the ascent, on a clear day the trip offers fabulous panoramas. Most passengers board at the Lower Terminus between Garden Road and Cotton Tree Drive. (The tram has five stations.) The fare is HK$28 one way, HK$40 round-trip, and the tram runs every 10–15 minutes between 7 am and midnight daily. Bus 15C shuttles passengers between the Lower Terminus and the Star Ferry.

STREET TRAMS

Old-fashioned double-decker trams have been running along the northern shore of Hong Kong Island since 1904. There is bench seating on the lower deck and seats on the upper one, although trams are now being renovated to replace the benches with single seating, and the entrance turnstiles with electronic barriers. Most routes start in Kennedy Town or Western Market, and go eastward all the way through Central, Wan Chai, Causeway Bay, North Point, and Quarry Bay to Shau Kei Wan. A branch line turns off in Wan Chai toward Happy Valley, where horse races are held in season.

Destinations are marked on the front of each tram and route maps are displayed at the stops; you board at the back and get off at the front, paying HK$2.30 regardless of distance (by Octopus or with exact change) as you leave. Avoid trams at rush hours, which are generally weekdays from 7:30 to 9:30 am and 5 to 7:30 pm. Although trams move slowly, for short hops between Central and Western or Admiralty they can be quicker than going underground to take the MTR. A leisurely top-deck ride from Western to Causeway Bay is a great city tour. Note, though, that there is no air-conditioning on trams.

Tram Information **Hong Kong Tramways** ☎ *2548–7102* ⊕ *www.hktramways.com.* **Peak Tram** ☎ *2522–0922* ⊕ *www.thepeak.com.hk.*

ESSENTIALS

▌ BUSINESS AND TRADE SERVICES

BUSINESS CENTERS

Hong Kong has many business centers outside hotels, and some are considerably cheaper than hotel facilities. Others cost about the same but offer private desks (from HK$250 per hour for desk space to upward of HK$8,000 a month for a serviced office). Amenities include a private address and phone-answering and forwarding services. Many centers are affiliated with accountants and lawyers who can expedite company registration. Some will even process visas and wrap gifts for you.

Harbour International Business Centre provides typing, secretarial support, and office rentals. Reservations aren't required. The Executive Centre and Regus are two international business services companies with several office locations in Hong Kong. They provide secretarial services, meeting and conference facilities, and office rentals. You can rent conference and meeting rooms at the American Chamber of Commerce. The Chamber also hosts regular Breakfast and Learn workshops, luncheons, seminars, and monthly networking cocktail gatherings.

Information American Chamber of Commerce ✉ Bank of America Tower, 12 Harcourt Rd., Room 1904, Central, Hong Kong, Hong Kong–China ☎ 2530–6900 ⊕ www.amcham.org.hk. The Executive Centre ✉ Two Exchange Square, 8 Connaught Place, Level 5, 7, 8, Central, Hong Kong, Albania ☎ 2297–2297 ⊕ www.executivecentre.com. Harbour International Business Centre ✉ Admiralty Centre, 18 Harcourt Road, 2802, Tower One, Admiralty, Hong Kong, Hong Kong–China ☎ 3748–3748 ⊕ www.hibc.com. Regus ☎ 2166–8000 ⊕ www.regus.hk.

CONVENTION CENTER

The Hong Kong Convention and Exhibition Centre (HKCEC) is a state-of-the-art, five-level complex located on the Wan Chai waterfront. The HKCEC houses six exhibition halls, two convention halls, two theaters, and 52 meeting rooms, totaling 920,000 square meters of rentable function space. The center is adjacent to the Convention Plaza, which includes the 825-room Renaissance Hong Kong Harbour View Hotel, the 549-room Grand Hyatt, office and residential towers, a shopping arcade, and an underground parking garage. The Hong Kong Trade Development Council (HKTDC) regularly organizes trade fairs, some of which are Asia's largest, at the Convention Centre.

Information Hong Kong Convention and Exhibition Centre ✉ 1 Expo Dr., Wan Chai, Hong Kong, Hong Kong–China ☎ 2582–8888 ⊕ www.hkcec.com.hk.

MESSENGERS

Most business centers offer delivery service, and you can sometimes arrange a delivery through your hotel concierge. Courier services such as City-Link International will pick up from your hotel, as will FedEx and DHL, who also have drop-off points all over Hong Kong (⇨ Shipping Packages, below). Price is based on weight and distance. Hong Kong Post (⇨ Mail, below) also has a dependable and speedy courier service. You can drop off your package at a post office or at any one of the local courier post boxes in the city.

Information City-Link International Courier Co. Ltd ☎ 2382–8289 ⊕ www.citylinkexpress.com.

TRADE INFORMATION

Information Hong Kong General Chamber of Commerce ☎ 2529–9229 ⊕ www.chamber.org.hk. Hong Kong Trade Development Council ☎ 1830–668 ⊕ www.hktdc.com. Hong Kong Trade and Industry Department ☎ 2392–2922 ⊕ www.tid.gov.hk. Innovation and Technology Commission ☎ 3655–5856 ⊕ www.itc.gov.hk.

TRANSLATION SERVICES

Information Polyglot Translations ☎ 2851–7232 ⊕ www.polyglot.com.hk. **Translation Business** ☎ 2893–5000 ⊕ www. translationbusiness.com.hk. **Venture Language Training** ☎ 2507–4985 ⊕ www. languageventure.com.

▌ COMMUNICATIONS

INTERNET

Going online is easy in Hong Kong. Free public Wi-Fi is now available at more than 400 locations, including public libraries, museums, large parks, indoor markets, MTR stations, ferry terminals, and popular tourist spots. Some buses, including those to and from the airport, also provide free Wi-Fi onboard—look for the Webus sticker by the door. Public libraries and many MTR stations also provide free access to computer terminals. Many fast-food outlets, cafés, and shopping malls offer free Wi-Fi service.

Pacific Coffee and Mix cafés have computer terminals; there is usually a 15-minute limit on computer use, and you'll need to buy food or a beverage first. Internet cafés, or cybercafés, can be found tucked away in small, hard-to-find corners of Wan Chai, Mong Kok, and Tsim Sha Tsui. PCCW, the Hong Kong–based communications company, has more than 10,000 Wi-Fi hotspots in the city, including areas near universities, convenience stores, public phones, and shopping malls. You can buy a 24-hour Wi-Fi prepaid pass for HK$20 or a 30-day pass for HK$158 at 7-Eleven and Circle K convenience stores, as well as all PCCW shops.

Contacts Hong Kong Public Libraries ☎ 2921–0208 ⊕ hkpl.gov.hk. **Mix** ⊕ www.mix-world.com. **Pacific Coffee Company** ⊕ www.pacificcoffee.com. **PCCW Wi-Fi** ⊕ www.pccwwifi.com.

PHONES

The good news is that you can now make a direct-dial telephone call from virtually any point on earth. The bad news? You can't always do so cheaply. Calling overseas from a hotel is almost always the most expensive option; hotels usually add huge surcharges to all calls, particularly international ones. In some countries you can phone from call centers or even the post office. Calling cards usually keep costs to a minimum, but only if you purchase them locally. And then there are mobile phones (⇨ below), which are sometimes more prevalent—particularly in the developing world—than landlines; as expensive as mobile-phone calls can be, they are still usually a much cheaper option than calling from your hotel.

Hong Kong was the first city in the world with a fully digitized local phone network, and the service is efficient and cheap. Even international calls are inexpensive relative to those in the United States. You can expect clear connections and helpful directory assistance. Don't hang up if you hear Cantonese when calling automated and prerecorded hotlines; English is usually the second or third language option. The country code for Hong Kong is 852; there are no local area codes.

CALLING WITHIN HONG KONG

Hong Kong phone numbers have eight digits: landline numbers usually start with a 2 or 3; mobiles with a 9, 6, or 5.

If you're old enough to talk in Hong Kong, you're old enough for a cell phone, which means public phones can be difficult to find; MTR stations usually have one. Local calls to both land- and cell lines cost HK$1 per five minutes. If you're planning to call abroad from a pay phone, buy a phone card. Convenience stores such as 7-Eleven sell stored-value phone cards (a PIN-activated card you can use from any phone). Some pay phones accept credit cards.

Some hotels may charge as much as HK$5 for a local call, while a few others include them for free in your room rate. Restaurants and shopkeepers may let you use their phone for free, as the phone company doesn't charge for individual local calls.

Dial 1081 for directory assistance from English-speaking operators; dial 10013 for international inquiries and for assistance with direct dialing; dial 10010 for collect and operator-assisted calls to most countries, including the United States; and dial 10011 for credit-card, collect, and international conference calls. If a number is constantly busy and you think it might be out of order, call 109 and the operator will check the line. The operators are very helpful, if you speak slowly and clearly.

CALLING OUTSIDE HONG KONG
International rates from Hong Kong are reasonable, even more so between 9 pm and 8 am. The international dial code is 001, followed by the country code.

The country code is 1 for the United States.

So to call the United States you dial 0011. You can dial direct from many hotel and business centers, but always with a hefty surcharge.

Access Codes AT&T Direct ☎ *800/96–1111 in Hong Kong.* **MCI** ☎ *800/96–1121 in Hong Kong.*

MOBILE PHONES
If you have a multiband phone (some countries use different frequencies than what's used in the United States) and your service provider uses the world-standard GSM network (as do T-Mobile and Verizon), you can probably use your phone abroad. Roaming fees can be steep, however—99¢ a minute is considered reasonable—and overseas you normally pay the toll charges for incoming calls. It's almost always cheaper to send a text message than to make a call, since text messages have a very low set fee (often less than 5¢).

To save on local and even international calls, consider buying a new prepaid rechargeable SIM card (note that your provider may have to unlock your phone

for you to use a different SIM card). You'll then have a local number and can make local calls at local rates and cheaper international calls using a phone card.

▇ **TIP➜** If you travel internationally frequently, save one of your old mobile phones or buy a cheap one; ask your cell-phone company to unlock it for you, and take it with you as a travel phone, buying a new SIM card with pay-as-you-go service in each destination.

Most GSM-compatible mobile handsets work in Hong Kong. If you can unlock your phone, buying a SIM card locally is the cheapest and easiest way to make calls. Local phone company PCCW sells them from around HK$50 from their shops and in convenience stores. Local calls cost around HK$0.25 a minute.

Otherwise, you can rent handsets from CSL (HK$35 per day with a HK$500 refundable deposit) with prepaid SIM cards (HK$48–HK$180). There's a stand at the airport and shops all over town. If you're in town for a week, this is a good-value option.

Cellular Abroad rents and sells GSM phones and sells SIM cards that work in many countries. Mobal and PlanetFone rent and lease mobiles and lease GSM phones (starting at $49) that will operate in countries around the world, though per-call rates vary and can be expensive.

Contacts Cellular Abroad ☎ *800/287–5072 in U.S.* ⊕ *www.cellularabroad.com.* **CSL** ☎ *2888–1010* ⊕ *www.hkcsl.com.* **Mobal** ☎ *888/888–9162 in U.S.* ⊕ *www.mobal. com.* **PlanetFone** ☎ *888/988–4777 in U.S.* ⊕ *www.planetfone.com.*

▐ CUSTOMS AND DUTIES

You're allowed to bring goods of a certain value back home without having to pay duty or import tax. But there's a limit on the amount of tobacco and liquor you can bring back duty-free, and some countries have separate limits for perfumes; for exact figures, check with your customs

LOCAL DOS AND TABOOS

CUSTOMS OF THE COUNTRY

Face is ever important in Hong Kong. Never say anything that will make people look bad, especially in front of superiors. However, you'll find that locals are comfortable commenting on things like weight and appearance that Westerners may balk at. Take it in stride; it's not meant maliciously. Hong Kongers like to talk about money—salaries, stocks, insurance, and real estate—so don't be surprised to be asked about these things.

GREETINGS

Hong Kongers aren't touchy-feely. Be discreet. Stick to handshakes and low-key greetings.

SIGHTSEEING

By and large Hong Kongers are a rule-abiding bunch. Avoid jaywalking, eating on public transport, and feeding birds. Legislation has banned smoking in restaurants, most bars, workplaces, schools, and even public areas such as beaches, sport grounds, and parks. A whopping fine of HK$1,500 should deter even the most diehard smoker. Littering is also frowned upon, and it's not unusual to see police handing fines (also HK$1,500) out to litterbugs. Hong Kong is *crowded*; most people walk quite fast on the street. When on escalators, make sure you stand on the right side, leaving the left side for those who are in a hurry.

OUT ON THE TOWN

Meals are a communal event, so food in a Chinese restaurant is always shared. You usually have a small bowl or plate in which to transfer food from the center platters. Although cutlery is common in Hong Kong, chopsticks are ubiquitous. Be sure not to mistake the communal serving chopsticks (usually black or a different color) with your own.

It's fine to hold the bowl close to your mouth and shovel in the contents. Slurping up soup and noodles is acceptable, as is picking your teeth with a toothpick while covering it with your other hand when you're done. Avoid leaving your chopsticks standing up in a bowl of rice—they look like the two incense sticks burned at funerals.

Young Hong Kongers dress quite smartly when going out on the town.

DOING BUSINESS

Make appointments well in advance and be punctual. Hong Kongers have a keen sense of hierarchy in the office. Let the tea lady get the tea and coffee—that's what she's there for. If you're visiting in a group, let the senior member lead proceedings.

Suits are the norm, regardless of the outside temperature. Local businesswomen are immaculately groomed. Pants are acceptable.

When entertaining, locals may insist on paying: after a slight protest, accept, as this lets them gain face. Conversely, you can insist on paying for drinks or a meal to signal your gratitude for the hospitality you've received.

Business cards are a big deal: not having one is like not having a personality. If possible, have yours printed in English on one side and Chinese on the other. Proffer your card with both hands, and receive one in the same way, handling it with respect.

department. When you shop abroad, save all your receipts, as customs inspectors may ask to see them along with the items you purchased. If the total value of your goods is more than the duty-free limit, you'll have to pay a tax (most often a flat percentage) on the value of everything beyond that limit.

Except for the usual prohibitions against endangered species, narcotics, explosives, firearms, and ammunition, and limits on alcohol, tobacco products, and perfume, you can bring anything you want into Hong Kong, including an unlimited amount of money. Visitors may bring in, duty-free, 19 cigarettes or 1 cigar or 25 grams of tobacco, and 1 liter of alcohol.

Information in Hong Kong Hong Kong Customs and Excise Department ☎ 2815-7711, 2545-6182 customs hotline ⊕ www.customs. gov.hk.

U.S. Information U.S. Customs and Border Protection ☎ 877/227-5511 ⊕ www.cbp.gov.

▌ ELECTRICITY

The current in Hong Kong is 220 volts, 50 cycles alternating current (AC), so most American appliances can't be used without a transformer. Exceptions are most laptops and mobile phone chargers, which are dual voltage (i.e., they operate equally well on 110 and 220 volts), and thus require only an adapter. The same may be true of some hair dryers and other small appliances. Always check labels and manufacturer instructions to be sure. Don't use 110-volt outlets marked "for shavers only" for high-wattage appliances such as hair dryers.

Most plugs have three square prongs, like British plugs, but you can buy adapters in just about every supermarket and at electronics stalls in street markets. If you travel frequently, consider making a small investment in a universal adapter, which has several types of plugs in one lightweight, compact unit.

Walkabout Travel Gear has a good coverage of electricity under "adapters."

Contacts Walkabout Travel Gear ☎ 800/852-7085 in U.S. ⊕ www. walkabouttravelgear.com.

▌ EMERGENCIES

Locals and police are usually very helpful in emergencies. Most officers speak some English or will contact someone who does. For police, fire, and ambulance, dial 999. There are 24-hour accident and emergency services at Caritas, Pamela Youde Nethersole Eastern, Prince of Wales, Queen Elizabeth, Queen Mary, Ruttonjee, and Tseung Kwan O hospitals. The following hospitals also have 24-hour pharmacies: Pamela Youde, Prince of Wales, Queen Elizabeth, and Queen Mary. Local drugstore/pharmacy chains Watsons and Mannings have shops throughout the city; closing times generally vary between 7:30 pm and 10:30 pm. Most private hospitals in Hong Kong have only primary and secondary medical services. Government-run public hospitals cover all three types. Most treatments in public hospitals are heavily subsidized or free.

Consulate U.S. Consulate General ✉ 26 Garden Rd., Central, Hong Kong, Hong Kong–China ☎ 2523-9011 ⊕ hongkong.usconsulate.gov.

General Emergency Contacts Police, fire, and ambulance ☎ 999. Hong Kong Police Hotline ☎ 2527-7177.

Hospitals and Clinics Caritas Medical Centre ✉ 111 Wing Hong St., Sham Shui Po, Kowloon, Hong Kong, Hong Kong–China ☎ 3408-7911 ⊕ www.ha.org.hk. Pamela Youde Nethersole Eastern Hospital ✉ 3 Lok Man Rd., Chai Wan, Hong Kong, Hong Kong–China ☎ 2595-6111 ⊕ www.ha.org.hk. Prince of Wales Hospital ✉ 30-32 Ngan Shing St., Sha Tin, New Territories, Hong Kong, Hong Kong–China ☎ 2632-2211 ⊕ www.ha.org.hk/pwh. Queen Elizabeth Hospital ✉ 30 Gascoigne Rd., Yau Ma Tei, Kowloon, Hong Kong, Hong Kong–China ☎ 2958-8888

⊕ *www.ha.org.hk/qeh.* **Queen Mary Hospital** ✉ *102 Pok Fu Lam Rd., Pok Fu Lam, Western, Hong Kong, Hong Kong–China* ☏ *2855-3838* ⊕ *www.ha.org.hk/qmh.* **Ruttonjee Hospital** ✉ *266 Queen's Road E., Wan Chai, Hong Kong, Hong Kong–China* ☏ *2291-2000* ⊕ *www. ha.org.hk.* **Tseung Kwan O Hospital** ✉ *2 Po Ning La., Tseung Kwan O, Kowloon, Hong Kong–China* ☏ *2208-0111* ⊕ *www.ha.org.hk.*

Pharmacies Mannings ☏ *2299-3381* ⊕ *www.mannings.com.hk/eng.* **Watsons** ☏ *2608-8383* ⊕ *watsons.com.hk.*

GOVERNMENT ADVISORIES

As different countries have different worldviews, look at travel advisories from a range of governments to get a sense of what's going on out there. Be sure to parse the language carefully. For example, a warning to "avoid all travel" carries more weight than one urging you to "avoid non-essential travel," and both are much stronger than a plea to "exercise caution." A U.S.-government travel warning is more permanent (though not necessarily more serious) than a so-called public announcement, which carries an expiration date.

The U.S. Department of State's website (⇨ *Passorts and Visas, below*), posts travel warnings and advisories, as well as consular information sheets issued for every country that contain general safety tips, entry requirements (though be sure to verify these with the country's embassy), and other useful details.

■ TIP ➔ Consider registering online with the State Department (https://travelregis-tration.state.gov), so the government will know to look for you should a crisis occur in the country you're visiting.

General Information and Warnings U.S. Department of State ☏ *888/407-4747 in U.S., 202/501-4444 from outside U.S.* ⊕ *www.travel.state.gov.*

■ HEALTH

It's a good idea to be immunized against typhoid and hepatitis A and B, and in winter, a flu vaccination is also advisable,

especially if you're infection-prone or are a senior citizen. Speak with your physician and/or check the Centers for Disease Control and Prevention (CDC) or World Health Organization (WHO) websites for health alerts, particularly if you're pregnant, traveling with children, or have a chronic illness.

Water from government mains satisfies WHO standards, but most locals don't drink water straight from the tap. Expect to pay HK$10 to HK$20 for a 1½-liter bottle of distilled or mineral water, or drink boiled tap water.

Condoms can help prevent most sexually transmitted diseases, but they aren't absolutely reliable, and their quality varies from country to country.

Health Warnings Centers for Disease Control and Prevention (*CDC*). ☏ *800/232-4636 24-hr hotline in U.S.* ⊕ *www.cdc.gov/travel.* **World Health Organization** ⊕ *www.who.int.*

HONG KONG–SPECIFIC ISSUES

Large-scale health threats in Hong Kong in recent years have included an outbreak of Severe Acute Respiratory Syndrome (SARS) in 2003, intermittent fears over Influenza A virus subtype H5N1 (avian flu), and H1N1 (swine flu) in 2009. A massive awareness program stopped the spread of the illnesses, but it's worth checking to be sure there have been no new outbreaks.

SARS, also known as atypical pneumonia, is a respiratory illness caused by a strain of coronavirus that was first reported in parts of Asia in early 2003. Symptoms include a fever higher than 100.4°F (38°C), shortness of breath, and other flulike symptoms. The disease is thought to spread by close person-to-person contact, particularly respiratory droplets and secretions transmitted through the eyes, nose, or mouth. To prevent SARS, the Hong Kong Health Department recommends maintaining good personal hygiene, washing hands frequently, and wearing a face mask in crowded public places. SARS hasn't returned to Hong Kong, but many experts believe that it or other contagious, upper-respiratory viruses will continue to be a seasonal health concern. It is also worth noting that the World Health Organization declared Hong Kong SARS-free in 2003.

Avian influenza, commonly known as bird flu, is a form of influenza that affects birds (including poultry) but can be passed to humans. It causes initial flu symptoms, followed by respiratory and organ failure. Although rare, it's often lethal. The Hong Kong government now exercises strict control over poultry farms and markets, and there are signs warning against contact with birds. Pay heed to warnings, and make sure that any poultry or eggs you consume are well cooked.

In May 2009 Hong Kong's response level to Influenza A (H1N1), commonly known as swine flu, was raised from "serious" to "emergency" when a man traveling from Mexico through Shanghai to Hong Kong was confirmed to be the first case found in the city—and the first case in Asia. The patient was isolated in a hospital, while the 173-room Metropark Hotel in Wan Chai where he had been staying was quarantined for a week. In June 2009 all primary schools, kindergartens, and special schools were closed for two weeks; by November 2009 more than 32,300 people in Hong Kong had tested positive for the virus, of which the overwhelming majority were under the age of 14. In May 2010 the response level was lowered from "emergency" to "alert," with the public advised to stay vigilant and continue to practice good personal and environmental hygiene habits.

All government and most commercial buildings now have hand-sanitizing dispensers by the lifts, and doors and other frequently touched areas are cleaned regularly. You'll also see people wearing face masks when they're ill to avoid infecting others.

Local Health Information **Department of Health Hotline** ☎ 2961–8989 ⊕ www.dh.gov. hk. **Travel Health Service** ☎ 2961–8840 on Hong Kong Island, 2150–7235 in Kowloon ⊕ www.travelhealth.gov.hk.

OVER-THE-COUNTER REMEDIES

You can easily find most familiar over-the-counter medications (like aspirin and ibuprofen) in pharmacies such as Watsons or Mannings, and usually in supermarkets and convenience stores, too. Acetaminophen—or Tylenol—is often locally known as paracetamol. Oral contraceptives are also available without prescription at Chinese pharmacies.

▮ HOURS OF OPERATION

Banks are open weekdays from 9 to 4:30 and Saturday from 9 to 12:30. Office hours are generally from 9 to 5 or 6, although working longer hours is common. Some offices are open from 9 to noon on Saturday. Lunch hour is 1 pm to 2 pm; don't be surprised if offices close during lunchtime. Museums and sights are usually open six days a week from 9 to 5. Each site picks a different day, usually a Monday or Tuesday, to close. Pharmacies are generally open from about 10 am until about 9 or 10 pm. For 24-hour pharmacies, go to Pamela Youde, Prince of Wales, Queen Elizabeth, Queen Mary, Tuen Mun, or United Christian Hospital (⇨ Emergencies, above).

HOLIDAYS

Public holidays in Hong Kong are: New Year's (January 1), Chinese New Year (three days in late January/early February), Ching Ming (April 4 or 5), Good Friday and Easter Monday (April), Labor Day (May 1), Buddha's Birthday (May), Dragon Boat Festival (late May/early June), Hong Kong SAR Establishment Day (July 1), Mid-Autumn Festival (late September/early October), National Day (October 1), Chung Yeung (October), and Christmas and Boxing Day (December 25 and 26).

▮ MAIL

Hong Kong's postal system is efficient and inexpensive. Airmail letters to any place in the world should take three to eight days. The Kowloon Central Post Office in Yau Ma Tei is open 9:30 am to 6 pm Monday through Friday and 9:30 am to 1 pm on Saturday; the General Post Office in Central is open 8 am to 6 pm Monday through Saturday and 9 am to 5 pm on Sunday and holidays. All other post offices are open from 9:30 am to 5 pm on weekdays and 9:30 am to 1 pm on Saturdays.

Airmail sent from Hong Kong is classified by destination into one of two zones. Zone 1 covers all of Asia except Japan. Zone 2 is everywhere else. International airmail costs HK$2.40 (Zone 1) or HK$3 (Zone 2) for a letter or postcard weighing less than 20 grams. To send a letter within Hong Kong, the cost is HK$1.40. The post office also has an overnight international courier service called Speedpost.

Main Postal Branches General Post Office ⊠ *2 Connaught Rd., Central, Hong Kong, Hong Kong-China* ☎ *2921–2222* ⊕ *www.hongkongpost.com.* **Kowloon Central Post Office** ⊠ *405 Nathan Rd., Yau Ma Tei, Kowloon, Hong Kong, Hong Kong-China* ☎ *2928–6247.*

SHIPPING PACKAGES

Packages sent via airmail to the United States can take up to two weeks. Airmail shipments to the United Kingdom—both packages and letters—arrive within three to five days, while mail to Australia often arrives in as little as three days.

You are probably best off shipping your own parcels instead of letting shop owners do this for you, both to save money and to ensure that you are actually shipping what you purchased and not a quick substitute—though most shop owners are honest and won't try to cheat you in this way. The workers at Hong Kong Post are extremely friendly, and will sell you all the packaging equipment you need, at unbelievably reasonable prices. Large international couriers in Hong Kong include DHL and Federal Express.

Express Services DHL ☎ *2400–3388* ⊕ *www.dhl.com.hk.* **Federal Express** ☎ *2730–3333* ⊕ *www.fedex.com/hk_english.*

▌MONEY

Very few shops or restaurants accept U.S. dollars, so either change in bulk or draw Hong Kong dollars direct from an ATM. Traveler's checks aren't accepted in most shops, and can be a pain to cash—avoid them, if possible. Getting change for large bills isn't usually a problem.

SAMPLE PRICES	
Cup of Coffee/Tea	HK$25/HK$20
Glass of Wine	HK$45–HK$70
Glass of Beer	HK$40–HK$60
Sandwich	HK$25–HK$40
Fresh Juice from a Stall	HK$10
Bowl of Noodle Soup	HK$20

Prices throughout this guide are given for adults. On public transport and for attractions, reduced fees are almost always available for children, students, and senior citizens.

▌TIP→ Banks never have every foreign currency on hand, and it may take as long as a week to order. If you're planning to exchange funds before leaving home, don't wait until the last minute.

ATMS AND BANKS

Your own bank will probably charge a fee for using ATMs abroad; the foreign bank you use may also charge a fee. Nevertheless, you'll usually get a better rate of exchange at an ATM than you will at a currency-exchange office or when changing money in a bank. And withdrawing funds as you need them is a safer option than carrying around a large amount of cash.

Reliable, safe ATMs are widely available throughout Hong Kong. MTR stations are a good place to look, where you'll always find at least one Hang Seng Bank ATM. If your card was issued from a bank in an English-speaking country, the instructions on the ATM machine will appear in English.

■ TIP→ PINs with more than four digits are not recognized at ATMs in many countries. If yours has five or more, remember to change it before you leave.

CREDIT CARDS

Major credit cards are widely accepted in Hong Kong, though they may not be accepted at small shops, and in some shops you get better rates paying in cash. When adding tips to restaurant bills, be sure to write "HK$" and not just "$."

It's a good idea to inform your credit-card company before you travel, especially if you're going abroad. Otherwise, the company might put a hold on your card owing to unusual activity—not a good thing at the beginning of your trip. Record all your credit-card numbers—as well as the phone numbers to call if your cards are lost or stolen—in a safe place, so you're prepared should something go wrong. Both MasterCard and Visa have general numbers you can call (collect if you're abroad) if your card is lost, but you're better off calling the number of your issuing bank, as MasterCard and Visa usually just transfer you to your bank; your bank's number is usually printed on your card.

Although it's often cheaper (and safer) to use a credit card rather than cash for large purchases you make abroad (so you can cancel payments or be reimbursed if there's a problem), note that some credit-card companies *and* the banks that issue them add substantial percentages to all foreign transactions, whether they're in a foreign currency or not. Check on these fees before leaving home, so there won't be any surprises when you get the bill. If you plan to use your credit card for cash advances, you'll need to apply for a PIN at least two weeks before your trip—but remember, most banks charge heavily for issuing cash advances.

■ TIP→ Before you charge something, ask the merchant whether he or she plans to do a dynamic currency conversion (DCC). In such a transaction the credit-card *processor* (shop, restaurant, or hotel, not Visa

or MasterCard) converts the currency and charges you in U.S. dollars. In most cases you'll pay the merchant a 3% fee for this service in addition to any credit-card company and issuing-bank foreign-transaction surcharges. Plus, the exchange rate is often less favorable than that offered by the credit-card company.

Dynamic currency conversion programs are becoming increasingly widespread. Merchants who participate in them are supposed to ask whether you want to be charged in dollars or the local currency, but they don't always do so. And even if they do offer you a choice, they may well avoid mentioning the additional surcharges. The good news is that you *do* have a choice. You can avoid the potentially costly practice altogether thanks to American Express; with its cards, DCC simply isn't an option.

Reporting Lost Cards **American Express** ☎ 800/528-4800 in U.S., 336/393-1111 collect from abroad ⊕ www.americanexpress. com. **Diners Club** ☎ 800/234-6377 in U.S., 2860-1888 in Hong Kong ⊕ www.dinersclub. com. **MasterCard** ☎ 800/627-8372 in U.S., 636/722-7111 collect from abroad, 800/966-677 in Hong Kong ⊕ www.mastercard.com. **Visa** ☎ 800/847-2911 in U.S., 800/900-782 in Hong Kong ⊕ www.visa.com.

CURRENCY AND EXCHANGE

The only currency used is the Hong Kong dollar, divided into 100 cents. There are bronze-color coins for 10, 20, and 50 cents; silver-color ones for 1, 2, and 5 dollars; and chunky bimetallic 10-dollar pieces. Bills can be confusing; there are a range of designs and issuing banks. There are new purple and a few remaining older green $HK10 bills in circulation, as well as bills for HK$20 (blue-green), HK$50 (purple), HK$100 (red), HK$500 (brown), and HK$1,000 (yellow). Don't be surprised if two bills of the same value look different: three local banks (HSBC, Standard Chartered, and Bank of China) all issue bills, and each has its own design. Although the image of Queen Elizabeth

II doesn't appear on new coins, old ones bearing her image are still valid.

The Hong Kong dollar has been pegged to the U.S. dollar at an exchange rate of HK$7.8 to US$1 since 1983. You can exchange currency at the airport, in hotels, in banks, and through private money changers scattered through the tourist areas. Banks usually have the best rates, but as they charge a fee of up to HK$50 for non-account holders, it's best to change large sums infrequently. Currency exchange offices do not charge fees, and they are open at conveniently late hours, but the rate of exchange is usually less favorable than it is at banks. Withdrawing money from your account at ATMs may be the least expensive option (⇨ *ATMS and Banks, above*).

▋ PACKING

Appearances in Hong Kong are important. This is a city where suits are still de rigueur for meetings and business functions, and women are expected to look elegant (or at least trendy). Slop around in flip-flops and shorts and you *will* feel there's a neon "tourist" sign over your head. Pack your nicer pairs of jeans, slacks, or skirts for sightseeing—there are plenty of fake handbags around to dress them up with if you're going to a nice restaurant.

From May through September conditions are seriously hot and sticky, but air-conditioning in hotels, restaurants, museums, and movie theaters can be arctic—keep a crushproof sweater or shawl in your bag or pack. Don't forget your swimsuit and sunscreen; many large hotels have pools, and you may want to spend some time on one of Hong Kong's many beaches. In October, November, March, and April, a jacket or sweater should suffice, but from December through February bring a light overcoat, preferably waterproof. Compact folding umbrellas can come in handy to protect against either rain or sun, but hotels will also lend you larger ones for the day.

▋ PASSPORTS AND VISAS

Citizens of the United States need only a valid passport to enter Hong Kong for stays up to three months. You need at least six months' validity on your passport before traveling to Asia. All minors regardless of age, including newborns and infants, must also have their own passports. Upon arrival, officials at passport control will give you a Hong Kong entry slip. Keep this slip safe; you must present it with your passport for your return trip home. If you're planning to pop over the border into mainland China, you must first get a visa (⇨ *Visas, below*).

PASSPORTS

U.S. passports are valid for 10 years for adults, five years for minors under 16. You must apply in person if you're getting a passport for the first time; if your previous passport was lost, stolen, or damaged; if your previous passport has expired and was issued more than 15 years ago; or if your previous passport was issued when you were under 16. All children under 18 must appear in person to apply for or renew a passport. Both parents must accompany any child under 16 and provide proof of their relationship to the child.

The cost to apply for a new passport is $135 for adults, $120 for children under 16; adults (over 16) may renew passports for $110. Allow four to six weeks for processing, both for first-time passports and renewals. For an expediting fee of $60 you can reduce this time to two to three weeks. If your trip is less than two weeks away, you can get a passport even more rapidly by going to a passport office with the necessary documentation. Private expediters can get things done in as little as 24 hours, but charge hefty fees.

TIP→ Before your trip, make two copies of your passport's data page (one for someone at home and another for you to carry separately). Or scan the page and email it to someone at home and/or yourself.

VISAS

A visa is essentially formal permission to enter a country. Visas allow countries to keep track of you and other visitors—and generate revenue (from application fees). You *always* need a visa to enter a foreign country; however, many countries routinely issue tourist visas on arrival, particularly to U.S. citizens. When your passport is stamped or scanned in the immigration line, you're actually being issued a visa. Sometimes you have to stand in a separate line and pay a small fee to get your stamp before going through immigration, but you can still do this at the airport on arrival. Getting a visa isn't always that easy. Some countries require that you arrange for one in advance of your trip. There's usually—but not always—a fee involved, and said fee may be nominal ($10 or less) or substantial ($100 or more).

If you must apply for a visa in advance, you can usually do it in person or by mail. When you apply by mail, you send your passport to a designated consulate, where your passport will be examined and the visa issued. Expediters—usually the same ones who handle expedited passport applications—can do all the work of obtaining your visa for you; however, there's always an additional cost (often more than $50 per visa).

Most visas limit you to a single trip—basically during the actual dates of your planned vacation. Other visas allow you to visit as many times as you wish for a specific period of time. Remember that requirements change, sometimes at the drop of a hat, and the burden is on you to make sure that you have the appropriate visas. Otherwise, you'll be turned away at the airport or, worse, deported after you arrive in the country. No company or travel insurer gives refunds if your travel plans are disrupted because you didn't have the correct visa.

Travel agents in Hong Kong can issue visas to visit mainland China and arrange trips; China Travel Service has more than 20 branches all over Hong Kong. Generally, expect to wait two to three days; Americans will pay a fee of about US$160. If you apply for a China visa before leaving home, the wait time is usually four to five days and the fee is US$140.

China Visa Information Chinese Consulate in New York ☎ 212/244-9456 ⊕ *www.nyconsulate.prchina.org/eng.* **Chinese Embassy in the U.S.** ☎ 202/338-6688, *202/337-1956* ⊕ *www.china-embassy.org/eng.*

Hong Kong General Information Hong Kong Immigration Department ☎ *2824-6111* ⊕ *www.immd.gov.hk.*

Hong Kong Travel Agents China Travel Service ☎ *2315-7171* ⊕ *www.ctshk.com.*

U.S. Passport Information U.S. Department of State ☎ *877/487-2778* ⊕ *travel.state.gov/passport.*

U.S. Passport and Visa Expediters A. Briggs Passport & Visa Expeditors ☎ *800/806-0581, 202/338-0111* ⊕ *www.abriggs.com.* **American Passport Express** ☎ *800/455-5166 in U.S.* ⊕ *www.americanpassport.com.* **Travel Document Systems** ☎ *800/874-5100 in Washington D.C., 877/874-5104 in New York, 888/874-5100 in San Francisco* ⊕ *www.traveldocs.com.* **Travel the World Visas** ☎ *866/886-8472* ⊕ *www.world-visa.com.*

∎ RESTROOMS

Big shopping malls, especially high-end ones, are your best bet for clean toilets that are well-stocked with toilet paper. If there isn't one nearby, you will likely find public toilets near indoor markets, parks, and MTR stations (a handy guide in the "Getting Around" section of the MTR website lists toilets near stations (⇨ *By Subway, above)*; however, only a few stations have toilets inside. It's best to carry tissue paper with you, and don't expect to find tampon or sanitary napkin dispensers in Hong Kong toilets.

SAFETY

Aside from a few random acid attacks in Mong Kok and Causeway Bay a few years back, Hong Kong is an incredibly safe place—day and night. The police do a good job maintaining law and order, but there are still a few pickpockets about, especially in Tsim Sha Tsui and Mong Kok. So exercise the same caution you would in any large city: be aware and avoid carrying large amounts of cash or valuables with you, and you should have no problems.

Nearly all consumer dissatisfaction in Hong Kong stems from the electronics retailers in Tsim Sha Tsui. Get some reference prices online before buying, and always check the contents of boxed items before you leave the shop. Have a good idea of what you're looking for before you shop, and keep all receipts.

TIP→ Distribute your cash, credit cards, IDs, and other valuables between a deep front pocket, an inside jacket or vest pocket, and a hidden money pouch. Don't reach for the money pouch once you're in public.

TAXES

Hong Kong levies a 10% service charge and a 3% government tax on hotel rooms. There's no other sales tax or V.A.T.

TIME

Hong Kong is 12 hours ahead of Eastern Standard Time and eight hours ahead of Greenwich Mean Time. There is no daylight savings time in Hong Kong, so remember to add an hour to the time

difference between the U.S. or other countries that observe it.

Time Zones Timeanddate.com
⊕ *www.timeanddate.com/worldclock.*

TIPPING

TIPPING GUIDELINES FOR HONG KONG	
Bartender	HK$10–HK$20 per round of drinks, depending on the number of drinks
Bellhop	HK$10–HK$20 per bag, depending on the level of the hotel
Hotel Concierge	HK$20–HK$50, more if he or she performs a service for you
Hotel Dorman	HK$10 if he helps you get a cab
Hotel Maid	HK$10 a day
Restroom Attendants	HK$2–HK$5
Porter at Airport or Train Station	HK$10–HK$15 per bag
Waiter	5%–10% if service was good

Tipping isn't a big part of Hong Kong culture. Hotels and restaurants usually add a 10% service charge; however, in almost all cases, this money does not go to the waiters and waitresses. In restaurants, add on up to 10% more for good service, or simply round up the tab. In hotels, tip bellhops and other helpful staff members. Tipping restroom attendants is common, but it is generally not the custom to leave an additional tip in taxis and beauty salons, and unheard of in theaters and cinemas.

▌VISITOR INFO

The *Standard* is a free English-language tabloid focused on business that you can pick up at MTR stations, and the *South China Morning Post* is Hong Kong's leading local English-language daily. *Time Out Hong Kong* is the local edition of the well-known city guide magazine.

ONLINE TRAVEL TOOLS

For a guide to what's happening in Hong Kong, check out the Hong Kong Tourist Board's excellent site. For weather info, check out the Hong Kong Observatory. For political information plus news and interesting business links, try the Hong Kong government site.

Business in Hong Kong is a government-run site packed with advice, and Centamap provides online Hong Kong street maps so detailed they give street numbers and building names.

For cultural activities check out *HK* magazine, the online version of a free weekly rag with the lowdown on just about everything happening in town. The government portal Hong Kong Leisure and Cultural Services Department (LCSD) is a useful resource that provides access to the websites of all of Hong Kong's museums and parks, as well as information on special events and festivals. You can also book tickets directly online at the LCSD site. Time Out Hong Kong online offers both features and detailed listings.

To discover bars and restaurants, try the online guide Eat Drink Hong Kong or Openrice.com, a popular site where locals rate and discuss restaurants. GLB Hong Kong is a catchall site to gay and lesbian resources and venues. Geoexpat collects wisdom from Hong Kong's large expat community. Hong Kong Outdoors is the authority on hiking, camping, and all things wild in Hong Kong. Love HK Film reviews the latest Hong Kong and mainland releases.

For currency conversion, go to Google and type in the amount and currencies to be converted (e.g., "600 HKD to USD"). XE.com also provides quick and straightforward currency conversion. Oanda.com offers comprehensive currency exchange rates and provides money transfers and other services.

All About Hong Kong Business in Hong Kong ⊕ www.gov.hk/en/business. **Centamap** ⊕ www.centamap.com. **Hong Kong Government** ⊕ www.gov.hk. **Hong Kong Tourist Board** (*HKTB*). ⊕ www.discoverhongkong.com. **Hong Kong Observatory** ⊕ www.weather.gov.hk.

Cultural Activities HK Magazine ⊕ hk.asia-city.com. **Hong Kong Leisure and Cultural Services Department** ⊕ www.lcsd.gov.hk. **Time Out Hong Kong** ⊕ www.timeout.com.hk.

Currency Conversion Google ⊕ www.google.com. **Oanda.com** ⊕ www.oanda.com. **XE.com** ⊕ www.xe.com.

Local Insight Eat Drink Hong Kong ⊕ www.eatdrinkhongkong.com. **GLB Hong Kong** ⊕ sqzm14.ust.hk/hkgay. **Geoexpat** ⊕ www.geoexpat.com. **Hong Kong Outdoors** ⊕ www.hkoutdoors.com. **Love HK Film.com** ⊕ lovehkfilm.com. **Open Rice** ✉ Central, Hong Kong, Hong Kong–China ⊕ www.openrice.com.

Newspapers South China Morning Post ⊕ www.scmp.com. **The Standard** ⊕ www.thestandard.com.hk.

INDEX

PHOTO CREDITS

1, Jose Fuste Raga / age fotostock. Chapter 1: Experience Hong Kong. 6-7, Walter Bibikow / age fotostock. 8, Li Wa/Shutterstock. 9 (left), Sze Kit Poon/iStockphoto. 9 (right), Khoroshunova Olga/ Shutterstock. 10, Hong Kong Tourism Board. 11 (left), Ian Muttoo/Flickr. 11 (right), Ella Hanochi/ iStockphoto. 14 (left), mary416/Shutterstock. 14 (top center), HU-JUN/iStockphoto. 14 (bottom center), K.C. Tang/wikipedia.org. 14 (top right), Hong Kong Tourism Board. 14 (bottom right), maveric2003/Flickr. 15 (left), karendotcom127/Flickr. 15 (top center), James Cridland/Flickr. 15 (top right), amybbb/Shutterstock. 15 (bottom right), Hong Kong Tourism Board. 16, oksana.perkins/Shutterstock. 17, Hong Kong Tourism Board. 18, John Leung/Shutterstock. 19, Hong Kong Tourism Board. 20, Hong Kong Tourism Board. 21, Michael Weber. 22, charles taylor/Shutterstock. 23 (left), Marc van Vuren/Shutterstock. 23 (right), Marek Brzezinski/iStockphoto. 24, Li lin hk - Imaginechina. 25 (left), Hong Kong Tourism Board. 25 (right), Victor Fraile/Hong Kong Tourism Board. 26, leungchopan/Shutterstock. 27 (left), winhorse/iStockphoto. 27 (right), Jess Yu/Shutterstock. 28, AndyYip/Shutterstock. 29, Hong Kong Tourism Board. Chapter 2: Central Hong Kong and Kowloon. 31, Hemis / Alamy. 32, Laoshi/iStockphoto. 35, Hong KongTourism Board. 38, Hong Kong Tourism Board. 41, Hong Kong Tourism Board. 43, Dallas & John Heaton / age fotostock. 45, Hemis / Alamy. 47, MAISANT Ludovic / age fotostock. 49, Hippo Studio/iStockphoto. 51, claudio zaccherini/Shutterstock. 54, Gavin Hellier / age fotostock. 56, LungSanLau/wikipedia.org. 57, James Montgomery / age fotostock. 59, Hong Kong Tourism Board. 61, Ian Muttoo/Flickr. 65, cozyta/Shutterstock. 66, Iain Masterton / Alamy. Chapter 3: Day Trips. 69, Pat Behnke / Alamy. 70, Hong Kong Tourism Board. 73, Let Ideas Compete/Flickr. 74, David Ewing / age fotostock. 76, Oksana Perkins/iStockphoto. 77, Hong Kong Tourism Board. 79, AngMoKio/wikipedia.org. 80, Ron Yue / Alamy. 82, Hong Kong Heritage Museum. 83, wikipedia.org. 85, Ella Hanochi/iStockphoto. 89, Doug Houghton / Alamy. 90, Ian Trower / age fotostock. Chapter 4: Shopping. 93, Ian Cumming / age fotostock. 94, Grotto Fine Art. 100, Amanda Hall / age fotostock. 104, VH / age fotostock. 106, Doco Dalfi ano/age fotostock. 113, Sylvain Grandadam / age fotostock.116, Hong Kong Tourism Board. 124, John Warburton-Lee Photography / Alamy. 135, Hong Kong Tourism Board. 138, Gavin Hellier / age fotostock. 142, Douglas LeMoine/Flickr. 147, Jochen Tack / age fotostock. Chapter 5: Where to Eat. 149, Picture Contact / Alamy. 150, The Pawn. 155, JTB Photo / Alamy. 159, 8 1/2 Otto e Mezzo.160, Hong Kong Tourism Board. 163, macglee/Flickr. 170, The Pawn. 174, Florian/Flickr. 179, BrokenSphere/wikipedia.org. 183, Hong Kong Tourism Board. 184, Aqua Spirit. 189, InterContinental Hong Kong. Chapter 6: Where to Stay. 203, Worldhotels. 204, fl owerego/fl ickr. 212 (top and bottom) and 216 (top), Michael Weber. 216 (bottom), Jia Hong Kong. 219 (top), InterContinental Hong Kong/flickr. 219 (bottom), bryangeek/flickr. 223 (top and bottom), Starwood Hotels and Resorts. 225, Graham Uden. Chapter 7: Nightlife. 227, Francisco Diez/ Flickr. 228, Hong Kong Tourism Board. 233, Fumio Okada / age fotostock. 239, The Globe. 241, K. Koroda / age fotostock. 243, Picture Contact / Alamy. 245, Peninsula Hotels. Chapter 8: Side Trip to Macau. 247, Steve Vidler / age fotostock. 248 (top), Lance Lee | AsiaPhoto.com/iStockphoto. 248 (bottom), Cloodlebing and Great Kindness/Flickr. 249 (top), Roger Price/Flickr. 249 (bottom), Lauri Silvennoinen/wikipedia.org. 250, leungchopan/Shutterstock. 259, Iain Masterton / Alamy. 262, Tito Wong/ Shutterstock. 269 and 270, Christian Goupi / age fotostock. 272, Barbara Kraft. 274, Jimmy Yao/ Flickr. 279, dbimages / Alamy. 281 (top), dadokit, INC. 281 (bottom), Starwood Hotels and Resorts. 286, George Apostolidis.

ABOUT OUR WRITERS

After earning her MFA from the Writing Division at Columbia University, Doretta Lau worked for the city magazines *Time Out Hong Kong* and *HK* magazine. She is currently a contributor to Artforum. com, where she reports on events and writes exhibition reviews. As a freelance journalist and writer, she has worked in print and radio for media outlets in Hong Kong, Canada, the United States and England. Doretta updated Hong Kong and Kowloon neighborhoods.

Samantha Leese was born and raised in Hong Kong. She was educated at Stanford University and the London School of Journalism. Sam is a contributing editor at *Glass* and *Prestige* magazines, and writes on arts, culture, and travel for the *Spectator*, *CNN*, and *Asia Tatler*, among other titles. She lives by the beach in Hong Kong. Samantha updated the Nightlife chapter.

Maloy Luakian moved to Hong Kong after watching *Chungking Express* in 1999 and, aside from a few years in Italy, has lived there ever since. She has written travel articles for both print and online newspapers and magazines, focusing mostly on food, subculture, architecture, and alternative activities for travelers, such as ghost hunting in Manila or visiting abandoned parks and cities in China.

Dorothy So studied in Los Angeles where she developed a passion for exploring different food cultures. Honing in on her interest in food, she moved back to her home city of Hong Kong in 2009 to work as a dining journalist. Her writing has appeared in many publications, including *HK* magazine, *Time Out*, and the *South China Morning Post*. Dorothy updated the Where to Eat and Experience chapters of this edition of *Fodor's Hong Kong*.

Jason Spotts is a food and lifestyle writer, born and raised in Hong Kong. He has spent years exploring both the colonial and local sides of Hong Kong's unique culture. Jason's work has appeared in the *South China Morning Post*, *Hong Kong Tatler*, *Crave* magazine, and *Time Out*.

Kate Springer is an American journalist based in Hong Kong. She focuses on travel, lifestyle, and environmental reporting and her work has appeared in *Fodor's*, *TIME*, *Forbes Travel Guide*, and *Smart Travel Asia*. When she's not ambling around Asia, you'll find her teaching English, dabbling in photography, and devouring *xiao long bao* dumplings.